1994

# The Transition to Independence in Namibia

## Lionel Cliffe

with

Ray Bush
Jenny Lindsay
Brian Mokopakgosi
Donna Pankhurst
Balefi Tsie

Lynne Rienner Publishers   •   Boulder & London

Published in the United States of America in 1994 by
Lynne Rienner Publishers, Inc.
1800 30th Street, Boulder, Colorado 80301

and in the United Kingdom by
Lynne Rienner Publishers, Inc.
3 Henrietta Street, Covent Garden, London WC2E 8LU

**Library of Congress Cataloging-in-Publication Data**
Cliffe, Lionel.
    The transition to independence in Namibia / by Lionel Cliffe  :
with Ray Bush . . . [et al.].
        p. cm.
    Includes bibliographical references and index.
    ISBN 1-55587-420-7 (alk. paper)
    1. Namibia—Politics and government—1946–1990. 2. Namibia—
Politics and government—1990– I. Title.
DT1648.C58 1994
968.8103—dc20                                          93-33326
                                                            CIP


**British Cataloguing in Publication Data**
A Cataloguing in Publication record for this book
is available from the British Library.


Printed and bound in the United States of America


⊗    The paper used in this publication meets the requirements
     of the American National Standard for Permanence of
     Paper for Printed Library Materials Z39.48-1984.

# Contents

# Illustrations

**Maps**

**Tables**

**Figure**

# Preface

This volume results from a real team effort. The authors spent time in various parts of Namibia during the transitional period in 1989–1990, and all the findings of their fieldwork have been pooled in the text. Original drafts of chapters or sections prepared by different individuals benefited from the comments of other authors.

The team first came together at Leeds with the intention of mounting an academic version of the observation that many monitoring groups were undertaking during those critical months of Namibia's history and then recording what happened. Some of us had undertaken a similar exercise in 1980, at the parallel moment in Zimbabwe's emergence to independence. With that as a model, we could not presume at the outset what kinds of systematic investigation would prove possible in exciting but still troubled times, and in the event attitude surveys were not attempted. But as with other such moments when there is a new political dispensation and a critical election, political life became transparent, and we found much to observe and record.

This book started life basically as a factual account of the events written down for the benefit especially of Namibians. As the writing progressed and time elapsed, and as the necessity arose to spell out the international, historical, and other background to events in 1989, a book began to take shape. These additions notwithstanding, the book still reflects our original emphasis on setting out a factual record that allows readers to make their own assessments and not simply rely on our analysis of the issues, which we have chosen as our agenda for discussion in Chapter 1.

In fact the structure of the volume is straightforward. Part I provides the background to events from 1989: Chapter 2, the Namibian historical and political economy contexts; Chapter 3, the international forces at work; and Chapter 4, the UN plan for the transition to independence that was shaped by these internal and external forces. Part II traces what went on in the transition leading up to the elections: the troubled climate, the actual running of the elections, and the parties and their campaigns are dealt with in Chapters 5, 6, and 7, respectively. Part III deals with the outcome: the election results (Chapter 8) and subsequent happenings in the Constituent

Assembly and in the politics of the country and the region immediately preceding and following independence (Chapter 9).

Preliminary drafts for Chapter 2, parts of Chapters 5 and 7, and the crucial story of the Constitutional Assembly were produced by Jenny Lindsay, who also did the most protracted stint of fieldwork, which explored postelection events. Chapter 2 also benefited from Brian Mokopakgosi's input and knowledge of Namibian history. Donna Pankhurst was responsible with me for drafts of Chapters 3 and 4 and parts of 8. Ray Bush drafted parts of Chapters 2, 5, 6, and 7. Other drafts and most of the blame for the final product have to be put at my door.

Many others, however, deserve credit for comments on the text, insights from their experience, and general support, which have improved on what would have come from our unaided efforts: Brian Wood provided detailed textual suggestions and crucial background from his own parallel work on the international context; Toré Linne Eriksen brought his compendious knowledge of the Namibia literature to our joint activities and the gleanings from a postelection fieldwork as well as liaison with the Norwegian end of the collective undertaking; we had hoped to benefit from the expertise on international peacekeeping of the acting director of the Norwegian Institute for Foreign Affairs, Dr. Kjell Skjelsbaek, until his untimely death. Among many who shared their firsthand knowledge with us, special thanks go to Colin Leys, Nai'em Dollie, Peter Manning, Susan Brown, Samuel Mushi and his colleagues from the University of Dar es Salaam team studying the election, Sarah Hayward, Murray McGuiness and many others of the Christian International Monitoring Service, Chris Tapscott, Da'oud Vries, Richard Moorsom, and Jon Craig.

The whole work would have been impossible without a grant from the Economic and Social Research Council of the United Kingdom (Grant No. R000 23 2126). The Norwegian Ministry of Foreign Affairs contributed financial support that enabled Jenny Lindsay to extend her fieldwork beyond the election and our two team members from Botswana to join us; thanks go to the University of Botswana for releasing them and for backing the whole project. A grant from the University of Leeds Research Fund made possible follow-up fieldwork in 1990. The several versions of this manuscript were typed with great and much appreciated care by Charlotte Williams, Anne Land, Pam Hampshire, and Alex Robson. The final text has benefited greatly from the thorough, meticulous editing of our copyeditor, Jan Kristiaansson, and the work of Gia Hamilton, project editor at Lynne Rienner Publishers.

*L. C.*

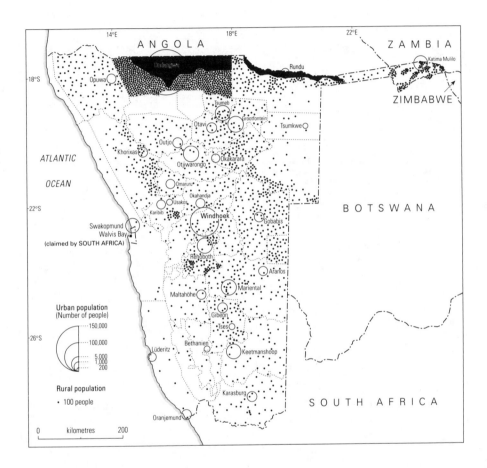

**Population Distribution in Namibia**

**Electoral Districts in Namibia**

# 1
# Introduction

The year 1989 was a historic and eventful milestone for Namibia. The final act of decolonization in Africa was at last to be played out. A cease-fire beginning in April heralded the end of the long-drawn-out war that had been waged by fighters of the South West African People's Organization (SWAPO) to dislodge the occupying South African security forces. The United Nations, which had been passing resolutions challenging South African overrule and had been acting to assert its own trusteeship, finally would establish a presence in the country to oversee a transition to peace and eventually, in 1990, to full independence. The culmination of this process would be the first fully open elections in Namibia, in November 1989, to choose an assembly that would write a constitution for the country. The elections and the work of the Constituent Assembly (CA) in turn would set the main parameters for the postindependence political system: they would shape the party system and the legal framework of the state structures.

This whole transition is reported here: the cease-fire, the UN presence, the campaigning and actual voting in the election, the deliberations of the Constituent Assembly, and other trends leading to independence in March 1990. In seeking to chronicle these events, we are aware that we were one small group among a very large number of other observers: representatives of interested governments and of international bodies such as the Organization of African Unity (OAU) and the Commonwealth, foreign correspondents by the score, and observers sent by churches, nongovernmental organizations, and other bodies interested in human rights and democratic practice. In fact, this volume draws upon many of their reports and assessments.

However, this book seeks to offer more than just an account of what happened, for the 1989–1990 transition was intriguing as well as exciting and provides many challenges to anyone seeking to *explain* what happened. We are concerned, then, with identifying the key analytical issues thrown up by these events, conscious that this will be only a preliminary effort but one that might at least set the agenda for future investigations of the transition to independence in Namibia.

It is instructive to see the transition in Namibia in a broader comparative and historical context. It marked the end of one historical phase in

Africa—the final ending of colonial rule and the culmination of an armed liberation struggle. It thus raised issues as to whose terms would govern the transition and where it would be sited on a scale between neocolonialism and national liberation. At the same time, the shape of the political outcome that emerged in 1990 suggested that Namibia could represent one of the early examples of a new trend—the installation of pluralist democracy in Africa.

A more immediate and obvious set of analytical questions involves explaining the results of the Constituent Assembly election. This was an especially challenging task in a country that was coming out of a liberation war and that had seen severe restrictions on people's freedom of political association. Just as in Zimbabwe, the Republic of South Africa (RSA), or the countries of Eastern Europe, the political affiliations of Namibians had never been revealed by an open electoral contest in which all parties felt free to stand. So all kinds of claims as to popular support had been made but would now be put to the test. The main nationalist party in exile, SWAPO, had claimed to be, and had been recognized by the United Nations as, the "sole and authentic voice of the Namibian people." Nevertheless, internally operating parties, several of them grouped in the Democratic Turnhalle Alliance (DTA), that had participated in the South African–backed interim government, had won large majorities in internal elections in which SWAPO did not stand. Whose claims would prove correct? Why in the event did SWAPO win a majority, but not as convincingly as many expected?

As with all competitive elections, analysts seek to answer such questions by identifying a party's backing in terms of shared characteristics or even group loyalties. In established systems, an analyst might typically refine the basic picture by distinguishing the parties' core support from marginal or fringe voters. Studies of elections in such systems often focus on the extent to which core support is confirmed or shifts and on which way swing voters move and why. In the Namibian case, however, predictions about the outcome of the 1989 elections were hard to make, as they marked a new departure; there was no established baseline. What stood to be revealed here were not marginal changes but the whole, previously hidden fabric of popular politics, the kind of identification existing between political parties and different sections of the population. What have to be documented and explained, then, are not just the results of one round of political competition but more fundamentally the very nature of the new politics emerging from the transition in Namibia.

If past experience offered few clues as to the level of basic support various parties enjoyed, it was even more difficult to anticipate what kind of people would give their vote to which party and on the basis of what calculations. To what extent would there be block voting, and would this be on the basis of class, race, or ethnic group? Local results would allow some analysis of regional variations in party support (see Chapter 8), but further analysis of such questions would prove methodologically difficult because the tense security situation and people's understandable suspicions would have made attitudinal surveys unreliable even if they had not been impracticable. Moreover, all that such voting patterns or surveys of attitudes show is the degree of correlation between party support and social groups; that such correlations occur is itself something that has to be explained. That was a challenging task in Namibia as, for instance, the degree of fit between parties and ethnic groupings was not great.

The whole electoral process would not only reveal this popular basis of parties but would also bring out and perhaps redefine their character, their structure and policy stances, and the interests they articulated. The two main contenders both had to reshape themselves for a new situation: SWAPO, returning from exile, had to switch from a movement for armed struggle to a campaigning political party; DTA had to transform itself from a grouping based on official South African patronage to one that sought popular support. At the same time, other parties came to the fore or were formed anew. Study of campaigns, their platforms, structures, and financing can reveal this emerging dimension of Namibian politics: the nature of the parties, their organizational capabilities, and their appeals and platforms are documented in Chapter 7.

Even more fundamentally, the election was a moment to take the political pulse of the people at large—not only how they would identify with the parties but also how they would generally perceive politics. Like all elections, the one in Namibia opened up a window to see into the deeper popular dimensions of political life that connected the mass of people to the main organs of politics. Moreover, the patterns that are revealed are etched more clearly at the moment of an election because of the heightened intensity of political activity. In Namibia the prospect of this revelation of the political base was even more intriguing. It was likely to be the decisive moment when, as in other African countries, the patterns were being set in a mold that would probably shape political affiliations and party bases of support, and even the nature of the future regime, for a generation to come. The voting would decide whether, at one extreme, a one-party state would be written into the constitution or, at the other extreme, Namibia would gain a functioning, sustainable, multiparty system with a loyal opposition. Or the permanent dominance of a kind of "one-and-a-bit party state," as in Botswana, might also emerge from the voting in 1989.

To examine these issues, we must sketch this social base for politics—the population, its distribution, its socioeconomic character, and its ethnic makeup (see Chapter 2)—not only to provide background but also to define the crucial actors who in the final analysis would determine the outcome of this critical transition. Of course, the people of Namibia are not just a set of individuals or a set of social groups, whose material circumstances automatically dictate their political stances. Namibians' consciousness of their social reality is the result of their shared interests, experiences, and perceptions in work, education, residence and migration, local culture, and decades of struggle against South African overrule. These crucial historical experiences have to be sketched in as background to understanding the transition. But the more transparent political climate that obtained during the transition also made possible a reassessment of what had been happening in earlier years, when secrecy and censorship dictated that the only accounts of events and of people's response to them were few, limited, and partisan.

The epic struggle of the last years could be seen as a contest between two different blueprints for a future Namibia: the models and stratagems of the South African government and its Namibian collaborators and those of the Namibian liberation movement. The explicit programmatic statements that the two contending forces made and the underlying aspirations they nursed more privately need to be laid bare, although this volume can do this only in a preliminary way. Chapter 2 documents how South Africa's conception altered from incorporation of Namibia in the 1960s, to an "internal solution" of a form of an "independence" orchestrated by South Africa itself, and then to a calculatedly ambiguous position toward an "independence which involved SWAPO." Chapters 3 and 4 address themselves to the manner in which the calculations of international actors imposed themselves on this basic conflict of paths and attempted some kind of compromise whose immediate political form was articulated in the UN plan that was ultimately implemented.

Also at issue were even broader matters than the political arrangements for a transfer of power. What policies would be pursued by a future government, and what efforts would be made to change the grossly unequal social and economic structures inherited from a century of colonialism? These prospects led to a widespread speculation among whites that their future status in an independent Namibia was also at stake, although more at issue was the status of the land and other property that they had monopolized in the past, and even that, like the one-party issue, was already settled in broad terms in the UN plan and the political context of the transition, as Chapter 4 makes clear.

The terms on which the transition took place, the long-delayed implementation of it, and the conduct of that transition, which was monitored by the UN but administered by South Africa, remained contested terrain to the bitter end—as did the final shaping of the constitutional structure of independent Namibia (through the deliberations of the Constituent Assembly), the critical politicking surrounding the formation of a government and the reformation of the civil service, and the realignment and reshaping of parties in the crucial few months just before and after independence. The contested nature of the transition raised a question that was very much at the forefront of observers' concerns: were the elections in fact free and fair? Most commentators gave them a clean bill of health in the immediate aftermath. In Chapter 4 we attempt to explore this issue by systematically looking at the provisions for the transition contained in the UN plan itself, arguing that it had some limitations and ambiguities. We also try later in Chapter 5 to document the climate in which the transition took place—the immediate aftermath of war is always likely to pose difficulties, and indeed the scheduled cease-fire was greeted by a minor bloodbath. Was the climate in which the campaign was conducted free of intimidation? Were the media fair, and did all parties have the same chance to get their message across? Was the presence of the UN as supervisor a sufficient guarantee that all was aboveboard? We also follow the different stages of the electoral process and their administration in Chapter 6: Were the rules for registering and for voting unbiased? Was the administration of these procedures by South African authorities, scarcely a disinterested party, evenhanded?

As with similar transitions after a liberation war, in Southern Africa and elsewhere, the outcome of this process was not determined on the basis of the explicit blueprints or private calculations of the main state or movement participants, even if it can be conceived as embodying some compromise between such formulations. The resulting trajectory can be understood as a product of complex social and political processes. Analysts of such transitions have suggested general models to which these emerging patterns of postindependence politics might correspond. One alternative, which some writers have discussed in relation to Namibia (Gottschalk, 1987; Simon and Moorsom, 1987), has been labeled *neocolonialism.* This process is usually posited as involving merely formal political independence with control of the economy still very much in foreign hands; but in Africa it has also involved some degree of diversification of control from the old metropolitan colonizer to a wider international consortium of powers and of capital. In Namibia's case, issues are raised as to whether such a conception does in fact help illuminate the future role of a nonmetropolitan, regional power such as South Africa. Other analysts have sought to understand the transition as embodying the logic of certain forms of struggle, in particular seeing to what degree a process of radicalization of political movements and the population at large had occurred, arguing that some such tendency could be expected to result from the popular mobilization involved in a guerrilla war (see Davidson, 1981; Saul, 1979; and Cliffe, 1986, for discussion of this issue in comparative perspective).

To explore such issues means asking questions about the past. Fortunately, the heightened activity and the emergence of open politics do offer a window on the future and the past. Thus, to assess the future prospects for independent Namibia prompts one to pose new kinds of questions about recent political history: How far and in what ways did the liberation struggle reach different parts of the country, and how did it affect people in them? To what extent were people mobilized and on the basis of what kind of appeals and with what kind of resulting consciousness? What kind of *political* organization and capacity did SWAPO and other parties develop in the course of the struggle? What kind of counterinsurgency methods did the South Africans apply and with what degrees of success? And what was the legacy of these trends for the transition, and what is it likely to be for the longer-term future? These, then, represent additional questions posed in Chapter 2 as we sketch in the background to the transition in 1989.

Studying these several dimensions of the transition helps situate Namibia in the pantheon of African national liberation struggles. A second set of intriguing comparative issues involve asking what the transition reveals about the prospects for pluralist democracy there and in Africa generally. There is a contradiction at the heart of any democratic system that provides regular elections based on universal suffrage. The essential principle underwriting this political system is egalitarian and thus runs counter to profound prevailing socioeconomic inequalities (Rueschemeyer, Stevens, and Stevens, 1992). Such a shift to some system of popular representation offers the prospect for classes and other interests that are disadvantaged to transform their oppressed and exploited conditions. For those whose social and economic benefits have depended on their access to state power, the problem is how to concede political equality while retaining as much of the status quo as possible. Southern Africa has merely exemplified a more intense, racially defined, and institutionalized version of this basic dilemma.

But there are also some variations within the region with respect to both the particular white interests whose dependence on state power makes them reluctant to concede any representative system of government and to the formulas that have eventually emerged as a temporary and partial resolution to the issue of demands for full political rights of all Africans. In Namibia, there is virtually no white working class, which in the South African case has been politically incorporated in return for benefits such as "job reservation" (Davies et al., 1976). But in Namibia there do exist interests, among farmers and some mining companies, that correspond to those class elements thought least likely to concede any democratization—those who depend on ultracheap and/or semiservile labor reproduced through political means (Rueschemeyer, Stevens, and Stevens, 1992). But the major distinction between the state in Namibia compared with South Africa or even the former Rhodesia is that Namibia was colonial, the dominant interests were external, and, unlike the rest of Africa, the ruling power was South Africa, which was also inhibited from passing on political control and on occasions taking a slightly different stance in what it would concede politically, compared with some indigenous white interests.

In the broadest comparative context, where democratization has been on the agenda, the potential for social transformation has been kept in check by some combination of generalized sociopolitical project that usually influences the character of political movements—the incorporation of (elements in) the working classes, for instance—through detailed manipulation of the system of representation and the outcome of elections. In developing countries, the resources and the acquisitiveness of privileged classes have not allowed the concessions of welfarism and livable wages that have characterized the political incorporation of working classes in developed countries in the second half of this century, at least until recently. Instead, the characteristic form of political incorporation has been *clientelism* (Charney, 1987). This familiar pattern whereby the political ambitions of local big noises depend on the clan loyalty they buy through their largesse certainly had its place in the underlying political structures that emerged in Namibia in the last two decades. But the localized, patron-client politics encouraged and institutionalized by the South African regime was not considered sufficient to withstand a completely open, one-person/one-vote election. In such a context of what the UN plan for Namibia saw as an essential element of the transition, the form of the electoral system and its operation would furnish a further mechanism for curbing the radical tendency inherent in democratization.

In the case of Namibia, the immediate political outcome was the establishment of a governing party faced with a significant opposition, a constitution, and, for the moment, political practices that guarantee pluralist competition. This outcome can be seen as another result of the balance struck among the contending forces and their views of Namibia's future. In particular, we argue that both sides had a different conception of representative government—two conflicting perspectives that Namibia shares with some other African countries in the period of transfer of power, especially some of the settler colonies. SWAPO articulated the orthodox African nationalist view that the people's aspiration could best be represented by a single national movement that would express their common Africanness and their common oppression. At the same time, such a perception would generate a national identity shared by all (black) people within the territory of the colonial state, thus overcoming tribalism and potential ethnic conflict.

The whites and the South African administration and their allies offered a conception of pluralism whereby different ethnic and cultural entities would be separately represented and would operate within some sort of confederal consensus. Of course, the whites and the South African state had manipulated such a model for years so as to perpetuate colonial overrule but had also modified its forms and even broadened the terms of this representation. These forces no longer offered a tiered structure of representation but sought to preserve their influence and that of local whites through domination of a coalition of parties representing such separate interests. However self-serving, this formula did correspond to a form of representation, which has been seen as appropriate to welding together fractured societies such as that of Ethiopia. Of course, this form of political representation has grave limitations, which have been observed in Africa: a patronage politics of local barons that is all too easily reduced to nepotism and corruption and the ever-present possibility of degeneration into open conflict.

These contending models, and the manipulative use of ethnic representation, have been a feature of the transition to postcolonial rule in most settler colonies in Africa since Kenya's transition in 1961 and are now central to the deals being struck about the future of South Africa (Szeftel, 1991). What has to be recognized is that negotiations about the essential type of representative government are always likely to be polarized, as they were for so long in Namibia, and yet, although the two formulas seem to be mutually exclusive, some agreement on the terms on which some new system will be constituted has to be a prerequisite for conflict to end and for a transition to be set in motion. In Namibia the outlines of the future political system that were the basis for the transition were a compromise between these two approaches, but these outlines were also fudged, with many of the significant emphases and details to be determined by the electoral outcome and the creation of the constitution.

In the event, the emergence of a pluralist representative system is itself a compromise among elites with competing appeals to some popular basis, rather than a result of those broadly based popular demands for government accountability that are necessary to sustain any kind of really representative system. This compromise between the minority forces of ethnic pluralism and the more widespread but not dominating forces of centralized national unity has for the moment produced a system that might head off the worst excesses of self-perpetuating elite rule that have been associated with the one-party state in many African countries. But it is necessary to explore how sustainable that compromise is: whether the ethnic or the national unity tendencies will ultimately be the more determinant. Also on the agenda is whether the compromise of a certain variety of pluralism may be partly at the expense of any significant transformation of an inherited socioeconomic system marked by racial and, increasingly, class polarization and by dependence on South Africa—themselves features that may affect the longer-run viability of the pluralist system.

Yet more fundamental explanations are called for in seeking to understand the transition in Namibia. Why did it take place, and why did it occur in the manner and at the time that it did? These are not straightforward questions because agreement to a UN-supervised transition and creation of an independence that would be acceptable to SWAPO and to the international community could not have been predicted with any certainty. As Chapter 2 reveals, South African authorities repeatedly seemed on the brink of imposing their own internal solution, and at times the fighting in Namibia and in Angola over Namibia as well as over other issues and involving many outside powers threatened to go on interminably. Moreover, once under way there was no automatic guarantee that the transition would actually be implemented successfully, and indeed there were at least two or three moments when the process might have come unstuck.

To explain all these outcomes, in Chapter 2 we consider the internal dynamic of political and other forces at work inside Namibia as well as external developments: the interaction between SWAPO's internal resistance and its diplomatic activities, in particular its relations with the Angolan government and its Cuban and Soviet allies, with OAU, and with the UN; the broader forces at work in the whole Southern African region; and the manner in which they interacted with the global politics of the Cold War and its eventual termination. And the tactics that South Africa pursued in Namibia and Angola have to be understood in the context of South Africa's broader "total strategy" for the whole region. Only then can we explain why South Africa delayed for ten years before implementing the UN plan that it and all parties had agreed to in 1978 and what circumstances and calculations led to the eventual initiation of the transition in 1989. These broader international issues are explored in Chapter 3.

A further set of questions arise in relation to South Africa's strategy. How far has Namibia been a proving ground for tactics to be employed in South Africa—either to slow down the implementation of meaningful political and social change or to test methods of political manipulation, such as the fostering of "third-force" black political groups that oppose the main national liberation movement and the building of black-white political alliances? These possible lessons of the Namibian experience for the transition under way in South Africa are discussed in Chapter 9.

Global events in the period following the transition prompt another set of questions about these international forces influencing events in Namibia. The transition can be seen with hindsight as the first of a string of attempts by the UN to play a role in resolving conflict, maintaining peace, and monitoring a transformation in political regime. Although by no means the first deployment of a UN peacekeeping force, the UN presence in Namibia was a new departure in that it involved civilian police monitors, election supervisors, and the central political backstop role of the UN Secretary-General's special representative and his staff. The UN's brief was also different: concerned with internal, rather than just interstate, conflict and with the putting into place of a political apparatus. In some of these dimensions, the UN's actions presaged UN interventions in the former Yugoslavia, Cambodia, and Somalia. Like those later instances, these actions raised issues of the UN's competence, readiness, and fitness to play a more invigorated and different, post–Cold War role. More generally, could the world community of states reflected in the General Assembly be the key mediator of conflict? Or would this role pass to the United States as the one undisputed superpower, on its own or with the major powers generally, acting directly or indirectly through the UN Security Council, operating as the world's police force? These questions were presaged in the tensions in the roles of the Western Contact Group (WCG) and of the UN in mediating the transition and in the assertion of the Security Council's role over that of the General Assembly.

The structure of this volume, then, is that Chapter 2 provides an outline of Namibia's geography and economy, its people and their recent political history, focusing particularly on the liberation struggle of the last decades and South African countermeasures to contain that struggle militarily and politically. The chapter also seeks to specify the conjunction of internal forces whose culmination brought on the transition in 1989. Chapter 3 complements that picture by sketching in the international forces at work that eventually led to the implementation of a UN plan for the transition to independence in Namibia and Chapter 4 details that plan, the provisions for a cease-fire, and the transition to independence. Chapter 5 explores the climate that characterized the transition period: the almost aborted cease-fire, the continued pattern of intimidation and media manipulation, and UN attempts to curb these and generally to regulate the transition. The electoral administration is the focus of Chapter 6. Chapter 7 offers profiles of the political parties and the emerging political scene in Namibia. Chapter 8 explores the voting patterns and the popular dimension of politics. Chapter 9 deals with the last stages of the transition: the work of the Constituent Assembly, subsequent political developments inside Namibia, and the country's relations with South Africa, the region, and the outside world.

# PART 1

# 2
# The Political Background

This chapter attempts to put the contending forces that would determine the transition to independence—South Africa's occupation of Namibia and the emergence of nationalist politics—in historical perspective, focusing in particular on three major themes. First, we review how the broader social and economic processes, and even the pattern of human settlement, were overwhelmingly shaped by German and then South African colonialism.[1] Then, we more extensively detail two processes that set the scene for much of the rest of this book: the character and dynamic of the Namibian nationalist movement and the changing stratagems and institutional forms of the colonial state. These latter maneuvers need to be seen as the South African response to the war for liberation and to international pressures following the ruling of the International Court of Justice in 1971 that South Africa's occupation was illegal.

## The Colonial Legacy

### The Early Impact

Namibia's inherited political economy, the very sparse but uneven spatial distribution of peoples, and how drastically they were shaped by colonialism are themes well documented elsewhere (Green, Kiljunen, and Kiljunen, 1981; First, 1963; Wood, 1988). But a brief review here is vital so as to lay out the character of class and other social, state, and regional forces that became part of the colonial legacy as a basis for assessing their impact on the whole transition.

Although Namibia is the size of the United Kingdom and France combined, it has a small population. Current estimates are 1.7 million (see World Bank, 1991: 204–206; and *The Courier,* May–June 1991), but the South African–conducted census of 1981 put the figure at 1,033,196 (excluding Walvis Bay). This latter figure, with an assumed 3 percent annual increase, was the basis for projections of the total and, in turn, the eligible voter populations for the 1989 elections. Jaster (1990: 6) suggests, however, that estimates at the time varied by as much as 20 percent. Another remarkable demographic feature is the extremely skewed spatial distribution, with more than half the people living on a thin strip of land on the northern border in the "reserves" of Ovamboland, Kavango, and Caprivi (see the map of population distribution in Namibia). Elsewhere people are sparsely dispersed in very dry environments as small groups of farm workers on vast white-owned ranches and farms and in other "communal" areas, notably among the Damara, Herero, and Nama. There are a few small towns, but more than 10 percent of the population lives in the capital, Windhoek (Simon, 1983). Whites make up just 6 percent of the total, and coloureds, 4 percent.

Between 1884 and 1915 the territory was a German colony. Invasion and occupation by South African and other Allied forces during World War I paved the way for a League of Nations mandate to South Africa to administer the area in 1920. After World War II South Africa refused to concede UN trusteeship responsibility for Namibia. For all intents and purposes, Pretoria treated Namibia as a fifth province from the 1920s until the 1970s (First, 1963; Fraenkel and Murray, 1985; Green, Kiljunen, and Kiljunen, 1981).

The Germans massacred the majority of the Herero and many of the Nama in the settled southern and central parts of the country (on precolonial Namibia, see Clarence-Smith and Moorsom, 1977). These indigenous people were dispossessed of their land and cattle. The German occupiers imposed a harsh discipline enforced by a paramilitary force within a police zone that excluded the far north of the country (Bley, 1971; Drechsler, 1980).

South African occupation reinforced the distribution and settlement of the population that the German colonial period had initiated. Yet the occupation began to use local peoples much more in the creation of a political economy that would serve the interests of capital and the South African state. People living in the south of the country came increasingly to provide the labor for white ranches and farms, some on a seasonal and temporary basis before returning to the barren and arid reserves between contracts. Many more remained on the ranches and lived in semiservile conditions. South African colonialism promoted two forms of agriculture—a commercial sector dominated by whites in the ranching of cattle and sheep, mainly for export, and a household agriculture in the African communal areas. About 50 percent of the economically active population are engaged in this latter, while about 8 percent became employed in the white-owned commercial sector (Green, Kiljunen, and Kiljunen, 1981). Almost five thousand large commercial farms occupy 77 percent of the viable farming land (Moorsom, 1982; Pankhurst, 1992; Oloya et al., 1984). Agriculture has been geared to the needs of South Africa for more than fifty years, supplying meat to the republic.

People to the north of the police zone lived under a different kind of administration, with seldom the same direct colonial intervention. They had no right to "unauthorized" residence in the rest of the country. Instead, they became earmarked for work in the mines as semiproletarians subject to a contract labor system organized through the chiefs, or they worked in the fishing industry. The pattern of control and administration in the north resulted in the northern reserves having an economy where most of the adult men were away and the remaining women, aged, and children were left to eke out an existence on their own.

*The Colonial Economy*

Mining became, and remains, the most significant sector of the economy. There are a large range of minerals to be found and some 152 mines, mostly small and some inoperative. The mines are spread throughout the country, but the major concentrations are at Oranjemund (diamonds), Rossing (uranium), Tsumeb (copper and other minerals), and between Tsumeb and Grootfontein (the Kombat mine) (Chamber of Mines of Namibia, 1991). Mining is the largest contributor to gross domestic product (GDP) (29 percent in 1989 and 22 percent in 1990) and accounts for around 75 percent of export earnings. Some major mines, including that at Rossing, are owned or controlled by Western multinational corporations, but the majority is controlled by South African mining houses (Economist Intelligence Unit, 1990–1991). Rossing is the only one to institutionalize a more permanent, resident labor force with family housing. The diamond giant De Beers, for example, at Oranjemund has retained a labor force of rotating contract workers, with one-third of those on contract repatriated for a four-month furlough at any one time—just like the patterns of recruitment in neighboring South Africa. Even though mining is a significant employer, its capital-intensive character means that it actually employs only twelve thousand mineworkers, 5 percent of the total employment, of whom three thousand are white. Moreover, large numbers of the unemployed (Dropkin and Clark, 1992), concentrated in the country's black townships, have often been miners at one time.

Despite a UN resolution stating that international companies are acting illegally in extracting minerals from the territory, there has been a tendency for mining houses to overexploit the deposits in recent years (Thirion, 1985; Pilgrim, 1990)—no doubt to enjoy the largest earnings possible before the appearance of an independent government. There has nevertheless been a decline in mineral production between 1982 and 1992 and overall prospects for production are unlikely to recover to earlier levels (Ericsson, 1992).

Northerners not recruited to work in the mining industry were often hired to work in the quickly growing fishing sector. Namibia's long coastline provides what were some of the richest fishing grounds anywhere in the world, but overfishing in the 1970s and 1980s by international fleets that did not recognize a 200-mile exclusion zone depleted stocks and reduced the importance of the fishing and processing industry. In 1989 fishing and fish products were contributing just 3 percent of export earnings (Oden, 1991: 11). Moreover, like the mining industry, most of the fish processing industry is owned by South African firms, and the major processing and canning plant is located in South African–administered Walvis Bay.

In 1989 the country's GDP was U.S. $1,650 million (World Bank, 1991: 206), but a large proportion of that wealth was not retained inside the country. The economic inheritance of resource extraction in the hands of foreign capital meant that at least 65 percent of the GDP consisted of merchandised exports, while merchandised imports made up 59 percent. Namibia's economy is therefore far more distorted and externally oriented than those of other countries even in Southern Africa and is thus more vulnerable. Because of a number of factors—recession, the collapse of fishing industry, falls in the prices of minerals, drought, and a lack of investment following sanctions—per capita income fell by more than 1 percent a year from 1980 to 1988.

### The Social Consequences

Colonial administration had major consequences for the manner and the degree of different people's incorporation and helped shape local societies and their politics down to the present. The division between the north and the south of the country and then the South African regime's restructuring of its administration in the 1970s (in response to proposals from the Odendaal Commission [1964] to bring Namibia in line with South Africa's apartheid structures) reinforced the colonial pattern of a stereotyped division of labor for the local inhabitants.

The South African administration reclassified reserves as "homelands." They had their own "independent" administrations; but these had little viability, based as they were on the old system of labor reserves, which had never been intended to provide all the means for people's survival. The Herero were restricted to poor grazing areas northeast and southeast of Windhoek. The Damara homeland was located northwest of Windhoek, and the Nama became scattered in an area between Mariental and Keetmanshoop in the south—islands within a sea of white-owned ranches. The northern border area, where much the greatest part of the African population lives, was devastated in the twenty years prior to 1989 by the war, which escalated rapidly after Angolan independence and South Africa's intervention to support Jonas Savimbi and his UNITA movement's campaign against the MPLA government.

The South African obsession with classifying the population according to race led the colonial administration to create townships as adjuncts to the larger towns: one for blacks and one for what South Africans term *coloureds.* Many of the latter are workers, and some are supervisors and technicians or minor functionaries in public and private sectors. Apart from any cultural distinction, coloured workers were in different economic circumstances from Africans: they simply did not have to rely to any extent on subsistence agriculture for their own reproduction, and they had a more completely urban existence, usually with better wages and securer rights. Their position vis-à-vis independence is likely, therefore, to have been more ambiguous, for in addition to gaining more rights, they also stood to lose relative privileges. Moreover, appeals to issues concerning land were likely to have little attraction for them.

Yet the major economic and social differences in Namibia are clearly between whites and the rest in terms not just of income differentials, estimated to be 17:1 in 1978, but in terms of employment and access to every aspect of social and health provision. One result of this income distribution is that at least 60 percent of the population lives in absolute poverty despite a relatively high per capita national income of more than U.S. $1,000 (UNIN, 1986: 77).

The final chapter addresses issues related to the prospects for transforming the inherited economic structure and inequalities. But this brief review highlights some of the options: Would Namibians be able to gain greater control of the economy and retain more of the mining and fishing revenues presently exported? Would they be able to halt the decline in national product? Would redistribution of land, income, and social facilities toward black workers, semiproletarians, and peasants prove possible? Much would depend on the political outcome of the transition.

### The Emergence of the Nationalist Movement

Organized political resistance to the South African regime, when it began in the late 1950s, came from two directions. From Hereroland it was articulated by the Chiefs' Council, and from Cape Town in South Africa it came from among migrant workers. These two initiatives gave rise to the formation of the South West African National Union (SWANU) and the South West African People's Organization. Indeed, many later strands of resistance emerged from these two parties. It is therefore important here to survey some of the background of these two earliest organizations and their shifting relationships. Doing so gives a sense of the dynamics underlying resistance to colonial rule and the ways in which it has changed over time.

#### South West African People's Organization

SWAPO had its origin in Cape Town in 1958 with the Owambo People's Congress, founded by migrant workers, among whom were Andimba Toivo

Ya Toivo, Peter Mueshihange (both to become ministers in the independence government), Solomon Mifima, and Andreas Shipanga. Associated with this group were Namibian students such as Jutundire (Fanuel) Kozonguizi, Ottilie Abrahams, and her husband, Kenneth Abrahams. In 1959 the organization moved to Windhoek and was renamed the Owambo People's Organization (OPO). From the beginning the intention was to form a national organization concerned not simply with the working conditions of Owambo migrants, although this was a central concern, but also with the ending of South African rule over the whole country. To this end branches were formed throughout the country, bringing different ethnic groups together in an effort to develop a nationalist movement following the African National Congress (ANC) model, not a tribal organization. Owambo migrants did remain leading figures, and Sam Nujoma, who has been SWAPO president since its foundation, was also the first president of OPO (Cullinan, 1982; Hamutenya and Geingob, 1972).

Because of this legacy, SWAPO has often been called an Owambo party, and indeed the 1989 election was the first major, public test of how far it had transcended its regional origins. From the beginning SWAPO had sought a wider panethnic composition and was by no means an exclusively Owambo organization. It was first and foremost an organization of workers, albeit migrants, who then sought to spread it among the semiproletarianized peasants of their home areas and other classes. Thus, in the late 1950s, Ya Toivo had discussions with Chief Hosea Kutako and with Kozonguizi, who was an adviser to the Herero Chiefs' Council. When SWAPO was finally founded in 1960, Mburumba Kerina became vice-president; and other non-Owambo members of the executive in the early days were Hans Beukes and Victor Dixab, from Rehoboth and Damaraland, respectively; Reverends Tjirimuje and Karauera of the African Episcopal Church; and Nama leader Hendrik Witbooi.

## South West African National Union

Founded in 1959, SWANU was technically the first nationalist party. In the beginning OPO was represented within SWANU, and Nujoma was on the first SWANU executive. SWANU was set up by a combination of two groups—the Herero Chiefs' Council and the South West Africa People's Alliance (SWAPA), a cultural and intellectual organization consisting mainly of Herero ex-students—meeting in a constitutional committee appointed by Chief Hosea Kutako to discuss the idea of a national organization. But the chiefs soon withdrew their support from SWANU. The new organization intended to create "a new movement with new symbols, transcending traditional loyalties," in contrast to the chiefs, who meant to "graft the modern machinery of a mass organization upon the traditional system of authority" (Ngavirue, 1972: 292). Kozonguizi was elected the first president of SWANU, and a sharp competition then developed between two educated Herero, Kerina and Kozonguizi, at the leadership level until Kerina left SWAPO in 1962 (SWAPO claimed he was expelled) to become first president of the (mainly Herero) National Unity Democratic Party (NUDO) in 1964. Kozonguizi also joined NUDO in 1966. NUDO was the political party of the Chiefs' Council and later became one of the main components of the DTA. Meanwhile, Gerson Veii became SWANU acting president in 1968.

SWANU did not at first participate in the Turnhalle constitutional talks organized by South Africa in September 1975 to bring together representatives from various ethnic groups according to the Odendaal proposals for homelands in Namibia. The participation of Chief Kapuuo, assassinated in 1978, in these talks was something of a victory for South Africa.

Peter Katjavivi (1988: 49), himself from Hereroland, argues that SWAPO and SWANU evolved along divergent paths. He suggests that SWANU, for instance, made no real attempt to win support from non-Herero communities, whereas SWAPO tried from early on to include people who were not simply former OPO members.

Certainly SWAPO did develop a broad mass base that included migrant workers as well as educated elites and clearly involved at least the passive support of some rural dwellers in Ovamboland and, to some extent, in other parts of the north. Otherwise the long war would not have been sustainable. SWAPO also offered the main symbol and focus for the protest against South African rule that continued throughout the 1970s and 1980s. These obvious attributes, plus the fact that SWANU had very little of either a mass popular base or an external presence as a national liberation movement, confirmed SWAPO's status. SWANU's recognition by OAU was in fact withdrawn in 1965. All these considerations are what probably induced the UN General Assembly to recognize SWAPO as "the sole authentic representative" of the Namibian people in 1973, even though SWANU continued to try projecting an international image and to challenge this claim right through the 1970s, and indeed up to the 1989 elections (SWANU, 1976). Although SWANU was not invited to the initial Turnhalle Constitutional Conference and stayed out of this process for some years, it did eventually participate in efforts toward such an internal settlement in 1985, thus generating a split in what remained of the party that persisted until the transition to independence.

We return to some of these issues concerning the character of SWAPO's popular base when we look at the election campaigns and results in Chapter 8. But to understand how some ordinary people were involved in the emergence of a nationalist movement in conflict with South African overrule, we need to explore some aspects of the war of liberation and assess its legacy. This is especially necessary if we wish to determine to what extent the liberation struggle radicalized Namibian political movements.

*The Politics of the Liberation War*

The Windhoek massacre of 1959 first raised the question of the necessity for armed struggle in the face of South African brutality. In fact, the decision to prepare for war probably stemmed from the early 1960s, the first SWAPO group having begun military training as early as 1962. In 1965 SWAPO had taken up the offer of money made by OAU and its Liberation Committee; that offer carried with it the condition that SWAPO be involved in armed struggle. The commitment to that struggle was finally made in 1966. Despite this, SWAPO was never a banned organization as ANC and PAC in South Africa or ZANU and ZAPU in Zimbabwe were. This had the advantage of allowing some kind of visible party apparatus in the country (although, arguably, it had the disadvantage of allowing the South African administration to keep the internal members under scrutiny). Yet members were constantly harassed: beaten up, dismissed from their jobs, put into jail, and, in Walvis Bay (where South African laws were in operation), placed under banning orders (SWAPO, 1978; Ya Otto, 1981).

This repression became particularly marked after the first military clashes took place in 1966. At this time Namibians were frustrated by their lack of success at the UN and the International Court of Justice. Thirty-seven SWAPO members were arrested and taken to Pretoria, where they were systematically tortured and finally put on trial under retroactive legislation in 1967. Andimba Toivo Ya Toivo and Tuhadeleni made defiant statements from the dock on behalf of the thirty-four convicted men, rejecting South Africa's right to be in Namibia and its legal jurisdiction over the territory.

After Angolan independence from Portugal in 1975, the number of clashes between SWAPO and the South Africans increased, and the way opened for larger numbers of Namibians to escape into exile in Angola and thence to Zambia and beyond and for the building up of support facilities in Angola from which to infiltrate fighters back across the Angolan border. Moreover, the guerrilla networks in northern Namibia, especially Ovamboland, were able to expand rapidly, no longer curbed by Portuguese forces on the Angolan side of the frontier—although the presence of UNITA in the remote southeast of Angola even before this period forced SWAPO into complex relations of partial collaboration and then, increasingly in the later 1970s, conflict with UNITA.

This engagement in the armed struggle was not the sole emphasis in SWAPO's external work. Its diplomatic efforts involved more than the usual lobbying for support from the OAU and the Non-Aligned Movement, the Eastern bloc, and sympathetic opinion in the West. The movement had a further trump card in Namibia's special status within the UN system. Indeed, at the very moment of SWAPO's birth, the UN began to take initiatives not only to wrest back the mandate that South Africa had assumed after World War I under the League of Nations, but also to promote Namibia's independence. The world body set up the UN Council for Namibia, which sought to take over South Africa's role in the transition to independence, and the UN Institute for Namibia, whose purpose was to train refugees; it also moved in the 1970s to urge the UN to use the imposition of sanctions as the major instrument for pressuring South Africa to withdraw. Certainly some of the leaders of SWAPO, like the older generation of nationalist leaders in most countries of Southern Africa, saw this international pressure for change as the decisive force for bringing about independence; for them the armed struggle was an adjunct, a crucial lever for pressuring the Western powers. This emphasis on fighting, not in the hope of ever ousting the South Africans by military means alone, but until the world at large, if not the South African Defense Force (SADF), was exhausted enough to want the fighting to stop, became perhaps the major strategic aim in the 1980s as the massive South African military presence in Namibia and Angola put the guerrilla struggle more on the defensive. Such an emphasis was perhaps inevitable given the objective relative power balance between the two sides: the small size of the Namibian population meant, to use only one gauge, that the white population of South Africa alone outnumbered Namibians by a factor of five. This leads Gottschalk (1987: 34) to argue that "unlike the insurgencies of east and south-east Asia, they [the Namibians] cannot hope to militarily defeat their enemy and drive the occupying power from the country."

One crucial feature of the political dynamics of the war, a feature shared with other liberation struggles, was that the war set in motion an evolution of the political movement itself. SWAPO came to see its objectives in broader terms. It shifted in the later 1960s from being a party of protest, addressing the UN as well as its immediate overlords, to being people bringing about their own liberation.

Like other national liberation movements, SWAPO sought to overextend and wear down its enemy by sustaining a protracted struggle, using mainly hit-and-run guerrilla tactics. To this end SWAPO had to build up a military able to continually recruit, train, and deploy fighters and the support structures that sustain them. These structures were first set up in Zambia, at that time with only a narrow corridor for bringing out recruits through the common border and returning them through Caprivi; then later, with much greater effect, the structures were located in Angola.

A further legacy of the early years of struggle and these attempts to recruit and restructure the organization was the major internal conflict that arose in the mid-1970s following the unexpected arrival in Angola and Zambia of thousands of exiles. Many of them were members of the militant SWAPO Youth League, and they expected more material resources and better organization as part of a more militant strategy giving more weight to the armed struggle. They demanded representation in SWAPO structures

and called for a congress as a means to give the movement some ideological direction and shake up the old leadership, which, they felt, was remote
from them and from the immediate struggle. Simultaneously, People's
Liberation Army of Namibia (PLAN) cadres demanded more food and better arms. The SWAPO leadership, afraid of a takeover bid, called in the
Zambian army, and mass arrests followed, although the situation was confused by opportunists among the SWAPO leadership, led by Shipanga, who
tried to take advantage of this discontent in a personal bid for power. Most
of the detained combatants and students rejoined SWAPO after their
release and were sent to Angola, but Mifima and Shipanga were not
released from Tanzania, where they had been sent to avoid a writ of habeas
corpus in Zambia, until 1978. Shipanga eventually returned to Namibia
from Sweden to form his own party, SWAPO-Democrats (SWAPO-D).
(There were similar happenings in both the Zimbabwe nationalist movements, which were Zambian based at the time and were infected by both
personality clashes and young fighter dissidence. In each case conflicts
were resolved by Zambian intervention in favor of a section of the leadership. See Cliffe, 1980.)

Further such episodes followed the SWAPO leadership's claim to have
uncovered a spy networ!. in the early 1980s. In fact, the leadership admitted
to having detained some one hundred suspects in 1984, one of whom was
said to have died in detention. Later allegations put the number at several
hundred. This detainee issue became central to the formation and campaigning of party alliances during 1988 and 1989 and may have had a dis-
couraging and inhibiting effect on SWAPO supporters themselves during
the campaigning period (see Chapter 7).

Whatever the shifts in fortune and in the internal cohesion of SWAPO,
it was able to maintain a war of some sort in Namibia's northern border
areas for more than twenty years. Insofar as our task here is not just to
record the events of 1989 and the elections but also to explain their outcome, it is necessary to explore some of the patterns of the war during its
distinct stages and to unravel their political form and consequences, not just
their military character and outcome, for these form the central backdrop
against which the elections and the transition to independence unfolded. It
is only when viewed against the war that the full significance of the events
of 1989 emerge, for first and foremost they involved a cease-fire and a
hoped-for permanent end to the disruptions and sufferings that had been
endured for so long.

There is no doubt that the war "profoundly transformed Namibian society" (Gottschalk, 1987: 34). Gottschalk documents the effect of repressive
measures in concentrating more than half of northern residents around a
periurban nexus among the three main towns and the shift of resources to
this area as part of the "hearts-and-minds" campaign and as a spin-off from

the military expenditure there (see also Herbstein and Evenson, 1989). But the effects were very unevenly spread. This long ordeal and the prospects for peace were likely to influence how people saw the election, what their expectations about independence were, and how they saw the parties. Yet such attitudes would also predictably differ depending on how particular groups of people in different regions experienced the war.

The combatants and other exiles (estimated later at almost seventy-five thousand) and their kinsfolk were obviously most directly affected by the war and the prospect of peace. The extent of the involvement in one community in Ovamboland can be gauged by the fact that all students at one secondary (boarding) school, a whole generation, disappeared across the border one night. There was thus a sizable increase in the voting age population when these young adults returned and a larger proportion still of families that were affected by their return (or sorrowed by their non-return).

The other group directly affected by the war and its end comprised the many thousands of Namibians who had been recruited to replace the South Africans' own conscripts, as well as their kin, who came to rely on their wages, perquisites, status, and political muscle. This group would tend to see the war and the prospects of independence in a different light. The first local detachment was set up in 1975, and most of these first Namibian recruits found their way into what came later to be called the 101 Battalion. At the same time, the 32 (Buffalo) Battalion was constituted from a complement of some nine thousand Angolans raised during South Africa's 1975 incursion into that country; this battalion continued to be engaged for the next dozen years primarily in Angola and chiefly against SWAPO bases and columns there. Then in 1980 the South West African Territorial Force (SWATF) was launched, and gradually sections were developed for Namibians from each ethnic group.

The San (wrongly and disparagingly called Bushmen) provide an obvious example of the kind of impact on the whole society: many were among the Angolan recruits who continued to operate in their country of origin, with their families set up as residents in special camps in Namibia. Other San were recruited as trackers and came to form special Battalions 201 and later 203, which operated from camps in Caprivi, to which their kin were relocated and which were run paternalistically by South African commanders as "total institutions"; these camps completely changing the San's customary way of life "from foragers to fighters" (Lee, 1986). As a result, a large proportion of their number (twenty-nine thousand in the 1981 census, plus seven thousand from Angola, of whom fifteen hundred were professional soldiers and fifty-five hundred were their dependents) became dependent on the war situation. Those living in the camps, mainly in western Bushmanland, continued to receive until April 1990 between R 600 and

R 1,400 a month (CIMS, 1990: 164). Some of the seminomadic pastoralists from Kaokoland were also recruited as professional soldiers, mainly to act as trackers.

In addition to these specialist units to which smaller ethnic groups contributed disproportionately, many thousands of recruits made up the several regular "ethnic" battalions that formed SWATF, and their number increased greatly with the extension of conscription to all Africans in 1981. There were separate battalions assigned to Ovamboland, Kavango, eastern Caprivi, and Kaokoland, and a catchall 911 Battalion was made up of recruits from ethnic populations in the center and south of the country. Altogether SWATF had built up to thirty thousand troops by 1989, and several times that number of dependents had their livelihoods related to the war. However, conscription requirements may also have indirectly worked to aid SWAPO recruitment because they forced young men to take one side or another.

The list of those recruited into the war on the South African side did not end with SWATF, for a number of counterinsurgency units came into existence under the South West African Police (SWAPOL), also created in the 1980s. These included a "guard force" designed to protect tribal authorities and other special individuals; a task force responsible for counterinsurgency in the police zone, as opposed to the northern border districts; and, most notoriously, the mobile counterinsurgency unit Koevoet (literally, "crowbar"). The latter came to have a large part in the follow-up operations that were such a crucial component of South Africa's counterinsurgency strategy: army units patrolled fixed sections of the border; they or the trackers could call up rapidly available air strikes or helicopterized or motorized columns when signs of guerrillas were spotted, as could the guard force or other informers in the northern communities. Very often it was Koevoet in its Casspir, armed vehicles that arrived with the firepower to finally dispatch the fighters or that forced the initial "intelligence" out of local people. Of those killed in Namibia, 80 percent were said to have been murdered by Koevoet (*New York Times,* 15 January 1989). Its infamous reputation is attested to by commentators who in no measure could be considered pro-SWAPO: a U.S. author writing for the establishment Institute for Strategic Studies in London refers to the unit's "brutal and indiscriminate behaviour towards the people of Ovamboland" and quotes "an eminent jurist familiar with court cases involving Koevoet" as characterizing it as "a state-supported murder unit" (Jaster, 1990: 41, 75); even a South African account notable for its sympathetic treatment of South African security forces has to admit that "there is no denying the fact that some members of Koevoet have been found guilty of such offences as murder and assault" (Steenkamp, 1989: 216). South African proclamations gave Koevoet and other personnel a high degree of indemnity from such offenses, and the formal position of Koevoet and other units within SWAPOL gave them an ambiguous status under the UN plan agreed to in the 1970s prior to their formation. This situation was to prove a bone of contention during the transition period leading up to the elections.

This kind of war also affected very large numbers of people indirectly. SWAPO's guerrilla methods involved mobilizing effective, widespread support among the population in operational areas, which would then supply intelligence about the regime's troop movements and such, logistical support in terms of transporting and hiding equipment and arms, food, and other resources, and protective cover so that when outnumbered or outgunned, PLAN fighters could just mingle among the locals. These changes in organization and tactics in turn had inevitable effects on many people other than the direct combatants and not just innocent bystanders who might be caught in the cross fire.

South African counterinsurgency tactics sought to combat this process in two classical ways: by trying to distinguish the guerrillas from the villagers and sever the sustaining links between them and by attempting to win over the hearts and minds of the people through the use of carrots of some services. Beginning in the late 1970s SADF took over more and more of the hospitals, schools, and other social facilities in northern Namibia; but SADF's tendency to indulge in overt antiterrorist propaganda was often seen as another form of repression and could well have been counterproductive on occasions (IDAF, 1982). The first task mainly involved repression—forcing people to inform on fighters and their whereabouts, tracking down possible guerrillas through search-and-destroy methods, and generally providing a level of terror that sought to bring home the lesson that the cost of aiding SWAPO fighters was too high. In practice, because the South African forces themselves, and even the Namibians they later used, could not easily distinguish fighters from residents, or supporters from innocent bystanders, the terror tended to be indiscriminate and widespread in operational areas. It thus was potentially counterproductive to the second tactic of winning support. Thus, whether the provision of medical treatment, education, and agricultural advice was sufficient to win over any but those on the direct payroll of the security services or local government would be important to discover. The outcome of liberation wars depends on those essentially political efforts of popular mobilization, on the one hand, and of counterinsurgency and countermobilization, on the other.

In the remote, arid, and mountainous northwestern district of Kaokoland, the several small ethnic groups there benefited from counterinsurgency efforts in other ways than the provision of services: they were able to use the three thousand rifles they received to "protect themselves against SWAPO infiltrators" to live more off hunting game, thereby earning cash to build up the cattle herds on which their livelihoods depended.

Because of this, and because the whole area and its few isolated water holes were easily sealed off, SWAPO made little headway in this district either militarily or politically.

The perceptions of those towns and rural areas farther south where there had been little actual fighting but probably some repression would be different again. Our task of trying to assess the political effect of the war on different communities and elements in them is, however, made more difficult because predicting how even those people most directly affected by the war might react to the changed situation of 1989 was not a straightforward matter. They might be likely to vote for peace, but would this mean identifying with the nationalist movement so that the fruits of the long struggle might be realized or rejecting the movement for fear that the war might go on, either because South Africa or local whites would never accept a SWAPO government or because some other obstacle intruded? How would different people and groups calculate their prospects under different types of independence governments? Would they be worried about revenge or the end of favors? Would they be concerned about securing a new deal? Such speculations concern us in Chapter 8, when we attempt to tease out the reasons people voted the way they did.

In practice it is always difficult to determine the political by-products of such struggles because by their nature they are seldom fought to the point where one side wins an outright military victory. Such was the case in Namibia. Yet how deep and how extensive the political mobilization had been are difficult questions that only future histories of the war will fully answer. However, some preliminary assessment is necessary to understand the exact nature of the agreements that led to the cease-fire, the elections, and the transition to independence and why the two sides entered into them at that time. Such an assessment also helps bring into focus the patterns of political consciousness and organization in different regions and among various strata of the population and suggests likely determinants of voting patterns.

Of course, the elections themselves can act as an entrance into this hitherto hidden realm of popular consciousness and grassroots organization. The results need to be read as a barometer of popular feeling and of how people were affected by the war. This evidence is all the more useful not only because much of what was going on was hidden, subject to state censorship and justifiable caution about self-disclosure, but also because what is on record is one-sided. There are now several books and articles published in South Africa that simply document, often in great detail, the military feats of the South African forces in a celebratory manner (inter alia, Steenkamp, 1983, 1989; Stiff, 1985, 1989; Heitman, 1990; Hooper, 1988; Norval, 1989). SWAPO statements or church reports tend to simply catalog the very real extent of the suffering rather than reveal the mobilization of the people. So what can be said about the political character of the war during its different phases, and what does the election help clarify about those phases?

In the early days of the war, from 1966 to 1975, SWAPO's armed wing, PLAN, had been forced to confine its activities to the eastern Caprivi strip and occasionally the Okavango River area, as access could be secured only from bases in Zambia. The guerrillas made quick sorties across this remote northeastern border, engaged in small-scale actions with SADF or acts of sabotage, and then withdrew. After Angolan independence in 1975, it was possible to extend activities from bases around Cunene and Cuande Kubange in Angola into Namibian territory much further west in Ovamboland and Kavango.

In 1976 reported actions increased to a level three times the total for the previous ten years and continued to escalate throughout the late 1970s. The three northern border regions were declared "security districts" subject to a kind of martial law: people could be stopped, searched, and held without trial. Torture was used extensively; a kilometer-wide swath of no-man's-land was cleared along the border with Angola by shifting people from their homes, a strip of it sanded to reveal tracks. Yet the guerrillas still moved in, and contacts between them and SADF spread, eventually becoming common in the white farming areas south of Ovamboland near Grootfontein and Tsumeb and occasionally even further south. As a result, vehicles and helicopters were damaged, roads and bridges were blown up, and land mines made certain local dirt roads impassable (and prompted the introduction of the fearsome, mine-protected Casspirs and other armed personnel carriers by the South African security forces). At the same time, Caprivi became less contested after South African raids into Zambia intimidated the government there to the point that all cross-border operations were stopped by President Kaunda in 1978.

During the period 1976–1981, especially in Ovamboland, PLAN fighters might have had a continuing presence for some weeks among the population and no doubt made contact with their kin and with SWAPO party activists. However, SWAPO tactics were still aimed at withdrawing guerrillas into Angola and then reinfiltrating them; SWAPO leaders thought they did not have sufficient freedom of movement to set up even clandestine bases or have fighters permanently lodged among the people— although some guerrillas did urge such methods, which may have been one issue of internal dispute.

In 1981 following the breakdown of what would have been the first talks between South Africa and SWAPO at the Geneva preimplementation (of United Nations Security Council Resolution [UNSCR] 435) meeting, South African forces increased the pressures on PLAN. First, they invaded southern Angola in force, doing battle from then on regularly with the Angolan army (FAPLA) and thereby destabilizing the Angolan government and undermining its ability to support SWAPO while at the same time destroying SWAPO bases and refugee camps. Moreover, in areas of Angola to the north of Kavango, UNITA, armed and supported by SADF, harried PLAN fighters and made it difficult for them to move up to the border. Through these and other methods, guerrillas were halted often before they reached Namibia, and indeed PLAN found itself contributing to battles with FAPLA to defend its own bases and supply lines within Angola and support its ally and host. At the same time, efforts were greatly stepped up to seek and destroy PLAN fighters inside Namibia—through greater border surveillance, increased use of trackers, greater airborne and armed vehicle mobility, and massive stepping up of repression against the population in the north and against "legal" SWAPO organs and supporters throughout Namibia.

The hearts-and-minds campaigns of civilian activities by SADF also date from this time, although the SWAPO presence in Ovamboland and the strength of popular feeling there led to the virtual abandonment of these services by the mid-1980s. Elsewhere, such efforts, coupled with measures to promote an indigenous political alternative to SWAPO via second-tier local administrations and local parties linked to DTA, did have some effect. In the most extreme instance, perhaps half the San people were settled and remained until 1989 in camps under direct SADF administration. As a result of these various measures, PLAN's presence, ability to move, and capacity to fight were reduced and severely constrained—at the price of the presence of tens of thousands of SADF troops in the north—but were never eliminated.

In central and southern areas of the country, the effects of war were not anywhere near as direct, although a constantly repressive police presence was felt throughout the country. Arrests and beatings were a common occurrence everywhere in Namibia. One SWAPO activist told us that he wore an anorak even in the hottest weather just in case he was arrested: the anorak offered partial protection from a beating, and jails were cold places! At demonstrations the dreaded Koevoet counterinsurgency force and its Casspirs made their appearances just as in the north, descending to beat up and sometimes kill demonstrators.

How far the different kinds of political repression in various regions and the limiting of guerrilla opportunities actually diverted people's (concealed) feelings and loyalties from SWAPO to collaborationist parties was not at all clear and only began to be revealed with more open political activity in 1989. The extent of this effect is an explanation of and is measured by the election results.

*The Political Legacy of the War*

To further gauge the effects of the long conflict, it is instructive to compare Namibia's experiences with those of others in the region. A war of liberation will have the greatest political impact on the people in areas that are fully liberated, as occurred in parts of northern Mozambique, where fully fledged political education and experiments in new forms of social and economic organization were possible (Saul, 1979; Munslow, 1983). Namibia's political geography and the power of SADF did not allow for such areas, not even for the creation of semiliberated zones as occurred in many parts of Zimbabwe, which sufficiently excluded security forces and local administration to ensure a continuing presence of guerrillas, even if they did their extensive political work only at night.

Even if no such dual power was achieved in Namibia, there was, however, a continual process of fighters infiltrating into the most populous area, Ovamboland, where some political interaction with local people no doubt occurred, even though guerrillas were seldom based within the country. There was also massive repression in that area—itself a process that could politically educate local people about the harsh realities of South African overrule. The same process of infiltration and the beginnings of interaction between fighters and rural dwellers had got under way in Kavango and Caprivi in the 1960s and 1970s. But that was greatly curtailed by attacks on bases in Zambia, the South African strengthening of UNITA across the immediate border area in southeast Angola, and the Lusaka Accords of 1984, which ended Zambia's role as a base for SWAPO, although there had been a virtual curtailment after SADF raids into Zambia in 1978.

Indeed, one pattern of war needs to be noted at this stage because of what it explains about the circumstances that led to UNSCR 435 finally being implemented more than a decade after it had been agreed to. The truth is that much of the fighting that was decisive for political events in Namibia occurred in Angola. SADF only finally and successfully contained the PLAN incursions that were escalating markedly between 1976 and 1979 when SADF troops invaded Angola in strength and provided backing for UNITA to take control of southeast Angola. As a result, Kavango and Caprivi were closed to SWAPO, which was thereby restricted to a much reduced and more easily policed border with a densely populated Ovamboland. In the mid-1980s it was the mounting capabilities of FAPLA, with the backing of SWAPO and ANC battalions, to threaten UNITA and even SADF's capacity to protect UNITA that became the crucial lever to get South Africa to the negotiating table.

Yet it is not only the geographical extent or depth of guerrilla penetration that future historians need to monitor to get a measure of the consequences of the war. Also important is the ideological content of the political consciousness and organizational effectiveness that developed in different regions, whether as a result of SWAPO's direct political education, South African repression or hearts-and-minds campaigning, or the dire underlying socioeconomic realities people faced as a result of the colonial situation and the war. There is less documentation about ordinary people's perceptions than about other aspects of the war, and it is possible only to speculate here on what was partially revealed during the elections. Here again, comparisons can yield insights. Ranger's study (1985) of popular consciousness in Zimbabwe, Kenya, and Mozambique suggests several dimensions that can be explored: the role of "traditional" values, especially (indigenous) religion; the basic grievance that was identified (in Zimbabwe it was the loss by blacks of land and farming opportunities to whites); and what class or other divisions, if any, among the African population were salient.

In the Namibian case, SWAPO, either as a severely constrained internal political party or as an armed movement, seemed to possess only limited opportunity to engage in political education like the nighttime *pungwe* in Zimbabwe and delivered little, if any, explicit message that attempted to give a specific key to the realities of local people's lives, other than a broad appeal to Namibian (and perhaps Owambo) identity and the wrongs perpetrated by the South African regime and whites. From what little is known, there seems, however, to have been little equivalent appeal to the supernatural as occurred in the Mau Mau ceremonies in Kenya (Buijtenhuis, 1982) or in the role of spirit media (Lan, 1985) in Zimbabwe. Instead, the role of the Christian churches as a vehicle was very extensive (Ellis, 1981; Frostin, Katjavivi, and Mbuende, 1989). At the same time, the loss of land was not the centerpiece of such mobilization as did occur in Owambo—land seizure did not correspond with the historical realities of their being partitioned off from the rest of the country and ignored, rather than removed from their lands as people farther south had been. And although labor migration had not sufficiently penetrated lifestyles and rural conditions in Zimbabwe to rule out what Ranger has called the return to the "peasant option," through better prices for crops and a fair share of agricultural inputs, the same was no longer possible in Ovamboland. The land issue did, of course, figure in SWAPO appeals in those other areas, but whether for reasons of its being muted or alternative appeals by DTA, land seems not to have had the same political resonance as in neighboring countries.

Local "enemies" of the struggle were certainly pointed out but were defined in political terms: the collaborationist chiefs who ran the bantustan administrations, recruits for SWATF, and informers on SWAPO, especially in Owambo, where some chiefs were assassinated. Even though an African middle class was actively emerging in the 1980s, there seems to have been little effort by SWAPO to point the finger at any broader class, strata, or other privileged group identified with the status quo, such as, for instance, occurred with the Kikuyu landed gentry in Kenya. In Ovamboland some very well-off traders and property owners who had undoubtedly prospered from the war economy still gave support to SWAPO in the elections, even if it was belated. In the other war-affected areas of the north, where

SWAPO clearly had only partial support, that seems to have come as much or more from educated professional and employed people as from poorer peasants.

A final issue to raise about the very different experiences of the liberation war among people in the dispersed area of Namibia is the overall effect of these experiences on Namibian nationalism. Anticolonial analysts have tended to generalize the image of SWAPO as the "sole, authentic" voice into a picture of the Namibian people united in struggle and held down only by South African repression and by ethnic collaborators of an apartheid system. In one of the few analyses that avoids this oversimplified perspective while similarly rejecting the colonial apologists, Dollie (1989: 30) suggests that these differential effects of the war combined with radically differing precolonial linkages to other parts of Africa and insertions into colonial administration and economy and a lack of any linguistic similarity or even a common colonial oppression meant that a "positive identity. . . has yet to be developed." The elections and other aspects of the transition would reveal how far this conclusion was accurate.

*Mass Organizations and the Nationalist Movement*

*The SWAPO Youth League and the student movement.* Throughout Namibia one of SWAPO's strongholds has been in the schools and colleges, among teachers, students, and young people generally, including such places as Hereroland and Damaraland. A student was killed at Okakarara in Hereroland in 1976, and there had been mass demonstrations before that at Ongwediva High School and Training College in the Owambo region, at the Augustineum High School in Okahandja, and at Martin Luther High School in Okombahe. Mass expulsions followed demonstrations and students left to continue their political activities elsewhere. Some went into the exile struggle or into the unions, thereby establishing a close relationship between students and workers, and some went into teaching, where they influenced a succeeding generation of students.

In the months before the independence elections, school boycotts all over the country grew to affect some two hundred thousand students despite the South African administrator-general's (AG) efforts to outlaw politics in schools. These had a profound effect on political awareness, especially in Kavango, where SWAPO organization had been weaker than in neighboring Ovamboland, and also served notice that the ethnic administrations had not won many hearts and minds among youth. The student organization NANSO, developed in the mid-1980s, came to play a key role in these events and functioned as a mobilizing agent for SWAPO, as did the teachers' union NANTU, which was formed in early 1989.

*The churches.* Throughout Namibia Lutheran, Anglican, and Catholic churches supported the nationalist movement from the outset and did so in circumstances where SWAPO's own overt efforts were often constrained. Church leaders were outspoken in their criticism of the illegal South African regime when the pulpit was one of the only public platforms allowed, and church organizations built up a network of publicity, communication, and organizational focus in support of SWAPO. In Ovamboland, as in other parts of Africa where congregations have suffered great repression, churches identified with the people's privations and were an important vehicle for protesting these conditions and mobilizing welfare. Thus, it was natural that the Council of Churches in Namibia (CCN) should be the body to undertake the reception of the returned SWAPO exiles and combatants, so many of them from the northern region. Elsewhere clergy and church leaders not only identified with SWAPO and the nationalist struggle but also in the south were often, with students, the only vehicles for articulating that position. One church leader interviewed in Kavango spoke of the tension of taking this position while still trying to avoid alienating those members of the congregation who were not SWAPO supporters.

During the campaigning period and the elections, CCN played a continuing role in providing a forum for voter education by promoting communications within the country and with the outside world and by organizing international observers to monitor the electoral process. This small army of observers, some of them resident in localities for months, who were ready to yell "Foul" if the South African election administrators or security personnel stretched the rules, were a crucial ingredient in ensuring the election was free and fair, and their observations have been published in an invaluable collection of firsthand reports of the election (CIMS, 1990). The detailed role of the churches and their close involvement in the struggle have been documented by a work, two of whose editors are senior SWAPO officials (Frostin, Katjavivi, and Mbuende, 1989).

*The trade union movement.* Black workers have always been at the forefront of resistance to colonial rule in Namibia—even SWAPO grew out of a contract workers' organization. The trade union movement was not, however, fully organized until the 1980s, partly because of repression and partly because of the dispersed nature of the workers in far-flung mines and coastal fisheries and the contract basis of their employment. However, strikes have been a powerful weapon in the hands of Namibian workers. The most famous was the 1971 contract mineworkers' strike, which brought the mining economy to a standstill and had far-reaching results in terms of developing a consciousness of popular resistance but which, significantly, was organized at the point of embarkation for work, not at the site of production (Cronje and Cronje, 1979; Gordon, 1977; Moorsom, 1979).

The partial repeal of the pass laws in Namibia in 1977 and the official (although not always actual) end of the contract system were in part due to the fact that workers had rendered the laws unenforceable. Between June 1973 and June 1975, there were another seventy strikes in all sectors of the economy, and the militancy of the workers continued. SWAPO took advantage of this situation to launch the National Union of Namibian Workers (NUNW), which had been planned in exile in 1972 but was not introduced within the country until 1977. It was at first a general union that followed where workers led, backing up strikes led by SWAPO activists in local areas rather than organizing on the shop floor. However, after the release of some younger SWAPO leaders from Robben Island in 1984, and under the influence of COSATU and the 1984–1986 resistance in South Africa, there was renewed vigor in the activity of trade unions. NUNW was relaunched, now separately organized in six different sector unions, under the leadership of people such as ex-combatant and Robben Island prisoner Ben Ulenga. Militancy occurred in late 1988 and early 1989 when NUNW organized protests and strike action against hurriedly announced plans by the departing South African administration to privatize certain public works and even social services. The radicalism of the unions in the late 1980s was greater than might be expected from their small size; NUNW had a paid membership of only fifty thousand. The shop floor militancy of 1989 was finally swallowed up by the trauma and controversy surrounding the abortive cease-fire in April and by the unions devoting all their efforts to supporting SWAPO in the election campaign.

However, this militant mood did spark two initiatives by the South African administration and employers. First, efforts were made to promote an alternative, less radical trade union movement that did not owe political affiliation to SWAPO: some of the small but influential unions for white workers, such as the South West African Miners Union, were encouraged to open their ranks to blacks, and a few new unions were promoted. Second, in 1987 a commission of inquiry into labor matters was set up under the chair of Professor Wiehahn, who had headed a similar body in South Africa in the 1970s. This body could be seen as preempting any independent government's policy in this area, and its proposals, while couched in terms of meeting "international standards," in fact proposed statutory conciliation procedures that would limit the right to strike (Wiehahn, 1989).

## South Africa's Response: The Politics of Collaboration

### Restructuring the Colonial State and Society

Although the UN was never prepared to enforce its revocation of South Africa's mandate over Namibia or the findings of the International Court of Justice, increasing pressure from inside and outside the country in the 1960s was sufficient to shelve South African plans for Namibia's full incorporation. Nevertheless, in defiance of international opinion, South Africa went ahead with the implementation of apartheid policies along the same lines as those being introduced in South Africa itself. The 1964 report of the Odendaal Commission (set up in 1962) advocated "separate development" delineating several prospective bantustans. In 1968–1969, the Development of Self-Government for Native Nations in South West Africa Act and then the South West Africa Affairs Act were passed to give effect to the report; these acts provided for the creation of tribal homelands and the eventual setting up of eleven legislative assemblies and executive councils. The plan was seemingly for the eventual "independence" of the ten black homelands and the incorporation of "white" Namibia in RSA. Meanwhile, an administration was provided for each of the eleven identified groups, which did exercise power over matters concerning education, health, and agriculture. These administrations had to be very largely financed by grants from the central government, for local taxes raised so little except among whites, who thus were able to establish facilities of a far superior standard exclusively for themselves. Control of the military, police, and foreign policy was excluded from the powers of these ethnic administrations and vested in the central South African administration.

However, beginning in 1973 extensive amendments to this plan were made by the South Africans themselves (Werner, 1987; Lister, 1987). This new strategy opted for a form of independence for Namibia as a whole but under a kind of federal structure, with the ethnic administrations acting as a second tier sending representatives to a central authority. Moreover, they would become genuinely ethnic administrations, extending their control and provision of services to those of their people in the towns. This formula was in part a concession to the UN, but it was mainly a stratagem for containing the national liberation struggle and finding an alternative (parallel to the internal solution in Zimbabwe that was engineered in the same period) to radical nationalism.

One further component of this approach was to foster not only administrations but also an alternative political movement to SWAPO that could eventually serve as a mechanism for mobilizing some support for such a solution. The form chosen encouraged the members of the administrations to form local political parties and then attempted to set up nationally a formal political alliance of the ethnic clients, what was to become DTA. But constitutional measures were also required: the South African parliament officially gave up its legislative powers over Namibia and the white members representing the territory in favor of a national assembly created from the DTA-dominated Constituent Assembly that was eventually elected (without SWAPO participation) in 1978. An internal central administration, acting under an administrator-general appointed by RSA in 1977, took over the running of national affairs, except for security and external affairs, which were left to the AG himself. The Council of Ministers thus set up was composed of DTA members. These various steps emanated from the Turnhalle Constitutional Conference, which was set up in 1975 at the time of Angolan independence and continued its work until 1977.

As part of the same process of restructuring, the military containment of SWAPO forces was also internalized. SWATF was built up on wage levels higher than most jobs and was later enlarged further through conscription of all Namibian male adults (which posed many youth with a stark choice of fighting or joining the nationalist struggle and thus helped fuel the ranks of PLAN). SWATF consisted of seven ethnically recruited battalions and various special force units plus tribal police, which gradually took on much of the direct counterinsurgency operation within the country. This left the SADF conventional forces free to operate in Angola, providing logistics and other support for UNITA there and attacking SWAPO guerrillas before they crossed the border. The containment of SWAPO thereby took on some aspects of a civil war between Namibians. At the same time, the addition of more than twenty thousand people to the payroll provided an avenue for patronage beyond civil service jobs and favors dispensed by the tribal administrations.

The new strategy also included some social and economic "reform" measures. There was a concerted effort "to expand and incorporate the black petty-bourgeoisie" (Werner, 1987: 73), which had been discouraged by strategies similar to ones followed in colonial Rhodesia before the mid-1950s and again by Ian Smith's regime, which relied solely on traditional authorities as the main allies of the regime. Pass laws and other apartheid-type restrictions, notably on owning urban land, were repealed. The salaries of professionals such as teachers and nurses were dramatically raised to parity with whites. The tight laws of influx control that dictated where Namibians could live were repealed, thus allowing for freer movement, more rapid urbanization, and some partial reduction of contract labor and migrancy. A further step in the revision of laws that had administered much of Namibia as a labor reserve came with the Wiehahn Commission appointed in late 1987. There was an effort to provide agricultural support for richer peasants and the beginnings of efforts in some areas to privatize communal land to their advantage. The fostering of the black middle class led Dollie (1989: 31) to conclude that compared with South Africa, "in Namibia [it] is relatively powerful and decidedly conservative."

In 1983 there was mass DTA resignation from the powerless Council of Ministers, resulting in the abolition of the National Assembly and the Council of Ministers by the AG and the eventual setting up of a new multiparty conference that culminated in the appointment of members to yet another transitional interim government, the installation of which was celebrated in Windhoek in 1985 under Proclamation R101. The government was once again boycotted by SWAPO and other noncollaborationist parties. DTA was one of six member parties (the others included one faction of

SWANU and SWAPO-D) in this transitional government and held three cabinet posts. The transitional government remained in power until it was dissolved in 1989 in preparation for the implementation of UNSCR 435.

## The Democratic Turnhalle Alliance

This federal alliance was founded in 1977 by representatives of the ethnic population groups that had staged a walkout from the Turnhalle Constitutional Conference (1975) over the insistence by the National Party (an offshoot of the South African ruling party) on maintaining certain apartheid legislation in the proposed new constitution. Dirk Mudge had already formed the Republican Party in September of that year, after he had left the National Party over similar issues. The most influential main DTA leaders were always these original white defectors from the National Party, even as it brought in elements from among black ethnic groups. Those leaders sought to do this in part by fostering a tradition of consensus decisionmaking that effectively gave the white groups a veto. DTA's "amended anti-discriminatory" constitutional proposals then became the basis of its policy and manifesto.

The original alliance included ten ethnic parties, each led by tribal, collaborationist leaders appointed originally by South Africa: the Bushman Alliance led by Geelbooi Kashe; the Kavango Alliance led by Chief Alfons Majavero; the Rehoboth Baster Association under the leadership of Dr. Ben Africa; the Caprivi Alliance Party of Chief Richard Mamili; the Tswana Alliance; the National Democratic Party led by Cornelius Ndjoba in Ovamboland; the "coloured" Labor Party led first by Andrew Kloppers and then by Joey Julius; Daniel Luipert's Nama-based party, the Democratic Turnhalle Alliance; and the white Republican Party. The final element in DTA, the SWA Democratic United Front led by Engelhart Christy, was a breakaway from the Damara Representative Council, which was the one ethnic administration political grouping to stay out of the alliance.

DTA thus had a federal structure of small ethnic parties variously built around the tribal administrations plus the small parties with which they had been involved in central government in the four years before the transition. It represented the second major strand in Namibian political groupings— one based on ethnic loyalties (which were themselves fairly artificial creations of the 1940s; see Gottschalk, 1987), patronage, and manipulation. Local leaders had been content to collaborate with the South African administration and indeed had gone along, some clearly with their eyes open, with South Africa's strategy of building up a political force that would dissociate itself from radical nationalism and be more amenable to mining and farming interests and to "big brother" next door. DTA did manage to gain some political base, although its numerical extent and depth could be questioned, based as they were on blandishments, patronage, and threats. Whatever legitimacy the ethnic elements of the alliance had in some localities was further undercut by the several charges of corruption that were under investigation from 1985 (Thirion, 1985), such as the well-known case involving Chief Riruako of Hereroland, and by the schools closure of 1988.

Popular perceptions of DTA were more generally going to be determined by the alliance's part in the government for some years, but these reactions were likely to be mixed. DTA might share the blame for repression in the north or be seen, especially in those regions, as having failed to end the war. Elsewhere among some segments DTA might be seen as experienced, as the provider of expanded services or even the guarantor of security. These latter appeals were certainly the basis of DTA's electoral strategy.

### Previous Electoral Experiences

Successive South African strategies involved bids to legitimize transitional structures via the ballot box. But none of these experiences boded well for the prospects of free and fair elections in 1989. Previous elections had been contested only by the collaborationist parties, plus the Damara Council; SWAPO refused to give them the implied legitimacy of participating. The first elections for tribal authorities were held in Owambo in 1973, but a successful campaign by SWAPO to get people to boycott them reduced the turnout to 2.5 percent (in any case only twenty-one out of fifty-four members were elected; the rest were nominated). In Kavango, in contrast, there was an estimated 65 percent turnout, and a Kavango authority was duly elected. Even the South African Broadcasting Corporation described these elections as a "farce": few seats were contested, and few votes were cast (quoted in Barber and Barratt, 1990: 127).

In 1975 in Owambo, it was another story. For a variety of reasons, SWAPO was unable to replicate the 1973 boycott, partly because many young activists had left the country for Angola and Zambia after Angolan independence made crossing the border more possible. Considerable pressure was exerted upon the people in Ovamboland: for example, collaborationist chiefs threatened loss of rights, jobs, or services. As a result, there was an estimated 76 percent voter turnout in Owambo. But in other parts of the country, only 4 percent of Owambo voted, making a total turnout of 55 percent (Serfontein, 1976; Ellis, 1979). When such threats were not enough, the regime resorted to direct coercion, such as beatings, to get people to the polls.

In the elections for a constitutional assembly in 1978, people were once again forced to register. There is much documented evidence of other electoral manipulation as well, which rendered the elections unacceptable to the international community (Ellis, 1979). A further feature of the elections was the great expense: DTA was reputed to have spent more than U.S. $5 million, from sources it refused to disclose, although there were suggestions of West German as well as South African finance (Leonard, 1983: 67). It is a known fact, revealed by a former South African Information Ministry official, Rhoodie, in the Muldergate scandal, that the ministry financed DTA (*The Guardian,* 28 March 1979). DTA won 82 percent of the vote, gaining forty-one out of fifty seats in the National Assembly. SWAPO and other noncollaborationist parties boycotted the election. The turnout was 80 percent of those registered. The registration process was again subject to coercion, to threats by headmen, and to the use of the voter registration card as a pass that could be demanded by police. Many refugees and temporary residents were apparently registered, and no one from a boycotting party could challenge the list. The South African regime claimed that 93 percent of the eligible population registered, but this figure depended on an estimate of the adult population at 440,000, almost certainly an underestimate. Others suggest it may have been nearer 600,000, implying a turnout of 60–70 percent (Ellis, 1979). DTA also gained power in many of the second-tier administration elections held later in 1980 in accordance with Proclamation AG8, not surprising considering the number of chiefs in the alliance and the lack of credible opposition. Indeed, the Tswana and Nama administrations had South African–nominated DTA majorities. The white administration had a National Party majority. The Damara voted for the Damara Council. It is significant that no elections were held in Ovamboland, although Peter Kalangula's Christian Democratic Action (CDA) was considered elected on the basis of the equally questionable 1975 elections.

These elections of the 1970s were the only previous electoral experience of the Namibian people, many of whom were forced to register and to vote against their will for a restricted set of collaborationist parties. Intimidation played a major role in these elections, police and special constables rounding up the voters, staffing the polling stations, and even filling in ballot papers for illiterate voters. The registration document (passbook) that every black Namibian had to carry and produce on demand also contained the voting record, so there was an effective instrument available to exert pressure on people to register and vote (Ellis, 1979). And although the pressures and the evidence of the pass could not dictate whom people voted for, the restricted choice of parties gave them little freedom. A measure of the resulting distortion is indicated by the fact that South Africa's own National Intelligence Service was still estimating in 1980 that in a free election SWAPO would win 80 percent of the vote (*New Statesmen* 22 August 1980).

It is against this background of intimidatory practices that the electoral processes of 1989 must be considered. Clearly, the South African administration, DTA (whose leaders had shared power and helped run this system nationally and locally for a decade), and the many activists on the payroll augmented by new recruits from the security forces expected that elections could be run on the old basis of patronage and coercion to obtain desired results. As Jaster (1990: 40) acknowledges, "There were reasonable grounds for [the] fear . . . that South Africa, through officials appointed as police and interim administrators of the territory, would try to rig the elections and the constitution." He adds that this fear was coupled with a fear of "an independent Namibia dominated by an Owambo majority." The two fears created, in the view of this establishment observer, a climate of mistrust among all those involved, Namibians and outsiders, in the transition process.

## Conclusion

This brief survey helps identify the social and political context in which the cease-fire, elections, and transfer of power took place in 1989. Namibian society was highly polarized: that 10 percent of the population that was white had a highly privileged separate status—the best jobs, the farms, the businesses, good educational and other opportunities; the black population was scattered, had been forced into ethnic identities that were partly artificial, and had had different experiences because of their location and the stereotyped role they were called upon to provide in the colonial labor economy. Namibia's was an exceptionally externally oriented economy in which minerals were the crucial resource, followed by fishing and farming, and were exploited by mainly migrant labor. Namibia had a history of a particularly repressive form of colonial rule, and its indigenous politics had for the most part been divided since the late 1950s into two quite divergent streams: armed opposition to that colonial presence and collaboration with it. During this time a violent war had brutalized the populous northern border areas, which led to their partial mobilization in support of SWAPO fighters and to the recruitment of a mercenary counterinsurgency force. This struggle in its various forms, and the repression and the attempts at social engineering and political manipulation designed to contain it, provided the immediate context of the war and accounted, among other things, for the bitterness between the two main contenders, SWAPO and DTA.

But the legacy of repression and containment was not simply one that implied a particularly pointed electoral contest and a vicious atmosphere. The managed transition leading up to the elections and independence heralded both the eventual end of the struggle of the Namibian people for liberation from South Africa and the continuation of that struggle into a new stage and in a different form. Thus, the election and the events leading to it have to be seen as a contest between the noncollaborationist, nationalist forces and the South African government, as well as among the actual registered parties, for South Africa was seeking to ensure its own desired outcome to the elections and its own preferred pattern of Namibian independence. These efforts involved various reform measures—promotion of black businesspersons, professionals, and rich peasants and partial relaxation of labor migrancy—designed to create a viable political alternative to SWAPO and reshape the political economy. In these respects Namibian experience became a precursor for measures that were introduced in South Africa some years later. One of the crucial analytical questions that we pose about the events of the late 1980s is how far Namibia was used as a testing ground for strategies that the National Party might seek to apply in the republic to end apartheid in a manner that suited its interests.

South Africa sought to dictate the basis for an independent Namibia and aimed to do so by trying to manage the transition. However, the role of controlling the transition was itself a matter of contestation because the transition was taking place within the context of a complex and much broader interplay of regional and international forces involving Angola, its own internal conflicts, the Cuban and Soviet presence there, and Western responses to that presence. These latter calculations were in turn premised on the other considerable interests that the West had in Namibia and the region, in particular Western concerns about what would emerge from the upheaval within South Africa itself—processes that obviously also affected South Africa's strategy and tactics in Namibia. But also at stake were the relations between RSA and all its neighbors. So for internal reasons as well as solidarity with a national liberation struggle, the Frontline States (FLS) and the other countries of the Southern African Development Coordination Conference (SADCC) sought to influence the transition in Namibia. The latter's best way for exerting influence was through the UN, which had sought to interpose itself as the manager of the transition—a role that both South Africa and the West contested.

How far South Africa's interests were motivated by a desire to manage its own geopolitical environment or by a more specific project for its own neocolonial solution in Namibia (Simon and Moorsom, 1987: 82) is at the heart of the complex field of contestation. Insofar as South African interests involved the latter, there would be some degree of conflict with Western interests, which had vacillated between a belief that a white South African government was and would remain the agency to protect these broader interests and a fear that the excesses of apartheid might threaten their long-term interests. These and other calculations as well as the complex international arena in which they were made are the focus of the next chapter.

# Notes

1. Britain was briefly a third colonial power, and its annexation of the only deep-water port at Walvis Bay gave RSA its argument for not including the area in the independence settlement (Berat, 1991).

# 3

# The Search for an Internationally Acceptable Transition to Independence

## The Determining Influence of International Forces

The old adage "Whether there will be meat in the kitchen is never decided in the kitchen" (Baran, 1957: 308) was true of Namibia. At many points in its history, the fate of this small population was decisively affected by forces at work elsewhere in the region or the global system. On the one hand, as we saw in Chapter 2, nationalist forces had played two different cards in their efforts to dislodge the colonial rule of South Africa: internal struggle and appeals to the international community. This last strategy involved them in close alliances with OAU, the nonaligned movement, FLS, and, through and with those bodies in broader diplomatic maneuvers, the UN system. Crucial for both the internal struggle and the diplomatic game were events to the north in Angola: the national liberation struggle there and the collapse of Portuguese rule in 1975; the fighting between MPLA and the other Angola movements, UNITA and FNLA, which were backed by the United States and supported by a South African invasion in 1975; the support the MPLA government had come from then on from Cuban troops and Soviet arms supplies; the continued incursions of SADF; the debates over these issues within the UN. From the start of the armed struggle, SWAPO had had links with MPLA but also (ambiguous) relations with UNITA, which had always had a presence in the southeast corner of Angola. SWAPO had had to cross that territory to infiltrate from Zambia into Caprivi and had located bases and routes there until they were betrayed by UNITA to SADF in 1975.

On the other hand, South Africa was also very much an international actor. From the late 1970s onward, its policy toward post-Turnhalle Namibia was always calculated within the context of a total strategy that sought definite outcomes at home and in the whole Southern Africa region. South Africa sought to get acceptance, if not support, for its regional policies; for its incursions into Angola; and for its delays in handing over power in Namibia by overtures to the major Western powers in which it presented itself as the upholder of the free world faced with communist expansion in the region. Given this situation, the Western powers themselves, but increasingly the United States in particular, took the whole issue of Namibia into their hands beginning in 1976 and continuing throughout the 1980s. Five governments—the United States, Britain, France (all permanent members of the UN Security Council with a veto), Canada, and West Germany—constituted themselves the WCG. Its purpose was to liaise—some would say collaborate—with South Africa (Landis, 1988). In the process, however, they had to contend with questioning from African and Third World governments and the UN system and with opposition from the other superpower.

So the complex interactions of the superpowers, the West, FLS, Angola and Cuba, and the United Nations are just as much part of the saga of Namibia's transition to independence as are the long internal war and the elections of 1989. These international forces are the concerns of this chapter, which seeks to explore how far they were responsible for the long delay in implementing the UN plan for Namibia's independence, for the plan's eventual implementation, and for the shape of the transition. Specifically, what was going on behind the scenes in the international negotiations in 1977–1978 that produced the UN plan? What were the different actors seeking to achieve? What was the balance of forces between them, on what did it depend, and how and why did it shift over the following years? Was RSA serious about accepting the plan, or did RSA agree to sign UNSCR 435/78 out of fear that international sanctions were a real possibility? Did the WCG countries' readiness to veto such proposals remove such fears? And if so, was RSA's eventual agreement merely nominal? And if RSA was not serious about implementing the plan, what was the country's game plan during the following ten years? If the point was to buy time, why was South Africa doing so? What kind of Namibian settlement was WCG itself after? In 1976 the Western powers had not been prepared to pay the price of sanctions for the implementation of an earlier resolution, UNSCR 385/76 (see Chapter 4), yet they evidently desired some settlement of the RSA/Namibia question and related issues in the region and were prepared to insist on major concessions to RSA in order to facilitate this. This prompts further questions: What then finally changed the minds of RSA leaders? What circumstances finally led to the implementation of the plan?

An account of the broader international context also helps clarify the political circumstances of the transition, its timing, the definition of the regulations under which it took place, and even why the election results and aftermath turned out the way they did. As will become evident, neither SWAPO nor the internal administration and parties were directly involved in many of the negotiations, and neither they nor the UN Security Council were informed of all the agreements struck. This international focus also brings home that the transition in Namibia was part of a broader process that settled some conflicts and issues in and between Angola and South Africa. To what extent it ushered in a set of changed circumstances for this whole region, for the survival of apartheid in South Africa, and for that country's relations with its neighbors are questions we return to in Chapter 9.

## The Politics of Delay and Negotiation, 1976–1987

For twelve years continuing deadlock did seem to be the likeliest outcome, and UNSCR 385/76 and 435/78 stood unimplemented, almost solely as a result of the recalcitrance of RSA and in spite of protracted negotiations. President P. W. Botha of South Africa is on record as saying in the early 1980s that the chances of a UN-approved settlement in Namibia were "exceptionally slim," and Dirk Mudge of DTA described them at that time as "very remote" (Chen, 1990: 346). Fathoming the intentions of WCG and RSA during this period is not a straightforward task. But the behavior of these major actors from 1976 to 1989 and the responses of forces allied to SWAPO give a feel for the whole politics of the transfer of power in 1989 and 1990. Inevitably much of this story can be traced by focusing on RSA itself: obsessed as it was by the aim of engineering events in the region, it was the main protagonist to whose initiatives and onslaughts the other actors more often than not found themselves responding.

### South Africa's International Calculations and Total Strategy

Early evidence of a lack of commitment to withdrawal from this territory or an acceptance of Namibia's independence was given in 1978 with the Kassinga massacre of Namibians in Angola by SADF just at a potentially critical phase of negotiations. That and many subsequent actions showed clearly that the fairly major concessions granted RSA in UNSCR 435/78 (see Chapter 4) were still not sufficient at that time to persuade RSA that giving up its colony was worth the risk, in spite of the mounting political costs of the war in the international arena and within Namibia and its human and financial toll.

Only future historical research will definitively establish the precise calculations made by South African decisionmakers during the long period before the implementation of UNSCR 435/78. Much of the literature, from different ends of the political spectrum, on the inner workings of South African ruling circles (Barber and Barratt, 1990; Lipton, 1986; Saul and Gelb, 1986; Grundy, 1986; Fraenkel, 1984; Cock and Nathan, 1989) suggests that there were different tendencies at work from the 1970s onward, even within SADF (what Price, 1991: 276, refers to as the "securocrats" and the "internationalist-reformers"). Some forces advocated indefinite delay; others urged acceptance of Namibia's independence. Jaster (1990: 11) argues that "by early 1978 . . . Namibian policy was causing serious discord in Vorster's Cabinet" and, moreover, that this discord meant that the South African leadership "was not prepared to negotiate seriously over the future of the territory." Other analysts, however, believe these disputes can be overstated and that there was a complementarity between the positions: the use of systematic violence by the securocrats being a means to give the bargainers the maximum leverage. But whether the controversy in the late 1970s, or the continued version of it in the 1980s, inhibited any change of policy, it certainly always gave the South African government two or more options. That government continued to implement its own internal solution and prosecute the war, but perhaps as part of what the then U.S. ambassador to WCG, McHenry, called a dual track strategy, whereby it continued to talk and string out the negotiations with WCG (Jabri, 1990: 60). An influential UN official involved in the process, Brian Urquhart, further suggests that not only were there two lines but there was also "a policy of calculated ambiguity towards the Namibian talks . . . (whereby) South Africa gave the appearance of cooperating with the Contact Group and moving the negotiations forward, while in fact avoiding firm commitments and blocking progress" (quoted in Jaster, 1990: 12).

The common element in any such differing tendencies was a preference for a Namibia that met certain conditions: it would not undermine South African objectives for Southern Africa as a whole, particularly by being a close ally of the MPLA government in Angola and by inviting Cubans to a territory on South Africa's own borders; it would not provide bases for ANC to use in its campaign of armed struggle in South Africa; it would not offer too radical a precedent for social and economic change in South Africa itself; and it would not jeopardize the economic interests of South African capital and of resident whites in Namibia. For some policymakers, the best guarantee of this kind of Namibia was to keep direct control for the time being or at least put into place their own internal solution, regardless of UNSCR 435. This latter step would have provided a regime sympathetic to South African and settler interests that would have excluded SWAPO (or made it peripheral) and that was content to run an economy and society still heavily dependent on South Africa.

The other tendency would point to the dangers of that approach as a long-run strategy, as it would not automatically neutralize the armed struggle and allow SADF to demobilize; nor would it win international acceptance or settle the regional conflict that had led to the Cuban presence in Angola. But these latter advocates of an internationally acceptable solution, which would have to be along the lines of UNSCR 435, would contemplate its implementation only when they could be sure that any more genuinely independent and representative government of Namibia would meet the conditions just outlined. Such an alternative prescription was premised upon a recognition that SWAPO could not be denied some place in government, but this prescription sought to limit the extent of SWAPO's predominance politically, to hedge any government with constitutional and diplomatic constraints, to reassert economic dependence on South Africa, and to ensure that an independent Namibia was weak strategically and had no strong allies.

A solution designed to give effect to these aims could well be labeled *neocolonial,* a formulation that, as was evident in Chapter 2, some analysts have applied to explain South Africa's long-term goals for Namibia. Usually they do not imply some of the connotations that would normally be read into a more rigorous theoretical use of the term: namely, that South Africa seeks to perpetuate economic advantage and the dominance of its capital after political independence and to do so by manipulating the inherited economic dependence. Wood (1992) does, however, offer a recent example arguing this harder position but dubs this scenario *semicolonial.* Rather, these analysts are simply indicating that South Africa sought to maintain its interests by using political and economic ties. But this view still leaves those interests undefined. What, however, is less debatable is that in the short to medium term, the dual-track policy did buy time, whatever the long-term outcome desired. The long years of negotiating arguably served to allow the creation of the preconditions that South Africa sought to achieve, so for the negotiators—especially for the hard-liners—the long delays in the process served a useful purpose (Wood, 1991).

Insofar as it is useful to think of two such tendencies, the faction that put security first could be seen as temporarily taking a back seat when the plan to go ahead with an internal solution was for the moment abandoned and RSA finally accepted UNSCR 435 in 1979. But that fact was once again in the ascendance with the emergence of P. W. Botha as president and the changes that he brought about that made the military politically central in the working of the state. This cautious line was reemphasized by ZANU's 1980 win in the election in Zimbabwe against the odds and the resulting fear that the same might happen in Namibia if there was an internationally accepted settlement straightaway. The hand of this cautious, militaristic faction, which now sought to delay implementing UNSCR 435, was strengthened by the coming to power of Prime Minister Margaret Thatcher in the United Kingdom in 1979 and President Ronald Reagan in the United States in 1981, who were less inclined to put pressure on South Africa to settle.

During the first phase of negotiations from 1976 to 1978, South Africa refused to withdraw its commitment to its internal Turnhalle solution, even while it continued to talk to WCG. Once South Africa had agreed to the UN plan contained in UNSCR 435 in 1978 and was officially committed to its own withdrawal from Namibia and to UN supervision of a cease-fire and elections, it dug in its heels over the specifics of the plan and its implementation. Nevertheless, agreement was reached on paper between 1978 and 1980 about SADF's withdrawal, SWAPO's demobilization, the composition and role of a United Nations Transitional Assistance Group (UNTAG) civilian and military force, and some elements of the system of elections, which would be for a constituent assembly, not a government. Ambiguity, calculated or not, remained, however, over whether the voting system would be on a proportional representation (PR) or single-constituency basis and over the confinement of PLAN forces within Namibia (see Chapter 4 for details of agreements and Chapter 5 for the consequences of this latter imprecision).

However, as some matters came to be regarded as settled in the early 1980s, RSA further shifted its ground by insisting that additional conditions be satisfied, "often about issues previously agreed" (Geldenhuys, 1984: 226), and by making some new proposals. One earlier instance of what U.S. Assistant Secretary of State for African Affairs Chester Crocker (1981) admitted was a "time-buying instrument" was the ill-fated preimplementation negotiations in Geneva in early 1981, which were supposed to be face to face for the first time. RSA attended but refused to talk, its inclination toward intransigence strengthened by more hard-line stances being adopted by the incoming Reagan administration. Among new proposals was an attempt to get a constitution agreed to by negotiation prior to elections. The UN's previous recognition and support of SWAPO was also raised to cast doubts about the UN's impartiality. On this issue Jabri (1990: 100–101) concludes that one UN proposal would have given "South Africans everything they wanted" but was not taken up by RSA, suggesting, she argues, that the impartiality issue served as a delaying tactic for RSA.

By 1982 most matters of substance had been agreed or at least relegated to the implementation phase, except for one matter on which RSA now started to insist: linkage, meaning that any progress on implementing the UN plan for Namibia should be subject to success in negotiations about the withdrawal of Cuban troops and the Soviet presence in neighboring Angola. Indeed, in 1982 the Reagan administration, but not the other WCG members, endorsed the linkage principle. Thus, the issue of RSA's withdrawal came to be seen internationally as only one part of the regional conflict in Southern Africa, rather than as an illegal occupation, and the interests of South Africa became diplomatically linked to those of the United States.

There was no basis in international law for connecting the two matters: South Africa's occupation of Namibia had been declared illegal; Cuban troops were in Angola at the invitation of a separate, recognized, sovereign state, requested precisely because of successive repetitions of the original incursion of SADF in 1975 and its support for UNITA rebels in southeast Angola. This fact indeed prompts the thought that the purpose behind the linkage demand was more than to buy time. Some analysts have even suggested that the South African strategy was to ensure, by the very fact of the incursions throughout the 1980s, the maintenance, not the removal, of the Soviet and Cuban presence. Playing up this "threat" would enable Pretoria to secure continued backing for its position from right-wing circles in the West and reduced pressure for change from the United States (Price, 1984: 25). Whether there was such an intention, the linkage of Cuban troop withdrawals to a Namibian settlement was the one remaining unresolved matter impeding implementation of UNSCR 435 and guaranteeing massive incursions into Angola and RSA support for UNITA until 1988, when the two matters were dealt with simultaneously, if not formally linked.

There is a copious literature that situates such maneuvers on Namibia within RSA's total strategy and the international interplay of political forces around it (Davies and O'Meara, 1985; Hanlon, 1986; Geldenhuys, 1982, 1984; Grundy, 1986; Fraenkel, 1984), but these analysts have said little about what purposes required this delaying tactic and about the relative success or failure of efforts to put an alternative structure into place in Namibia. A full history of South African calculations during those "lost" ten years cannot be attempted here, but the efforts in that direction that are just beginning are certainly badly needed. RSA's record over a long period, its articulation of a total strategy, and its use of linkage as the final piece in the game plan do indicate that South Africa was determinedly seeking certain outcomes. These delay tactics did give the RSA administration time to set in motion within Namibia plans to establish an indigenous administration and a viable political alternative to SWAPO, which were outlined in Chapter 2. RSA's uneven pattern of success is explored in Chapters 5 and 7. The election was to be the ultimate test of the success of these efforts.

Some of the measures designed to obtain what we have surmised to be South Africa's project (Jaster, 1985) had already been secured by agreements surrounding UNSCR 435: the requirement that there be an election of a constituent assembly in which a two-thirds majority would be required and constitutional principles protecting property rights and inhibiting one-party rule. South Africa also had broader objectives relating to the security situation in the countries around Namibia, and these were secured in the 1988 Brazzaville Accords and in South Africa's determination to hang on to Walvis Bay (see letter from RSA to Secretary-General, 31 July 1978, UN document S/12797). The final piece in this game plan seemed to involve efforts to secure a preferred result to the elections themselves (without this being done in a manner so crude that international acceptability would be withheld). How far RSA went in this regard in specifying the rules governing the election and in the running of it and how much or how little UNTAG's actual performance of its supervisory role allowed South Africa to shape events is explored in the next chapters. How much scope RSA had for this manipulation depended in turn on what rules and procedures it had managed to get written into the final specifics of the UN plan.

Whatever the changing interplay of international and South African factors, RSA's policies within Namibia over the next decade continued the strategy of restructuring Namibian society and politics by aggressively pursuing an internal settlement and fostering a politically conservative alternative to SWAPO (like the Muzorewa option in Zimbabwe). RSA had confidence in its own ability to carry this off given time. The West was not so ready to countenance indefinite delay, recognizing that one of the risks of a strategy of delaying independence was the resulting further radicalization of the population, as was witnessed in Zimbabwe.

RSA appears to have interpreted the lesson of Zimbabwe differently—that holding national, free elections too soon before having restructured society along desired lines is too dangerous. UN-supervised elections at this point would have brought a complete SWAPO victory, and so delaying tactics were needed. Indeed, Dirk Mudge was reported at the time of the abortive Geneva talks in 1981 as saying that an extra two years would be needed to mount a credible alternative to a SWAPO government. Immediately that implied a minimum time for RSA to foster the ethnic, second-tier authorities, plus DTA and other agencies of patronage politics sufficiently, while at the same time violently forcing people to participate in elections and presenting the result as democracy to the outside world. As an interim delaying measure before final acceptance of the inevitable implementation of UNSCR 435/78, let alone as a final solution, this strategy required a peculiarly arrogant view of the possibilities for social and political engineering by the colonial state, although arguably some minimum degree of success was achieved in some parts of the country. But Wood (1991: 760) points to further and concomitant objectives aimed at the consolidation of a "semi-colonial state, material base and ideology in Namibia." Pursuit of these objectives involved manipulating voting patterns, consolidating a black middle class, and battle-strengthening SWATF so that there was a more effective internal force than the weak and indisciplined auxiliaries that Abel Tendekayi Muzorewa had had at his disposal in Zimbabwe.

Another element in the strategy was clearly concerned with SWAPO itself—"not only to contain [it militarily] but to destroy it as a credible guerrilla force in order to diminish its appeal inside Namibia and to weaken its claim to international support" (Jaster, 1990: 12). To this end counterinsurgency in Namibia was coupled with massive incursions into Angola to attack SWAPO bases and supply routes. Indeed, some of the bloodiest fighting between SADF and PLAN, some of the most decisive events that were finally to settle the future of Namibia, occurred not inside the country but in Angola, and arguably the greatest suffering of the war over Namibia was experienced by the Angolan people. These tactics of undermining

SWAPO's position and promoting alternatives continued to be the basis of South Africa's policy right through to the election in 1989.

Support among the white population of RSA for a political ideology of white supremacy and anticommunism unique to South Africa further underwrote the military and political actions necessitated by the government's total strategy. The lessening hold of this ideology over all but hard-line Afrikaners was later to underlie changes in RSA's strategy toward Namibia in 1988.

Such political, ideological, and military reasons for the importance of Namibia in RSA's overall calculations perhaps outweighed any considerations about the more direct economic interests that South Africa had within the country. The maintenance of Namibia's colonial status actually cost RSA from the mid-1980s onward. The extraction of Namibia's minerals and the use of the country as a captive market for consumer goods were clearly significant to RSA's economy but were not vital or strategic, and, arguably, the nature of these economic relationships would not necessarily change by virtue of independence even under a SWAPO regime. In many ways the example of Zimbabwe should have provided RSA with reassurance over that possibility.

Eventually several changes helped strengthen the hand of the faction in South African ruling circles that ultimately wanted an internationally acceptable settlement: the check to SADF military superiority in Angola, the new international climate, and the imminence of changes inside South Africa itself. The conjunction of all these factors also allowed this faction to stress the ever-mounting costs in terms of economics, politics, and white casualties (Ohlson, 1989; Seery, 1989). Before we explore how these changed circumstances and calculations in South Africa interacted with the other interests and forces to create the prospect of implementing the UN plan, we first turn to a second group of major global actors.

## The United States and WCG

When WCG was formed in 1977, its original motivation was to resolve the dilemma of having to support or veto the growing international pressure for UN sanctions against South Africa while at the same time continuing to put pressure on RSA to go along with an internationally acceptable, rather than an internal, solution in Namibia. But that dilemma was self-created by the vetoes of the three Western powers on the Security Council to prevent mandatory arms embargoes on RSA for its noncompliance with UNSCR 385/76. (FLS and Soviet-bloc supporters of ANC were urged by it to back an arms embargo only on the grounds of RSA's apartheid policies, not those in Namibia.) It is also clear that WCG was not prepared to back an immediate move to independence for Namibia under a SWAPO government, although whether WCG's preferred solution automatically and permanently precluded that, as commentators such as Landis (1988) argue, was to be revealed by the events of 1989–1990. Beyond a readiness to accommodate RSA, each of the five WCG governments had its own interests and calculations. These fine distinctions are usefully drawn in Jabri's (1990) account. In the early years one such difference of emphasis was between Britain, which even under a Labour government indicated that its trade and business links with South Africa precluded sanctions under any circumstances, and the United States and probably the other three WCG members, which were initially prepared to use at least the threat of supporting sanctions as a means of pressuring South Africa to stick with the negotiations and make some concessions (Zartman, 1989).

However, with Reagan's election and the U.S. policy of constructive engagement toward South Africa (Crocker, 1981), any real threat of sanctions was removed from 1981 onward, giving RSA more confidence that carrying out its strategy toward Namibia (and the rest of Southern Africa) according to its own internal political logic and demands would not bring punishments from the West. The other departure in U.S. policy in the 1980s was the growing insistence, fueled by mounting right-wing clamor for an aggressive policy of standing up to and even rolling back perceived Soviet expansion in the Third World, on imposing linkage between regional conflicts and global issues, here by making a Namibian settlement dependent on Cuban withdrawal from Angola. However, the other four members of WCG never subscribed to the notion of linkage, and disagreement over this issue led first to the French withdrawing and then to the virtual end in 1982 of the group as an effective coalition.

From then on, the initiative passed to the United States acting on its own. The Reagan administration continued to carry on parallel negotiations on Namibia with Angola and RSA about the withdrawal of Cuban and South African troops from Angola. The U.S. failure to get the Cubans out of Angola through negotiation was followed by a more aggressive policy of resuming direct military aid to UNITA in 1986 for the first time in ten years (after the repeal of the Clark amendment, by which Congress had prohibited any further clandestine or other involvement in Angola after the 1976 adventure) in the hope of forcing the Angolan government to negotiate with UNITA and accept linkage.

### SWAPO's Diplomacy and the Frontline States

From its inception, SWAPO consistently maintained that it wanted the withdrawal of RSA's illegal occupation of Namibia. But in seeking this goal, SWAPO always set great store by its efforts, and those in Africa and elsewhere in the world, to get the UN to implement the decision that under international law South Africa should give up the position it had obtained in Namibia under the League of Nations and hand over to the UN responsibility for seeing the country through to independence. In one sense the legal status of the colony and the availability of a UN option strengthened SWAPO's hand and gave it a diplomatic card to play in addition to its own struggle inside the country. But SWAPO's reliance on the UN and on getting support of countries for such diplomatic action was also a measure of the limits to which it could take the armed struggle.

As was made clear in Chapter 2, a combination of factors—the massive armed strength of SADF, the small gap available only in the extreme northeast for SWAPO to infiltrate until the 1970s, the willingness of RSA to wreak havoc in Angola, the small population, and limited educational and other opportunities—all acted to reduce the armed struggle to a point where it was merely, but with determination and great human cost, kept on to provide a bargaining counter. SWAPO was thus in a position, like other liberation movements in Africa but perhaps to a greater degree, of dependence on FLS and the particular states that provided sanctuary and bases. Thus, in the mid- to late 1970s, SWAPO's strength inside Namibia was curtailed by Zambia pursuing détente with RSA and then by that country getting cold feet after some SADF raids, after which PLAN fighters never again crossed from there into Caprivi.

As a result of being susceptible to pressure from African states, SWAPO had to demonstrate in negotiations a willingness to make concessions. It even returned to the negotiating table after the brutal Kassinga massacre in 1978. It then agreed to UNSCR 435/78 before RSA did, even though it was compromising some elements already agreed in UNSCR 385/76. This compromise was achieved only at the firm behest of the Frontline States, pressured as they were by massive RSA intervention and destabilization in their own countries. Thereafter, SWAPO fought a rearguard diplomatic action to try minimizing the concessions WCG and the United States were prepared to make to RSA. But routinely, as Jabri (1990: 95) acknowledges, "SWAPO's allies were used to gain such acceptance [by SWAPO]."

SWAPO did successfully resist a voting system that would have had a separate roll for whites and from 1982 to 1987 got support in holding out against linkage. SWAPO also made a big issue of the matter of its bases, eventually agreeing to UNTAG monitoring of those in Angola but insisting on a right to a presence inside Namibia. But this issue was also fiercely resisted by RSA and was never resolved by agreements acceptable to all sides. It was dealt with, like other matters, in WCG or U.S. negotiations with RSA, whose "successful" outcome (meaning South Africa's acceptance of some formula) was then reported to the UN and SWAPO. In this way SWAPO and its supporters among the African and nonaligned countries were deliberately marginalized from some of the most crucial agreements. Eventually, too, SWAPO was unable to have a voice in the discussions and agreements in 1988 wherein linkage was finally conceded; they involved only RSA, Cuba, the United States, and the USSR.

*Angola, Cuba, and the Soviet Union*

Namibia's northern neighbor and its allies, the USSR and Cuba, were in no official sense parties to the agreements surrounding UNSCR 435/78, but Angola and Cuba were signatories to the accords that eventually initiated the implementation of the UN plan in 1988. The stance of the three countries thus deserves scrutiny.

Soviet involvement in the affairs of the southwestern part of Africa dates back to the 1960s, when both MPLA in Angola and SWAPO were given political and diplomatic backing and eventually military and other training and arms. In Namibia, as in Mozambique, this support for the liberation struggle meant simply backing the one movement that was taken seriously by OAU and the international community, while in Angola, as in Zimbabwe, the USSR was taking sides between rival movements. Not surprisingly, the Soviets threw their support firmly behind MPLA in 1975 when fighting broke out between it and the rival movements, UNITA and FNLA. The decision to intervene strongly not only with major arms supplies but also with troop reinforcements from Cuba and with logistical support and strategic direction from the Soviet Union, following the invasion of Angola by South Africa and the covert support for UNITA/FNLA by the CIA, seemingly stemmed from a strong initiative by Cuba with which the USSR went along (García Márquez, 1977).

After MPLA was able to consolidate its rule and end the intervention in 1976, the Cuban troops stayed in Angola helping to resist the several waves of South African incursions over the next twelve years and train the Angolan army, FAPLA. The Soviets continued to supply arms to the Cuban forces and FAPLA and advisers to the latter. In the escalation of fighting beginning in 1985, the Soviets not only quickly replaced all FAPLA's losses but also built up an air force capability for defense and attack.

The position all three countries took with regard to Namibia itself was not to get involved in direct negotiations, rejecting the idea of linkage as contrary to international law; in this they were supported by Security Council resolutions, notably in 1983 (UNSCR 539). They did involve themselves in talks with South Africa about avoiding direct confrontation between SADF and Cuban troops and about possible withdrawals from Angola, and agreements were made in early 1984 between RSA and Angola for SADF withdrawal from Angola and the specification of a ceasefire zone in parts of southern Angola, which in return neither Cuban nor PLAN forces would enter. These provisions were to be policed by a joint monitoring commission (JMC) set up by Angola and South Africa, and for two years thereafter there were only minor incidents between the two sides.

The Soviets, caught up in the tensions of a "second Cold War" and a period of more direct confrontation with the Reagan administration, seemingly had their doubts about such an agreement. They reaffirmed their military support for SWAPO at the time and probably encouraged SWAPO in its policy of respecting the accord but not observing truce in its efforts to insert fighters into Namibia, a truce agreement to which SWAPO had not been a party.

The Soviet and Cuban position of not negotiating on Namibian issues finally changed in 1988 (Adamichin, 1990) when Cuban and South African withdrawal from Angola and Namibian independence were finally negotiated together (see Chapter 4). Of course, the two issues were never unconnected. The three countries supported the aim of full Namibian independence, and the fighting inside Angola did have direct Namibian involvement and implications: part of the purpose of UNITA and SADF was to hit SWAPO bases and to curb its infiltration across the border; in turn, PLAN fighters fought alongside Cuban and Angolan troops in the major engagements of the 1980s. The Cuban and Soviet presence in Angola, although mainly for protection against SADF, was also seen as contributing to the Namibian struggle. Fidel Castro promised Namibians in 1985, "We will be there until Namibia is independent" (Deutschmann, 1989: 104) and he kept his word. More broadly, it has to be recognized that "the costs to Angola of the war in Namibia far exceeded those suffered by the main protagonists, namely the South African government and SWAPO" (Jabri, 1990: 165).

The motivation for this commitment also needs to be explored. For the Angolan government, the issues were simple: it had little choice but to resist SADF invasions of Angola, and unless the government was to give up the capital, the source of much of its support, and go back to the guerrilla methods of the 1960s, it had to rely on military support on the kind of scale that could resist the South Africans. The MPLA government had resisted the initial insurgency mounted by UNITA; it was even less inclined to negotiate with a movement that showed itself more and more clearly to be an agent of foreign powers and that was itself seemingly disinclined to negotiate in any serious way. For the Angolans, the prospect of a genuinely independent Namibia was also very much in their own interests: it would remove the SADF threat 800 kilometers to the south of Angola's own borders and give Angola a sympathetic southern neighbor.

For the Soviet Union, as for the United States, Cold War issues of a broader, global-strategic sort no doubt figured in its calculations, especially in the period of the second Cold War in the late 1970s and early 1980s. Thus, in addition to an ideological commitment to an MPLA regime that was at the time avowedly Marxist-Leninist (Belikov, 1991), the Soviet Union's involvement in Angola embodied the geopolitical power game typical of the realpolitik of the Brezhnev era. The USSR asserted its diplomatic and military presence for the first time in Southern Africa and on the Atlantic seaboard to match the naval presence it had already established on the Indian Ocean littoral of eastern Africa and thereby pose potential threats to the West's monopoly of control over the resources of the region and its strategic sea-lanes.

South African claims, echoed by the far right in the United States, that this was part of a grand design for a Soviet takeover of the whole continent and of international resource supply lines were never sustainable, but the USSR thereby gained significant leverage to bolster its position vis-à-vis the United States so as to face off in the more confrontational phase of superpower politics in the 1980s or win concessions over disarmament or trade. The first signs of a change in the Soviet bloc's stance predated the critical fighting of late 1987 and 1988 and reflected the new moves toward détente initiated after Mikhail Gorbachev came to power. In July 1987 the United States was receiving signals that the USSR was interested in considering linkage (Jaster, 1990: 29). The Soviets' dilemma, however, was how to reduce their commitment in the region in accordance with the new dictates of national economic policy and global strategy without losing face in a situation where "their 'clients' would inevitably have to make substantial concessions" (Jaster, 1990: 29). Their willingness to compromise was given final illustration when they went along with last-minute proposals by the United States to reduce the UN monitoring force in Namibia (see Chapter 4).

Cuba, however, stood to gain little apart from some respect among progressive Third World countries from its commitment of personnel, which was massive in terms of its own limited resources. The record from Cuban circles (Deutschmann, 1989) and those in the West (Stockwell, 1978) also confirm that Cuba was not simply acting as a Soviet surrogate; rather, it took the initiative to come to Angola's aid. It is thus hard to escape the conclusion that Cuba was motivated mainly by a "socialist internationalism."

## The Final Moves to Implement the UN Plan, 1988

The year 1988 marked a turning point: South Africa finally ended its by-then-interminable delaying and accepted that UNSCR 435/78 had to be implemented. At the same time, agreements for the simultaneous withdrawal of SADF forces and Cuban troops from Angola were reached. The previous five years had been marked by heavy SADF incursions and support for UNITA, which, reinforced from 1986 onward by U.S. support for the latter, including the supply of strategically important weapons such as the Stinger ground-to-air missiles and mercenaries, harassed SWAPO and confronted the Angolan army. It is tempting to explain the shift to diplomacy and the breaking of the impasse to the relative successes of the contending military forces on the ground. Although they do not provide a complete explanation, we consider them first.

*Military Stalemate*

Analysts who are sympathetic to one side or the other have triumphantly held up the agreements as evidence of the victory of one of the sides in the fierce and sustained battles that occurred in the second part of 1987 and early 1988 in Angola, many of them around the strategic southeast town of Cuito Cuanavale. Thus, Fidel Castro says, "When you meet a white South African, a racist, the only thing you have to ask him is: what happened in Cuito Cuanavale? . . . The battle and its outcome are of historic importance. . . . There has been a total change in the balance of power. . . . Why does South Africa want to negotiate?" (quoted in Deutschmann, 1989: vii). At the other pole, Heitman (1990: 337), in an account written from an SADF perspective and sources, sees a "defeat inflicted on the FAPLA forces . . . [that] was so crushing, that it changed the strategic situation beyond recognition."

Some of the issues about the actual outcome of the 1986–1988 campaigns in Angola and their strategic significance and political implications are clearly still in contention, and this episode of history needs to be further researched. But a careful reading from both sides of the conflict of the record of the campaigns that led up to the major battles around Cuito Cuanavale in 1987 and early 1988 and the further military escalation that continued in 1988 does allow some tentative balance sheet to be drawn up.

It is clear that in late 1985, after a two-year lull in direct fighting between FAPLA and SADF and a partial withdrawal of the latter, the Angolan government, with strong backing and a buildup of sophisticated tanks, aircraft, and other weaponry from Cuba and the USSR, embarked on an offensive against UNITA. This offensive was a response to UNITA's actions in 1984 and 1985 of spreading some of its sporadic attacks beyond its main base area in the southeast corner of Angola. UNITA's headquarters were at Jamba in the triangle between the Zambian and Caprivi borders, and the movement had the run of Cuando Cubango Province in the southeast. Its main logistical base was in that province but slightly farther toward the center of the country at Mavinga, some 150 kilometers southeast of Cuito Cuanavale. This latter town was thus the ideal advanced base for the MPLA government in its campaign, which it hoped would provide the key to open up Cuando Cubango Province and Jamba.

In the second half of 1985, a FAPLA force did advance slowly from Cuito Cuanavale, pushing UNITA back toward Mavinga, where, in an unanticipated move for which there was no overall air cover, SADF intervened with massive air strikes and mechanized columns; the Angolan offensive was turned back with considerable loss of personnel and weaponry. The armaments lost were replaced by the USSR in a matter of weeks, and a sophisticated radar defensive system and an air attack capability were built up around Cuito Cuanavale and elsewhere in the southeast in 1986. A new offensive toward Mavinga, the gateway to Jamba, was postponed until after the rains in 1987 for a variety of reasons, including the U.S. decision to aid UNITA overtly with, among others, Stinger surface-to-air missiles.

In August 1987 FAPLA again moved out in force from Cuito Cuanavale, this time with air cover against SADF, and did push back UNITA. But then as FAPLA attempted to cross the Lomba River some 50 kilometers from Mavinga, it was met by a very considerable force of SADF and SWATF, which had already reinforced UNITA with tanks, artillery, and aerial support. They engaged FAPLA in major battles over several weeks, and the latter was once again forced back to fight defensive battles over the next three months around Cuito Cuanavale. The loss of life and armaments to both sides was considerable, and the South Africans eventually withdrew early in 1988 with the town still intact.

Herein lies the basis for one of the differences in interpreting these events: South African propagandists like Heitman now argue that SADF's objective was not to take or destroy Cuito Cuanavale, its base, and its airstrip with its complex equipment. Rather, SADF intended merely to settle for what it achieved: pushing FAPLA back to the west of the Cuito River and keeping the town and airfield under attack to render them inoperative. Nevertheless, it is hard to escape the conclusion that if those were the South African objectives, then the four-month siege of the town in 1987–1988 and the further two months of artillery bombardment were "a long and costly effort for so modest and impermanent a result" (Jaster, 1990: 19). Just to deny the use of Cuito Cuanavale would have won only temporary respite from FAPLA attacks on UNITA's base area; surely the temptation was to deal a blow that would remove this gateway for good. That would have offered more long-term protection to South Africa's ally, and thereby avoided another fear of the South Africans—the reopening, as in the 1970s, of the northern borders of Caprivi and Kavango to SWAPO incursions. Given these more probable and larger aims, the Angolan effort, backed at the last by direct Cuban involvement, was indeed a "stalwart defence."

Whatever the aims of the two sides, the campaigns around Cuito Cuanavale were costly to both sides and no doubt prompted reassessments of whether those costs in human, military, and financial terms (and the much greater ones that would be involved in any further pursuing of the aims of either side now that both sides had airpower and there was a greater overall parity) could be justified. In particular, it was during this bout of intense fighting that Angola, Cuba, and the USSR first made concessions about linkage and indicated a willingness (in January 1988) to consider total Cuban troop withdrawals from the whole of Angola rather than the phased withdrawal from southern Angola that had been their earlier position. In return, they demanded a guaranteed SADF withdrawal from Angola and Namibian settlement as the best way of ensuring an end to conflict in Angola. In the following weeks, the South African government withdrew from the siege of Cuito Cuanavale not so much because of defeat but because of the high cost in white lives and the difficulty it would encounter in replacing aircraft and weapon systems if fighting continued. The South Africans no doubt began to contemplate how they might withdraw totally from Angola by actually securing what they had always proclaimed they had wanted but might have prevented by their own actions: Cuban withdrawal. But despite such reevaluations, both sides offered few concessions and maintained hard-line stances. Indeed, fighting continued until the eve of the first face-to-face talks among the United States, South Africa, Angola, and Cuba (with the USSR in close attendance) in London in early May 1988. The breakthrough to a diplomatic solution was by no means clearly established.

Insofar as military events on the ground had an impact in forcing genuine concessions toward agreement, arguably the further effect of the opening of a second theater of confrontation some 400 kilometers west of the Cuito Cuanavale theater was the more decisive episode. In an initiative that has been widely attributed to Fidel Castro, after a sobering assessment of the costs of the Lomba River catastrophe in 1985 and of the strategy behind it, a large detachment of fifteen thousand newly arrived Cuban recruits with 270 tanks was dispatched in May 1988 directly toward the Namibian border north of Ovamboland, much further to the west than Cuito Cuanavale. The ensuing buildup of a front along 300 kilometers of land that was 15–50 kilometers from the border posed a threat to South Africa of renewed PLAN incursions behind this shield. It also posed a direct threat of air and artillery strikes against SADF detachments in Angola and bases in Namibia and even of actual invasion across the border. Although not realized in the world outside, the fear of this latter possibility was emphasized by a senior military commander later interviewed by Jaster (1990: 23): "Had the Cubans attacked [Namibia] they would have over-run the place. *We could not have stopped them.*" In the event, there was only one actual (and apparently unintended) clash, at the Calueque Dam, but it underscored the scope for a massive further escalation and may have been a "major catalyst in moving the two sides to seek ways of avoiding further clashes" (Jaster, 1990: 23). The buildup continued into July and August 1988, so an Angolan peace and a Namibian settlement were still not in evidence, but serious talks had got under way.

Our account of the military operations thus far has brought out that the conflicts around Cuito Cuanavale and the confrontation that led to the Calueque clash were inconclusive and ended in standoffs. But the changed character of the fighting had brought home the dangers and greatly escalating costs of continued fighting. Specifically the point had been reached where the elimination of the threat posed to the MPLA government by UNITA was possible by military means, but not so long as SADF was prepared to intervene. At the same time, South Africa's containment of the struggle in Namibia could be seriously threatened in the east along the Caprivi and Kavango borders, unless RSA continued to step in to back UNITA, and now in the west by the Cuban/Angolan buildup to the north of Ovamboland. South Africa's ability to contain the struggle in Namibia while at the same time localizing the counterinsurgency was brought into question by mutinies within SWATF of several hundred black troops apparently not wishing to be cannon fodder in Angola (Wood, 1991: 751). Moreover, the readiness of Cuba and the Soviet Union to promote the buildup of FAPLA forces on the ground and to provide for the first time an air capability to match that of SADF brought home the escalating costs of continuing war.

These military calculations reverberated with other developments and reassessments going on in Namibia, South Africa, and the wider world. The details of the behind-the-scenes diplomacy and the successive meetings at which final agreement about the phasing of withdrawals from Angola were hammered out have begun to emerge in studies such as those of Bender, (1989) Jaster (1990), Jabri (1990), and Wood (1991), although little has so far been documented from the Soviet, Cuban, and Angola sides. The main specifics of what emerged about the implementation of the UN plan—some of which were matters already settled, whereas others were products of the various 1988 agreements—were spelled out in this chapter and in Chapter 4. However, our explanation of why and how the long delay in implementation came to an end and how the shift from military confrontation came about needs to be completed by bringing in factors apart from developments inside Angola and weighing their relative significance.

*Changing South African Calculations*

In Namibia the second half of the 1980s had seen a growing popular political mobilization, especially among students, youth, workers, and church members, and an increasingly radical stance by many of these groups. The political costs of containing and repressing this trend were thus beginning to loom large just at the moment when it became clear that increased escalation would be necessary to maintain the military status quo in Namibia and Angola. Other trends, however, seemed to augur well for South Africa's plans to stage-manage an alternative decolonization. The extra time that Dirk Mudge had asked for in 1981 had been used to some effect in fostering clientelist support for the ethnic administrations and DTA coalition of parties. And even if such popular support was still limited, it might have been thought to be at its zenith by 1988—likely to decline in the teeth of emerging scandals about the second-tier administrations and mounting radicalism among youth. Strategists in South African circles might well have calculated that the time for a negotiated end to RSA rule in Namibia on their terms was not likely to get any riper. Wood (1991: 756) does argue that RSA made such calculations about timing, although he gives primacy to the establishment and blooding of SWATF.

Any such calculations would strengthen the hand of those in ruling circles who had all along seen the intransigent, "military security first" option as a high-risk strategy (Davies, 1989). They could point to the achievement of some restructuring of the state, with the prospect of it being reversed and of mounting costs if South Africa did not change policy. The changing global situation was also advanced as grounds for a switch. Apart from RSA's own annual military costs of the operation in Namibia and Angola, which have been estimated at R 4 billion in 1988 (Price, 1991: 277), RSA was subsidizing Namibia's budget to the tune of U.S. $180 million a year throughout the 1980s, made necessary by the vast expansion in government expenditure from only 12 percent of GDP in the late 1970s to 27 percent in 1987. That decade also saw South Africa's own gross national product (GNP) grow at only 1 percent a year on average, representing a net decline in per capita levels (Jaster, 1990: 30). Debt-servicing demands were escalating, and there was a need to seek rescheduling, both at a time when there were renewed calls in the international community for sanctions. Public revenues were thus in jeopardy just as pressures were mounting in South Africa to provide social services to blacks and absorb the quarter-million young blacks entering the job market every year.

Decisive in South Africa's policy switch were the remorseless pressures of the popular movement in South Africa, which in 1988 led to the ouster of Botha in favor of de Klerk's administration, the release of Nelson Mandela, and moves toward a negotiated settlement in South Africa. The rise of this group of National Party politicians to leadership almost automatically led to a change in stance over Namibia because of the weakening of the previous Botha alliance with the military. Meanwhile, changes within South Africa made the continuation of a policy of hanging onto Namibia irrelevant: a buffer was not needed to contain ANC's armed struggle once it became an internal political struggle under a legally recognized movement. (But for a cautionary note skeptical of the extent of such changes, see Szeftel, 1991.)

*The Changing International Context*

These changes in South African personnel, policies, and calculations in turn owed something to the new international climate, which was to herald the end of the Cold War. Gorbachev's speech at the UN in 1986 had already begun to signal a willingness in the USSR to seek accommodation with the West and to look for solutions to regional conflicts in which the superpowers were involved. As this move continued, it implied an ongoing desire of the Soviet Union to disengage from Africa and from its support for revolutionary struggles (Kramer, 1991; Lister, 1987). This new stance induced the Soviets to pressure ANC into eventually following a strategy of dialogue as an internal civil rights, rather than an armed struggle, movement and helped propel SWAPO and the Angolan government toward compromise. However, this process did not involve a headlong dismantling of Soviet and Cuban support for Angola's resistance to South African incursions and South African–backed UNITA insurgency. Indeed, unlike Afghanistan, where the Soviet army simply withdrew and left the warring factions to themselves once the USSR had secured some limited agreement from the West to end military supplies to the insurgents, Soviet policymakers decided that increased military pressure was needed in Angola to create the changed circumstances that would make withdrawal possible. Soviet objectives were to curb and, if possible, eliminate UNITA's military capability and then reduce South Africa's commanding position in southern Angola to make RSA more ready to negotiate.

The Soviet hand in signaling a willingness to consider political solutions, while at the same time promoting some breakthrough in the military situation after the initial reversals of the 1985 FAPLA campaign against UNITA and the 1987 campaign, was seemingly strengthened by the Cuban government's insistence that "it was necessary to change the correlation of forces," as Castro put it in 1987 (quoted in Jaster, 1990: 21). As has been noted, FAPLA losses had been immediately more than made up in 1985 and 1987, and there had been a 50 percent increase in the number of Cuban troops from 1987. This military buildup and the fact that after Cuito Cuanavale the Angolan government was talking from a position of some strength probably gave RSA's statements of a "willingness to go for settlement greater credibility" (Jabri, 1990: 165). At the same time, the economic pressures on Angola, facing drought and a drop in oil prices after 1986, and on Cuba, facing Soviet cutbacks and the prospect of rescheduling its debts to Western governments, also made a political solution attractive to them.

Meanwhile, the West was entering into a new relationship with the USSR in the last part of the Reagan presidency. The United States was inclined to take the USSR seriously and enter into dialogue about regional conflicts. Afghanistan had shown the way. The Soviet Union under Gorbachev was no longer the "evil empire," and this meant that the United States was less likely to be influenced by South Africa playing the card of the "Red threat" in Angola. These recalculations were being made at a time when pressure was again mounting worldwide for sanctions and other measures against South Africa following the state of emergency there. Thus, as the costs and risks of further escalating the war and the impossibility of either side finding any major breakthrough in military terms in the short run became more apparent, the new international climate was one that fostered genuine negotiation.

It was, however, still not a foregone conclusion that talks would be successful when the negotiating process got under way tentatively, which it did in 1987 with the United States talking to Angola and RSA separately or then in May 1988 with the first face-to-face talks involving Angola, Cuba, South Africa, and the United States (with the USSR in attendance). As Jaster (1990: 22) notes, "Up to a point, the Botha government . . . had offered no serious concessions in the talks, either at Brazzaville in May, or at Cairo in June," where U.S. observers noted "yawning gaps" between the two sides. The fact of talks itself however implied one concession in the Angolan/Soviet/Cuban position: the three countries were implicitly accepting linkage in their willingness to bargain over Cuban against South African withdrawals from Angola and a Namibian cease-fire and independence. The Angolans and Cubans in turn linked these issues to ending RSA support to UNITA. But the initial bargaining positions of each side demanded, unrealistically, the prior withdrawal of the other.

The real breakthrough occurred at the July round of talks, just after the standoff between South African and Cuban troops at Calueque near the Namibian border, and at subsequent separate talks between the military commanders. The New York talks laid out fourteen "Principles for a Peaceful Settlement on Southwestern Africa," including a commitment by Angola and South Africa to fix a date for the implementation of UNSCR 435/78; the staged withdrawal of Cuban troops, most of that to follow a South African withdrawal from Angola; and the ending of RSA backing of UNITA and Angolan sanctuary for ANC. These principles, plus a cease-fire in Angola and Namibia to begin almost immediately, and an actual timetable (detailed in Chapter 4) for implementing the UN plan for Namibia, to begin 1 November 1988 were incorporated into the Geneva protocols signed in August by the Angolan, Cuban, and South African governments.

What these protocols did and did not include, their status, and the specific circumstances of their creation were to become significant in a number of respects. They did not make specific mention of UNITA or ANC beyond a general commitment by both sides not to support hostile acts against other states from their territory and noninterference in internal affairs. And although RSA support to UNITA was subsequently greatly reduced, if not eliminated, thus easing the situation on Namibia's borders during the transition and into the immediate postindependence period, these 1988 agreements did not secure any U.S. commitment to ending support for UNITA. An unstable situation to Namibia's north thus continued, as did the grave disruptions suffered by the Angolan people.

More fundamentally significant for the immediate transition in

Namibia was the absence of SWAPO even from the talks, let alone as a signatory, even though the protocols committed Angola and Cuba to "use their good offices to press SWAPO to move its bases in Angola north of the 16th Parallel," some 150 kilometers north of the border. SWAPO did signal its agreement to a cease-fire "in accordance with the spirit of the Geneva agreement" in a letter to the UN Secretary-General on 12 August 1988 (UNS/20129), but this did not subscribe to all the protocols nor mention the withdrawal north of the 16th parallel. There seems some doubt as to whether all the terms of the protocol were made available to SWAPO at the time; they were certainly not made public. Indeed, just as with the agreements secured by WCG before and after 1978, only the outline of the protocols was communicated to the UN Secretary-General for the benefit of the Security Council.

Further difficulty was put in the way of SWAPO and African states influencing the transition arrangements and monitoring their implementation by the U.S. strategy of seeking to confine discussion of the UN plan's progress to the Security Council rather than the General Assembly, in which all countries were represented. This partial disclosure and the resultant obfuscation and denial of a broader international opinion remained true of the subsequent agreements about the exact phasing of Cuban redeployment farther north and eventual withdrawal from Angola and of South African withdrawal, which were not completed until December 1988.

Thus, by the end of 1988, when the process of implementing the UN plan had already officially begun with the informal cease-fire starting on 1 November 1988, the main elements in the plan, whose original provisions we look at in the next chapter, and the manifold surrounding agreements that were supposed to give it definition were finally in place. In February 1989 the operational phase of the implementation within Namibia was to begin with the arrival of the advance party of UNTAG in Windhoek. That story is taken up in Chapter 5.

# 4
# The UN Plan for Namibian Transition

## The Provisions of the UN Plan

There were three main elements in the transition that got under way in 1989 and 1990: arrangements for a cease-fire, the holding of an election, and the drafting of a constitution leading to independence. These were all supposedly to be implemented in line with a blueprint drawn up under the auspices of the United Nations. The various actors all appealed to this UN plan as the point of reference to justify their actions and to criticize those of others. The plan even included a timetable specifying the steps to be followed—UN preparations, a cease-fire, demobilization of the armed forces, return of refugees, election registration and campaign, convening of the Constituent Assembly—and their exact timing once the clock was running. It was this program that was followed, with the countdown beginning from February 1989, not the originally specified 1978 starting date (see Appendix A).

The plan itself was actually set out in more than twenty resolutions and subsequent documents, letters, memoranda, and informal understandings (see NCC Documents, 1989; Manning, 1989b). This set of international agreements came to be labeled, in shorthand fashion, by the name of one of the central statements and one that all UN actors accepted: UN Security Council Resolution 435 of 1978 (UNSCR 435/78—see Appendix A). The plan made provision for three elements: cessation of fighting, free elections, and achievement of independence. The first step in articulating such a plan had been contained in an earlier UN Security Council resolution, 385 of 1976 (UNSCR 385/76), which required RSA to withdraw its illegal occupation in favor of a UN administration that would hold elections prior to handing over to a representative government.

South Africa refused to accept UNSCR 385/76 and continued to pursue the internal option represented by the Turnhalle conference. Vetoes in the UN by the United States, the United Kingdom, and France, notably to draft resolutions to the Security Council in 1975 and 1976, had until then prevented the imposition of punitive international sanctions as a means of forcing the end of South African occupation, which all powers agreed was illegal and which was restated in UNSCR 385/76. WCG, faced with international disapproval of vetoing or going along with the increasing pressure for sanctions, set about "persuading" RSA to withdraw from Namibia by setting up new negotiations with it and separately with SWAPO. WCG eventually secured the agreement of both parties and then communicated the details to the UN Secretary-General in a document (S/126236) that was then given UN Security Council approval. In some ways this Security Council document was the core of the settlement plan (see Appendix A). It did not formally replace UNSCR 385/76 but supposedly merely set the conditions under which the transfer of power (the need for and legality of which were set out in UNSCR 385/76) might be implemented. But in practice this document represented a compromise with the terms of UNSCR 385/76 to make it more acceptable to RSA.

UNSCR 435/78 was itself short and general but, among other things, gave the Security Council's approval to the agreements that WCG had worked out with RSA and SWAPO. These agreements already incorporated concessions to make the plan acceptable to RSA but thereby achieved the West's aim of preempting the sanctions implied in UNSCR 385/76. In particular these new proposals implied a departure from earlier provisions that downplayed the role of the UN in administering the country in the transition. UNSCR 385/76 would have charged the UN, not South Africa, with directly running the election and being responsible for law and order.

The hard bargaining to work out detailed agreements continued after the 1978 presentation of UNSCR 435/78. These subsequent settlements sought to give arrangements a specific form, and both sides sought specifications that would maximize the advantages to them. Indeed, SWAPO only agreed to UNSCR 435 "with regrets" after two months of pressure from its own backers and WCG; RSA took three more months before indicating that it was "willing to cooperate on implementation of UNSCR 435," but subject to further conditions. In every specific deal that was struck, about everything from the nuts and bolts of registering voters to the size of the UN presence, the two resolutions were interpreted in almost all cases to the benefit of RSA. Notwithstanding these concessions to South Africa in 1977–1978, it still took ten long years of delays and negotiations, and of fighting in Angola and within Namibia, before the plan was implemented.

Focusing on the differences between the two main resolutions and on the particular outcomes of later attempts at specification helps shed further light on the political pressures operating behind the bargaining over technicalities: on the motivations and calculations of the different international actors (our focus in the last chapter) and the internal struggles going on within Namibia between the South African colonial state and the national liberation movement (our focus in Chapter 2).

## The Reinterpretation of UNSCR 385/76

A useful measure of the concessions initially made to South Africa can be found by noting the more significant decisions written into the various agreements under UNSCR 435/78 that modified UNSCR 385/76 (see Landis, 1988). These include:

1. The insistence in UNSCR 386/76 on the termination of RSA's "illegal occupation" of Namibia and on "free elections under UN supervision and control for the whole of Namibia as one political entity" could reasonably be taken to imply, and probably was by SWAPO, that the administration of the elections, the ensuring of law and order, and the observation of the cease-fire would be directly undertaken by some UN body running the territory until independence. The basic document (S/12636) approved under UNSCR 435/78 made clear, however, that RSA would be allowed to maintain power and specifically to run the elections through its AG. This "neutral" figurehead (installed in Namibia in 1977 to preempt the provisions of UNSCR 386/76; see Chapter 2) and SWAPOL were to be the bodies for maintaining law and order. Their activities were to be merely "supervised and monitored" by a UN force.

2. Walvis Bay (the only deep-water port on the Namibian coast) was regarded as part of Namibian territory in UNSCR 385/76 but, at RSA's insistence, was regarded as part of RSA territory in UNSCR 435/78 and was therefore excluded from all transition arrangements.

3. SWAPO's UN privileges, its recognition as the "sole and authentic representative of the Namibian people," and its membership in certain UN bodies were to be removed, which meant that SWAPO would lose an important source of funding and legitimacy. The UN also undertook not to prejudice free and fair elections to the extent that it would not take sides in any conflict or campaigning that might arise in the transitional period.

4. Whereas UNSCR 385/76 did not specify what the elections were to be for, the new resolution stipulated that they would not be for an independent government, but for a constituent assembly that would be empowered to enact a constitution. A prior step was thereby inserted before the emergence of an elected government, thus allowing more room for RSA to reduce the possibility of SWAPO's complete dominance of a future government.

This latter possibility was further undermined by two proposals about the Constituent Assembly that surfaced in 1982 (S/15288 Annex); these further modified the UN plan by reducing the assembly's freedom to maneuver through the inclusion of some preagreed "constitutional principles" that the UN plan accepted as binding. The United States had made a proposal in 1981, which was seized on with obvious relish by South Africa, that all Namibian parties should meet to draft a constitution. This proposal was in direct opposition to UNSCR 435/78, which called for a cease-fire and elections before the drafting of a constitution, and was opposed by other governments in WCG as well as by African states. The principles were a compromise to get out of this impasse. A second provision in the same document (S/15287 of 1982) stipulated that any constitution would require a two-thirds majority, thus making it even more difficult for SWAPO to come to power under a structure of its own choosing; a mere majority was not going to be enough.

The exact balance between the RSA administration's ability to continue setting the rules and the UN's ability to exert effective control was also at issue in all the subsequent agreements, in the specific provisions for electoral and other laws made in 1989, in the day-to-day practices of the AG and SADF, and in their interaction with UNTAG throughout this later period. Moreover, the exact outcome of these contestations about the fine print of the rule book was determined not by technical calculations or legal rights or wrongs but by the balance of political and military forces on the ground or in the international arena.

What was more generally at stake during this long drawn-out process, and what remained in some doubt throughout this period, was whether and when Namibia's decolonization from South Africa would take place. Nevertheless, the negotiations themselves revolved around other, more mundane matters: "the issues came to centre on the details of the *process* leading to decolonization and the *nature* of Namibian self-determination" (Jabri, 1990: 40). What would determine those specific outcomes, and what the underlying conflict was about, was the competition about *who* would play the major decolonizing role—the South African administration or the UN. In this conflict the WCG countries were not simply neutral arbiters; they were, in Jabri's insightful phrase, "interested third parties" that wanted to see a certain kind of decolonization.

Brief reference to other earlier African experiences can shed light on what WCG sought. In much of the continent the departing European colonial powers had "managed" the decolonization. The process had escaped their grasp, however, in Mozambique and Angola, as it had in the early 1960s in the Congo when there had been similar competition between the UN's role and the West's; the collapse of the Portuguese dictatorship in 1974 allowed power to pass directly and without much constraint to the main liberation movement—to the consternation of the Western powers. Similar difficulties were likely in the then-remaining white-dominated territories of Southern Africa, whose regimes were regarded as illegitimate by international opinion and even by international law. In Zimbabwe the matter was resolved by the formal reimposition of British colonial rule, which had not existed since 1923, as a means of effecting a compromise transfer of power worked out at a constitutional conference at Lancaster House in

London. In Namibia there was no similar legal fiction for involving an out-side decolonizing power: to call in the German excolonizers would have been absurd, and the actual colonial power was certainly seen as illegiti-mate. South Africa had its reasons for wanting to stage-manage the transfer of power. Yet however much the West wanted South Africa to get out, a Western, rather than a UN, decolonizing agent no doubt seemed less of a risk, of which the UN operation in the Congo would serve as a reminder, that the decolonization would be more to the liking of the national libera-tion movement and FLS. In essence the plan brokered by WCG down-played the role of the UN in the transition to that of linesman, with South Africa, itself a protagonist, as stage manager (for an insightful critique of their role, see Landis, 1988).

The concessions made to RSA in the new UNSCR 435/78 and later agreements curtailing the power of the UN and restricting the freedom of the Constituent Assembly could be seen as favoring an outcome to the elec-tion and to the whole transition that would allow some greater degree of continued white privilege by protecting property and existing private busi-ness and thereby limiting the sovereignty of a future Namibia. RSA also gained respectability and a semblance of semilegality by being allowed to retain administrative power and responsibility for law and order during the transition period and responsibility for Walvis Bay. RSA offered few con-cessions in return other than actually signing the agreement.

Despite the long bargaining process, however, several issues regarding the arrangements for the transition remained unresolved by 1988. Beyond stating that the UN had to be satisfied by the AG's proposals, no clear regu-lations were set out as to the running of the election, the exact role and deployment of the police, the method of voting, or what legislation should be repealed, nor were arrangements stipulated for the transfer of power after the CA. Most crucially, confusion remained about the monitoring of SWAPO fighters inside Namibia (see Chapter 5). All these omissions creat-ed further problems when these issues were finally defined in 1989.

This section has detailed some of the bargaining chips that the West gave away to RSA as a result of the tortuous wheeling-and-dealing process and the changing balance of forces detailed in Chapter 3. It is important to ask what differences these concessions made to the outcome of events in 1989. Indeed, this is one of the litmus tests we try to apply to the analysis of the events of 1989 in the remaining chapters.

## The UN Provisions for a Cease-fire, Elections, and the Transition to Independence

### Monitoring the Cease-Fire: The Military Component of UNTAG

The first task that had to be managed and monitored was the ending of hos-tilities, specifically a cease-fire on the part of SADF and SWAPO, their confinement to base, and the repatriation of SADF. The UNTAG military component was charged with handling these tasks and, like UN peacekeeping forces elsewhere in the world, was enjoined not to use force except in self-defense, although this could cover cases of resistance against UNTAG's attempts to prevent intimidation. The component's agreed and specified tasks included:

1. Monitoring the cessation of hostile acts by all parties
2. Monitoring the restriction of SADF troops to base and their subsequent reduction to the agreed strength of fifteen hundred troops, which would be restricted to certain agreed-on locations
3. Monitoring SADF military personnel performing civilian functions during the transition period
4. Monitoring the dismantling of the command structures of citizen forces, commando units, and ethnic forces, including SWATF; the withdrawal of all SADF personnel attached to these forces; the confinement of all the arms and ammunition of such forces to agreed locations; and the disbanding of the counterinsurgency units, including Koevoet
5. Keeping the borders under surveillance and preventing infiltration
6. Ensuring that all military installations along the northern border were deactivated or placed under UN supervision and providing security for vital installations in the northern border area
7. Monitoring the restriction of SWAPO fighters to base in Angola and Zambia (UN S/20412, para 43—but note that this document did not make provision for SWAPO fighters inside Namibia)

The specification of the numbers of UNTAG personnel to oversee these and other tasks became a matter of some dispute. UNSCR 435/78 had specified that 7,500 UNTAG soldiers and 1,860 civilians would be required to make up the UNTAG personnel, but the UN General Assembly in a last-minute decision in January 1989 (S/20457) voted for funding for only 4,650 soldiers and 500 police monitors. The Western powers chose this eleventh hour to decide against financing the extra forces, but the USSR also voted for these changes, even in the face of evidence from NCC as to the likely extent of RSA's intimidation and the risk if UNTAG personnel were too scattered (Anon, 1989: 12). This was the first occasion in the United Nations in which the USSR voted against the Third World on a major issue; if it had voted for the extra finance, that might well have switched the decision (*The Guardian,* 18 January 1989).

The Soviet vote could have reflected a belief in statements by the Western powers that a vote for increasing the forces would delay the transfer of power unduly. But given that SWAPO was not concerned about an additional short delay at this stage, and indeed made protestations to the

USSR (reputedly by Ya Toivo in one stormy meeting), that explanation seems unlikely. It may well have been more a reflection of the new Soviet post–Cold War stance of accommodating the United States and backing off from anti-imperialist struggles. Whatever deals might have gone on backstage, the vote indicated a slackening of the commitment to SWAPO, which had been substantial in the mid-1980s, and a less antagonistic attitude toward RSA.

Why the Western powers themselves did not vote for the extra forces is still not clear. Did they want to make it easier for RSA to retain effective control of Namibia during the election, or did they believe arguments that suggested the lower amount would be sufficient? The British experience in Zimbabwe pointed to relative success without anything like the number of monitors proposed for Namibia, and the UN itself was indeed under financial strain (after the imposition of budgetary constraints in 1987–1988). But this hair-splitting did carry implications that monitoring would be less than effective in a country much larger than Zimbabwe with a more dispersed population.

*The Extent and Limits of the*
*Plan's Provisions for Monitoring the Transition*

It is notable that UNSCR 385/76 and 435/78 and related documents from the late 1970s did not specify details concerning the definition of citizenship and thus eligibility to vote, the voting system and the regulation of the election itself, the convening and functioning of the Constituent Assembly, or other postelection arrangements leading to independence. These still substantive details were to be determined by the AG, but under UNSCR 435/75 would have to pass the scrutiny of the UN Secretary-General's Special Representative (UNSGSR) for Namibia. The various regulations were finally spelled out in several election proclamations drafted by the AG but requiring the UNSGSR's approval; these appeared once the election process had begun (see Chapter 5).

The key office of UNSGSR was established because of the unique role the UN had played in Namibia's history. He was to oversee every stage of the process, which could be halted in the event of his not being satisfied that all the UN preconditions for free and fair elections had been met or if the actual conduct was unfair. Indeed, in this reduced role, the only lever available to the UN was to use this ultimate sanction of halting the whole transition process. But the international political climate, where détente between the superpowers was in the air, where all actors including FLS were keen to breathe a sigh of relief that the whole issue of Namibia was over after such long delays, and where considerations of the enormous cost of the operation were crucial, made such a call of foul play and abandonment of the plan in practice quite a remote possibility.

The supervision by the UNSGSR was to be conducted with the assistance of a large body of professional personnel seconded from the UN bureaucracy and with military and police components of UNTAG, supplied by member governments of the UN, which were directly answerable to him. The UNSGSR himself was to be directly answerable to the Secretary-General of the UN and, in the last resort, to the Security Council itself. In effect, the extent of his power lay in UNTAG's ability to ensure effective monitoring of actions of the AG's office or personnel of the previous administration now under the AG's direction or, in the last resort, to order or condone military action by UNTAG itself. His was to be a highly sensitive and potentially influential post, then, as so many key decisions about the election and the transfer of power had not been made by the UN by the time the representative, Martti Ahtisari, arrived in Windhoek in February 1989. (The extent to which he used the powers available to him is assessed in Chapter 6.)

UNTAG supervisors of police (CIVPOL) had the role of monitoring SWAPOL, which in theory would be the only security force in operation, once SADF was confined to base, and which would be responsible for maintaining law and order. The UN police monitors would thus have a crucial part in the election period:

> The duties of the UNTAG civilian police component will include taking measures against any intimidation or interference with the electoral process, accompanying the existing police forces in the discharge of their duties and assisting in ensuring the good conduct of the existing police forces and their suitability for continued employment during the transition period. Arising from these duties is a secondary responsibility of monitoring the maintenance of law and order in Namibia from the cease-fire until the end of the transition period. (Manning, 1989b: 11, summarizing provisions in UN S/12636, para 9; S/12827, para 9)

The limited and passive, merely supervisory nature of this brief and the particular interpretation put on it by the UNSGSR were to cause some considerable problems in the monitoring of intimidation (see Chapter 6).

## Preconditions for a Free and Fair Election

The UN plan stipulated a range of preconditions that had to be met in order to guarantee that the elections would be free and fair (which are clearly set out in Wood, 1989) and established certain provisions for the type and running of the election and the role of the Constituent Assembly. These included:

1. The impartiality of the UN and RSA, to be ensured through the UN not giving preferential treatment or funding to SWAPO; RSA

refraining from supporting its collaborative political parties (although this was always going to be much more difficult to guarantee and monitor because of the close identity of such parties with the existing state apparatus, which was responsible for running the election; there was also a related problem of guaranteeing the impartiality of the media, when radio and TV were monopolies run by the outgoing administration)

2. Security measures: cease-fire and restriction of RSA and SWAPO forces to base, phased withdrawal of South African armed forces, disbanding of RSA's locally recruited militia, and suitability and impartiality of the police

3. The return of exiled Namibians under conditions where they were free from intimidation or imprisonment (no specific measures for their protection were specified, so that the vigilance of UNTAG was the only guarantee)

4. The repeal of all discriminatory legislation

5. The release of all political prisoners and detainees

The last two conditions were defined in only the vaguest terms, which again meant that the onus of interpretation and monitoring lay with the UNSGSR in responding to the proposals and actions of the AG.

In the event, there were delays and difficulties in ensuring all the required preconditions, which may have impaired a further precondition about adequate timing. UNSCR 385/76 called for time enough "for the purpose of enabling the UN to establish the necessary machinery within Namibia to supervise and control such elections." A further document (S/12636) stipulated that "The date for the beginning of the electoral campaign, the date of the elections, the electoral system, the preparation of voters rolls, and other aspects of electoral procedures will be promptly decided upon so as to give all political parties and interested persons, without regard to their political views, a full and fair opportunity to organize and participate in the electoral process." The most complex preconditions, and arguably the most contentious, were those relating to the security situation. As these later became further disputed in the light of the events of 1 April, we consider these now in more detail.

*Security Requirements*

As soon as UNSCR 435/78 was signed, there were disputes about where the opposing forces were to be allowed in the event of a cease-fire. Various UN documents summarize some of the proposals, objections to them, and counterproposals; a list of the most important is included in Appendix A. The task of actually implementing the UN plan was complicated by several factors. It was difficult even to keep track of the various communications because of the mediation of WCG, which had brokered most of them and did not keep even the Security Council fully briefed about their contents. Then having acted independently of the UN, WCG handed over to the international body responsibility for working out the implementation arrangements for the agreements. In addition, agreements were made among the governments of Angola, Cuba, and RSA with regard to security arrangements (specifically, the withdrawal of Cuban troops from Angola) and were not signed or agreed to by SWAPO or the UN. As a result, there was room for considerable ambiguity about the legality and relative primacy of different agreements.

Yet these documents and their ambiguity are crucial to understanding the politics behind what was agreed, and especially the bloody events of 1 April 1989, when the planned cease-fire instead led to major fighting. Those in question refer to regulations about where the military forces of SWAPO and RSA were allowed to be, whether they were allowed to move, whether they could be armed, and whether they had to be monitored by the UN or another authority. One crucial issue was whether the rules allowed PLAN fighters to be armed and within Namibia, in the country at all, or north of the 16th parallel, 150 kilometers across the border into Angola. All the documents specified that SWAPO forces, like SADF, had to be "restricted to base" at the time of the cease-fire and under the supervision of the UN or the governments of Zambia or Angola. The particular confusion and controversy that became critical in April 1989 surrounded the issue of what provision, if any, should be made for SWAPO forces inside Namibia at the cease-fire date. One crucial document (S/12626 and Annex—see Appendix A), which set out the basis of WCG's proposals and was specifically approved by UNSCR 435/78 itself, certainly implies that bases to which SWAPO had to be restricted would be in Namibia, as there was no provision for a UNTAG role outside the country. A later report from the Secretary-General (S/13120) proposed that "any SWAPO armed forces in Namibia at the time of the cease-fire will . . . be restricted to base at designated locations inside Namibia to be specified by the Special Representative after necessary consultation." SWAPO had agreed to this in 1979, and for it, that is where the matter rested. However, the South African government challenged this proposal, and it was the subject of negotiation among RSA, WCG, and the Secretary-General, the latter arguing that it was a practical provision in the event of there being any such forces. Efforts to get RSA's acceptance of a formula for restricting and monitoring PLAN fighters involved proposals for a demilitarized zone just on the other side of the Angolan border, but although FLS accepted this proposal, it was finally dropped, and the matter was left undefined. The resulting confusion was such that Jabri (1990: 98) concludes from her researches that even different WCG ambassadors had conflicting viewpoints on the issue: the United States assumed that SWAPO had at least temporary bases inside Namibia; Britain did not. There were also different interpretations of what was agreed: RSA would later refer to documents drafted by the prospective UNTAG commander but later rejected by the UN.

The Geneva protocols that established the final cease-fire in southern Angola were signed by RSA, Angola, and Cuba in 1988, and it stipulated that SWAPO armed forces in Angola should be withdrawn north of the 16th parallel. This document was quoted and interpreted by RSA as stipulating that PLAN fighters should *all* be to the north of this line in Angola at the time of the cease-fire and that there was therefore no need to arrange for them to assemble and be disarmed and monitored within Namibia. The location of the PLAN fighters and the "bases" from which they operated were always a hotly contested propaganda matter between SWAPO and RSA. The former was not a signatory to the protocol of 1988 and was later to claim that it was operating according to its own interpretation of UNSCR 435/78 and that by 1 April it was expecting UNTAG to monitor PLAN fighters inside Namibia. In fact, UNTAG was totally unprepared for this role (see Chapter 6), and none of the "consultations" between SWAPO and UNSGSR specified in UN S/13120 so that he could "designate locations" for bases inside Namibia had taken place.

There was also confusion about what was actually to happen to all the SADF troops in Namibia, although these regulations are clearer than those for SWAPO. According to UNSCR 629/89, SADF troops were supposed to be reduced in stages and confined to base from the time of the cease-fire according to this schedule:

| | |
|---|---|
| 1 April: | cease-fire and restriction to base |
| Mid-May: | reduction of SADF in Namibia to twelve thousand |
| Early June: | reduction to eight thousand |
| 1 July: | reduction to fifteen hundred; border installations under UNTAG supervision |
| Mid-November: | completion of withdrawal from Namibia of last fifteen hundred SADF |

Regulations also covered all militia locally recruited by South Africa, which were to be demobilized and their command structures dismantled. In particular, Koevoet and SWATF were supposed to be disbanded. The dismantling and removal of weapons were supposed to be implemented by the Administrator-General and only supervised by UNTAG. This particular monitoring operation was complicated, however, by virtue of two facts: that SWATF had been formed in 1980, after most of the agreements around UNSCR 435/78 had been made, and that Koevoet, which had taken on the major search-and-destroy role in northern Namibia, was officially classed as part of SWAPOL, with resulting confusion as to whether it should be disbanded and whether its demobilization should be monitored by the UNTAG military component or CIVPOL. The UN Secretary-General took the position in a January 1989 report (S/20412) that Koevoet was a paramilitary unit and should therefore be disbanded and that RSA had informed him that it would be.

## Voting Procedures

As long ago as 1985 during negotiations between RSA and WCG, it had been agreed that the independence elections in Namibia would be by proportional representation rather than a single-member constituency system (S/15776, S/18767, S/17658; see also Appendix C for details of the system used). But further details regarding the type of system were left to be determined once the process was begun and so were decided by proclamation from the AG's office and monitored by the UNSGSR, with power of veto, (see Chapter 5). However, the UN plans did include some general guiding principles for the election process, which were to be followed in the drawing up of detailed regulations and can be summarized as follows:

1. There would be a "proper registration" of all adults who were eligible voters under conditions that guaranteed the absence of fear of intimidation of any sort.
2. The election campaign would not begin until the UNSGSR was satisfied with all the election procedures and certain that the prevailing conditions were such that all individuals could campaign freely.
3. Voting would take place by secret ballot, with adequate provision for those who could not read or write. There would be approximately four hundred voting stations, whose precise location and number would be decided by the AG to the satisfaction of the UNSGSR.
4. There would be a proper and timely tabulation and publication of the voting results, which would be conducted to the satisfaction of the UNSGSR.

## The Constituent Assembly

The UN role was not to be limited to overseeing the election and its preparations but would also include the effective transfer of power, including the establishment of the CA. The UN plan offered only the vaguest indication of when the effective transfer of power might be deemed to have been accomplished; the length of the supervisory period after the establishment of the CA was to be determined by the UNSGSR.

The role of RSA in the establishment of the CA after the election was also only vaguely defined by the UN, although UNSCR 435/78 clearly stated the illegality of the South African administration. The stated intention of the UN was that after the election, the Constituent Assembly would meet, draw up a constitution for an independent Namibia, and then adopt it, thus excluding the AG from any guiding or overseeing role. This did not prevent the AG from trying to have some say over the assembly's activities (see Chapter 9).

The UN proposed that a document agreed during negotiations between WCG and RSA in 1982, *Principles Concerning the Constituent Assembly of an Independent Namibia* (S/15287), should form the basis of the future constitution. The principles included the following:

1. Separate legislative and executive branches of the government to be constituted by periodic and genuine elections
2. An independent judiciary
3. A declaration of fundamental human rights and civil liberties that included protection against deprivation of private property without compensation
4. Freedom to associate and to form political parties
5. A prohibition on retrospective punitive legislation
6. Equal access by all to recruitment to the public service

The constitution itself was to be written in the assembly and had to be passed by a vote from two-thirds of its members, as set out in S/15281. The need for the two-thirds vote then set the goal for the election: a simple majority would be insufficient to monopolize the writing of the constitution. How the need for two-thirds support was to interact with the polarized character of Namibian politics, with its lineup of nationalists and collaborators, would not be revealed until the election campaign was under way and the results were in.

# PART 2

# 5
# The Political Climate
# of the Transition

## The Politics and Administration of the Transition

Any transition from armed conflict to a constitutionally bounded political competition is complex and difficult. The process generally emerges from complicated and delicate negotiations and compromise, which in the Namibian case were especially long and tortuous and which could easily have been disturbed and put into reverse. The chances of success are likely to be heightened when there is a clear set of ground rules governing each stage of the transition to reassure the suspicions of former mortal enemies. However, agreement may have been reached only by virtue of there being some intentional ambiguities and some unspecified matters. Chapter 4 indicated some of the gaps and imprecisions in the UN plan as well as specifying the plan's requirements for acceptable preconditions with regard to the political climate during transition. In any such still imprecise circumstances, the warring factions are likely to continue seeking to translate whatever edge they inherited from the period of struggle into bankable electoral or other advantages. If there is a situation of dual power, where each side controls some areas or sectors of the population, their mutual efforts might cancel each other out but are more likely to be a formula for conflict. Where, however, the former authorities retain control of the electoral process, they will have scope to shape the outcome. Yet if they take too much advantage of the situation, they risk jeopardizing the whole delicate process of transition. What will be judged "going too far" will depend on the pressure coming from opponents and the influence of observers, not just the self-restraint of the contending parties. Thus, in addition to the existence and comprehensiveness of ground rules, the overall climate is also determinant—the willingness to compromise, the degree of trust or mistrust, the readiness to eschew violence and stick to the rules, the degree of influence of outside monitors and international opinion. These latter themes are the focus of this chapter; the further definition of the ground rules for the election and their administration is the subject of the next.

In the Namibian case, SWAPO saw its crucial trump card as the overwhelming popular support it thought it could count on. SWAPO believed any minimally open political process would allow it to translate that support fairly automatically into votes and into power—and to an extent SWAPO was prepared to risk competing against a partially stacked deck. This did not stop it trying to steal a march at the start of the transition by infiltrating guerrillas into northern Namibia ahead of the cease-fire in April.

But what of the other actors? The national liberation movement had been opposed by a coalition of the South African state and its administration, plus South African and locally recruited security forces, allied with internal ethnic administrations and the local parties related to them, most affiliated to DTA. Their main leverage lay in the perquisites and resources of the state structures at different levels, including their coercive power. Moreover, the compromise that led to the UN plan and to its implementation left the South Africans in unambiguous control of the administration and, of course, the running of the election. What was crucial, therefore, was how far the South African regime would push home its advantage using its coercive and manipulative power or how far it would be willing or pressured to moderate its dictates in accordance with its supposed role as neutral administrator of the decolonization. What would in turn be revealed was the closeness of any continuing linkage between the South African state and the internal parties.

RSA and its appointed administrator-general, who took over absolute power from the transitional government on 1 March 1989 at the beginning of the transition, maintained a rhetoric that they were just being the administering and arbitrating authority. The AG's staff was formally committed to cooperating with UNTAG. The staff and DTA itself claimed that no official support was given to any parties, and at the time no financing could be proven. Their supposed neutrality was always open to question, however, for, as Jaster (1990: 40–41) argues,

> the realpolitik of the A-G's position, however, meant that he was not a neutral party disinterested in the outcome of the November elections. Pienaar and his staff, including registrars, lawyers, bureaucrats and 6,000 police were . . . answerable only to Pretoria. Most would be seeking transfers to the South African civil service once Namibia became independent. There could be no doubt in their minds that the South African government remained strongly opposed to a SWAPO-dominated Namibia. Not surprisingly, therefore, many of the Pienaar Administration's actions appeared biased against SWAPO.

They asserted that they were just maintaining law and order, but there was much evidence assembled at the time by UNTAG, by observers, and by researchers (including us) suggesting that the patterns of repression by state security bodies of the war years continued. Subsequently, however, information from South Africa in mid-1991 revealed a much clearer picture of an orchestrated campaign by the South African state wherein brutalities by a range of official agencies amounted to systematic intimidation, which was supplemented by massive financing of parties, manipulation of political events, and South African control of reporting in the media to shape the election and the whole transition process. The political dirty tricks were revealed to involve RSA, through its Military Intelligence and other agencies, in an Operation Agree designed to harass SWAPO and its efforts to mobilize support, to bolster DTA and other groups that could distract support from SWAPO, and to manipulate events to deny SWAPO a majority or at least the two-thirds support it needed to dominate the Constituent Assembly. Nico Basson, formerly of South African Military Intelligence (SAMI), who was paid to set up a public relations firm from which he ran the operation, came clean in June 1991 and pointed to three areas where he thought their tactics had been successful: "exploitation of the scandal over the torture by SWAPO of its own members; whipping up of anti-SWAPO sentiment over the incursion into Namibia of SWAPO guerrillas from Angola in April 1989; and building up the credibility of the DTA" (*The Guardian,* 11 June 1991).

This public exposure of South African intentions in 1991 led finally to an admission by the RSA government of its funding of parties, which was justified on the grounds that "SWAPO had been the enemy." This exposure also points strongly to what many observers suspected: that there was some overall strategy that orchestrated the actions of the security forces and the AG's office with the political tactics and methods of DTA and perhaps other political parties and groups. But the detailed evidence of what happened during the transition needs to be scrutinized to help confirm this interpretation, to clarify just what the specific tactics in this strategy consisted of and aimed at, and to evaluate how effective they were when people's responses are taken into account.

These tactics can be divided into three categories: the covert manipulation of the overall situation in the transition through intimidation and other state security actions, the leverage used by the South African administration of the transition, and the support for and even direction of political parties. This continuation of South African attempts to influence the transition, under the changed postconflict circumstances, and the responses of SWAPO, other parties, and ordinary Namibians are the focus of this and the next two chapters. The issues of the degree of violence; how far it was perpetrated by the public, party campaigners, or official organs; in what ways it could be constituted systematic intimidation; how effective such efforts were made; and what other indirect methods of influence and manipulation of voters were used are the focus of this chapter. (The possible leverage over the electoral process is explored in Chapter 6; the parties are the focus of Chapter 7.)

## A False Start: The Aborted April Cease-fire

The implementation of the provisions of UNSCR 435 officially began on 1 February 1989 with the arrival of the UN advance party in Namibia. But the actual assembling of UNTAG was seriously delayed as a result of the acrimonious debates at the last minute in the United Nations Security Council and between it and the General Assembly over the resourcing of the UN operation. These prolonged arguments meant that the UN military did not begin to arrive until late March, just before the crucial moment in the plan: the cease-fire that was to come into operation on 1 April. By then fewer than 1,000 of the intended 4,650 military components were on the ground, most of them logistics and support personnel, and only 12 of the expected police monitors were in place; they were short of equipment and still trying to arrange the leasing of mine-protected vehicles from the South Africans themselves (another disputed economy measure). In the event, they were too little and too late to cope with the emergency that immediately ensued. UNSGSR Martti Ahtisari did not arrive himself until 31 March. (For details of the UN debates and delays, see Jaster, 1990.)

The arrangements for the cease-fire in the UN plan and for stage-by-stage demobilization of all forces under the monitoring eye of the UNTAG military component did not go off as smoothly as UNTAG had expected. With hindsight, it is possible to see the seeds of the tragedy of 1 April in the ambiguity over demobilization arrangements for any SWAPO fighters inside Namibia. In the early hours of that morning, SADF reported an "invasion" of PLAN fighters; immediately the supposedly disbanded Koevoet initiated hostilities. There followed in the next few days some of the bloodiest fighting seen in Namibia in the whole long war, with more guerrillas, civilians, and SADF troops killed than in any other engagements inside Namibia—perhaps 250 or more deaths.

These events threatened the peace process and the transition itself and certainly colored the whole period up to the elections. The South African government warned that it was considering suspending its participation in the peace process and asking for the withdrawal of UNTAG (*The Guardian*, 5 April 1989). Exactly what was the order of events? Why did the PLAN fighters move into Namibia and when? How far were SADF and Koevoet poised to take advantage of such a situation? These are issues still shrouded in confusion, but some preliminary attempt to set the record straight has to be made here, if only as a basis for considering the significance and repercussions of these events for the outcome of the election and the transition. (One important source of information we use in making sense of these events was extensive interviews with Brigadier Opande, the Kenyan deputy military commander of UNTAG [8 and 9 September 1989], who was the first UNTAG official on the scene in the north of the country where these episodes occurred.)

Signs of the impending tragedy were visible on the evening of 31 March when the AG stated that he had definite, "confirmed" information about an impending incursion by armed PLAN guerrillas, which he described as "a major invasion." The same kind of "intelligence" had been contained in similar RSA statements for some two weeks before (Jaster, 1990: 36). During the early hours of 1 April, SADF troops engaged guerrillas in battles in the border areas, to the west of Ruacana, in remote parts of Kaokoland, and at Okatana and other parts of Ovamboland. In the next few days some thirty such battles were fought across much of the northern border from Kaokoland through Ovamboland to the western border of Kavango. Some 140 PLAN fighters were reported killed in the first three days (according to a Legal Assistance Center report, SADF, which claimed more than 300 in the first nine days, has always tended to overrate what it terms its "kill factor"). Most reports suggest a common pattern to these engagements: some SWAPO fighters would be spotted and surrounded, usually by helicopter gunships and by the highly mobile Koevoet units in Casspir and Wolf armored vehicles, and although they returned fire, these SWAPO fighters were simply killed. In later incidents South African security forces were more effectively resisted—altogether SADF sustained an estimated 35–40 casualties—and the two sides reached a kind of standoff by mid-April, according to Opande. During those days UNTAG and FLS representatives were rushing among the northern areas, Windhoek, and Angola trying to arrange an actual cease-fire, but it was not until mid-May that the plan's implementation was officially resumed and SADF and SWATF were once more confined to base.

The most far-reaching consequence of these incidents was a result of a decision late in the day of 1 April when the UN Secretary-General "reluctantly" gave his approval to some SWATF units being released from bases to provide minimum required backup to the police. The next day UNSGSR Ahtisari approved six SWATF battalions being reactivated and rearmed with Casspirs and SADF helicopter gunships to assist SWAPOL (mainly Koevoet) in curbing what Margaret Thatcher (fortuitously in Windhoek at the time) called a "challenge to the authority of the international community" by SWAPO (*Financial Times*, 3 April 1989). Thus, not only were the South African security forces back in business; so also were their "brutal and determined assaults" on PLAN fighters (Jaster, 1990: 39), which had been given the backing of the UN. The UN Secretary-General justified this action by claiming that he was faced with "the alternative of accepting a decision by the RSA to decide that it could no longer be bound by UNSCR 435, and the settlement proposal" (statement by UNTAG spokesperson Cedric Thornberry, 5 April 1989); the former meant that SADF then would deal with the threat in its own way and without any restraint. The delays in agreeing on UNTAG's finances and the reduction in its full complement certainly meant that UNTAG itself, with so few troops in the country, could not act, or even obtain its own independent sources of information, and thus was inclined to take RSA reports at face value.

RSA's threat to act on its own once again raised the possibility that it, or at least one faction in Pretoria, was still looking for ways to avoid implementing UNSCR 435. RSA leaders were dissuaded, according to one press report at the time, by Thatcher's strong advice that she could not deliver international support if RSA reneged on the plan (*The Guardian*, 3 April 1989). The South Africans were certainly intent on reactivating SADF, but here again Thatcher's role seems to have been decisive in persuading Foreign Minister Pik Botha that any such release of security forces from their bases had to be done "under UN cover, even if that cover was only a fig-leaf" (Jaster, 1990: 36, quoting a "senior Western diplomat"). Thatcher was directly involved in negotiations with RSA and the UNSGSR to keep the peace plan on track. They agreed there would be an immediate UN investigation into the events—although this did not prevent Thatcher from condemning SWAPO, in the terms we noted, before that investigation began (*Financial Times*, 3 April 1989).

Other interpretations of the incursion were to surface in the next few days: SWAPO claimed not only that the relatively small number of fighters were not bent on aggression but also that they had not infringed on the agreements. There was confusion about the provision for the disarming and monitoring of PLAN fighters within Namibia, which was at the root of the controversy about what happened and how. SWAPO claimed the right under UNSCR 435/78 to restrict its forces to bases inside Namibia, whereas the 1988 Geneva protocols specified that PLAN fighters withdraw some 150 kilometers north of the border with Angola—a proposal that conveniently ignored the possibility of PLAN fighters being in Namibia itself and that had always been hotly contested by SWAPO. The South African government, of course, always wanted the propaganda advantage of denying that any PLAN fighters had established bases. This issue of what exact presence SWAPO had in the country was thus of substantial symbolic and political significance in the election period ahead.

The South Africans claimed that the PLAN fighters had "invaded": that is, they had not been in the country before 1 April, had crossed the border on the fateful night, and had done so for belligerent purposes. How far does the necessarily incomplete evidence we have support these or SWAPO's counterclaims about the fighters involved in the fighting in April? It is clear that, according to the Geneva protocols, those who were in Angola on 1 April should have withdrawn north of the 16th parallel, and many of them did do so, to be disarmed by the Angolan army and to be monitored by UNTAG military until they eventually returned to Namibia as part of the "returnee" contingent of SWAPO, under the auspices of the UN High Commissioner for Refugees (UNHCR). SWAPO claimed that as it had not been a direct party to the protocols, it was not bound by them.

Nevertheless, no concrete provision was made for any PLAN fighters in Namibia before 1 April. The Geneva protocols, because they were among RSA, Angola, and Cuba, obviously could not take on what was to go on inside Namibia. UNSCR 435 acknowledged there was an issue here but did not make any specific agreed provision for PLAN fighters to be assembled.

This situation was in contrast to what had happened in the similar cease-fire agreed in Zimbabwe between the liberation movements and the Rhodesian colonial authorities, where in 1980 some sixteen assembly points were specified in different parts of the country to which guerrillas made their way, to be disarmed only when they were within the points by neutral forces that then monitored (and protected) the former fighters. Relatively small numbers of mainly political cadres and refugees came back directly from neighboring states. Moreover, the Lancaster House conference on Zimbabwe's independence incorporated a recognition of the "theoretical equality" of the Rhodesian and the guerrilla armies (Tamarkin, 1990: 268); both were supposedly responsible to the British-appointed governor for observance of the cease-fire. In the event, the British governor remobilized the Rhodesian forces to track down what were claimed to be cease-fire violations by ZANU forces—in the same way as was to occur in Namibia with the AG reactivating SADF and SWATF, with the UNSGSR's approval. But in Namibia PLAN fighters did not receive even a notional recognition from RSA that they might have a legitimate presence in the country.

The transition from Rhodesia to Zimbabwe is instructive not only because it points up some of the particularities of the Namibian experience but also because it most likely figured in the actual calculations of both RSA and SWAPO. The South African government had borne in mind the unexpected outcome of the 1980 Zimbabwe elections. The result had been different from what RSA as an interested party, the British government as the decolonizing power, and the United States and other Western nations had thought they had set up: namely, an independence government that would include "internal" leaders (Bishop Muzorewa and Reverend Sithole), the white political bloc led by Ian Smith, and one faction of the liberation movement, Joshua Nkomo's ZAPU. They thereby thought to exclude ZANU, the wing of the liberation movement that had done most of the fighting and was considered more radical. The attempt to set up this outcome was done partly through the system of representation: a guaranteed white contingent in parliament with a veto plus a different form of proportional representation for Africans that would supposedly give the internal ethnic forces full weight.

But a further element in the tactics was the remobilization of the security forces almost immediately after the cease-fire on the grounds that it was being violated by ZANU. There was thus a continued repressive presence at the local level that sought to bring home a certain political message, chiefly through intimidation. This strategy was fairly successfully countered by many ZANU cadres, who remained unarmed in the villages rather than going to the assembly points, politicized the locals, explained voting procedures, and so on. It was no doubt with the example of this kind of preemptive strike to prevent the rural areas being "contested," under dual power, during the transition to the elections that SADF and SWATF stood poised to take action immediately before 1 April but also in late June. On the very eve of the poll on 31 October, the South African authorities were again to claim that they had evidence of a "further SWAPO invasion." By that time, however, RSA had finally cried wolf once too often, even for UNTAG and international opinion—and even for the AG, who reported no basis for RSA's claims.

Events were further influenced by Zimbabwe precedents, for the conventional explanation in Rhodesia and Western circles of why ZANU had foiled the game plan was that ZANLA guerrillas who stayed in the villages succeeded by "continuing to terrorize." RSA was to claim after April that such had been the intention of SWAPO (see the account by Stiff, 1989, which was written from the RSA point of view). These ZANU cadres had thus provided political education and the nucleus of a newly formed political structure and also challenged the presence of the security forces on the ground. Moreover, they and their comrades in the assembly points provided a visible symbol of unbowed liberation fighters. Not only was RSA intent on foiling this pattern in Namibia; RSA also did not want to allow SWAPO the symbolic gains of "freedom fighters" coming into any assembly points. At the same time, SWAPO probably hoped to follow something of ZANU's lead. Indeed, we were informed in Harare in August 1989 that some joint seminars with SWAPO had been held in mid-1989.

The evidence does suggest that whatever PLAN presence there may have been in the north during the preceding months, there was an influx of PLAN fighters into the country just before the 1 April deadline when SWAPO had agreed all incursions across the border would cease, possibly continuing over the night between 31 March and 1 April. The political logic of such an attempt is clear: it would give these fighters, and SWAPO generally, more kudos as victorious returning liberators and would also make available some cadres locally to help in political education work. But at issue are the circumstances of the PLAN fighters' incursions into northern Namibia: was this an invasion with military objectives? Brigadier Opande interviewed the only two PLAN fighters to be captured and survive, who said they had come over the border on 29 March. One claimed he was one of a platoon of twenty-nine that "came to be monitored by UNTAG"; the other was a scout who was checking out where UNTAG was and whether SADF troops were in base as they were supposed to be and was then ambushed by them. An Owambo farmer who was an eyewitness to another ambush told Leys (1989a) a similar story about seeing some guerrillas who were trying to find UNTAG to give themselves up. Two human rights lawyers who visited Okahenge on 3 April concluded on the basis of eyewitness reports that "the SWAPO forces in that area had no hostile intentions and that the skirmish there had not been initiated by SWAPO" (Legal Assistance Center, 1989: 3). The South African *Weekly Mail* (7 April 1989) reported that SWAPO forces "were apparently under orders to look for UNTAG and to surrender themselves."

However, the advantages of having organizers on the ground would have accrued only if they had gone to ground and not given themselves up to UNTAG. In fact, accounts all seem to agree that the infiltrators wore very visible uniforms, were heavily laden with arms and other equipment, and carried propaganda materials. Thus, even a book-length account of this "Nine Day War" that was a highly partisan celebration of the military feats of the men of SWAPOL "who saved the day and the peace with their courage and their blood" (Stiff, 1989) notes how different these displays of large groups ("we saw about fifty SWAPO, not even in cover" [p. 86]) were from the normal mode of infiltration that had been anticipated by SADF: "infiltrators . . . singly or in pairs, probably wearing civilian clothes and lightly armed with pistols and grenades . . . [not] large numbers of run of the mill PLAN fighters."

It is this kind of evidence that conversely led some observers to a very different conclusion from Stiff's: that SWAPO forces did come with the intention of giving themselves over to UNTAG and handing over their weapons and that "they had no hostile intentions" (Legal Assistance Center, 1989: 3). This last report also concluded that SWAPO had certainly not initiated the skirmishes. Now that the dust has settled a little, there is not much evidence to suggest that an invasion was occurring—a belated and ultimately ill-advised, symbolic incursion perhaps.

These incursions provided the ideal opportunity to remobilize the security forces, especially Koevoet, which was first on the spot in many engagements. The circumstances whereby Koevoet was available to resume its counterinsurgency task are themselves a continuing bone of contention. What is clear is that these dreaded forces were once again let off the leash and continued to operate under some kind of claim to legitimacy, with only very limited monitoring, until the eve of the elections, thereby becoming the single most serious intimidating factor and calling into question the freeness of the elections. Moreover, the remobilization of SADF and SWATF forces after they had withdrawn to base was authorized by the UNSGSR. This gave credence to the RSA version of events; legitimized the massacre that took place; made monitoring the activities of Koevoet thereafter more difficult; generally placed UNTAG in a position of responding to RSA initiatives, as was to be the case for much of the electoral process; and delayed all UNTAG's other preparatory tasks until mid-May. In sum, as was observed at the time, "UN officials agreed . . . to arrangements which significantly enhance[d] Pretoria's control over the transition process" (*Financial Times,* 3 April 1993). In immediate military terms, the UNSGSR no doubt thought he had no alternative; but that was in part because he had only RSA sources of intelligence available to him to know what was going on. In addition, there were only ninety UNTAG troops on the ground at the time, with virtually no vehicles available to them. They were taken by surprise and took a long time to recover their ability to initiate action. However, if there had been a greater UNTAG complement in place from February, or had an airlift been possible, the longer-term political costs of bowing to RSA security demands might have been avoided.

These underlying shortcomings are hard to excuse: the UN had ten years to prepare the timetable, and the military component was required first and foremost on the day of the cease-fire. In the event, the delay in the component's arrival was occasioned by last-minute reconsideration of its provisions during January and February by the permanent members of the Security Council before the long-agreed plan was given the go-ahead for implementation. Moreover, in a last-minute decision, occasioned, they said, by lack of finances, the UNTAG components were reduced from the planned 9,200 "full strength" to 6,450 personnel.

That these tragic events had such political benefits to RSA and the parties it supported tempts speculation that somehow this preemptive move was contrived by SADF. This hypothesis is given some credence by Brigadier Opande's observation that SADF had already said in mid-March that its intelligence expected a "PLAN incursion on 1 April" and that on reflection he could recollect a great increase in border surveillance and an intensification of Koevoet control points and mobile operations in the days before—even though there had been no actual fighting since August 1988. In any case, the South Africans were clearly intent on using these April events to advantage. At first, it seems, there was a strong lobby for using it as an excuse for aborting the whole plan of UNSCR 435. Pik Botha was apparently dissuaded by Margaret Thatcher. But thereafter the South Africans simply used the events to capture the initiative. Indeed, in revelations some two years later of a concerted operation to manipulate the transition, one of their secret agents listed the "whipping up of anti-SWAPO sentiment over the incursions . . . in April 1989" as one of the three successful features of that part of the campaign (*The Guardian,* 11 June 1991).

However, in speculating on the implications of the April events for the transition, Jaster (1990: 39) perceptively suggests that "the incursion may have lost SWAPO some votes among whites and other ethnic groups, but it may have enhanced its status among its chief constituency, the Ovambo majority . . . [for] local residents blamed the security forces, rather than SWAPO's incursion, for the ensuing bloodshed and devastation." This accords with our own conclusion that the overall pattern of South African strong-arm measures, which certainly received a positive injection in April, were probably as often counterproductive in Ovamboland even if they had more effect on their cause in other parts of the country. Another possible interpretation of South African utilization of the April events was to point to them as justification for oft-repeated SADF speculation that SWAPO might resort to force following the elections or not accept the result, which in turn gave RSA both the excuse and means to pressure any future SWAPO government into accepting the administrative, security, political, and economic status quo (Leys, 1989b).

A final implication for subsequent events should be noted. The incursion was sparked by a decision somewhere in the PLAN high command to send fighters back home. Even if this act could be claimed to have been in accord with UNSCR 435, and to that extent did not represent a contravention of the cease-fire agreement, it was nevertheless extremely ill-conceived in its operation. No attempt was made to consult with UNTAG or to consider the likely reactions of SADF or the fate of the fighters and locals. This decision was therefore ill-advised in terms of its immediate personal and political costs. The circumstances in which such a decision was taken in turn raise questions about the manner in which SWAPO conducted the war and its general character, especially in terms of the relations between commanders and fighters, issues that were to resurface time and again during the campaign and after, especially in relation to the detainees issue (Chapter 7).

## Monitoring the Demilitarization

The fighting in the north continued for ten days, fueling a crisis as to whether the settlement process would be aborted. The AG announced that the plan had been suspended and that arrangements for the elections were indefinitely postponed. Intense diplomatic activity sought to defuse the conflict: FLS proposed a cease-fire under which the PLAN fighters would be disarmed and allowed to remain in the country, but RSA rejected this last aspect. The Angolan, Cuban, and South African members of JMC met on 8–9 April in Namibia and finally hammered out the Mount Edjo Declaration, by which SWAPO fighters would be guaranteed safe passage to UNTAG-monitored assembly points and then escorted north of the 16th parallel in Angola, the process to be completed by 15 April. Although this was accepted by SWAPO, word did not always reach guerrillas and counterinsurgency forces in time; some fighting continued, and few PLAN fighters followed this process. Most instead withdrew to Angola under their own steam. Some, however, did remain undetected—four hundred according to SADF claims, half that according to UN officials. This withdrawal was proclaimed complete by 15 May, and the elaborate process once again cranked uneasily forward.

By that time the UNTAG military monitors had been hurriedly assembled, and the demobilization of the South African–controlled forces was once again under way. The Secretary-General had been informed (S/20883) that some 30,743 of them were deployed in Namibia at the time of the cease-fire: almost 10,000 were SADF, although 1,000 of them provided the command structure of SWATF; another 11,500 were locally recruited "citizen forces" and "commando units," more than 9,000 made up the ethnic battalions of SWATF. SADF personnel were back in base under UN monitoring by mid-May and thereafter withdrew as laid down in the plan's timetable (see Chapter 4). The citizen forces and commando units had been demobilized by 31 March. The ethnic forces were being demobilized at that time, but this process was not completed until the end of May. Their arms were repatriated to RSA or put under UNTAG lock and key, but that was not officially accomplished until September. The troops themselves were eventually dispersed, although they continued to receive pay twice a month until February 1990. In these respects the demobilization of SADF and SWATF went broadly according to plan (one exception was the two Bushman battalions that had become so estranged from their hunting and gathering life-style that they remained in camps with their families and were given the choice of going to South Africa after independence).

However, all was not as it seemed. In early 1989 the AG set up the Department of Defense Administration, whose only formal duties seemed to be organizing the fortnightly payments to SWATF and looking after the few SADF troops that were allowed to continue in civilian occupations. Yet for these tasks some 156 SADF personnel, many of them former commanding officers, were seconded to this new department; they used their former battalion headquarters for the pay parades, which often lasted two or more days a month. Only after the UNSGSR's protests and some considerable time were these functions assigned to accounting officials. Thus, to all intents and purposes the demobilization and the dismantling of command structures prescribed in the plan were very considerably delayed. Moreover, the only weapons that were adjudged to belong to SWATF troops, rather than SADF, were personal hand arms, not any heavier equipment; there was no proper accounting for these small arms, and the numbers UNTAG later reported implied that several troops must have shared one rifle (Leys, 1989b)!

Similar processes governed the treatment of ex-Koevoet, who also continued to receive pay, but with them there were further complications. As no explicit provision had been made for this paramilitary unit created after UNSCR 435/78, its demobilization was negotiated between the Secretary-General and RSA at the end of 1988. Early in 1989 the AG claimed that Koevoet had been disbanded as a unit but that some eighteen hundred of its three thousand personnel had been reabsorbed as individual members of the police force. These latter were clearly on hand to be reactivated within the reconstructed unit on 1 April to deal with SWAPO incursions. Although it is a matter still shrouded in obfuscation (we interviewed the deputy military commander and the head of the police monitors of UNTAG to seek clarification), it seems likely that some of the twelve hundred who were not absorbed within SWAPOL were also remobilized. By mid-May the South African authorities were stating that Koevoet was disbanded but with the same number reabsorbed into SWAPOL. That this was a fiction was confirmed in late September when some twelve hundred "ex-Koevoet members of SWAPOL" were demobilized (again!) at Oshakata in Owambo, but without UNTAG monitoring, and so further demobilization parades were held under CIVPOL's supervision, one as late as 30 October in Kavango. The UNSGSR had told the South African authorities that most of the ex-Koevoet were not "suitable"—by virtue of their limited education and training and experience only in counterinsurgency—for normal police work. But the actual monitoring of their activities posed problems for UNTAG as this task fell between CIVPOL, which was supposed to scrutinize the ex-Koevoet's activities and even accompany them on their patrols, and the military component, which was to monitor their demobilization and keep an eye on those confined to base. There was one group that was eventually confined to base under UNTAG military monitoring, but this scrutiny was limited in practice to office hours; at night the ex-Koevoet were free to move out with their equipment.

The actual situation that existed until October is described in these terms by a report of the Secretary-General to the Security Council (S/20883, 6 October 1989):

> Although ostensibly members of SWAPOL, many of the ex-Koevoet personnel continued to operate in the same manner as they had before the disbandment of Koevoet. This included the use of the armoured personnel carriers known as "Casspirs" mounted with heavy machine guns. UNTAG received many complaints of intimidation and other unacceptable conduct by ex-Koevoet personnel and UNTAG police monitors were on a number of occasions themselves witnesses of such behaviour. The use of Casspirs and heavy machine guns was inconsistent with the provision in the settlement plan that "the police forces would be limited to the carrying of small arms in the normal performance of their duties."

Continued representations were made by the UNSGSR: he wrote to the AG in June that Koevoet was "behind a campaign of terror which, if continued, would make free and fair elections impossible" (*Times of Namibia,* 21 June 1989), but even so the campaign continued. The eventual demobilization announced by the AG on 28 September had to be done again and anyway only included some 45 percent of ex-Koevoet in that district. The later demobilizations in October were finally monitored by UNTAG, which observed the handing in of personal weapons (although of a very small number for so many men) and checked the names of those who paraded for the last time. But this was still not an exhaustive identification as SWAPOL did not provide records of those who supposedly made up Koevoet against which these named individuals could be checked.

Even after that a Koevoet presence and command structure seemed to be in evidence. In Kavango the demobilization parade at the end of October was followed by extravagant marching into the townships. These personnel continued to be very visible in uniform-style T-shirts emblazoned "Koevoet Kavango" and carried handguns in public places, even, as observed by one of our team, in DTA campaign headquarters in Rundu Town on 5 November. When this team member also reported to CIVPOL the presence of a handful of young white men dressed in civilian clothes ferrying these ex-Koevoet around in two pickup trucks with South African number plates, the UNTAG police monitors said they knew these men and vehicles well and suggested that these were former commanders.

The overall picture then is one whereby ex-ethnic battalion and especially ex-Koevoet were kept on a payroll and in touch with their former commanders throughout most of the election period, through the AG's Department of Defense Administration and its regional offices. Koevoet took on the protective coloring of SWAPOL. Some further details of the activities of these (former?) security personnel and their relationship to the parties is detailed in the next section and in Chapter 7.

## The Electoral Climate: Violence and Intimidation

One of the preconditions, as was noted in Chapter 4, that the UN plan sought was the existence of a general climate conducive to the conduct of free and fair elections. In the event, the social and political atmosphere was tense and full of hostilities during almost the entire period between April 1989 and independence in March 1990. The start of the transition process was marred by the bloody events of 1 April and repeated threats by RSA authorities that the election would be called off if intimidation of the decolonization process by SWAPO was not halted. The AG and his masters in Pretoria sought, with a large measure of success, to prevaricate and delay the whole range of electoral and voting ordinances that formed the necessary legal framework to the transition proceedings, as is documented in Chapter 6. They were only partially inhibited in this by the UNSGSR, who tended to adopt passive, rather than active, interventionist stances. Yet although he was caught off guard by the events of 1 April, UNTAG staff throughout the electoral districts were in general much more insistent that, once agreed, the regulations for registration of voters and parties be met and that intimidation of voters and party rallies be minimized. In those tasks UNTAG staff were assisted by hundreds of foreign observers from the region and beyond who monitored every aspect of the transition process and kept all the authorities on their toes. In this, the Churches Information and Monitoring Service (CIMS) and several international monitoring groups were particularly important in producing reports and in continually monitoring key areas. In so doing, these groups often minimized the most serious threat to the election process—the persistent violence and the systematic intimidation of voters and parties.

Concern had been expressed internationally about the possibilities of either a breakdown in the whole transition as a result of spiraling violence or a sufficiently widespread scale of systematic intimidation that the validity of the election results would be called into question. And a climate of violence certainly haunted the election process: shootings, kidnapping, throwing of hand grenades, beatings, and even assassinations. But the use of the abstract noun *violence* often obscures more than it reveals: it does not say who was doing what to whom. It is important to explore how far this violence was a matter of excesses in the political campaigning by supporters of political parties that had until recently been on opposite sides of a war and how much it was part of directed strategies to intimidate. Detecting the latter element requires going behind the actual incidents to uncover, if possible, the intentions and calculations motivating such tactics. Then efforts must be made to assess the effectiveness of such activities in influencing potential voters and to estimate the extent to which violence distorted the election outcome and the nature of the transition, an issue that is carried forward into the discussion of results in Chapter 8.

In addition, consideration is given not only to the intimidation by force or threat of force that was visible and overt but also to that which was less transparent and direct, particularly to what might be called "structural intimidation" arising from the subordinate and dependent social and economic relationships in which many people were deeply embedded. People who had got jobs or received pensions from a particular ethnic administration or who were caught up in patron-client relationships, indebted to officials, chiefs, and headmen in various ways, might well not wish to vote in any way that would jeopardize their situation. As was already discussed in Chapter 2, the ethnic political structures set up by the South African administration had fostered such patron-client political relationships. Employees, especially farmworkers, trapped in semiservile relationships with their employers, were also subject to pressure, either to vote for the party suggested by their boss or to refuse the opportunity to vote at all. We attempt to assess the extent of this structure of intimidation in the last section.

In one sense the electoral process itself was an example of structured intimidation. Registration and voting took place in magistrates' courts, at white farms, in old army bases, all places with associations of oppression by the colonial regime. Registration and electoral officials were from the AG's administration, not always people sympathetic to the local black population and sometimes aggressive toward voters. Indeed, the actual voting administration involved South African officials and UNTAG observers but almost no Namibians. In some places police were prominently placed at registration points/polling stations, often with guns, a not very encouraging sight for voters. Any apprehension would have been fueled by people's memories of the kind of heavy-handed and biased electoral experiences in earlier years.

Violence alone then, especially if it is a result of spontaneous loss of temper between supporters of different parties, may have no systematic influence on the way votes turn out, however regrettable that violence may be. So one must investigate how far acts of violence, or even indirect pressures, were accompanied by specific threats, especially if part of orchestrated campaigns. Moreover, one must discover what explicit tactics parties or officials did indeed use to induce voters to vote differently from what they had intended or to not vote or register at all: What sanctions did these provocateurs employ to ensure this outcome beyond the initial threat? How effective was such intimidation? Of course, crucial to the latter question was the issue of how far the vote was, and was perceived to be, secret; only if there were doubts would intimidation alone have resounding impact. In exploring violence and the systematic use of force as well as the possibility of official intimidation, one must consider, finally, whether the specific and pointed acts could be said to add up to a general climate of violence or fear of it, whether a result of deliberate strategy or not. An overall atmosphere of anarchic and seemingly pointless violence could itself contribute to the effectiveness of threats against specific people or communities. Such measures were not unknown in Southern Africa and in RSA's total strategy, which in Mozambique and Angola involved the total destabilization of communities.

The South African administration itself pointed a finger in another direction: to the threat from SWAPO, suggesting that it would parallel the "terrorist" tactics of which the Rhodesian authorities had accused the Zimbabwe nationalist movements. It is hard to untangle whether this was a genuine fear, a deliberate camouflage of the administrations's own actions, or a reflection of the fact that RSA's own rhetoric would not allow any acknowledgment that SWAPO had popular support out of commitment rather than threats. The AG, Louis Pienaar, actually claimed to have set up the (O'Linn) Commission for the Prevention and Combating of Intimidation and Election Malpractice in May 1989 in order to deal with cases of intimidation perpetrated by SWAPO, although he himself admitted that, as it happened, SWAPO "had not put a foot wrong" (interview, 26 January 1990). The United Nations refused to become involved with the O'Linn Commission, reserving the right to make up its own mind about intimidation. On 22 July the AG also published a new "Prevention of Intimidation" proclamation, introducing heavy penalties for election malpractice including verbal threats, although there were very few prosecutions under it. By mid-August the O'Linn Commission itself had handled only 57 complaints, although 403 had been reported to UNTAG. By the time of the last sitting on 17 November, the O'Linn Commission had had 215 cases brought to it but had made judgments on only 128, 10 having been referred to the AG's office for possible prosecution. O'Linn's own conclusion was that the "malpractice" side of the commission's deliberations did not "become a real threat to free and fair elections," despite the "many vague allegations of fraud, bribery and corruption." However, "intimidation was a serious problem which always had the potential to escalate to such dangerous proportions that free and fair elections could have been aborted." His own overall assessment was that "the Commission's contribution lies mostly in the fact that it was an alternative option, particularly for those who suspected existing institutions of bias" (*The Namibian*, 17 November 1989).

By the end of August the level of violence was such that foreign observer missions, churches, the UN, and various political groups were all worried about whether the election should go ahead. Legal assistance centers in Windhoek, Walvis Bay, and Rundu continued to accumulate complaints about intimidatory behavior. Our scrutiny of their files after the elections revealed details of 130 cases that had been reported to them or that had been reported in detail in *The Namibian* during the five months from March to July 1989. Of these cases, 44 involved harassment or attempts to intimidate, another 44 involved actual assault, and 16 involved shooting. The rest did not involve physical violence but included 8 cases of people dismissed from jobs. Of the 120 cases where the alleged perpetrator(s) were specified, 86 were attributed to security forces: members of SWATF or SADF (59), ex-members of the ethnic battalions (14), Koevoet (6), and other SWAPOL (7). Another 17 cases involved employers or administration personnel and 16 DTA supporters. By virtue of the origins of these cases, supported as they were by churches, cases brought to the centers and reported in *The Namibian* would be unlikely to include many cases brought by DTA supporters, so this sample cannot be taken as evidence that SWAPO was not involved in any intimidation at all. It does, however, offer an indication of the scale of violence and threats perpetrated in the early part of the campaign period. It also provides specific details indicating that most threats and violence emanated not from the political parties, not even DTA, but from the security forces, although the activities of the latter two were not always distinguishable. Similar indications were contained in a report (*The Namibian*, 31 May 1989) from UNTAG that it received 120 complaints of misconduct in April and May, "most of which were directed at members of the security forces."

The brutalities committed by security personnel were a continuation of their unlicensed behavior over several years. It had become customary for them to be issued certification of immunity from prosecution by the South African state president under the RSA Defense Act No. 44 of 1957. Some efforts were made with the return to some degree of rule of law in 1989 and UNTAG pressure to make them more answerable to the courts. The Supreme Court of Namibia invalidated certificates in March 1989 against six members of the security forces who had murdered a SWAPO former Robben Island prisoner; ten charges were brought against such personnel in the north, one for murder (*The Namibian,* 24 March and 24 June 1989, respectively). But such efforts were put into perspective when two SWATF soldiers were sentenced to fines of R 200 or fifty days in prison for beating to death a sixty-five-year-old pastor, the magistrate having been swayed by their contention that they thought they were dealing with a "terrorist" (*The Namibian,* 21 April 1989). They were given further indirect protection by a decision in mid-1989 that would have curtailed the work of the Legal Assistance Center, which had brought 150 cases of such complaints before the courts in the previous twelve months and which charged the complainants no fees, by withholding its right to legal aid (*The Guardian,* 20 August 1989).

UNTAG was seen by those "Namibians who did not wish to address themselves directly to SWAPOL" (S/20883) as an alternative channel for complaints. There does seem to have been a great reluctance to complain directly to the police, for as one man from Owambo said, "If you are bitten by a snake, you don't go back to the snake for a cure" (*The Namibian,* 8 September 1989). But many people discovered that reporting incidents to UNTAG did not yield many results either, for UNTAG could only pass on complaints to SWAPOL for investigation, although CIVPOL did seek to monitor the progress of these investigations. The Secretary-General's report of 6 October 1989 (S/20883) acknowledged that these "proceeded very slowly" in most cases, a finding confirmed by the director of UNTAG in Ruacana, who said that SWAPOL had not brought a single case of reported violence to any kind of conclusion all the time he had been in Ruacana (interview, 8 November 1989). The same UN report refers to complaints made "against SWAPOL, especially its ex-Koevoet elements, and against former military personnel of SADF and SWATF, political parties and private citizens."

The actual evidence on violence and intimidation is partial and episodic, but these sources, as well as the published reports of various official and unofficial observers, do allow some sort of overall picture, area by area, to be put together of who was perpetrating what kind of offenses and with what effect. One of the most substantial of these sources is the compilation of reports by the forty-five monitors from many countries fielded by the CIMS (1990). This network was set up by CCN "to maximize scrutiny of the transitional dispensation . . . in the hope that the implementing parties (South Africa and UNTAG) as well as the Namibian participating political parties would adhere to the letter and spirit of the independence plan." Given CCN's orientation as broadly supporting the national liberation movement, much of the attention of these monitors was directed to the activities of the administration, although, arguably, that was where other observers also saw the greatest transgression of the rules. In any event, as what has been collected and printed is a set of raw materials, rather than an analysis, commentators can make their own use and assessment of it, as we do in looking at the electoral climate in different areas.

Instances of SWAPO violence and intimidation did occur, although on occasions it was also clear that incidents were carried out by groups dressed and appearing as SWAPO or PLAN cadres (CIMS, 1990: 104). In one notable case, a DTA organizer, Lukas Pedro, was killed in a fight at Onepandaule in Ovamboland in October by a crowd of SWAPO supporters, and that incident precipitated widespread retaliatory violence by DTA. In other incidents DTA supporters responded to threats and provocations in kind. In Owambo, where SWAPO had considerable strength, there were many returnees, and SWAPO might have been thought likely to display its strength: out of 102 cases reported to UNTAG during September, 30 were complaints by DTA against SWAPO and 69 by SWAPO against DTA; in an escalation in the first week of October, 41 complaints out of 43 were against DTA supporters (CIMS, 1990: 102). However, the fact that considerable restraint was by and large exercised by SWAPO is borne out by Pienaar's comments and much other evidence. The party was clearly determined not to offer any excuse for delaying or calling a halt to the independence elections.

This does not exclude more general pressure being used. We document some of the threats of loss of privileges or livelihoods used by local chiefs and headmen, and although the overwhelming majority of these officials were DTA (or United Democratic Front [UDF] in Damara), there is no reason to believe that those significant few who were known or covert SWAPO supporters refrained from using such leverage. The ex-detainees of SWAPO and their organization no doubt were conscious of the possible further attention they were inviting then or in the future from SWAPO security chiefs or a future SWAPO government. Such worries and a pervasive influence of massive support for SWAPO in Ovamboland might account for the fact that UDF, which included the Patriotic Unity Movement (PUM), got a smaller percentage of votes there than it did nationally, even though there must have been some ex-detainees in that electoral district (ED) given the depth of SWAPO's recruitment there (see Chapter 8 on results).

Against the fact that Lukas Pedro was the only known case of someone killed by SWAPO supporters, there was significant loss of life by SWAPO supporters. Examples taken at random of this most serious form of violence include someone killed when a vehicle coming away from a SWAPO rally was fired at and several cases of members of security forces shooting people in streets, bars, and elsewhere, often for chanting slogans or sporting party symbols. Several were killed when houses and vehicles were bombed. But the targets included not only ordinary supporters: the brother of Peter Mueshihange (SWAPO's defense minister) and two brothers-in-law of Hidipo Hamutenya (information minister) were killed; the latter's house was hand-grenaded, as was the home of Vice-President Hendrik Witbooi; the SWAPO chief of staff for the western region was killed in the April events; Anton Lubowski, SWAPO's top legal aide and best-known white leader, was assassinated. Clearly the leadership itself was put under threat.

In moving on to consider the actions of DTA, one must recognize the degree to which it recruited (ex-?) members of the security forces. In Ovamboland and Kavango especially, ex-members of SWATF battalions and of Koevoet were mobilized by DTA to do the grassroots work. They were apparently organized in military-style units of twelve under a leader, usually white, and maintained a high profile throughout the campaigning period. The mere existence of such personnel in campaigning activities must have been threatening to local people, who very often could recognize them and remember their past brutalities. Their actual tactics in their new party roles were predictably intimidatory. Indeed, according to CIMS monitors, many former "Koevoet places are full of red white and blue" (DTA colors), and on the weekend they would openly carry weapons of intimidation such as sticks and knives (CIMS, 1990: 111). SAMI defector Nico Basson was later to assert contemptuously that his employers assumed that "intimidation is the only thing that works in Africa" (*The Guardian,* 11 June 1991). He further intimates that these elements through their command structure were to some degree orchestrated with the activities of those who remained in Koevoet inside the police. In addition, CIMS monitors on a number of occasions felt SWAPOL was reluctant to take action against rioters or people causing disturbances because "a big number of SWAPOL men are DTA supporters and they don't want to intervene against other DTA supporters" (CIMS, 1990: 111).

The existence of so-called cultural organizations, such as Rzuva, also pointed to a further, not very covert political role of former security personnel and provided a threatening background to the election processes (Gottschalk, 1987). These police and paramilitary groups justified their activities by pointing to the fact that ex-PLAN combatants were campaigning for SWAPO.

Other agencies that were kept more at a distance from the security establishment and DTA and that used other personnel were also involved in intimidation or other more overt activities. There was, for instance, a petition signed by almost fifty thousand people in the north drawing attention to thirty-three atrocities, several of which involved murder, perpetrated in the border areas of eastern Ovamboland by UNITA "bandits" (*The Namibian*, 30 October 1989). On the southern borders of Ovamboland, special teams were operating during 1989 in the Etosha Pan game reserve against elephant and rhino poachers, as also in Kavango and Caprivi. This exercise in wildlife preservation was undertaken by two British-based security companies, one staffed by former members of the British antiterrorist Special Air Service, with twenty-six personnel in Etosha and others in Damaraland; this operation required R2 million of equipment and was supposedly financed by "private interests" in Europe and the United States concerned about wildlife. (However, *Africa Confidential*, 28 July 1989, in reporting this suggests that a company such as Lon Rho might be a more likely paymaster than RSA, although no such operation could be mounted without South African approval. Ironically, revelations inside RSA later implicated SADF in ivory poaching in the region; see *Independent*, 23 February 1992.)

With the arrival of UNTAG in full force after the events of 1 April, there was some attempt to monitor and perhaps curb the official and the informal "security personnel" within DTA, who had operated for years without constraint. But the difficulties inherent in these efforts was indicated by Commander Fitzgerald, who was in charge of UNTAG police monitoring in Ovamboland. He was in constant argument with SWAPOL and with "Major General" Hans Dreyer who was previously in the counterinsurgency forces in Rhodesia, was a former commander of Koevoet, and was still essentially in charge of its operations in Ovamboland because he had been placed as head of SWAPOL there, about intimidatory behavior. Typical of this dialogue was the dismissal by Dreyer of the random firing of guns by ex-Koevoet and police after dark as "only high spirits" (interview with Fitzgerald, 4 November 1989).

## The Climate in Ovamboland

Ovamboland was the scene of probably the most widespread, overt, and bloody intimidation. CIMS observers chronicled its extent. One report from the weekend of 30 October–1 November alone contained the following catalog: "15 people treated in hospital after a grenade explosion at a school in Ondangwa and 12 from a similar explosion some miles away, and 15 were injured and two killed in a crowd singing SWAPO songs at Omuganda; 17 other people were hospitalized during the same week-end after several incidents, all of them SWAPO supporters injured by DTA activists, with one DTA exception wounded by a grenade thrown by another DTA member in a quarrel over a woman, which also killed a security policeman" (CIMS,

1990: 97). Another report highlighted the plight of a small village, Okanjota, where an informant declared that strangers were not very welcome "because many DTA men came from outside and beat up people"; as this information was being given, a Casspir passed through the village quickly without the required UNTAG monitor (CIMS, 1990: 102).

One target of such threats comprised the many returnees who had been part of the SWAPO and PLAN operation based in Angola and who came back into Namibia in June. They were easy targets as they were lodged at first in camps and were also identifiable—and isolated—when they returned to their home villages. One report (CIMS, 1990: 88) quotes local teachers about a group of about fifty "pistol-carrying DTAs . . . walking around the village asking for returnees." The aggression was even directed against UNTAG. In one incident on 7 October 1989 Mary Kelly, wife of UNTAG staff member Brian Kelly, was attacked in her car by a flare rocket and by a group "armed with clubs," some of whom "were wearing DTA hats and/or T-shirts" (CIMS, 1990: 113–114).

On the weekend of SWAPO's Star Rally at Oshakata, where Sam Nujoma spoke in Ovamboland for the first time after his return from exile, considerable violence broke out, directed toward a school in Ongwediva and toward UNTAG personnel who attempted to intervene. On the Sunday morning there was the funeral of a DTA supporter, Lukas Pedro, killed by SWAPO supporters after a grenade-throwing incident at Onepanda. That weekend the atmosphere in Oshakata was tense, and violence persisted in a number of different ways throughout October and November and even broke out after the election results were announced.

Some reports give a feel for the role in this intimidation played by Koevoet, SWATF, and SWAPOL. One case brought to the O'Linn Commission in July alleged that a bus of SWAPO supporters was fired on by DTA supporters under the eyes of SWAPOL, which eventually arrested thirteen of the SWAPO supporters and let DTA go. The UNTAG regional director in Ovamboland is quoted as the source of a story of a man singing SWAPO songs being arrested and having his tongue ripped out (both reported in CIMS, 1990: 5–6). Chief Taapopi was arrested by SWAPOL for intervening in the arrest of a SWAPO mobilizer and was subjected to considerable indignities (*The Namibian,* 1 September 1989), while at the same time Chief Kautuima, leader of the National Democratic Party (NDP) within the DTA alliance, was protected by an ex-Koevoet bodyguard heavily armed with machine guns and grenade throwers. Further indication of the degree of the official role in intimidation is offered by Ahtisaari reporting that the UNTAG office in Oshakata, which covered the whole of Ovamboland, had received two hundred complaints of intimidation by June and that "quite a number of those complaints were against SWAPOL" (CIMS, 1990: 68).

## The Climate Elsewhere in the North

There was also considerable intimidation in the neighboring northern districts of Kavango and Caprivi. These were heavily militarized districts, and reports about the conduct of the election focused on the consequences of the widespread presence of ex-SWATF and Koevoet, making Kavango in particular seemingly a stronghold for the DTA with a "high rate of intimidation" (CIMS, 1990: 9). There were three hundred Koevoet in Kavango throughout the registration and campaigning period within the police force but in a separate unit; they constituted 50 percent of SWAPOL's total force and were not confined to their base, retaining their Casspirs for patrolling purposes and taking part in roadblocks. They were even purportedly "doing a good job preventing poaching in Western Caprivi" (interview with National Patriotic Front [NPF] electoral agent, 16 September 1989).

Many ex-202 Battalion combatants were also incorporated into DTA after demobilization: one of the district DTA leaders was Major Gende of 202, now a member of the National Assembly. Numerous reports associated intimidation with these ex-combatants and with ex-Koevoet personnel. In early October, for instance, ex-Koevoet troops were reported on the rampage in Kavango. A DTA truck carried forty people, most dressed in DTA colors and Koevoet T-shirts, east of Rundu singing, "Today we beat SWAPO down!" The truck stopped at the village of Utoka, and the people it carried started beating the inhabitants with *sjamboks* (rhino-hide whips); about ten people were beaten, and one, Romano Ndango, twenty-five, who was wearing a SWAPO T-shirt, was badly injured (CIMS, 1990: n.p.). In another report, CIMS noted that on 5 November 1989 Dirk Mudge, chair of DTA, was seen "huddled together with DTA party workers at the Kavango Motel in Rundu. These campaign workers were wearing T-shirts proudly displaying the words 'Kavango Koevoet' in DTA colours" (CIMS, 1990: n.p.). A CIMS monitor thought that the former South African commanders of 202 Battalion and the local Koevoet had come up from South Africa in the days before the election.

Although the UNTAG office in Rundu did not seem to think there had been any intimidation of consequence (interview, 4 October 1989), the SWAPO office had a large file of complaints, many of which had been sent to the O'Linn Commission, and there was a steady stream of critical press and CIMS complaints during September, October, and November. A police monitor admitted that after dark anything could happen out in the bush and that UNTAG could not be everywhere. One of our team was actually stopped at a roadblock that was searching cars just outside Rundu Town, staffed by a large armed group of plainclothes police, not accompanied by CIVPOL as it was supposed to have been, just two nights before voting began.

These pressures apparently operated at several levels directed at different sections of the population. In early September a DTA smear campaign against church leaders in Rundu claimed that Catholics were preaching SWAPO politics; Father Wirth complained that his telephone was tapped, presumably by police in Rundu (*The Namibian,* 5 September 1989). As in Ovamboland, chiefs connived at such violence and even took part in it. In one incident a local chief known for his DTA support led a busload of DTA supporters in a vicious *sjambok* attack against two women who, when greeted with the DTA sign, refused to return it. The women received multiple injuries. The chief, Alfons Majavero, was eventually elected to the Constituent Assembly (CIMS, 1990). Like the situation in Ovamboland, intimidation in Kavango continued up to the voting itself. On 10 November 1989 CIMS observers were called to the Sambya Mission, where eighteen people were hiding from Koevoet forces that had beaten people in the area. According to a further CIMS monitors' report assessing the levels of intimidation during the voting period, the "beating up of people in rural areas by supporters of DTA and ex-Koevoet members is still going on. Every hour wounded people arrive at Rundu hospital" (CIMS, 1990: n.p.).

One of the most serious incidents was the killing by police in August of Josef Petrus, a former PLAN fighter who had been tortured and turned so as to work for Koevoet. Police officers claimed that he had pointed a pistol at them, but the O'Linn Commission was dissatisfied at its preliminary hearing, and there was delay until February 1990 before the final hearing—by which time the elections were well past. In September Isak Daniel, a friend of Petrus, fled to Ovamboland with his family in fear of his life (*The Namibian,* 28 September 1989). The Petrus case is an indication of the kind of intimidation by the police/Koevoet in Kavango. Koevoet forces were still terrorizing people up to the demobilization parade on the eve of the election. Immediately after these forces went on a provocative march through Rundu and neighboring areas and boasted that they were "still in business;" they finished with a rampage that culminated in the death of a woman in a bar.

In Kaokoland the level of DTA intimidation against both SWAPO and NPF was such that it was very difficult for these parties to operate at all in this region. Located in the northwest corner of Namibia bordering Angola, the region was almost completely cut off during the war, except for a strong military presence. The army maintained and kept close watch over watering holes in this barren and sparsely populated area as Koevoet befriended the indigenous Himba and other ethnic groups. Often without any national news reports and where even radio transmissions were rare, local people, except perhaps in the regional center of Opuwo, were dependent upon DTA propaganda (CIMS, 1990). The continued military presence in Kaokoland led CIMS observers to note that the police/Koevoet remained active and were "feared by the local population" and "that there is a concerted campaign to squeeze SWAPO out of the region" (CIMS, 1990: 133). That paramilitary activity raised serious questions about maintaining the security of local residents during the implementation of UNSCR 435, something reinforced by the observation that "the role of UNTAG in the Kaokoland region leaves much to be desired. Most of the residents we spoke to complained that they do not see UNTAG in action and that police move alone mostly" (CIMS, 1990: 133). One reason for this may have been that even by the end of October, UNTAG was still waiting for delivery of two Casspirs to monitor and keep an eye on Koevoet, which was not confined to base (CIMS, 1990: 139).

In many areas of Kaokoland, local headmen refused SWAPO permission to open offices. Chief Kakuhire Mbaumba of the Orumana told CIMS monitors, for example, that SWAPO could not open an office, and he also asked SWAPO to "remove a house" that had been designated for a suboffice. SWAPO also experienced similar difficulties from headmen in Korosave, Otavi, and Ongano (CIMS, 1990: 127–128). SWAPO speakers were also liable to be physically abused. A returnee was detained by police and subjected to interrogation for no apparent reason, and a SWAPO mobilizer was killed while he was sleeping in his house in the week before the election (CIMS, 1990: 129–130). A large proportion of the population was either employed by the security forces or benefited from their presence; as was noted in Chapter 2, SWAPO had little established presence among the people during the war and could make little headway during the campaign as a result of the institutional pressures.

## The Climate in Central and Southern Areas

There was intimidation in southern and central areas of Namibia as well, although it was of a different character and intensity; it was not so much a continuation of patterns of counterinsurgency as in the north. It often took the form of confrontations between party supporters and might involve stone throwing and disruption of party rallies or scuffles and threats between gangs of activists. At Lüderitz, for example, an inflammatory speech by Barney Barnes of DTA led to skirmishes between DTA and SWAPO supporters. Elsewhere in the south intimidation by DTA supporters of SWAPO took both an overt disruptive form where police and local whites patrolled township areas, as in the town of Bethanie, and a covert, tension-filled form where petty apartheid practices were still in place in shops and local hotel bars. In nearby Keetmanshoop this institutionalized racism was less extreme, but the election campaign was conducted by SWAPO under recurrent threat of physical attack and abuse. On one occasion, all pick ax handles were rumored to have been purchased by whites from the town's stores to threaten SWAPO supporters before local rallies (interviews with SWAPO and UNTAG, Bethanie, Keetmanshoop, and Lüderitz, September 1989).

Violence extended to the capital, Windhoek, where in one incident many were injured as a result of a DTA march in September in which stone throwing at houses and cars was the main form of assault on the SWAPO area through which marchers proceeded (CIMS, 1990: 365). One of the most serious incidents during the election was, however, the assassination of Anton Lubowski outside his home in Windhoek, thereby depriving SWAPO of one of its most valuable white leaders. The ramifications of this murder, with accusations and counteraccusations about who was responsible, continued for many months. One man was arrested but when charged it was only with being implicated; whether the real assassin will ever be brought to justice is by no means certain. Another case in which the assassins are still at large is the killing of a security guard in an attack on the UNTAG office in Outjo.

As noted, it was not uncommon for UNTAG to be on the receiving end of violence, and there was some discussion about arming UNTAG police monitors in October after the outbreak of violence at Oshakata on the weekend of Lukas Pedro's funeral. It was decided not to arm UNTAG, a courageous decision that carried a risk but that may have finally contributed to bringing down the level of violence until after the election, when it burst forth in a final attack on SWAPO after the results were known.

Finally, mention can be made of intimidation of an overt kind by both political parties and state officials at registration points and at polling stations. The police stood armed outside polling stations, and administrators interpreted electoral regulations in such a way that black voters were put at a disadvantage. Some of the most sustained examples occurred in the enclave of Walvis Bay, which RSA still claimed, and the neighboring town of Swakopmund. Border police harassed black voters coming from Walvis Bay to register and later made it difficult for them to go to Swakopmund to vote. At the same time, the administrator in Swakopmund seems to have attempted various forms of harassment of black voters, from registration onward; his actions ranged from insistence that black voters be thumbprinted, whether literate or not, to the restriction of opening times of the registration point in the magistrate's office, making it difficult for black voters to get there from Walvis Bay. There was even a refusal to permit Mondesa, the black township, to have a polling station at all. Moreover, SWAPO was not allowed to have an office in Walvis Bay or to hold rallies there although such restrictions were not placed on other parties.

*The Effect of Intimidation and Violence*

The final question is, of course, how far various forms of intimidation affected the election results. Strangely enough, it would appear from the pattern of voting that structural intimidation may well have had considerably more effect than the direct and visible forms of intimidatory violence. The activities of DTA thugs ("rent-a-thug," as one UN official called them) and ex-Koevoet within the police, and even of the chiefs in places such as Kavango who exerted considerable pressure on voters, may sometimes have been counterproductive. Perhaps the previously quoted assumption that intimidation "is the only thing that works" implies such an overre-liance.

The remarkably high turnout and the SWAPO majority, although with-out the hoped-for two-thirds majority, seemed in the end to have silenced most observers' reservations about the conduct of the independence elec-tions, and certainly UNSGSR Ahtisaari proclaimed the elections free and fair. Other observers who were aware of the intimidation perhaps felt that even if the election was not especially free, the *result* could be adjudged fair. However, the only obvious conclusion that can be drawn about the effect of violence and intimidation from the results is that it did not dent SWAPO's massive support in Ovamboland. Perhaps this was a result of the extra security that people felt in communities that were virtually unani-mous. Of course, the huge SWAPO percentage there also implied that peo-ple felt secure in the knowledge that the vote was indeed secret. Perhaps there was also sufficient critical mass.

In the other northern areas, apart from Kaokoland, where there had been much official and DTA intimidation, SWAPO managed to get signifi-cant proportions in spite of the harassment of the population, even in Caprivi, which was the home of the DTA president. But it is hard to know whether SWAPO could have expected only that partial degree of support or whether threats and attacks coupled, as they seemingly were on occasions, with hints that the way people voted would be known did scare some voters into voting against their intentions, especially where the common security and effective voter education about the secrecy of the ballot that seemed to have countered the violence in Ovamboland were lacking.

Elsewhere in the south and center of the country, the evidence does not suggest that intimidation alone was a sufficient explanation for why SWAPO got relatively small percentages. As we discuss in Chapter 8, reac-tions about the SWAPO detainees, existing DTA footholds through patron-age and other means, and possibly ethnic identifications may have been more decisive, even if intimidation had reinforced these factors.

*Structural Intimidation and Manipulation:*
*Farmworkers and Other "Clients"*

In addition to the vivid, obvious intimidation, there was also substantial structural intimidation, which was less overt than the shooting and other kinds of physical abuse so far discussed. This was particularly noticeable in Damaraland, where flying the blue, green, and white UDF flag was a demonstration of loyalty to Chief Justus Garoeb. Old-age pensioners at Okombahe and other places in Damaraland may well have felt that a vote for Garoeb was a vote that would protect their pensions. The dependence of those employed by ethnic administrations was also directly shown when sixteen secondary-school-teachers were sacked from their posts at Dibasen Secondary School in Okombahe for their political activities. They were replaced by unqualified but politically acceptable teachers (interview, Okombahe, 8 December 1989).

In Hereroland it was difficult for SWAPO to campaign because chiefs and headmen simply said that their people were DTA and refused access to their land. Even UNTAG was refused access by one headman on the Aminius Reserve, declaring that the only political party he wanted on his land was DTA (interview, 29 November 1989). The deeply embedded patron-client relationships of people in Hereroland made it difficult for them to vote for anyone except DTA.

Much of the fear about voting contrary to the wishes of tribal chiefs or employers turned on the question of the secrecy of the ballot. Illiterate voters could be intimidated only if they could be convinced that their votes were not secret and that retribution would follow if they voted for the wrong party. Stories about this means of intimidation from white farmers were common. In addition, employers often refused their workers permission to take time off to vote, as in the Walvis Bay enclave, although many workers ignored their employers and went to the polling stations anyway, some getting the sack in the process (*The Namibian,* 12 November 1989). Many more may have been sufficiently intimidated into not going to vote, although just how many we cannot know. Earlier on in the electoral process, workers in Tsumeb at the Henning Stone Crusher Works, were given the sack for not going to a DTA rally, including a foreman who had worked for the firm for nine years (CIMS, 1989).

Chapter 2 indicated that the estimated five thousand white-owned farms in Namibia occupy 77 percent of the viable farming land, employ perhaps forty thousand workers, and are home to perhaps three or four times that number of dependents. Pay and conditions on these farms have been notoriously bad, and the workers have been isolated from contact with the outside world, often caught up in dependent, patronage relationships with the farm owners.

Moorsom (1982: 33–34) estimates that the number of farmworkers had gone down from more than 50,000 in 1970 to "probably under 40,000" in 1977, fencing and camps having allowed farmers to save on labor for grazing, with karakul farmers using more casual labor. He says that by 1970–1971 more than 30 percent of farmworkers were casual labor employed for only part of the year. According to the 1981 census, there were some 75,000 "living on farms." Some researchers suggest that the number of workers' dependents is much greater than the one-to-one ratio that the census figure suggests and that the resident population maybe as high as 250,000. Accurate estimates are difficult in view of the extent of casual labor and the difficulty of estimating dependents, in addition to workers, because dependents may also move in search of work elsewhere. The Wiehahn Commission (1989) did give a very specific figure for farmworkers, which, if correct (its source is not indicated in the report), represents a further fall during the 1980s. With that figure as a basis, the number of voters on the farms would include more than 30,000 workers, depending on whether one assumes the one-to-one ratio in the census or the same proportion of people of voting age among the farm residents as in the population at large, anything between 30,000 and 130,000 additional residents.

A newspaper report after the election paints a typical picture of conditions on the farms: wages between R 40 and R 60 a month (£10–£15 in a country where the cost of living is about the same as Europe), plus a weekly food ration to supplement the miserable wages. The boss of this farm, visited by the reporter, admitted that he supervised his workers' voter education: "He supplied mock ballots and taught them how to vote for the DTA. Mr Louwer (a worker) explains that he understood that the ballot was secret but when asked for whom he voted he says DTA, explaining, 'I'm an old man now. I need that R60 and I'm not sure how much longer I will get it'" (*The Namibian,* 2 December 1989).

Reports from throughout Namibia from CIMS (see 1990: 199, 212–213, 359, for reports from Otjiwarongo, Gobabis, and the Windhoek rural district) and other observers, from our own interviews and farm visits, and from the press all indicated that this story was not untypical and that there were a number of ways in which farmworkers could have been pressured by their bosses:

1. Farm-owners provided transport to registration points for their workers and then kept registration cards "for safekeeping."
2. DTA was often the only party that obtained access to farms (Action Christian National [ACN] seems not to have bothered with workers). Access was often difficult for SWAPO and other parties, and even when they obtained access, farmworkers were often too afraid to participate in meetings and in voter education, although SWAPO managed to contact many workers by means of a whole range of appeals and subterfuges plus occasional intervention by UNTAG.
3. Farmworkers were dependent on their employers for transport to polling stations, and their bosses were often behind them in the queue.
4. Farmers gave their workers "voter education" that often amounted to instructions to vote for DTA or ACN if they wished to keep their jobs.

5. Even the fact that many polling stations were on white farms and occasionally old army bases constituted a kind of intimidation, for who could feel free to vote in such places?

During election week observers at many polling stations recorded the active presence of farmers keeping an eye on the way their workers were voting. In Tsumeb these farmers were threatening toward CIMS observers who were taking an exit poll and also objected to the taking of photographs outside a polling station (CIMS, 1990: 351). Farmworkers in Gobabis came with the DTA section of the ballot paper sticking to their T-shirts or caps and even fixed to their foreheads so that it would be clear which party they were voting for. Some simply handed the DTA slip to the electoral officer as if they understood this action to be the exercise of their right to vote.

Farmworkers were at a disadvantage, being without proper voter education and electoral information and still locked in a feudal relationship with their employers. This is a problem for farmworkers the world over, of course, and in planning for the future, SWAPO needs to consider these farmworkers, important as voters but also as human beings living in appalling conditions.

It seems likely that farmworkers voted overwhelmingly for DTA (see Chapter 8) because of the structural intimidation they faced. However, it is clear from the 1981 census figures that farmworkers are drawn from a wide range of ethnic groups: Nama and Damara in the south, Herero and San in the central areas, and a considerable number of Owambo migrant laborers. The farmworkers' vote therefore must be explained in terms other than ethnicity.

## The Media

Media coverage has become central in all present-day elections. What was especially critical in Namibia was the inherited pattern whereby there was strict state control of radio and television, plus a few newspapers in Afrikaans, German, and English aimed almost entirely at whites. Overcoming this inherent bias was a change that the UN had seen as a precondition for a free and fair election. To be sure, a few newspapers that were not collaborationist had emerged—*The Namibian* in the 1980s and then others during the campaign, including a SWAPO weekly, *Namibia Today*—but the printed word would always be less influential than radio and television among a largely unschooled and very scattered African population. Indeed, neither newspapers nor television was readily available outside Windhoek. In Ovamboland a limited number of copies of *The Namibian* circulated, often one or two days late. In Kavango and

Kaokaland even this service was not available, and the first question that greeted travelers was a request for a paper.

### The South West African Broadcasting Corporation

The South West African Broadcasting Corporation (SWABC) had a broadcasting monopoly and was a parastatal organization answerable ultimately to the AG and run by a board appointed by him, most of the members in 1989 having been recommended by the outgoing transitional government. Indeed, it was the last essentially political body that had not been dissolved. SWABC tended to offer a very restrictive coverage of events within Namibia and more generally in the region. Throughout most of the transition period, it remained blatantly biased in favor of the RSA regime's view of events and antagonistic toward SWAPO, which it continued to describe as terrorist. The challenge of reform had been well stated by the UNSGSR in a 13 September 1989 statement: "SWABC has a monopoly of the electronic media, on which a large proportion of the population, many of whom are illiterate, depends for its knowledge of Namibia and the world. This demands a meticulous standard of objectivity. The basic problem is that of editorial policy, editorial decisions, the essential question of objectivity in the coverage of news and current affairs." Ahtisari further elaborated on the problem when he stated that, although there had seemingly been attempts at "self reform" of SWABC, they had "not been sufficient and satisfactory." Indeed, he concluded that he was "not satisfied with the impartiality of the state-controlled media in Namibia."

The task of assessing the role, the impartiality, and the possible impact of the broadcasting media is made easier by the findings of *An Investigation into the Extent of Impartiality of the South West African Broadcasting Corporation* (Radio and Television News) (Namibia Peace Plan Study and Contact Group 435, n.d.). During the campaign SWABC bias was evident not only in its treatment of events but also in its unequal treatment of political parties and what they represented. This independent assessment of sixty-five radio and twenty-seven TV SWABC news broadcasts, carried out between 18 June and 3 July 1989, shows that in both media DTA had significantly more time devoted to its activities and more mention on news reports than did SWAPO and that some of the smaller parties had almost as much exposure as SWAPO. The report goes on to argue that the bias in the electronic media aimed at both limiting the coverage and, wherever mentioned, being critical of SWAPO and UNTAG. The overall conclusion of the monitoring of radio news broadcasts is that "the SWABC has a distinct bias against SWAPO and UNTAG (14.45 minutes of negative comment) as opposed to a positive bias towards the AG, DTA and SA (10.25 minutes of positive comment)" (p. 6). Similar observations are made by the report on TV coverage of SWABC. The report notes a "selective choice of content in editing and compiling of news bulletins aimed at supporting the current status quo." It also concludes that SWABC used "a style of reporting which is one of purely passing on pre-selected information without verifying, examining or criticizing what is being broadcast, thus not giving the general public their right to analyse the same story from different perspectives."

The situation in the north was continually referred to as being "complicated" and "unstable," yet these statements were not accompanied by detail of what these terms meant (p. 4). Moreover, there had been lengthy mention of the events of 1 April and unsubstantiated reports of more incursions, but no mention was made of hostile action by ex-members of Koevoet (p. 6). The report also notes that whenever SWAPO was criticized, the party's name was used. When other parties were criticized, they were referred to as "a certain political party" (p. 4). The report further notes that all SWAPOL releases given airtime were negative about UNTAG and SWAPO. And in discussions of the specific policy of different parties, the bias, this time in favor of DTA, was stark. In a broadcast on 28 June, SWABC reported on an overseas trip made by DTA. The radio commentary noted that economic aid would be forthcoming only if voters made the correct choice, implying a free-market system (p. 6). The report's final conclusion is that there was no alternative offered "by the SWABC to the current status quo, even though there would appear to be no doubt that the existing order will change, no matter who wins the election. The electorate is therefore not being prepared for any alternative to the South African–imposed order" (p. 10).

In the face of this kind of evidence and despite "repeated representations" by the UNSGSR (S/20883, 6 October 1989), it was not until mid-September that SWABC agreed to concede equal access to all political parties and then only for the last six weeks of the election period. Nor would equal time for official party statements "resolve the underlying problem of editorial decision-making" by the SWABC board, as the same report notes. Eventually the board was advised by a liaison committee with broader representation, but only from September onward. Some degree of impartial information, especially about the mechanisms of the election, was provided by an UNTAG information program, which included daily radio broadcasts, and also some television, videos, inserts into newspapers, and special leaflets.

*The Press*

By the time of the transition, there were four daily newspapers in Namibia: *The Namibian* had the largest circulation, about twelve thousand; *The Times of Namibia,* somewhat less; the *Windhoek Advertiser,* an independent and somewhat eccentric paper, a tiny circulation; and the Afrikaans-language *Die Republikein,* about nine thousand. There were also some German-language papers coming out less frequently; the most popular, *Allgemeine Zeitung,* reportedly had a circulation of four thousand. Although the combined circulation was less than 5 percent of the electorate, actual readership was much greater, especially given the custom in small communities of a paper often being passed around at some bottle shop or other informal reading center.

*Die Republikein* was proclaimedly a supporter of DTA, with which it shared offices; Dirk Mudge was the chair and occasionally an editorial writer. *The Times of Namibia* was an independent and lively paper until mid-1989, when its local businessman owner sold it to *Die Republikein,* which then forced the whole editorial staff to resign over an advertisement placed by the Parents' Committee that termed SWAPO a "gestapo" and that was included without a qualifying editorial. Nico Basson, who was operating the public relations firm Africa Communications Project (ACP), as a cover out of the DTA–*Die Republikein* office building, claimed to have engineered and financed this coup (*Top Secret,* September 1989). After this takeover the *Times* started to appear five times a week instead of one.

# 6
# The Administration of the Transition and the Elections

## Electoral Regulations and Their Administration

The actual provisions and regulations governing the conduct of the elections and the way they were administered were always likely to have an effect on the overall result and were thus a matter for contestation and controversy. Some of these conflicts were resolved in the batch of agreements put together before 1986 to give substance to UNSCR 435/78. These specified that what was to be elected was a *constituent assembly,* not a parliament. They provided for some system of *proportional representation,* rather than single-member constituencies, although the details were left to be worked out following implementation of the UN Plan. The South African regime had sought a system whereby voters would have two votes and/or there would be two lists, thus assuring some direct representation of ethnic "groups," especially whites (A similar provision in Zimbabwe in 1980 ensured that 20 percent of parliamentary seats went to whites). However, this was one of the issues on which the international community prevented RSA having its way; there was to be a single vote for each elector. What remained to be settled was the specific form of PR: a single national constituency or several regional constituencies, as in Zimbabwe; whether parties would have to meet some minimum threshold to have any representation, as in most European systems; and the formula for calculating what should happen to the small "remainders" over and above the "quota" that would entitle a party to a whole seat. (The one actually adopted did give two small parties the benefit of the doubt—under a different formula the Namibia National Front (NNF) would not have got the one seat.) Appendix C provides an explanation of how PR systems work and the details of the system actually implemented in Namibia with a single national constituency, whereby each party would put forward a single list of candidates from whom a number proportional to the votes received over the country as a whole would be deemed elected.

As we noted in Chapter 1, the definition of the electoral system as well as its administration by the powers-that-be can be used manipulatively to curb the potential impact of democratization for societal change. At an early stage of the negotiations over UNSCR 435/78 the WCG proposed a hybrid system of allowing each voter two votes, one on an ethnically defined constituency basis to elect half the CA, the other half to be on a national PR system. Such a system would have given the white minority and some of its allies in the ethnic parties protected status. It would have been a variant of the two rolls; the white on a constituency; the black on PR, foisted on Zimbabwe in 1980. However, SWAPO, backed by FLS, rejected this proposal in 1982 and stated it would support either a PR or single-member constituency system but not a combination and for once won its point. A subsequent UN Institute for Namibia study (UNIN, 1989: 23) suggested that South Africa would pursue a strategy of "maximising the fractionalisation of the CA" and felt the "fractionalisation will be worse if the STV [Single Transferable Vote] or PR method applied in the bogus 1978 elections is applied." Insofar as this study of options for the electoral system went on to advise "all the political parties interested in a stable independence government . . . to reject any PR system that tends to frac- tionalise party representation," it had in large measure missed the boat (189). A PR system of some sort was the last substantive issue in the plan to be agreed in 1985. The most effective detailed measure to minimize frac- tionalization that SWAPO or any other party could have attempted to add to the actual rules drawn up in 1989 would have been one that instituted a minimum ceiling. But no such proposals were put forward by the UN, and none of the parties made an issue of this point.

We attempted a small simulation exercise of what might have hap- pened if the election had been run on a first-past-the-post, single-member constituency basis rather than PR. It was assumed that each ED was divid- ed into a number of constituencies proportionate to the "quota" of regis- tered voters in the ED (see Appendix C) and that the proportion of votes in each constituency was the same as the actual voting in the ED to which it belonged. This somewhat rough-and-ready system of allocating winners of constituencies certainly would have reduced the CA seats won by small parties from ten to between two (UDF could have had two in Damara) or four (if ACN had won one or two "white" seats in Windhoek). But this pre- diction would result in the six to eight seats that would have been reallocat- ed from small parties being evenly divided between SWAPO and DTA. Hence, SWAPO would have had forty-four to forty-five seats, still short of the forty-eight needed for a two-thirds majority; DTA would have gained more in proportion to its actual seats. So the PR system might well repre- sent a miscalculation from the perspective of South Africa!

Other crucial matters governing the eligibility and registration of vot- ers had not been specified in agreements, nor had arrangements for regis- tering parties, for actual polling, and for counting. RSA's and WCG's suc- cess in gaining control of the transition meant that all such matters were left to be solved by proclamations of the AG, subject, of course, to the appraisal and approval of the UNSGSR, but the AG certainly held the initiative. In the event, the AG took until 21 July to draft the regulations for voting; political parties were invited to comment and propose amendments to the draft (all did, often at length—SWAPO produced a forty-page document; NNF, twenty pages). The AG's proposals were highly contentious, and the final election regulations resulted from an intense bargaining process between the AG and UNTAG and were not officially proclaimed until 13 October 1989, four months behind the schedule in the UN Plan and only three weeks before the first of the election days. The registration of voters and of parties that were necessary preliminary to the campaigns and voting was the subject of separate proclamations made before the voting rules were known.

*Registration of Voters*

Two big issues that would affect the role and nature of the electorate remained unresolved in the UN Plan: whether Namibians could vote at eighteen or twenty-one and how Namibian citizenship and thus the eligibility to vote were to be defined. Proclamation AG19 of 27 June 1989 made provision for eighteen years to be the voting age—despite DTA and AG's proposals that it should be twenty-one. This arguably benefited SWAPO as most opinion seemed to think it had more support among youth. But what was far less welcomed by SWAPO was AG19's provision that in addition to people who themselves or whose parents had been born in Namibia, anyone who had been ordinarily resident for four years or more prior to 1989 would be allowed to register. Under this latter formula many South African and Angolan residents, including those who had been engaged in counterinsurgency operations, refugees, and other immigrants, were eligible.

The effect of the registrations of South Africans was especially felt in Windhoek and in the south. The RSA's Bureau of Information launched a campaign in early July encouraging South African residents who themselves or whose parents were born in Namibia or others who were eligible by reason of past residence to travel to Namibia to register. Registrations in Karasburg were a massive 263 percent of the estimates of those eligible, and UNTAG confirmed that 20,000 registration cards had been sent to registration centers near the border posts (NCC, 1990). In the border town in that district, Ariamsvlei, the arrival of more than forty buses with white South Africans was reported on election days, and the Friends of South West Africa (FSWA) welcoming body is said to have slaughtered 120 sheep as hospitality. FSWA also chartered eight planes, five buses, and one train to transport voters. Although it claimed to be nonpartisan, one of the organizers in South Africa was also listed on a pamphlet of ACN (*The Sowetan*, 26 October 1989). One estimate (Wellmer, 1990) suggests that these "extras" who voted in the six southern electoral districts amounted to between 5,800 and 8,750. (These estimates are obtained by subtracting the two estimates of potential voters made by UNTAG from the much larger number who turned out.) The *Windhoek Advertiser* (21 September 1989) reported that some 9,481 South Africans had registered at Ariamsvlei and Noordoewer, the two border points. A report of the Secretary-General to the Security Council on 6 October 1989 (S/20883) indicated that some 450 RSA officials working in Namibia had also registered. Certainly the white-only ACN gained its biggest share (25.8 percent) in the border district of Karasburg. In Windhoek there was not such a large percentage of actual voters over the estimated eligible population (only 105 percent), but South Africans did fly in for registration—indeed, life was made easy for them by a special registration point at Windhoek airport—and voting.

Of course, the rule about South Africans being allowed to vote with parent or own birth or minimum residence also applied to many people in Walvis Bay, still claimed by South Africa despite UN resolutions proclaiming it as part of Namibia, claims that were accepted for the time being as part of the 1988 agreements. However, Africans from the enclave who sought to register found that they did not enjoy anything like the same welcoming parties and help with transport and regulations. Rather, they found that their movement was restricted: they had to travel 30 kilometers to register, and many were not given time off work. Many were employed on a contract, seasonal basis in the fishing industry and had to wait until the end of the fish factory season in September before they could get to register; but at that moment they were whisked out of the enclave in which they became "illegal" immigrants once work was over (CIMS, 1990: 257). As they then went north, they may have been able to register in other EDs in the last few days of registration.

The registration practices also seemed to have required them to offer abundant documentary proof of residence or of their or their own parents' birth outside the enclave. Many births are not registered in Namibia, people born in Walvis Bay of Namibian parents did not have "South West African" identity cards, and CIMS (1990: 232–260) reports several cases of such people being turned away and of people with UN refugee documents or with accompany parents willing to swear statements (proof of eligibility commonly accepted elsewhere) being asked to come back with "extended birth certificates." This latter treatment even happened to the daughter of the acting president of SWAPO, Julia Maxuilili. It is possible to make some estimate of how many Namibians living there were or were not registered by working out how those who did manage to register in nearby Swakopmund inflated registration there. South African and UNTAG election officials were reportedly planning on some nine thousand extra "eligibles" from Walvis Bay. The proportion of those registered there compared to the estimate of eligible voters was 181.2 percent, eleven thousand above the projected figure (although that calculation assumes that growth in the populations of Swakopmund and Walvis Bay was only the same as the national figure; it was likely to be more, in which case the number of Walvis Bay registrants was likely to be less). It was this that led a senior UNTAG official to suggest that eleven thousand from Walvis Bay had registered and that this represented the expected number (interview, 30 October 1989). He also suggested that perhaps 90 percent of them were workers in the fishing industry, mostly from Owambo. However, a survey carried out by an Anglican minister in the enclave (CIMS, 1990: 238) suggests the number of eligible Namibians there at more than sixteen thousand, thus implying that five thousand or more Namibians were not registered.

Another distortion in registration might have come from "Angolans," several categories of whom could benefit from the eligibility rules that required only short-term residence. There were an estimated 40,000 Angolans who had become refugees in the country over several years. Many of these had in the past been issued Namibian identification cards, and they were clearly eligible. Others with lesser claims included more recent "refugees," some of whom were recruits in special SADF or ethnic battalions or their families. One CIMS report suggested that of perhaps 20,000 of them in Kavango, most had originally not wanted to register, but that at least in the case of the 5,000 in one resettlement village, Delta in western Caprivi, efforts had been made by DTA to persuade them. However, only 250 had any documents that allowed them to register or met residence requirements (CIMS, 1990: 29). More disputable was the trucking into Kavango of people ordinarily resident on the Angola side of the border. That was reportedly stage-managed by South African's ally, UNITA, which controlled much of the southeast of Angola, and then by DTA local personnel who were ex-SWATF. In the words of a CIMS (1990: 29) report, "A Lutheran minister told us about his talk with an Angolan headman. He and many people had been called to a UNITA post and told to register for the Namibian election. He had refused because he was an Angolan—unless there was a good reason. The reason he was given by UNITA was: 'Savimbi was told by the South African government that he should send his people to Namibia to register and vote for DTA because if DTA would lose the election there would be no support for UNITA any more.'"

The UNTAG assumption was that only a few would be able to get documentary proof: identification document (ID) showing birth in Namibia or evidence of residence (driver's license, clinic attendance card). Some "proved" eligibility by having someone in authority swear an affidavit to their residence or birth. A group of South African lawyers, the Nadel Group (CIMS, 1990: 31), reports that a headman on the Angola side testified under oath that he was induced under threat from UNITA to go and swear in his eighty villagers. Another CIMS report (1990: 18) quotes an eyewitness's account of a crossing of the river that forms the border at Sekondo, naming those who organized it and giving registration numbers of the vehicles involved, which had been given to UNTAG in Rundu, the administrative town of Kavango. There is clearly some possibility that such things happened on a significant scale. Estimates of the number of Angolans registered vary: there were some initial SWAPO statements suggesting as many as forty thousand, almost certainly an overestimate; UNTAG officials in Rundu suggested fifteen hundred to two thousand, which could well be an underestimate. The three CIMS monitors who were in the Kavango district, one for several months, suggested that as many as 10 percent of the votes cast in that electoral district were Angolans, which if correct would account for some 6,000 actual votes (DTA received a total of 24,817), for their impression was that not all of those so registered turned up to vote (CIMS, 1990: 32). Some were seemingly bused in, however; at one polling station where the registration point had registered only one thousand voters, some twenty-seven hundred actually turned up to vote.

To put the whole matter in some perspective, however, one has to remember that the population of the north is heavily concentrated along the border, and in Kavango especially people live close to both banks of the river that marks the border. Thus, distinctions between Namibians and Angolans are somewhat arbitrary. There was nothing legally improper about the registration of most South Africans and Angolans under the registration proclamation, but in the cases of the latter in particular, it was often difficult for registration to be checked. Indeed, SWAPO complained that it could not challenge those that were irregularly registered as the rules required notification of those challenged, and they could rarely be found, having often returned to Angola.

UNTAG, only partially in place and unsettled by the events of 1 April, could not respond with the same scrutiny of the registration proclamation as it did toward later proposals from the AG (interview with John Truman, UNTAG deputy election director, Windhoek, 9 September 1989). Moreover, if UNTAG had had executive, rather than supervisory, responsibility, the law might not have provided such a wide opening to non-Namibians. In the event, the number of additional voters from South Africa and Angola cannot be easily estimated. The two journalists who infiltrated DTA-SAMI felt this registration was "so massively successful . . . that the South Africans don't need any other help" (*Top Secret,* October 1990). Our own best guess is that perhaps some twenty thousand cast their votes, predictably for ACN and DTA, whereas three thousand or more likely SWAPO supporters in Walvis Bay may have been disenfranchised—amounting to a swing of three CA seats.

Overall, the actual registration process was a somewhat complicated one that was carried out for a period of twelve weeks from 3 July to 23 September. Prospective voters were required to present themselves for registration at either 36 fixed registration points established in urban centers around the country, 35 temporary ones in places where there was some concentration of people, or 110 mobile registration teams that moved to another location after a day or so. People had to bring with them to these registration points proof of their identity and their eligibility. A valid ID issued by the South West African administration would automatically establish both, but it was anticipated that perhaps a quarter of all applicants would not have IDs. That would be especially so in the north, and so other documents, such as passport, UNHCR document, driver's license, or residence permit, could be accepted as proof of identity. If none of these certified birthplace or established residence, documents such as a birth certificate, pension card, immigration document, certificate of military service, or title deed would also be required. Other documentation could be accepted as proof of residence (tax receipts or hospital records) or birth (parents' or own identity cards; repatriation certificates, which did not require any birth certificates or other supporting documentation, birth certificates, and so on), including some registered voter or someone in authority who was prepared to testify to one's residence, birthplace, and/or age.

The AG's staff running the registration points was then supposed to record the number and details of the ID or other identification and the date of birth as a basis for later checking of any voters who were challenged or who had lost documents. Registrants who satisfied the officials were then issued registration cards, which they were supposed to present when coming to vote. During these processes the AG's registration officers were monitored by UNTAG election supervisors. Their presence did avert some inconsistencies, ensuring, for instance, that blacks and whites from Walvis Bay were treated according to the same procedures (CIMS, 1990) and preventing AG officials from being too rigid; in general, these supervisors ensured that the practices accorded with articulated procedures. Thus, one UNTAG team in Kavango prevailed upon the AG's registration officers not to continue accepting the affidavits of the *kuta* and *induna,* the tribal authorities, because, they felt, these people were too closely linked to one party (CIMS, 1990: 14).

There were nevertheless some anomalies: another CIMS report from Ovamboland (CIMS, 1990: 88) identifies a registration team that was not accepting school or church documents to validate residence but was sending people who offered them on an extra journey to the magistrate. Moreover, UNTAG's "monitoring" role seems, from available reports, to have been passive: cases where AG officials were considering withholding registration were routinely referred to the UNTAG registration supervisors, which would effectively have prevented bias *against* those whom RSA officials might have wanted to exclude. Yet apparently the supervisors did not review even a sample of those allowed registration. Thus, anyone with less than full documentation whom AG personnel may have let in went undetected. UNTAG officials clearly prevented any tendency to *exclude* eligible voters who presented themselves in a biased or systematic way, and UNTAG reports indicate that very few were turned away from the registration centers and that only some seven hundred were rejected by the central registration office. Nevertheless, UNTAG may not have spotted ineligible *inclusions.* The original draft regulations would have made the task of scrutinizing those registered even harder because it did not allow for any publicly available lists. UN pressure ensured that such lists were produced, but in practice very few challenges to names on the list were made—probably because of the cumbersome requirement that the challenger had to seek out and inform the person challenged before a magistrate could go into the matter.

Whether anyone who so wished was denied the opportunity to register depended most crucially on the thoroughness of the registration process: was there enough time, were people aware of the procedures, and were remote areas reached? Concern was initially expressed by some observers that the time allowed for registration was too short, that the coverage in this vast sparsely populated country was not widespread enough to reach everyone, especially in the more remote areas. But considerable effort was made to seek out all those eligible: in Kaokoland helicopters were used to find some of those thought eligible to vote. There was a particular worry in Ovamboland, the largest electoral district by far, which had a mere forty-one registration teams of which only two were on permanent sites. In some remote areas special "sweep" teams were urged on the AG's office by UNTAG; one UNTAG officer even prevailed upon her RSA counterpart to register sick people in their homes (CIMS, 1990: 92). The registration period was extended an extra week largely because of representations from Owambo, where registrations suddenly accelerated from about 300 per day to more than 1,000 on each of the last five days of the original registration period, although the regional election director there, John Rwambuya, had urged two weeks' extension (interview, 30 October 1989; CIMS, 1990: 101). In that additional week between 17 and 23 September, a total of 1,381 registered to vote in Ovamboland (CIMS, 1990: 101).

At the end of the registration process, UNTAG concluded that no significant numbers of eligible voters had been denied access to registration. UNTAG, the AG's office, and many observers cited the seemingly incontrovertible evidence of registrations as a percentage of the estimated voting age population (see Table E.2 of Appendix E). These favorably compared the total registration of 701,483 with the estimated eligible population of 645,308, a rate of registration of 108.7 percent. Because these comparisons were so widely used as an indication of how free and fair this part of the process was, this yardstick must be looked at critically.

The estimates of eligible population can be questioned. They were calculated from the figures of total population enumerated in the 1981 census.

They thus did not make any allowances for returnees or for those from South Africa and Angola who registered. The number of people eighteen and older in 1981 was then multiplied by a factor of 1.247 to estimate the increase up to 1989—representing an assumed growth rate of adult population of 2.9 percent. UNTAG's guidelines to its officials who were involved in monitoring the registration included a further calculation for each electoral district: that another 5 percent across the board be added to the eligible population to compensate for the widespread feeling that the 1981 census had undercounted. UNTAG's calculation was probably more accurate but still an arbitrary yardstick against which to measure the "success" of registration. This second marker gave a total of 677,656. The detailed figures for each ED obtained from the two estimates are given in Table E.1, Appendix E. Table 6.1 also indicates the number of voters registered and expresses this as a percentage of the estimated eligible population (using the second estimate, which added 5 percent to the extrapolations from the census). Using even these revised figures as a baseline, the AG and UNTAG congratulated themselves that the overall registration reached 103.5 percent of the estimated eligible voters. However, two sources of doubt remain: the reliability of the estimates as a baseline for the eligible voters and the unevenness of the registration performance.

The AG's estimate of eligible voters was based on a 1981 total (all ages) population of 1,033,196. Other estimates put the population higher: the UN Institute for Namibia suggests at that time a figure of 1.125 million. Demographers consider such underestimations likely, especially in colonial situations. In Zimbabwe, for instance, estimates were made of the population eligible to vote in the April 1979 "internal" elections, which had excluded the national liberation movements, ZANU and ZAPU; there was no registration of voters either then or in the February 1980 elections that heralded independence, but the Rhodesian administration proclaimed the "success" of the 1979 election using the yardstick of an actual turnout of 64 percent of those estimated to be eligible. This was accepted as plausible at the time, until an extra 1 million voters turned out just ten months later, which would have meant a colossal turnout of 93 percent of the estimated population. It was much more likely that the 1979 figure of eligibles was an underestimate.

If one uses, just as an illustration, UN institute's estimate of the 1981 population (which would have grown to 1,890,000 by 1989) and then added returnees and South Africans registered, that would give an eligible population of 945,000, which would imply a rate of registration of only 74 percent. Such numbers are no more likely than the official ones, but neither they nor a wide range of others could be completely ruled out as implausible. Also, the estimates did *not* include returnees (the adults among whom may have totaled 50,000) or eligible residents of Walvis Bay, South Africa, or Angola (who together, from previous extrapolated figures, might have

**Table 6.1  Registered Voters and Estimated Eligible Voters in Each Electoral District**

| Electoral District[a] | Estimated Eligible Voters[b] | Registered Voters | % Registered[c] |
|---|---|---|---|
| Ovamboland | 280,436 | 248,272 | 88.5 |
| Lüderitz | 13,917 | 10,740 | 77.2 |
| Swakopmund | 13,996 | 25,363 | 181.2 |
| Tsumeb | 16,089 | 14,651 | 91.1 |
| Kavango | 61,125 | 64,156 | 105.0 |
| EDs SWAPO > 50% | 385,563 | 363,182 | 94.2 |
| | | | |
| Windhoek | 87,592 | 105,382 | 120.3 |
| Caprivi | 21,267 | 28,096 | 132.1 |
| Okahandja | 9,973 | 11,233 | 112.6 |
| Karibib | 5,700 | 6,955 | 122.0 |
| Matlahohe | 3,615 | 2,635 | 72.9 |
| Grootfontein | 17,793 | 20,510 | 115.3 |
| Otjiwarongo | 12,595 | 13,287 | 105.5 |
| Keetmanshoop | 21,042 | 20,039 | 95.2 |
| Damaraland | 15,559 | 15,127 | 97.2 |
| Omaruru | 4,027 | 6,008 | 149.2 |
| Mariental | 14,212 | 14,630 | 102.9 |
| Bethanie | 2,074 | 2,464 | 118.8 |
| Outjo | 6,249 | 7,219 | 115.5 |
| Rehoboth | 16,873 | 17,346 | 102.8 |
| Hereroland | 16,892 | 16,317 | 96.6 |
| Gobabis | 17,485 | 19,250 | 110.1 |
| Karasburg | 6,942 | 18,257 | 263.0 |
| Kaokoland | 12,203 | 13,546 | 111.0 |
| EDs SWAPO < 50% | 292,093 | 338,301 | 115.8 |
| | | | |
| Total | 677,656 | 701,483 | 103.5 |

*Notes:* a. The EDs are listed in descending order of % vote for SWAPO.
b. The higher estimate was made by AG's office on the basis of 2.9% annual growth on 1981 census plus 5%.
c. Column 3 represents Column 2 as % of Column 1.

totaled 30,000 or more). If these numbers are included, then the rate of registration of those eligible was only about 93 percent. So all that can be said is that the evidence of registration rates of 100 percent or more of estimates of eligible voters is based on calculations that are somewhat arbitrary and omit some data. At best, then, these rates can be only indicative and do not constitute *proof* of the thoroughness of the registration process.

A second doubt, this time about bias, arises from other circumstantial evidence obtained from analysis of the district breakdown of registration figures. Table 6.1 shows that the attainment varied from 150 percent or more in some EDs, even those not inflated by the influx of "South Africans" (Karasburg, Keetmanshoop, Swakopmund), down to less than 80 percent in others. This may simply reflect that even if the estimates of total population increase were reasonably accurate, the rates of increase would vary from one region to another—tending to be less in areas of high outmigration. One, more disturbing explanation of these very different success rates in registration is, however, suggested if one compares, as does the last column in Appendix Table B.2, the registration rate with the later voting pattern: a clear bias exists against those areas that were to vote strongly for SWAPO. Measured by the AG's estimates of eligibles, the registration rate in those areas in which SWAPO had an absolute majority was 94.2 percent, whereas in all other areas it was 115.9 percent. One possible effect of this on the election has been calculated in these terms: "There were 52,233 more votes cast and counted than the official estimate of voters in districts later on won mainly by the DTA, and there were 48,087 *less* votes cast and counted than the population estimate in areas later on won by SWAPO" (Wellmer, 1990: 5).

In seeking to explain this pattern and in particular to explore whether it was a result of a deliberate anti-SWAPO manipulation of the registration process, one can first recognize that the influx of South Africans and Angolans would account for some of the high registration measures, as we have noted, but these include Swakopmund, which had a SWAPO majority, and Windhoek and Kavango, where SWAPO won the largest share of the votes, even if still a minority. But what would account for the underregistration? It may be the case that Owambo lost population because of the war, although there is little evidence of *increased* rates of labor migration from there, and this could have been compensated by the many returnees there. Other areas such as Lüderitz and Tsumeb that were to get strong SWAPO support and that had registration rates well below the national average may have suffered from reductions in mine employment or the temporary absence of contract workers, but that latter eventuality would have swelled the voters registered in Owambo. These possible factors seem hardly enough to explain the great unevenness in the registration. Thus, a systematic distortion against SWAPO in the registration process cannot be ruled out on the basis of an analysis of the statistics, although overall the circumstantial evidence does not point to a bias against *all* areas that were strongly pro-SWAPO. Wellmer (1990) suggests that it might be as high as 12 percent of all votes cast (although this figure includes the influx of legally eligible South Africans and Angolans). To give another indicator: if registration had reached 100 percent of that estimated in Ovamboland (which level was achieved in many places and might have been possible by further extension of the registration period and wider reach), there would have been thirty-five thousand extra voters, and if, as elsewhere in Owambo, 92 percent of them had been for SWAPO, that would have given that party almost four extra seats. The extra voters would have numbered sixty-three thousand for all five EDs with a SWAPO majority if the same percentage (115.8 percent) had registered as in the other areas.

There is some evidence of how the procedures for registration might have led to some difficulties in registration in Owambo. The very fact that it was one among twenty-three districts, even though it had an estimated 40 percent of the population, may have led to proportionately less administrative provision not only for the registration but also for other parts of the electoral process. Thus, a UNTAG official in charge of monitoring registration in Owambo is quoted as being concerned about "the lack of educational material. . . . All such material seems to end up in the South" (CIMS, 1990: 104). Such shortages were also to recur during the voting. Some concern was expressed by CIMS monitors about such things as "long queues outside offices for registration at Oshakata . . . and Ondangwa" as late as 15 September; the fact that registration was delayed a week in some parts of the district because mine-protected vehicles were required; the case of the police using Casspirs to block SWAPO vehicles en route to a registration center at Osifo near Ruacana to impose a ban on SWAPO providing transport. Monitors also reported worries that not all the more than one thousand registration cards that had been sent away to Windhoek to have errors corrected would be returned (although half had come back by late September, according to UNTAG). However, CIMS monitors' overall summary report did conclude that "after a difficult start the registration process went on fairly well, and the extension period satisfied the political parties as a positive action" (p. 104). SWAPO even complained that the many errors of dates of birth, address, and so on that found their way onto cards might be a deliberate ploy by South African–appointed administrators. A U.S. lawyers' group partly confirms evidence of "intentional errors on the part of local registrars," citing one case where one-quarter of completed forms were spoiled (TWIN, 16–23 July 1989). The group also quotes UNTAG monitors' reports that "registrars frequently arrived late and left early, even when long queues were waiting to register, and that registrars moved from place to place arbitrarily and without notice." Some evidence of registration practices in handling Walvis Bay eligibles also indicates how some of the bias may have crept in: the excessive documentation required and the general atmosphere in registration centers there, described by two different CIMS observers as "tense" (CIMS, 1990: 241, 251).

If such bias was the result of deliberate policy, rather than of the additional factors just explored, in administrative inefficiency, or undercapacity, we have to ask on what kind of basis might any registration procedures or officials have excluded people. No previous electoral records were available to reveal SWAPO party loyalties, and officials could not have known with any certainty the voting outcome, especially as only in three or four of the twenty-three EDs was there any approximation of overwhelming sup-port for one party or another. The only possible calculation on which a *general* biasing could have been based is that of presumed ethnic loyalties in voting, more specifically a recognition that the Owambo people were likely to vote predominantly for SWAPO. The pursuance of such a strategy is compatible with the low registration in Ovamboland itself, and in Swakopmund and Lüderitz, which both had a predictably high proportion of migrants from Owambo. Any discrimination making it difficult to regis-ter in any other area would have run counter to the hopes of the South Africans and the strategy of DTA, which was based on the supposition that DTA and other parties could make major inroads into SWAPO support in areas and among people other than Owambo.

*Registration of Parties*

In any electoral system based on proportional representation where people vote for parties, provision has to be made for the registration of the political bodies themselves. As with the other regulations, the AG delayed on a for-mula, but eventually on 4 September 1989 he issued, with UNTAG's agree-ment, Proclamation AG43 to Provide for the Registration of Political Organizations with a view to Election of the Constituent Assembly. This required an application for registration of a party's name and symbol (important for illiterate voters) to be accompanied by a deposit of R 10,000 and nominations signed by two thousand registered voters. These were not heavy restrictions, but they were enough to exclude the tiniest groups and to encourage alliances among the smaller parties. In the event, eleven par-ties submitted applications to the registration court by its first sitting only a week later on 12 September; nine were officially approved. The court allowed the Christian Democratic Action for Social Justice and the Namibia Christian Democratic Party a further two weeks to obtain the required number of signatures; only the former succeeded. (These ten qual-ifying bodies and their characteristics are explored in the next chapter.)

*Campaigning Regulations and Practices*

Apart from the normal law governing public activities, and particular efforts to curb intimidation, the only specific rules governing the conduct of public campaigns were contained in Proclamation AG23 of 17 July 1989 for the Provision for the Protection of Public Peace and Order at Public Gatherings. The only significant provision in it required political parties to notify the police of rallies or public meetings of more than twenty people three days in advance and gave the latter some power to cancel them. The AG argued that this was necessary to curb violence, even though similar legislation was one of those repealed under the UN plan as being discrimi-natory. In the event, almost no controversy arose with regard to official notification of meetings, although in one or two places the local administrators provocatively allowed meetings of the two main rivals on the same day. Parties did meet some official interference with campaigning, and "observers supported SWAPO's claim of selective enforcement" (NDIIA, 1990: 49), but this seems to have occurred at a more local level. For instance, a three-thousand-person SWAPO rally was dispersed at Arandis after organizers filed their intention with the magistrate instead of the police; reports from Kaokoland indicate that some local chiefs would not allow SWAPO to open an office or engage in other activities (CIMS, 1990: 127, 135). SWAPO relied on holding mainly a few of its star rallies but otherwise held small, informal meetings chiefly concerned with voter instruction. (The actual campaigns mounted by the different parties are discussed in Chapter 7.)

The only other attempt to regulate the campaigning was through a voluntary initiative brokered by UNTAG to which all the parties subscribed. After some considerable negotiating, all the parties signed a code of conduct at a meeting on 12 September convened by UNTAG; this bound them to avoid violence and provocation and set out some ground rules for what was and was not acceptable behavior. This action did seem to reduce some of the interparty violence somewhat in the last weeks of the campaign.

## Voting Regulations and Procedures

The regulations governing all aspects of the running of the election were supposed to be made public by mid-May, according to the UN plan timetable. In the event, the AG finally issued a draft proclamation on 21 July 1989 that automatically sparked widespread concern: the regulations were "condemned as 'outrageous,' 'completely unacceptable' and 'even worse than we could have expected' by legal delegations from Britain and the US, and by Commonwealth, African and non-aligned experts" (*The Guardian*, 23 July 1989). The draft regulations were referred to all parties for their written comments and objections, and a lengthy and tough bargaining process began between the AG and the UNSGSR. The New York office of the Secretary-General saw what was at issue as serious enough that it became involved, sending a senior legal adviser to strengthen Ahtisari's hand and his resolve because the AG was refusing to make any amendments.

There seem to have been three main areas of contention about what was an extravagantly complex voting and counting procedure. First, the proposed verification procedure would have required all voters to place their votes in envelopes with their registration numbers on the outside, ostensibly so that their eligibility could be checked afterward; but this would have been a potential violation of the secrecy of the ballot. Second, voters were going to be allowed to vote anywhere in the territory; the UN thought this gave too much leeway for manipulation and wanted them to vote in the ED where they had registered so that they could be checked against local lists. In the event, voters were "expected" to vote in the same ED; but if they had moved to another district, they would have to complete a more elaborate exercise of a "tendered ballot," which would be forwarded (sealed) to Windhoek with identification documents or registration card to be checked off against central, computerized lists but in a manner that did not prejudice the secrecy of these votes. Other votes that were in some sense in contention as to voters' eligibility or identity would likewise be tendered. This proposal also meant that the counting would have to be done in one central place; the UNSGSR argued that this movement would increase the opportunities for tampering and would also lead to some weeks of delay before results were announced.

Third, only illiterate or disabled voters who sought assistance would have the chance to receive an explanation or help in writing in their vote, and this would be offered exclusively by RSA electoral officials. (One of our team remembered seeing how Rhodesian election officials had taken advantage of their right to "advise" illiterates in Zimbabwe's independence elections in 1980.) The final regulations stipulated that a UNTAG supervisor would always be present when help was being given in the voting booth itself. However, the UNSGSR did concede something on this last issue; the U.S. Lawyers Committee on Civil Rights under the Law claim that it was asked to comment on what UNTAG said was a final draft it had approved in which some means of impartial assistance was specified but that these elements, apart from provision for blind voters, were left out of the published version. A further revision that the UNSGSR had written in was to provide additional oversight of South African electoral officials by allowing each registered party to nominate a polling agent who would be allowed in to the polling station to cast an eye over officials and who could challenge voter's eligibility or identity.

Considerable bargaining between Ahtisari and the AG and mounting international pressure occurred before an agreed proclamation was finally promulgated on 13 October 1989, less than four weeks before polling began, little enough time to organize accurate voter education. The provisions in the draft were almost identical to those that had been used in the internal election of 1978, which was declared null and void by the UN; UN officials involved in the 1989 transition remembered telling RSA officials that such an electoral system would be "totally unacceptable" (NDIIA, 1990: 32). The UN Institute for Namibia also published a report on electoral systems options that systematically critiqued the mechanisms of the 1978 election (UNIN, 1989). Despite that background, according to one report (NDIIA, 1990: 33), the initial UN response was that "the Special Representative appeared ready to endorse the AG's basic framework, provided that it guaranteed ballot secrecy. . . . These matters under discussion were not sufficiently important, in Ahtisari's view, to jeopardize the schedule for the transition."

However, in the next few weeks international pressure mounted to modify the draft proclamation much further. The African subcommittee of the U.S. Congress in July formed a consensus that the proposals were unacceptable. A resolution of the Commonwealth heads of government in August adopted a resolution calling for amendments. There was similar pressure from FLS, the Africa group at the UN, and the nonaligned nations. All these pressures culminated in a resolution (640) of the UN Security Council at the end of August that explicitly called on on the SG to "ensure that all legislation concerning the electoral process is in conformity with the provisions of the Settlement Plan . . . [and] internationally accepted norms for free and fair elections." This decision led to a renewed round of intense bargaining between the AG and UN officials, whose resolve and bargaining power were beefed up by an additional legal expert sent from UN headquarters and the appointment of a deputy special representative, before final agreement on 6 October. These extended negotiations are evidence of a difference at least in emphasis between the Secretary-General's office in New York and the UNSGR, who was thought too ready to make concessions to the South African formula.

Given these delays, some crucial arrangements were not in place until the eve of the election. Polling station sites, some of which were fixed and open for the five days of polling and others of which moved to new venues at appointed times, were agreed for all EDs except Owambo; there they were not designated until four days before polling, greatly complicating the tasks of party agents and organizers. SWAPO in Owambo remained skeptical enough of the procedures to discourage its supporters from voting at "mobiles," where the ballot boxes would not remain visible all the time.

The Namibian elections began on Tuesday, 7 November. Throughout the country people turned out in the thousands, eager to participate and cast their vote. SWAPO had instructed its supporters not to wear party colors in order to avoid any provocation, and this instruction was scrupulously obeyed, contrasting markedly with DTA policy, which was to turn out decked in party colors and to decorate the roads leading to polling stations with party posters and flags; even the polling stations themselves were often plastered with the DTA red, white, and blue. Thus, DTA continued its strategy of a high-profile, visible presence even where support was small, as in Ovamboland. In addition, DTA set up tents as close to polling stations as it dared, providing loud music and free food and drink for its voters. In Karibib the UNTAG team leader threatened to halt the polling process unless DTA provided food for *all* political parties; DTA was forced to acquiesce. Such a strong line was rare, however, and in many places, particularly in the south, voters expected to be rewarded for voting DTA by free food. "Where do I go to get my food?" they asked UNTAG officials as they came out of the polling booth. In Gobabis voters turned up with a strip of paper taken from photocopied ballot sheets, just the strip with the DTA sign, so that they could match it to the ballot paper. Some had such strips stuck on their T-shirts or even talked to the electoral officials as if that was what voting meant.

Chapter 5 already mentioned observers' concern about the intimidating presence of white farmers around polling stations. It was also intimidating for black voters that so many polling stations were based on white farms and even on ex-army camps (we visited two of these), and electoral teams were placed under obligation to farmers for their hospitality. One report spoke of farmers leading their workers in the chant "What do we vote? DTA! Second one down!" The combined effects of DTA partying around the polls and pressure from white farmers must have had enormous influence on hungry voters in the south where there was severe drought. SWAPO countered by its call to "Eat DTA, but vote SWAPO," but the DTA vote in many southern areas was more substantial than SWAPO had expected.

At Karasburg and Ariamsvlei in the far south of the country, voting was dominated by the buses bringing in white voters from South Africa. Similarly, at Windhoek Airport, a "holiday atmosphere" prevailed among the whites who flew in to vote, but uproar broke out when there was an attempt to limit the numbers of other voters from inside Namibia in order to cater to these white voters, even to the point of having separate queues. UNTAG quickly settled this dispute, which it attributed to an "unfortunate error of judgment on the part of electoral officials" (*The Namibian*, 9 November 1989).

DTA was also active in the Windhoek area, distributing glossy, comic-style anti-SWAPO booklets entitled "SWAPO hell camps" (Nadel Observers Report, 1989: 5). Partying there sometimes included intimidation of voters by drunken DTA supporters. We observed at Dordabis voters having to run the gauntlet of DTA tents set up on the narrow road leading to the polling station. The Nadel observers conclude, "It was our impression that the presence of this encampment and the over-boisterous conduct of the partially intoxicated supporters could have had an intimidating effect/undue influence on voters."

In Swakopmund the permanent polling station at the Magistrates' Court was under stress because voters from Walvis Bay had to be accommodated, as did those from the black township of Mondesa, which had not been permitted to have a polling station of its own. Huge queues gathered outside the polling station as voters arrived from Walvis Bay on specially hired buses and trains, and a tense situation developed on the afternoon of the first day, the crowd threatening to get out of control, because many voters feared they would not be able to vote and many of those from Walvis Bay had been given only one day's leave of absence from work, while others had taken the day off without permission. However, the police, closely watched by UNTAG monitors and observer teams, handled the situation well, and there was no serious trouble. At Tamariskia, in the "coloured" township, there was a nasty incident, which had no serious consequences, when voters in front of the polling station were intimidated by a low-flying helicopter bearing ACN and FCN posters; CIMS observers filed a complaint with the UNTAG director but noted that this intimidation was certainly counterproductive. This helicopter appeared again in Swakopmund later in the week, distributing leaflets denouncing DTA and commending UDF, and again complaints were registered.

In Ovamboland nearly all bottle shops and *cuca* shops were closed during the first two days of voting, and this helped to keep the atmosphere calm, although there was a real holiday feeling, everyone out in Sunday best. However, there were problems. As people arrived at the polling stations early and in huge numbers on the first day of polling, it was difficult to control the waiting crowds when polling started at seven o'clock. Many electoral teams found it difficult to sleep, people crowding round the small school buildings that served as polling stations from as early as one o'clock in the morning. Some teams had not arrived until four or five o'clock the evening before, and polling on the first day was sometimes delayed until nine or ten o'clock in the morning, so that the waiting crowd grew even bigger. At Oshikuku it was reported that a baby had been killed in the crush, but this fortunately turned out to be untrue and the baby recovered. As the day wore on the crowds continued to wait patiently in the hot sun, and the elections were without any scenes of violence. On the second day, however, many polling stations had run out of election material, and calls were coming in over the radio reporting shortage of ballot papers, printing ink, ballot boxes, and envelopes for tendered votes. By nine o'clock in the morning, many polling stations were already closing for long periods of time.

Another problem arose in relation to the tendered ballots. During the first day and in some places the second, voters without an official ID were being required in several Ovamboland polling stations to vote by tendered ballot, contrary to UNTAG's instructions, so that more than 40 percent of the voters in some stations had voted in this complex and time-consuming way. However, this practice was corrected after complaints by observer groups, such as the American lawyers' group the Commission on Independence for Namibia. But the Americans were still worried about the relationship between UNTAG officials and AG officials, which had been an underlying factor in the matter of the tendered ballots: UNTAG officials were taking a subordinate and secondary role, which the lawyers considered "completely vitiates the concept of UN 'supervision and control'" (7 November 1989 letter to John Rwambuya, UNTAG director in Oshakata). This situation was heightened by the fact that UNTAG did not have its own interpreters. The American lawyers also noted that illiterate voters in many polling stations were given inadequate help, or no help at all, and predicted a large number of spoiled ballot papers as a result. Literate voters also had problems as all the literature was available only in Afrikaans and English, but no African language. These lawyers also drew attention to the passive role of party agents.

Western Caprivi was the scene of the most serious elections incident, at Omega base where ex-army San units were still stationed. A man who claimed to have been chosen to help illiterate voters in the community was actually accompanying voters into the polling booth, contrary to electoral law and with the acquiescence of both the UNTAG team leader and AG officials. Observers from OAU and FLS objected, and the UNTAG team leader and the AG official were relieved of their positions and replaced the next day. The Kavango River to the west was the scene of DTA parties encouraging Angolan voters crossing over to vote, but observers drew attention to the large numbers of such voters who had been brought across before the election and held in tribal offices or DTA offices against their will; a deposition was taken from one such headman at the Legal Assistance Center in Rundu, making clear that such voters had previously been forced to register and had been given voter education in Angola by DTA. However, according to UNTAG, all such voters had been properly registered, which was formally correct.

In the end the remarkably high turnout, even without SWAPO's hoped-for two-thirds majority, seemed to silence observer reservations about the fairness and freedom of the elections, lack of time for voting, adequacy of the number of polling stations, and so on. In the event, 83 percent of registered voters had cast ballots on the first three days, so polling stations handled only a few on the last two days. Ahtisari proclaimed the elections free and fair on 14 November, consistent with his desire to see the thing through and get it over with, but most observers also called it free and fair. And certainly, despite some irregularities, the conduct of the voting itself, if not beyond reproach, was unlikely to have led to many distortions. Nor was there much evidence of intimidation outside the polling stations to get committed voters to stay away or alter their allegiance. However, as the concluding section argues and our review of the electoral system, the registration process, and the effect of earlier intimidation has intimated, there are factors other than events on the voting days that might have been taken into account in proclaiming a verdict. What many observers were probably finding was that even if parts of the process were certainly not free, the overall result was roughly fair.

## The Role of UNTAG

We wish to assess the UN contribution to the transition: the role of the UNSGSR and the activities of UNTAG. As well as exploring the UN's strengths and weaknesses, an analysis of its role involves posing the question, What difference did its presence and intervention make? In the specific international context of the transition in Namibia, as we documented in Chapter 3, posing a more particular counterfactual question yields some insights: what difference would it have made if the UN had directly administered the transition and run the election rather than merely monitoring the South Africans? Answering that question is tantamount to summing up the overall effect of the whole set of factors explored in this chapter and the last: what difference did the intimidation and other aspects of the climate and the various stages of administering the election have on the result, the future government, and the political and constitutional form of an independent Namibia?

UNTAG was set up by the UN to help "usher in Namibia's Independence" (UN: DPI/963, n.d.). Its immediate task in 1989 was to "help the Secretary-General's Special Representative (SR) . . . *oversee* free and fair elections in the territory, to be held by the South African Administrator-General under United Nations *supervision* and control." However, this oft-quoted formula seemed to downplay the broader role the UN plan had specified of UN responsibility for ensuring the transfer of power to the Namibian people (Leys, 1989a). As compared with numerous other UN missions, the UN's role in Namibia was seen to be unique. In part this stemmed from the long association of the UN with Namibia's planned decolonization, and in particular this was the only case where the UN assumed, in formal terms, *direct* responsibility for a colony when it revoked South Africa's mandate. This role was also unique in that it combined two familiar UN operations: election monitoring and peacekeeping. This long UN involvement with Namibia was also reflected in the ten-year period of logistical and organizational arrangements for UNTAG, although that was not to be any guarantee of UNTAG's efficiency or success.

Given these combined and thus complex aims, UNTAG had to take on a wide range of functions. One set of objectives concerned the monitoring of a cessation of hostilities and the maintenance of peace. Another consisted of those operations of supervising and monitoring the South African administration of the transition—ensuring a political climate that was conducive to free and fair elections, being satisfied with the electoral law, making certain that the conduct of the election was in accordance with international standards. As was noted in Chapter 4, ambiguities remained in the specification of these functions.

The composition of UNTAG reflected these two sets of tasks and consisted of military and civilian components. Their organizational structure is delineated in the diagram in Appendix D. Elements from 109 countries made up UNTAG and were spread throughout the country in almost two hundred different duty stations. The military component numbered some 4,650 troops from twenty-one countries, almost 3,000 less than the complement originally envisaged in UNCSR 435. The main force consisted of three battalions from Kenya, Malaysia, and Finland, plus communications, engineering, and other specialist units. Their preliminary task was to monitor the cessation of hostilities and the confining to base of SADF, SWATF troops, and SWAPO fighters and to monitor the frontiers and ensure there was no intervention. They were not in place to perform either of these roles at the critical moment on 1 April, but confinement to base of SADF was accomplished by mid-May. Their subsequent role was mainly to "monitor the restriction of SADF troops to base, the withdrawal of most of those troops to South Africa and the restriction of the remaining 1,500 (known as the 'Merlyn Force') to base at Grootfontein and Oshivello" (S/20883). UNTAG military forces also monitored some remaining South African troops that continued to carry out essential civilian functions as doctors and teachers. This task of monitoring withdrawals of SADF properly was largely completed by the end of June—the original target, despite the delays in April.

Importantly, however, there remained the vexing issue of the demobilization of the "citizen forces, commando units and ethnic battalions." UNTAG was to monitor the dismantling of the command structure of these SWATF units, made up mainly of Namibians except for some commanders, and observe the confinement of their arms; and these tasks were eventually accomplished after considerable frustration. The ethnic battalions continued to assemble to receive payment after the elections. The problem of disbanding Koevoet proved an even greater stumbling block, complicating UNTAG's task, as these personnel being technically police were not part of the military component's remit. In northern areas the military component continued to monitor the border and the bases, guarded UNTAG offices, and assisted UNHCR in the guarding of reception centers. UNTAG's military role also extended to Angola, where monitors were stationed at Lubango to help supervise the confinement to base of SWAPO and Angolan forces. But essentially the military component's main tasks were largely completed some three months before the November elections.

The civilian component, which had the most onerous roles thereafter, was scattered throughout the country in more than forty district and regional centers and had a number of units whose jobs were quite different. The election unit was concerned with scrutinizing the electoral legislation, and thereafter with help from seventeen hundred election supervisors from twenty-six countries, with supervising the registration of voters and the smooth organization of the election in Namibia's twenty-three electoral districts. They checked that electoral legislation was adhered to and that the ballot took place under circumstances agreed between the UN and the AG. Most of the amendments made to the AG's original draft of the electoral laws did in fact give UNTAG a more prominent presence in the registration, voting, and counting process. CIVPOL (something unique in UN operations) was concerned with monitoring the activities of Namibia's existing South African–organized police force. This job became plagued with very great difficulties because CIVPOL's role had to cover the activities of the former members and units of Koevoet that, according to RSA, had been disbanded as a separate outfit but half of whose members had been absorbed into SWAPOL. Although these personnel continued to act in the same vein as a paramilitary, counterinsurgency force, they were within the CIVPOL, rather than the military component, remit. The original proposal was that the CIVPOL component would number 360. When the extent of its daunting task soon after April 1 was recognized, however, the UNSGSR requested an additional 500. By August 1989 the proposed strength of CIVPOL had risen even further to 1,000, although its actual strength then was still just 904, made up of police from twenty-two different countries (address by UNSGSR, Institute of Directors, 13 September 1989; UNTAG press release, 9 August 1989). An additional 500 were requested later in August, and by early November 1,498 from twenty-five countries were in Namibia.

The specific tasks this monitoring entailed in the north, where former Koevoet were active, included supposedly being notified of "police" operations and being present at any investigations or interrogations, if CIVPOL chose. This in turn necessitated CIVPOL accompanying SWAPO on their forays and thus required the same bush-bashing, mine-protected vehicles— which were not initially available to UNTAC and were always in short supply. CIVPOL did not have authority to initiate investigations, question witnesses, or make arrests. It did listen to complaints but could only pass these on to SWAPOL. In addition, CIVPOL performed some ancillary functions: its presence at political rallies and demonstrations was seen to have a "consistently reassuring and calming effect" (address by UNSGSR). Coordinating both election supervision and CIVPOL activities and more generally "providing the backbone of the UNTAG operations" (NDIIA, 1990: 67) by contributing to an appropriate climate for the election, including some role in voter education, were forty-two regional and district political offices, generally staffed by two or more professionals from within the UN system.

This whole operation was extremely costly. The Secretary-General projected the final budgeting costs at $416 million early in 1989, and that figure was approved by the General Assembly. By the end of 1989, the Secretary-General had reported a net saving of $42.8 million, mainly on shorter stays and savings on accommodation and transport. The budget was divided in the normal way, with more than 60 percent to be met by the permanent members of the Security Council and most of the rest by other developed countries. The election supervisors' salaries but not travel and related expanses were met by contributing governments, and a few countries made additional voluntary contributions, the most significant being $13 million from Japan.

We turn now to assess how UNTAG performed its role and what difference it made to the outcome of the transition. One source of difficulty for UNTAG was the differing perceptions Namibians had of the UN and UNTAG's intended role. When UNTAG began its monitoring roles, it was often confronted by Namibians asking questions such as "Is UNTAG a political party?" and "When is UNTAG going to take over the farms and redistribute the land?" (address by UNSGSR, p. 5). Yet if these were some of the naive questions asked by some ordinary Namibians, many whites were less than welcoming and enthusiastic about UNTAG's presence. There were numerous incidents, not least the horrendous bombing in August of the UN offices in the town of Outjo, home of the "white wolves," and the shooting up of CIVPOL headquarters in Ovamboland. UNTAG officials were subjected to verbal and physical abuse and proclaimed as unwelcome in some hotels and restaurants. Invariably UNTAG was linked with the long history of the UN's recognition of SWAPO. Even though the settlement plan required the UN to end that commitment, it proved extremely difficult for many white bodies and anti-SWAPO forces—DTA, ACN—to recognize UNTAG's neutral role. Against that, other Namibians often expected more of UNTAG than it was allowed or able to deliver, particularly expecting it to intervene in or redress situations of violence, official bias, or injustice.

UNTAG's basic difficulty, however, was that in many ways it was placed in an impossible situation, one rooted in the character of the settlement plan itself, which gave UNTAG monitoring and supervisory roles where the active powers were in the hands of the AG, SWAPOL, and the South Africans. In part these difficulties stemmed from the ambiguities (see Chapter 4) in what the monitoring role entailed—for instance, in defining which UNTAG body should monitor Koevoet and how this might be done. This role forced on the UN by WCG in the plan was a "compromise between actual administration and no UN role at all" (NDIIA, 1990: 74) and one that was hard to maintain in practice. These problems were perhaps intensified in the first few months by the UNSGSR's interpretation of what UNTAG could and could not do and what it should attempt to do—for instance, his initial readiness to accept the AG's draft proclamations on registration and the voting system with little amendment. When his resolve was strengthened by a stronger line from the Secretary-General's office and the creation in New York of another original organization feature in the UN system, a task force on Namibia, this nevertheless weakened his position and led to delays as he had to refer to the Secretary-General's office. His position was also prone to structural limits. His only effective tool for getting the compliance of South African or other actors was the threat to halt the process or withhold his approval. Weak as this leverage was, it was rendered even less credible by the profound diplomatic and political pressures on him and on the UN from the West, the international community, and even FLS to advance the process, keep up the momentum, and stick to the timetable so as to settle the Namibian issue once and for all.

Despite acknowledgment of these difficulties, a number of question marks have been raised about the actual performance of the UNSGSR and UNTAG. The first concerns the events of April. UNTAG's work began with an inauspicious start. It was caught unprepared by the massacre of SWAPO members in Ovamboland after 1 April before UNTAG had people on the ground and its own acceptance of the AG's version of events and of SADF's and Koevoet's mobilization. The UNSGSR and UNTAG, especially in regard to incidents of intimidation, found themselves thereafter reacting to events and to South African initiatives rather shaping their own agenda for the transition period. But the issue must be posed as to whether they had any alternatives.

The events of 1 April were clearly a critical moment in the whole process. UNTAG's remit did include responsibility for "infiltration prevention and border surveillance." Yet UNTAG was not in a position to monitor and disarm SWAPO fighters on the Namibian side of the border or intervene to prevent the clashes that occurred, despite the UN Secretary-General's promise in a report of 23 January 1989 (S/20412) that he would "do everything possible to have UNTAG in place *and operational* by 1 April 1989" (emphasis added). The failure to mount a presence in the border areas was attributed to delays in deployment and financing occasioned by the rows in the UN over the proposed reduction in the number of UNTAG military personnel to be deployed. But with the benefit of hindsight, one must ask why the proposal for reduction was voiced only at this very late stage, despite ten years of discussion and preparation. This was clearly a failure attributable to the West and especially to the United States, not to the Secretary-General and certainly not to UNTAG itself, which was dependent on the many funding governments. Equally, one can question why with this delay in assembling UNTAG did not prompt a proposal to delay the 1 April deadline for the formal cease-fire. This action would have been within the powers of the UN to suggest—although that would have been difficult given the diplomatic pressures from all sides not to slow down the clock. Continuation with the original timetable may also have been considered a significant risk even without UNTAG deployment, given that a de facto cease-fire between the two sides had been in operation since August 1988. But that justification is not wholly convincing given the reports that SWAPO had been sending queries to the UN for the two weeks prior to 1 April about arrangements for the demobilization of its fighters within Namibia and had not had replies (NCC Documents, 1989) and given SADF's claims that it expected an invasion.

Another justification that has been advanced is to suggest that "even with a full contingent . . . UNTAG could not have prevented the infiltration" (NDAIIA, 1990: 75). But this argument can also be challenged: even if the whole, long border could not have been patrolled, some limited presence there prior to 1 April might have enabled PLAN fighters to present themselves to someone, as that seemed to have been their intention. There could also have been a UN presence within a short time of firefights instead of days after. In the actual circumstances, the argument that the UNSGSR had little choice but to sanction the remobilization of counterinsurgency units carries weight even if not proved to everyone's satisfaction, but in other circumstances of some UN deployment in the border areas, that crucial step might have been avoidable.

If another outcome had been possible in April, the UN task might have been different in several respects. In the event, it took almost the whole seven months up to the election before that genie could be put back into the bottle. The timetable was disrupted and delayed, and attention was diverted from preparations for elections. UNTAG and Ahtisari himself suffered an erosion of confidence in some circles because of the manner in which the April events had been handled.

A second major question has been addressed to the manner in which UNTAG handled the disbandment of Koevoet and some of the ethnic battalions. The final demobilization was not announced by the AG until 31 October, despite the efforts of the UNSGSR and an explicit call for their disbandment in UNSCR 640 of 29 August 1989. This avoidance by the South Africans of the requirements of the settlement plan was achieved in part by sheer defiance, in part by deliberate obfuscation. In this latter respect, their efforts were made easier by UNTAG not clarifying quickly the relevant responsibility of the military component and of CIVPOL. One report by the Secretary-General (S/20412) had specified the "monitoring the disbandment of counter-insurgency units, including Koevoet, will be the concern of the Military Component of UNTAG." But the component did not take on this responsibility, even refusing to monitor an element of twelve hundred Koevoet who were confined to base by the AG at the end of August at Oshakata in Ovamboland on the grounds that this confinement was not provided for under the plan and stating that it would monitor only if they were fully confined in a closed camp elsewhere in the country. The actual confinement undertaken by the AG was only monitored between 8 A.M. and 4 P.M. (Leys, 1989a). After these times Koevoet units were free to leave their bases. They were often, it seems, taken in their Casspirs, and in uniform or wearing DTA or special Koevoet T-shirts, to their homes up and down the main roads in the populated areas of northern Namibia.

In practice the main responsibility for monitoring Koevoet was eventually taken up by CIVPOL. In what it is hard not to see with hindsight as a preemptive move, the AG informed UNTAG in February 1989 that a proportion of Koevoet numbers had resigned or been demobilized and that the rest had been absorbed as individual officers undertaking normal duties in SWAPOL. The UN had been informed in October 1988 that there were three thousand Koevoet within a SWAPOL force that had expanded from three thousand in 1978 to eighty-three hundred in 1988; so UNTAG assumed that perhaps fifteen hundred Koevoet were absorbed within SWAPOL early in 1989. But these numbers were never verifiable and did not match other official figures. Indeed, part of the obfuscation that greatly complicated UNTAG's monitoring of any disbanding of Koevoet, by whichever component, was the lack of precise information about numbers, personnel, or arms.

It is an acknowledged fact that some Koevoet were reactivated as distinct units for counterinsurgency in April, but it is unclear how many and whether they were from the demobilized or SWAPOL halves. Equally, UNTAG was never able to verify whether the 1,200 eventually confined at Oshakata in August were those remobilized in April, which was the presumption, or whether they were elements who had been operating within SWAPOL. In another act of prestidigitation, the AG announced in late September that a further 1,500 Koevoet had been demobilized, but this had been done without any UNTAG supervision, so after further negotiation the operation was repeated, twice. Eventually in the last few days of October, UNTAG personnel observed parades in which 1,207 Koevoet were stood down in Ovamboland, 129 in Kaokoland, and 314 in Kavango. After weeks of pressure to check Koevoet demobilization against personnel records, files were furnished against names on these later occasions, but the absence of photos still meant identification was not foolproof (interview with CIVPOL regional head of police monitors, Oshakata, 30 October 1989). Koevoet forces were observed to hand in their weapons, but there were no records made available to UNTAG about the original issuing of arms against which to check these. In earlier demobilizations, such as of SWATF battalions, either few weapons were handed in comparison to those likely to have been issued (Leys, 1989a), or those demobilized were encouraged to take out licenses for private arms. Indeed, by the time these Koevoet elements were finally demobilized, some observers and even UNTAG officials had begun to question whether releasing these armed, trained thugs into the volatile preelection population at large was more advisable than confining them where they could be monitored. "Demobilisation only transferred the problem of intimidation. . . . Ex-Koevoet members, often wearing DTA colours or hired as DTA party organisers, continued to terrorise and intimidate SWAPO supporters" (NDIIA, 1990: 78).

Koevoet elements in SWAPOL did continue to engage in what amounted to counterinsurgency operations, teams taking off in their

Casspir vehicles on patrols—presumably of surveillance but with intimidatory impact—until October. Gradually CIVPOL was able to broker some reduction in these operations; to get agreement on reductions in the number of Casspirs and on UNTAG's right to be informed of, and to accompany in their own vehicles, any such movements; and UNTAG's right to be present at interrogations. But CIVPOL could not get SWAPOL agreement to be allowed to visit any detainees. In these and other ways UNTAG sought to keep some tabs on these activities; but it did not secure an end to them, even on paper (interview with UNTAG senior liaison officer in charge of civil police monitors, 7 September 1989).

In practice these monitoring arrangements often broke down; the Secretary-General reported on 6 October 1989 (S/20883) that "ex-Koevoet personnel . . . have often categorically objected to being monitored by CIVPOL." More generally, he pointed to "a certain lack of cooperation by SWAPOL," including failure to give schedules of patrols and prevention of CIVPOL presence at police stations during interrogations. UNTAG officials saw this obduracy as a legacy of a situation where Koevoet was "used to a free hand, even in relation to the AG" (CIVPOL monitors supervisor, 7 September 1989), and "did what it liked, without being answerable" (regional CIVPOL director, 30 October 1989).

The whole story relating to Koevoet in the transition stands testimony to a more deliberate duplicity on the part of the South African administration. In a context made difficult, CIVPOL and regional offices of UNTAG in the north did gradually whittle away at the Koevoet presence and the level of intimidation, especially in the later part of the election campaign. But it is difficult not to agree with the verdict of a U.S. observers mission that "in the early days of the transition, the UN's response to the on-going Koevoet problem was inadequate" (NDIIA, 1990: 78).

In many other respects the other elements in UNTAG's civilian component—the electoral division, the regional and district offices—overcame the severe limits on their monitoring role and did modify the climate for the elections. Apart from scrutinizing formal practices of registration and voting and listening to complaints, even if they could not investigate or redress these complaints, the civilian component was responsible for some significant initiatives. Nationally, it brought together nine of the ten contesting parties to sign a code of conduct on 12 September 1989 wherein they foreswore intimidation and dirty tricks and set up a commission to investigate allegations of these practices. At the local level, it pursued campaigns of voter education, often with significant imagination and/or courage: personnel accompanied parties refused access to farms and factories by employers, spoke at church and other public gatherings, tried to impress that the vote would be secret, and chaired panel meetings of candidates of all parties.

The other area involving these elements of the civilian component that

became critical was the scrutiny of and amendments to the electoral legislation. As we have noted, critics suggested that this component had been less
than thorough in influencing the registration proclamation, whereas after
some hesitation it did insist on some reshaping of the law about voting and
counting, even at the cost of some lateness in announcing the arrangements
for voting. UNTAG's most notable success, to which the many other
observers contributed, was to ensure that the actual casting of votes went
ahead with only minor infringements and complaints and was substantially
fair in the sense of allowing no significant distortion. This achievement
owed much to the large number and experience of the election supervisors:
two Swedish officials we interviewed on the eve of elections had also been
present for the registration and had considerable background knowledge of
and interest in Africa; in the remote polling station in a small primary
schoolroom at Endola in the north of Ovamboland we chanced upon the
cool presence in sweltering conditions of our own deputy electoral officer
from Leeds!

The most significant success UNTAG had in calling a halt to the South
Africans' ambitions to write laws to shape the transition in Namibia was
with respect to a draft proclamation the AG put out in August to define the
powers of the Constituent Assembly. These proposals exhibited a major
effort to exert control over the deliberations of the CA and their outcome.
They sought to have the AG as president of the assembly, to write in the
constitutional principles agreed in 1982 through WCG into the term of ref-
erences, and to subject the constitution to review by South African–
appointed courts and reduce it to the level of "proposals" to the AG, which
would have given him a veto. RSA's proposals were seen by many in the
international community as a "ludicrous" (Jaster, 1990) overreaching by
South Africa, and after a long stalemate a proclamation was made the day
before the elections reflecting the UNSGSR's position that there should
just be an enabling law to guarantee an independently functioning CA in
which no attempt would be made to tie its hands.

UNTAG was also instrumental in scotching one of RSA's last scenar-
ios for intervention. On 1 November 1989 Foreign Minister Pik Botha
issued warnings at a press conference that SWAPO troops were massing on
the Angola side of the border for another invasion of Namibia. This was the
last in what a UNSGSR's report on 6 October 1989 (S/20883) had referred
to as the "often made unsubstantiated allegations of imminent infiltration
by SWAPO combatants from southern Angola." On this occasion, not only
did UNTAG border monitors dismiss this; even the AG had to say that,
although he had to take any information seriously and had asked the joint
committee with Angola to report, he had no evidence to confirm such
reports. SADF claimed that its source had been intercepted UNTAG messages, which UNTAG reviewed and insisted were not its own. Their credi-

bility was further reduced when it was reported just after the elections that the tapes with copies of these messages had been destroyed.

We have suggested that the AG's relatively free hand in the registration may have had marginal significance to the result, which together with the requirement of a two-thirds majority and a PR electoral system without a minimum ceiling and a remainder formula (both of which benefited small parties) came close to making the difference between SWAPO having a mere majority and having the two-thirds to control the CA, quite apart from any indirect effects of intimidation or political manipulation. In this context the historical issue is not whether UNTAG could have followed different practices and taken a firmer line, which would have eliminated some of these distortions, but how different outcomes might have been if the UN had indeed been exercising its legal mandate over Namibia during the transition. Not only might the scrutiny of voter eligibility and registration, say, have been more thorough; the legislation on all matters would also have been quite different. The overall climate of intimidation and patronage would also have been very different if the South African officials, with their links to ethnic politicians and SWAPOL, had not had the final authority in all day-to-day activities. The UNTAG shortcoming that mattered most was not the blemish in its record but the limits to its ability to influence events and the calculated ambiguities that we noted in the UN plan in Chapter 4.

It has been suggested that UNTAG's scrutiny of the electoral laws provides a legacy that might have relevance elsewhere in the world. The improvements it made in the final election law and even more the criteria it applied in reviewing the laws and monitoring practice might "provide a basis for analysing standards for what the international community perceives to be a free and fair electoral process" (NDIIA, 1990: 80). The standards that were asserted were seen as "secrecy of the ballot, reasonable speed in counting . . . and accountability and openness of the process to the competing parties." It is indeed important to recognize that the nuts-and-bolts practicalities of election administration are central to any process of democratization. There is certainly an important body of case law from Namibia that ought to enter the lexicon of comparative, international experience—not least to inform the transition in South Africa. And if, as this U.S. source suggests, as a result of the Namibian experience, such standards have become established under international law, that is not a negligible by-product. However, the more abiding lesson of Namibia is the weakness of the leverage available to the UN to influence the outcome of a transition from conflict to peace, a political transition, and an election administered by one of the parties of the conflict. That any UN or other international peacekeeping and/or monitoring body should have only a limited role is an all-too-likely component of the numerous conflict situations in the post–Cold War era: agreements to end conflicts internal to a country always involve compromise and thus calculated ambiguities, and the mandate of international bodies is likely to be predicated on the assumption, usually unrealistic, that the contending forces are genuinely committed to the letter of the agreements. But in the Namibian case, the UN's potential role in ensuring a free and fair outcome was greatly reduced by the diminution of that role engineered in previous years by the intervention of WCG to strengthen South Africa's hand, by UNTAG's unpreparedness at the start of the transition, and by the UNSGSR's at times overcautious interpretation of his mandate, with a resulting overly indulgent position toward South Africa.

The ironic paradox of the Namibia experience of a "transitional, conflict-resolving election" is that, despite a significant UN role, the administering power was able to manipulate sufficiently the process at the margins so as ensure that the CA and possibly the future political system would not be under the uncurbed dominance of one party—thereby creating one of the possible preconditions for a future, more democratic system. This paradox is discussed further in the concluding chapter, but that consideration was perhaps in the minds of the many observers who did call the election fair.

# 7
## The Parties and the Issues

### The Main Contenders for Power

The origins of the two main political party groups, SWAPO and DTA, the personalities involved in their formation, and their social bases were discussed in Chapter 2. These two parties did eventually share 85 percent of the total votes. Here we want to look at the further shape these two bodies took in 1989 as they prepared themselves to appeal to the public through an electoral process. Two particular features of any party are crucial to understand in the context of an election: their program and their organization. The first feature offers the basis on which a party appeals to voters (although image, gimmicks, and style can affect how it is actually perceived) and in turn offers some indication of what the postelection policies of the government will be. In the Namibia case the party manifestoes could be read as offering evidence on even more basic issues, as blueprints for the constitutional structure and development path of the independent country. Later on in this chapter, we review the official programs of all the parties as they were set out on paper.

The second feature affects parties' ability to promote their cause. Moreover, in Namibia the holding of these historic elections demanded some further evolution of parties' inherited structures as they rose to this challenge. So analysis of these emerging structures is both a critical part of explaining their relative effectiveness and the election outcomes and a revelation of the kind of political organizations that would form the crucial basis for future political life and culture in Namibia. A further determinant of the strength of party organization is the resources and the support that they command. In the Namibian case, especially, the sources of funding indicate to which interests the parties ultimately owe favors, if not allegiances. Again, some material on campaigning activities and organizational capacities of all parties are presented later on. But developments in each of the two main parties as they entered the election phase need exploring as they made their campaign entrances from quite opposite sides of the stage, having had vastly different formative experiences and thus bringing quite distinct capabilities and problems to this transitional stage.

*SWAPO*

In early 1989 SWAPO was in a sense two separate structures that were seeking integration: one returning from exile, one emerging from internal repression. The external wing had developed organizational forms appropriate to the tasks of conducting international diplomatic representation and promoting armed struggle. Its leaders had lived in exile for twenty-five years or more and had not submitted their position or program to a congress or any other forum of answerability in that period. However, they had been involved, with international advisers, in policy formulation through the UN Institute for Namibia in Lusaka, which had produced weighty studies of Namibian realities and position papers (e.g., UNIN, 1986). The other personnel of this wing consisted of fighters, party functionaries, intellectuals, and students. They began to return to the country only in the five months before the election, Nujoma only in mid-September. Tensions within the movement—between generations and between fighters and intellectuals—during the long exile had been and might again be significant, as might any tensions that emerged between internal and external wings.

SWAPO had always maintained an internal wing with a legal existence, but that had been so repressed and harassed by the South African administration that it had never been able to develop a fully visible, formal organizational structure throughout all parts of the country or even much of a presence in parts of the southern and central regions. Its workaday contacts with the external wing were at best tenuous. Yet many leading figures in the churches, professions, and schools and among mineworkers and students had chosen to identify with it and its symbols and message, and their number grew rapidly in the late 1980s. The churches and unions also in part substituted for a specific party organization, as was made evident in Chapter 2.

The challenge for SWAPO in 1989 was to build up a viable machine in a very short time and also weld together its very disparate memberships with their radically different experiences and styles of work and with little knowledge of one another. SWAPO quickly acquired a large headquarters building and set up an election directorate. But it also had to concern itself with external representation (links with FLS, for instance) and with problems such as those of the returnees. Although CCN relieved SWAPO of much of that latter burden organizationally, its pool of personnel overlapped that of the party. SWAPO posted key cadres as local electoral directors in each of the country's districts. Only a few of them operated in an area where they did not know the scene or the language, but going back to an area after perhaps twenty years' exile, some were out of touch; others adjusted quickly to a return to local realities. In the north especially, the local organization could draw on the large number of returnees as well as local internal members and the church and other groups with which they were associated. Harmonious working relations among them were made easier as the returnees moved out of reception camps into the community. Few tensions surfaced, but they did exist. However, two young returnees interviewed as they acted as party agents at a polling station in Ovamboland said that in their area they were welcomed by older generations and were far more on the same wavelength with their parents than DTA activists, "of whom their parents were ashamed." An observer in Kavango also suggested that there was less of a gap between returnees and the young student activists who had become the backbone of local party organization in the last couple of years than between them and the party leadership; the electoral director for the district, although from the area, had spent much of his life in Windhoek before exile.

SWAPO in exile had built up a significant resource base with support from the UN, OAU, and nonaligned and socialist states. But the party was impeded by the South African administration as it sought to bring its vehicles, so crucial in such a vast country, and its office equipment and files back from Angola. Little has been made public about funding during the election period, but support through OAU no doubt continued: one reported contribution was U.S. $200,000 from the Iranian government (*The Guardian,* 11 September 1989). SWAPO received the use of a fleet of vehicles and drivers during the final election period from the Congress of South African Trades Unions. It also benefited indirectly from the fact that many of the tasks of voter education and dissemination of information broadly supportive of its position were undertaken by private groups, including some churches and *The Namibian* newspaper.

*DTA*

DTA had had the experience of contesting and prevailing in elections for ten years and also had very considerable resources of funds, vehicles, and supplies; almost all its meetings, activities, and offices were characterized by free food, elaborate publicity material, and music. Much of its infrastructure and its lavish style of hospitality were legacies of earlier elections. Ellis (1979) reports that for the 1978 campaign, DTA was helped by the South African government to train and employ 425 fieldworkers and open thirty-six offices and was supplied with 132 vehicles. Its personnel, finances, equipment, and transport were supplemented by inputs obtained from South Africa and the security forces (see Chapters 2 and 5). In Ovamboland there are reports (CIMS, 1989) of some 90 privately registered pickup trucks being at DTA's disposal. In Kavango one of our team noted two jeeps with young white occupants providing support to local DTA cadres.

Although benefiting from this source of personnel, DTA thereby suffered from its own internal tensions—especially in the north, where DTA's ex-security personnel tended to rely on the bullyboy tactics with which they had coerced the population (not always successfully) for years. These tactics were only slightly sweetened by the carrot of handouts in a style not always to the taste of the ethnic politicians, which often bypassed them. There was almost open conflict in Kavango, for instance, between these thuggish elements that had increasingly taken over running the show and the chiefly elements that had originally built up the constituent ethnic parties and depended more on patronage and on status. In the central and southern areas, the local DTA took many differing forms, and the ex-security element was not so much in evidence.

The source of DTA's considerable finances was never revealed during the transition period, and indeed the alliance denied it received any funds from the one source that was publicly known to bankroll many small parties, the Namib Foundation. However, information surfacing in July 1991 from within South Africa in what was called the Inkathagate scandals revealed that the South Africa government had funded several anti-SWAPO parties. Foreign Minister Pik Botha was pressed into admitting the allocation of more than R 100 million for this purpose. His justification, that "we were against SWAPO, we were at times at war with SWAPO," of course confirmed not just the channeling of money but also the existence of an intention to swing the election. Faced with this evidence, DTA finally admitted that it had received South African government funds; its justification was that "there's nothing wrong with getting money from other countries; SWAPO also received money from other countries. It's history now, and I think nobody can complain" (*The Guardian,* 26 July 1991).

The implication that the South African government was dictating overall strategy not only for DTA but also for an alliance involving other forces can be read into some of the other revelations. The main source of this information was Nico Basson, who during the transition worked for the public relations firm African Communications Project, which happened to have offices in the same building as DTA and the *Die Republikien* newspaper. His role and that of ACP were revealed at the time by two Western journalists who penetrated the central offices of ACP and DTA as "volunteers" in August 1989 and revealed their findings at a press conference in Windhoek (15 September 1989) and in a joint publication of the German *Geheim* and *Top Secret.* They stated at the time that Basson claimed he had in the past worked for SADF and that he "had connections" with SAMI. What was confirmed in 1991 was that he was working for SAMI during the elections as part of a coherent program. He also stated, in what seemed to be a change of heart, that Pik Botha's final admission of a contribution by RSA of R 100 million was a "half-truth" and that "hundreds of millions were spent" (*The Guardian,* 26 July 1991). He also claimed, "Namibian political parties were still receiving funding from the South African government: not as much as before the elections, but enough to keep them going" (*The Guardian,* 27 July 1991).

The 1989 penetration of DTA's headquarters and of Basson's ACP also revealed some of the calculations behind the South African–DTA election strategy. The tactics in any one area were based on regular opinion polling and on information supplied by the South African Council for Scientific and Industrial Research, which was described as a "parastatal." The *Geheim* story (September 1989) suggests that Basson's internal intelligence estimated DTA support in Ovamboland as only 7 percent, which was to prove remarkably correct. It would be logical, if this figure was accepted, for RSA-DTA to have pursued a strategy that would limit the delivery of that potentially massive support for SWAPO if they could, perhaps by limiting registration and turnout. Elsewhere it would have made sense to build on the DTA support that did exist and to undermine SWAPO's support. The former tactic involved presenting an image of DTA as a "wealth-creating party"—presumably the calculation behind its "giveaway" style of campaigning. Basson thought that the latter task would be greatly enhanced by "the detainees issue eroding SWAPO support." But the strategy recognized that not all doubts about SWAPO from the detainees issue or from other propaganda would necessarily generate support for DTA and that "the DTA's biggest handicap is voters' fear of its South African connections" (*Geheim,* 1 September 1989). Thus, the back-room planners also promoted smaller parties that were trying to undercut SWAPO's claim to monopolize the struggle against South Africa—an image that DTA could not project—and thus promoted a bloc of parties that might get 50 percent of the vote, thereby control SWAPO, and in turn provide a "block to the one-party state and socialism."

## The Political Roots of the Small Parties

When the UN plan and the process of the transfer of power first got under way early in 1989, a very large number of parties were already in or quickly came into existence. Some observers estimate that there were more than fifty. The *Political Who's Who of Namibia* lists forty-five, one of which in turn comprised six groups; another, two (Putz, Von Egidy, and Caplan, 1989). The party registration requirements (see Chapter 6), the costs of electioneering, and the realities of seeking votes whittled down this plethora of parties into a smaller number of serious contenders, a process largely the result of the coming together of several parties into coalitions, fronts, or alliances. In the event, ten came up with the necessary resources to sustain a challenge. Apart from SWAPO and DTA, those entered for the election included three single parties—the Christian Democratic Action for Social

Justice, the National Democratic Party, and SWAPO-Democrats. There were six fronts, which involved between them no less than thirty-six separate parties. The five minor fronts in addition to DTA each obtained at least one seat in the Constituent Assembly. The fronts each were put together in 1988 or 1989, obviously to contest the election, although some of the constituent parties had had a considerably longer existence.

In terms of political roots, the electoral contestants represented a broad spectrum of interests and positions. One category, which was labeled *collaborationist* by opponents, consisted of the three competing single parties (CDA, NDP, and SWAPO-D) and the National Patriotic Front of Namibia, all of which had agreed to join DTA in the interim government formed by the South Africans in 1985. Of NPF's three component parties, the main one was a descendant of SWANU and had emerged as a result of a split around the issue of joining the interim government.

The other faction emerging from the split in SWANU formed the backbone of the Namibia National Front, which incorporated four other parties, made much of its noncollaborationist position, and even made an explicit "socialist" appeal, although it also defined itself as "centrist" between DTA and SWAPO. NNF sought territorywide support rather than an ethnic base. A similar centrist appeal was made by the United Democratic Front, which linked its explicitly leftist urban parties with the Damara Council and other ethnically based parties. It had remained in opposition to all interim regimes in Windhoek.

Two party groups did not fit neatly into this collaborationist/noncollaborationist categorization and came to represent specific interests. The Federal Convention of Namibia (FCN) brought together a disparate group of six parties, some with a record of collaboration, others with a distance from South African solutions, but all with a concern to limit the centralist character of the Namibian state and retain some federalist structure that would enshrine ethnic entities. Also articulating "group rights" was the Action Christian National, an alliance among Afrikaans- and German-speaking right-wing white parties, the Namibian rump of the National Party of South Africa, and the German speakers' Deutsch Aktion/Deutsch-Sudwester.

The ability of many of these parties and alliances to sustain an election challenge depended on the funding they received, mainly through the Namib Foundation. This secretive body (its officials refused to be interviewed by our study team) came onto the scene suddenly in 1989 to dispense money to parties that declared support "for multiparty democracy" and for some notion of "group rights." Widely perceived as a body that was anti-SWAPO, DTA claimed at the time that it had no such funding, but we confirmed that the foundation financed at least one party in every one of the other electoral fronts, except NNF and NNDP, but not the fronts themselves. Thus, our interviews with UDF officials established that of its affiliates, the Damara Council and the Labor Party received funds, but the Workers' Revolutionary Party (WRP) and PUM apparently did not.

The seemingly bottomless war chest provided for parties to set up offices, print glossy publicity material, and provide transport, even to charge their petrol to an account—but this facility was quickly withdrawn after the election, leaving many garages vainly trying to recover funds from the tiny rump of these small parties. In general this funding was one important factor in spawning a large array of parties—a factor that would clearly contribute to a strategy of grabbing support from SWAPO in an election based on proportional representation.

The source of the Namib Foundation funds was never officially disclosed; the presumption at the time was that they were from South African private and/or public sources, although one UDF informant (interview, Arandis, 1 November 1989) suggested that there were American and German as well as other sources. The public record over the Muldergate scandal of the 1970s (e.g., Rees and Day, 1980) indicates that it would not have been the first occasion on which RSA revenues had funded Namibian parties. The Inkathagate revelations in July 1991 confirm the extent and vast scale of this support and imply that the Namib Foundation was but one of the channels for South African government funds. The ACP office under Nico Basson seemingly promoted some of these smaller parties and in particular handled publicity for the parties and groups that were built up around the detainees issue. Thus, the two journalist "moles" (*Geheim,* September 1989) claimed that they saw propaganda about a "Patriotic Unity Movement" in Basson's office two weeks before the launch of PUM (which was later to join the UDF alliance in the elections, along with some other explicitly left-wing but anti-SWAPO parties) at the end of July 1989 and that the PUM statement was printed on the same word processor as ACP material. This launch statement did attempt to distance itself from both SWAPO and DTA, "with its links to Pretoria," and so to project a "third force."[1] And this claim was not just a fabrication, nor was the organization simply a South African front: witness Basson's reportedly contemptuous dismissal of the seriousness of PUM's Eric Biwa and the labeling of him as sharing SWAPO's ideology (*Geheim,* September 1989). There was, however, a tactical marriage of convenience. Two pressure groups built up around the detainees issue and related to PUM, the Parents' Committee, which had been set up in 1985, and the Political Consultative Council (PCC), which had been formed by detainees on their release from Angola, also accepted this kind of support from ACP and, indirectly, South Africa.

*The Noncollaborationist Parties/Fronts*

*UDF.* UDF was an alliance of eight parties founded in Windhoek in February 1989. And although it was disparate in origins and aims, the front represented the main third-force element, attempting to distance itself from the collaborationist parties as well as SWAPO. Six of the parties were tribally based, but in August 1989 two other parties joined the alliance: WRP, with Erica and Hewat Beukes, ex-SWAPO Youth League activists, of the Parents' Committee in its leadership, and PUM, organized by a group of ex-SWAPO detainees and led by Eric Biwa. UDF saw itself as offering an alternative to the major contenders, advocating a mixed economy, a guaranteed right to own private property, and the representation of traditional chiefs in a council of chiefs, with the protection of cultural and language rights.

The leading element in this alliance was the Damara Raad, a group around the Damara Council, led by Chief Justus Garoeb, originally formed as a tribal council in 1971 but transformed into a party in 1980 to fight the second-tier elections. It remained the dominating element in Damara but opposed all interim regimes in Windhoek. It even explicitly allied itself with SWAPO in the mid-1980s but stopped short at merging its members into SWAPO when the latter refused to consider incorporating the council as a distinct element within SWAPO. The coloured Labor Party, another partner, was led by Reggie Diergaardt, one of UDF's four elected candidates, who has since accepted a post as deputy minister of trade and industry in the SWAPO government. Other tribally based parties in the alliance were the Original People's Party of Namibia, a San organization led by Theophelus Soroseb; the Namibia National Independence Party, a breakaway from the Kavango Party under the leadership of Rudolf Ngondo; and two small parties from Caprivi: the Caprivi Alliance Party, led by Gabriel Siseho, and the section of the Caprivi National Union (CANU) that refused to join DTA, led by George Mutwa.

The alliance between the tribally based parties and the more militant WRP and PUM was a strange one from the beginning. In an interview Japhet Isaack of PUM and the Beukas of WRP explained the decision to join the UDF alliance as tactical: UDF was the alliance on the left of the political spectrum most likely to win votes; they considered NNF, which had approached them, to be an organization of "armchair intellectuals without grassroots support." This alliance in the end paid off for PUM, as Eric Biwa did get a place in the Constituent Assembly and on the standing committee that debated the constitution.

*NNF.* This alliance was established formally in February 1989, claiming to follow anti–South African policies, like its predecessor, the old NNF. It set itself up as offering a progressive alternative to SWAPO. It combined the leftist, urban-based Namibia Independence Party, under the leadership of Albert Krohne, Ottilie Abrahams, and Kenneth Abrahams, with the faction of SWANU that had refused to enter the interim government, led by Vekuii Rukoro and Nora Chase, together with three other small parties: the

Mmabatho People's Party, representing the Tswana people of Namibia; the Rehoboth Volksparty; and the United Namibia People's Party, a group that broke away from SWAPO-D in 1980 over collaboration with transitional authorities. Support for NNF was expected to come from Hereroland, where SWANU had its traditional base, and from southern Namibia, among the coloured and Rehoboth communities in particular, but also Windhoek, where NIP has worked among communities for some years, although in the event it managed to scrape one CA seat on the basis of a small scattering of support across the country.

## The Collaborationist Parties

*NPF.* This alliance was founded in Windhoek in March 1989 by the other faction of SWANU plus CANU and the Action National Settlement. NPF sought an image as the party of reason, advocating a mixed economy and calling for Namibia to be neutral and nonaligned in the future. CANU was established in 1963 by Brendan Simbaye and Mishake Muyongo, now president of DTA. Actually, there are two claimants to the title of both SWANU and CANU: SWANU-NNF was expelled from SWANU-NPF for refusing to take part in the multiparty conference (MPC) and the interim transitional government set up in 1985. CANU-UDF is composed of members of CANU who refused to take part in the interim government.

Moses Katjioungua is the leader of this SWANU faction and the leader of NPF (and became its sole candidate elected to the Constituent Assembly). He succeeded Gerson Veii as president of SWANU in 1982, when he returned from exile in Sweden and led a SWANU delegation to MPC. In the ensuing split, Nora Chase and Gerson Kangueehi attended the Lusaka conference as part of the SWAPO delegation and not under the MPC umbrella, accusing the SWANU leadership of "selling out" and being puppets.

*CDA.*    Peter Kalangula left DTA in 1982 to found this party, which remained the main party in the Ovamboland Legislative Assembly until that assembly was disbanded in 1989. He had spoken out against the military and police repression in Owambo and was responsible for the introduction of Owambo into the administration wherever possible and the introduction of English as the official language in Owambo schools. Despite this record of a degree of independence from South African officialdom and the patronage that could be dispensed, the election demonstrated that SWAPO had overwhelming support in Ovamboland; CDA was obliterated. Kalangula disbanded the party after the election, donating all its assets to an organization for the handicapped.

*Namibian National Democratic Party.*    This party was founded early in 1989 by Paul Helmuth and Tara Imbili as a breakaway group from

Kautuima's DTA party, NDP, although Imbili joined SWAPO a few months later. Helmuth has had a long political career. He carried messages between Lüderitz, Walvis Bay, and Cape Town at the time when OPO was formed; went into exile in 1959 to Dar es Salaam, the USSR, and then Scandinavia as SWAPO's first representative; and left the party in 1971. He returned to Namibia in 1979 and joined NDP within the DTA alliance, eventually taking part in the interim government between 1985 and 1989. The party clearly had little political support, polling only 984 votes.

*SWAPO-D.*  SWAPO-D was founded in 1978 by ex-SWAPO information secretary Andreas Shipanga, and Solomon Mifima after their release from Tanzanian custody in 1977. They had originally been imprisoned by the Zambian government at the request of SWAPO and transferred to Tanzania to avoid an action of habeas corpus being brought by Shipanga's wife. They had been accused of plotting against the SWAPO leadership when they and two hundred others called for a party congress to discuss party problems. Mifima and the Abrahams left in 1980. Shipanga went on to participate in the interim government as minister of nature conservation, mining, trade, and tourism. He led the party in the runup to the 1989 election and was expected by some observers to gain SWAPO votes by default as SWAPO-D used the old SWAPO torch symbol and the SWAPO colors— with an added touch of yellow. However, they gained only 3,161 votes, not even half the votes needed for a single seat, most of those in Owambo. The party's poor performance in the election prompted Shipanga to merge with NPF in August 1990.

*The Group Rights Parties*

*ACN.*  The ACN alliance of the National Party of SWA and the Deutsche Aktion/Deutsch Sudwest Komitee was formed specifically to contest the independence elections in 1989, believing that whites have an "exceptional contribution" to make to the future of the country. The National Party has a long history in Namibia, campaigning together with the United National South West Party for the full incorporation of SWA into South Africa, using the slogan "South Africa First." In 1949 they achieved limited success, when white South West Africans were given direct representation in the South African parliament. However, in 1975–1977 the National Party took part in the Turnhalle Constitutional Conference and acceded to the notion of an independent Namibia and a measure of power sharing with "nonwhites," setting up the three-tier constitutional proposals based on the Odendaal findings (Odendaal was himself a member of the National Party).

Dirk Mudge left the party in September 1977 as a result of insistence within the party on the retention of apartheid laws within the constitution. He formed the Republican Party in October, followed by DTA in November, which brought together traditional chiefs from a whole range of ethnic groups. The National Party formed its own multiracial alliance (ACTUR) in order to fight DTA and SWAPO in the proposed elections in 1978 and won six seats in the internal elections, which were held after SWAPO's withdrawal, but walked out of the assembly accusing South Africa of tricking them. The National Party has been relatively successful in the various ethnic elections held subsequently. In the transitional government set up in 1985, the National Party held a number of ministerial posts: Jacobus "Kosie" Pretorius was minister of water affairs, Ewart Benade was his deputy, Jan de Wet was minister of agriculture and fisheries, and there were others in posts and telecommunications.

The National Party was based on the principle of the protection of group rights and thus had always been opposed to UNSCR 435/78, which was based on the principle of one person, one vote. ACN eventually had to accept the implementation of UNSCR 435/78, albeit under protest, and was able to obtain three seats in the CA.

*FCN.* Six parties came together under the FCN umbrella in 1988, one of which, the Namibia People's Liberation Front (NPLF), already incorporated five groups. The disparate origins of the party's elements are indicated by its title. "Convention" seemed to invoke echoes of the short-lived National Convention (1972–1974), which sought to forge an alliance of all proindependence parties but split between pro- and anti-SWAPO elements when the latter was recognized by the UN. But FCN's "federal" character reflected the commitment to some autonomy by the constituent parties, most of which had an ethnic base. Indeed, all but one were local opposition groups to the ruling DTA-federated parties in the second-tier authorities of the Nama, Herero, and Caprivi and to the Damara Council. But the most influential group was the Liberated Democratic Party/Liberation Front, which was the ruling party in Rehoboth. Although it could deliver only 29 percent of that ED's vote to FCN, this accounted for half the total FCN vote. This Rehoboth Baster vote virtually guaranteed one CA seat, which, ironically, was filled by the president of NPLF, who was a Damara.

## The Party Platforms

### The Manifestoes

The most obvious place to look for a party's program is in its manifesto. The contents of the party/alliance formal electoral documents can be compared for points of agreement and conflict along three broad subject headings.

*Constitutional Proposals and the International Status of Namibia.* As the election was for membership of an assembly that would write the country's constitution and, in practice, for a government, issues of what kind of state was envisaged were prominent in the manifestoes. In addition, the larger parties also prepared complete draft constitutions; SWAPO produced a sixty-page outline document at the end of 1988, which was later revised and expanded. All parties stated their commitment to a democratic and sovereign state, with SWAPO, SWAPO-D, NNDP, and NNF emphasizing its unitary character. ACN and FCN stood for the legal protection of minority rights, proposing that group rights be defined regionally and enshrined in law. DTA, UDF, CDA, and NPF emphasized their commitment to multiparty democracy, whereas SWAPO offered a vague formula of leaving the decision on a future political system "to the people of Namibia themselves." All parties except ACN paid specific attention to the issue of human rights, with proposals from different parties for a bill of rights to protect against various types of discriminatory practice and to protect particular interests.

DTA favored a ceremonial president, an executive prime minister, and a two-house parliament, whereas SWAPO, SWAPO-D, NNF, and UDF preferred an executive presidency, and SWAPO, SWAPO-D, CDA, and NNF preferred a single-chamber legislation. SWAPO, NPF, SWAPO-D, and NNF all emphasized the importance of traditional leaders in different ways.

The general political system proposed would also be reflected in what parties indicated about future external relations—especially given that Namibia would be entering the global stage for the first time after colonial rule and the issue of relations with South Africa would loom so large. A neutral and nonaligned state of Namibia was proposed by NPF, SWAPO, SWAPO-D and NNF, with friendly relations with all nations of the world (especially neighbors) being emphasized by SWAPO, FCN, CDA, ACN, NNDP, SWAPO-D, and NNF. NPF, UDF, SWAPO-D, NNDP, NNF, and SWAPO all stated that Walvis Bay and the islands within the territorial waters of Namibia formed an integral part of the country and should be incorporated into it. SWAPO's draft constitution started with a strongly worded preamble referring to the history of South African colonialism and called for greater independence from RSA.

*National Economic Policy.* In spelling out national macroeconomic policy, a free market was explicitly mentioned by CDA, ACN, and NNDP, whereas a mixed economy was proposed by SWAPO, UDF, DTA, FCN, SWAPO-D, and NNF, which all offered slightly different details of what such a mixed economy would look like. SWAPO emphasized the need for great change in the economy in order to increase national economic independence, especially from South Africa, and reduce income inequalities; a significant role for the state was envisaged in bringing this about, although stopping short of any wholesale nationalization of mines, land, or other productive sectors. SWAPO's manifesto thus marked a significant shift in wording from the reference to scientific socialism in the party constitution adopted by the Second Enlarged Central Committee in April 1983 and in content from some of its own programmatic statements or those put together by advisers close to it (e.g., UNIN, 1986). Such statements fueled claims from small left-wing groups such as WRP (interview with E. and D. Beukes, 25 October 1989) and NNF that the SWAPO leadership had become antisocialist. Nevertheless, other self-professed socialists, such as the authors of a pamphlet from activists within the Congress of South African Trades Union entitled "Why Socialists Should Support a SWAPO Victory" argued this position as the most progressive alternative while expressing concern that SWAPO was moving away from "genuine [economic] independence."

All parties considered *agricultural development* to be a high priority, with considerable importance being attached to *land reform.* SWAPO committed itself to a total redress of the inherited, racial land allocations, promising a program of land redistribution; declared its opposition to the wholesale expropriation or nationalization of land; and announced its intention to promote a mix of state, peasant, cooperative, and private commercial farms. DTA emphasized the ownership of communal land by traditional communities. SWAPO, SWAPO-D, NNDP, and NNF all emphasized the central role of the state in agricultural development. SWAPO's stance with regard to land and the transformation of economic structures was more explicit and radical than that of the other contenders, although less radical than proposals that had been considered in the years of exile (e.g., UNIN, 1986). SWAPO was now proposing that "some of the land," mainly of absentee (white) landowners, be transferred to the African landless. Although clashes over such basic issues might have been expected to be central in the election campaigns, they did not become major concerns or become polarized in a contentious way, which may help explain the ease with which consensus around property rights was found in the CA after the election.

All parties highlighted the importance of the *mining sector* to the economy as a whole, and none proposed nationalization, but SWAPO took a somewhat more clear-cut position than the others in proposing means through which the wealth generated by the industry would be used to restructure the economy as a whole, stating that it "reserved the right" to state as void treaties and concessions made by colonial authorities. Parties addressed different aspects of the *manufacturing industry* in their manifestoes, but in spite of contrasting emphases, there were only narrow differences in their approaches in terms of the type and degree of state involvement proposed. All the parties mentioned the *rights of workers,* with the need for independent trade unions being supported by NPF, SWAPO-D, UDF, NNDP, and NNF; SWAPO merely recognized the right of workers to organize themselves in trade unions.

*Social Policy.* CA, NPF, SWAPO, NNF, SWAPO-D, and UDF proposed that the state should play an active role in the provision of adequate and affordable *housing.* The need for adequate *social security* was mentioned by SWAPO-D, NNF, NPF, and NNDF; SWAPO alone emphasized that there was a need to improve the *position of women* and proposed full equality between women and men; NNF was the only other party to focus on women's rights. SWAPO also called for fundamental changes in the migrant labor system, promising to abolish "all remnants of the contract labour system" and remove restrictions on residence and population movement, thereby allowing workers to live with their families in their work area.

*Education* was mentioned by all the parties, either in terms of expanding access (SWAPO, SWAPO-D, CDA, NNDF, NNF, and UDF) or ensuring the preservation of existing standards and working through existing structures (ACN and FCN). SWAPO, NPF, SWAPO-D, UDF, and NNF stipulated that *English* should be the official language of Namibia, whereas NPF and NNF proposed that Afrikaans should remain official through some period of transition.

## The Election Campaigns

A party's program is not adequately described by the contents of its manifesto. Even coverage of the issues raised through various media reporting and advertising does not provide complete insight into that party's priorities and appeal—in this case because of the relatively small proportion of the electorate to which such media were directed. Among a largely illiterate population with no experience of free elections, speeches given at political rallies were perhaps the most important formal avenues for the transmission of ideas, opinions, advice, promises, and proposals. Analysis of such occasions also affords considerable insight into how the parties went about their business, how they structured their appeal to the voters, and what the election results might mean. In practice in the Namibian case, the contents of the manifestoes of all parties contrasted quite sharply with what formed the main issues of the campaigns, where any policy issues were overshadowed by the stance the parties took vis-à-vis one another.

But it is not enough to consider both the official platforms and the informal appeals; the issue is how to judge their *impact,* especially in the absence of detailed survey data. In no election can the analyst conclude simply that if this party stood officially for a certain position and won, then the voters supported that party because of that aspect of its program. The explanation for the popularity of a party may be in the issues, in personality, in symbols, or in quite extraneous factors. How parties campaigned will not itself provide the key, but it will at least be instructive about what issues they prioritized or indeed whether they dealt with issues at all, what matters were in contestation among them, and what their style and the potential basis of their appeal were.

Political campaigning in Namibia was far more than what the managers instigated. It was a colorful business. All the registered parties produced T-shirts in party colors and flags that were flown from rooftops and even from trees, so that townships and rural areas took on a festive air for months on end. Some supporters even had special outfits in party colors for wearing to rallies and political occasions. Women in the striking, ankle-length Herero-style dress looked magnificent in SWAPO or DTA colors. Yet visible signs of party allegiance also led to unpleasant incidents, such as when T-shirts were torn from the backs of supporters or flags were torn down. In Ovamboland some people defended their flags with guns, and in Kavango a SWAPO supporter was jailed for sixty days for burning a DTA flag put up to replace a SWAPO flag outside his house (interview, 7 October 1989). Feelings ran high, and even refusal to respond to a party salute could lead to trouble, as two young women in Kavango found out when they failed to give the DTA sign to a van full of DTA supporters, who then descended from the van and beat them with whips (*The Namibian,* 15 November 1989).

*SWAPO's Campaign.*   One major emphasis in SWAPO's campaign strategy, as in DTA's, was to promote major rallies featuring national leaders, mobilizing mass attendance from locals, and often bringing in supporters from afar. SWAPO's first such star rally on 23 September was launched by Nujoma himself at Windhoek Stadium. People came pouring into Windhoek two or three days beforehand. After a speech outlining the history of colonialism and the liberation struggle, Nujoma brought the crowd to its feet for a minute's silence in memory of the tens of thousands of Namibians who had died in the fight for independence. At this first rally Nujoma started the theme of "reconciliation," which was to be such a main plank throughout SWAPO's political campaigning, urging white Namibians not to leave the country and stating clearly that "SWAPO has no intention of imposing a one-party political system against the will of the people." He promised changes in health, education, and the economy to right the wrongs of the past and bring about a fair distribution of resources and facilities.

Nujoma spoke not only of SWAPO's political program but also of the continuing intimidation in the country, evidenced by the assassination of Anton Lubowski and attacks on SWAPO offices. He also remarked on the unfairness of an electoral system that allowed South Africans to vote in the Namibian independence election. He pointed out in anger, "I have been living in Tanzania for ten years, Zambia for eight years and Angola for a further ten years, and I have never voted in those countries" (*The Namibian,* 24 September 1989).

Other such large rallies followed: at Oshakati (Nujoma on his home territory after thirty years), Rundu, Swakopmund, Katima Mulilo, Keetmanshoop. In Kavango an enormous crowd gathered to hear Nujoma speak even though DTA had scheduled a rally at Rundu for the same day. Nujoma's speech was directed at the concerns of the Kavango people, but he continued the themes started in Windhoek at the first rally. He spoke of the agricultural potential of Kavango but asked, "Instead, what do we see? Large military barracks!" He promised that a SWAPO government would embark on irrigation schemes along the Kavango River and promote fish farming to create much-needed employment. And this was one of the few occasions on which he mentioned land reform, promising to try for a "fair balance" of ownership of land. He also called on former Koevoet and SADF members to join SWAPO and be part of a peaceful future. "Come quickly! Come join! Come vote for us in order to bury colonialism." At this point the rally erupted into applause. Nujoma had clearly hit on a key concern in Kavango (*The Namibian,* 23 October 1989). One of the largest rallies was an eve-of-poll gathering in Katatura, the African township outside Windhoek, at which the South African antiapartheid leader, Reverend Allan Boesak, spoke along with Nujoma and other SWAPO leaders.

SWAPO rallies emphasized the need to reject collaborationist parties, projecting an image as the only truly nationalist party, one consistently opposed to South African rule. SWAPO emphasized its own role as a party of peace willing to take power with hands untainted by collaboration. At the same time, it recognized the pressures on people from intimidation and largesse, urging people who felt they "owed" a vote to DTA to realize that the ballot was secret and arguing that DTA would accept a defeat because of reconciliation (as Nujoma urged in Kavango). Hendrik Witbooi in the South used the slogan "Eat DTA, but vote SWAPO!"

In some areas there was an explicit promise to find solutions to the land problem, but in areas outside the north, this was played down, presumably in an effort to avoid antagonizing whites and to counter the image of SWAPO as a party that might confiscate property once in government. SWAPO's ambivalence toward the land question was to become apparent in the CA and in policy after independence.

In remote areas it is hard to know exactly what message the campaigns contained; in many areas outside Ovamboland there were considerable amounts of disinformation, such as in Caprivi, where people thought that SWAPO was planning to sell their land (Adams, 1990: 133). It was not uncommon for disinformation to be blatantly put about by white farmers and DTA campaigners.

The detainee issue was played down by SWAPO in favor of emphasizing the need for reconciliation. For example, in the south, where arguably the detainee issue might have most political effect, Vice-President Hendrik Witbooi emphasized his personal connection to the history of Nama resistance by staging a major rally on an anniversary of his grandfather's struggle. By identifying SWAPO as the party of resistance against colonialism, he hoped to bring the Nama vote to SWAPO. He emphasized the need for national reconciliation over any southern perspective on what happened during the war and focused on why southerners in particular should support SWAPO (interview with Hendrik Witbooi, October 1989). He did comment on the detainee issue and argued that, although SWAPO had been criticized for having dirty hands, "It is easy to keep your hands clean and do nothing." He added that SWAPO had deliberately stressed reconciliation and avoided attacking other parties in order not to drive people away, but, he said, most other parties had no such scruples, and their methods of campaigning centered on attacking the opposition, which usually meant SWAPO.

*DTA Campaigns.* DTA's central message seemed to be to project an image of a patron sufficiently experienced in government and with enough access to resources to be trusted with people's security and welfare. The flamboyance and trappings surrounding DTA's rallies and permanent and well-appointed offices and camps, with music and other entertainments, free refreshments always on tap, and well-produced flags and posters everywhere, continually underlined this image. In areas such as Hereroland, DTA was sufficiently well entrenched in the local power structures to offer itself as *the* local party and not simply as a national alliance (and thus external to the locality). The fact that land titles had recently been registered in that ED and that poorer people were dependent on the largesse of tribal authorities, who were also large cattle owners, for work as herders or for borrowing stock gave these notables two further levers for clientelist networks (personal communication, W. Werner; field trip, December 1989). They also looked for support to the security personnel and others on the payroll of the various administrations, sometimes explicitly; thus Mishake Muyongo, DTA president, at the party's biggest rally in Ovamboland at Oshakata on 4 November, said, "Countrymen, whether you have been in Battalion 101 or Koevoet, you are welcome in DTA." In other respects DTA tried to downplay its collaborationist role by cloaking itself in nationalist symbols, even appropriating some associated with SWAPO: the raised hand in salute (although with two fingers rather than the fist) and the chant of power, the playing of the nationalist hymn "Nkosi Sikilele Africa" used throughout the subcontinent, and even the general claim that it was DTA that had brought independence. There was also similar rhetoric painting a future of national development now that self-determination was to be achieved—all that was needed was "hard work." Seldom were any more concrete promises or prescriptions articulated.

The big DTA rally in Oshakata just before the election was typical of many, with a gigantic marquee set up for food and drink and a South

African band providing entertainment. A large crowd assembled, many of them transported from the south. Children were running off with bags of sugar and cans of food that were being distributed, and a few Himba people wandered about sporting DTA caps and flags. Muyongo's speech strongly resembled the rhetoric of SWAPO rallies: in place of the incantation of "comrades," Muyongo started each new topic by calling on his "country-men" (*alicana*). His theme was a bland one of general encouragement but little programmatic content: "If you all work together we can have paradise here in Namibia." He emphasized the significance of their vote: "When you make your cross remember there can be no new Namibia without you. Everyone must vote at the polling station."

One of DTA's main planks was to denigrate SWAPO rather than to present any alternative platform. These spoiling tactics helped build on fears that people in the south and center, where DTA had established support, had of SWAPO as a northern and Owambo party, and a potentially ruthless one. But such tactics could also be adapted to northern areas where DTA was mainly concerned to limit SWAPO's majority to less than two-thirds overall. A crucial means here was to use the detainee issue to present SWAPO as an organization with no respect for human rights, and this negative image of SWAPO was not successfully countered by its own campaigning, which merely emphasized the need to "forgive and forget." Attacking SWAPO on its human rights record also undermined its image as a party of peace. DTA sought to portray SWAPO as "warmongers," thereby playing on fears of whites and (some) blacks, especially after the April incursions. Glossy comic books were distributed around rallies depicting SWAPO's "secret" plans for a military takeover or graphically depicting tortures in "SWAPO hell-camps." On the eve of elections in one area of Ovamboland, we saw phony leaflets, purporting to be a call to arms by Nujoma to the faithful in his home area, being dropped from a plane.

One common tactic was to provoke SWAPO supporters into violence: parading with loud music (and often guns) on the fringes of SWAPO rallies,[2] around SWAPO offices, or, earlier in the campaign, around the reception camps in Ovamboland for newly returned SWAPO exiles (CIMS, 1990: 67). One of their chief tacticians and later a member of the CA, Barney Barnes, deliberately provoked SWAPO supporters at a Lüderitz rally by taunting with insults about Nujoma, leading to the eventual arrest of three local SWAPO officials who had in fact sought to restrain their supporters.

*Campaigns of Third-Force Parties.*  UDF certainly put itself forward as a third party, stressing its noncollaborationist credentials but its opposition to SWAPO. UDF's main component group, the Damara Council, had been the one party around an ethnic administration that had stayed outside the interim government, but its overtures to become an element within SWAPO had been rejected, and this was a cause of resentment in the area, assuring the UDF of some real prospect of a significant local base. The other components consisted of small organized groups, mainly of intellectuals or professionals, some of them ideologically radical, who proffered a critique of SWAPO's program simultaneously from both a centrist position urging a "middle way" and from the left—the need to go beyond mere nationalism. Not surprisingly, UDF made the detainee issue more of a central issue than any other party. Ex-detainees figured prominently in UDF's campaigning. UDF also stressed the need to "break the mold" of political contestation, which it characterized as being between the corrupt, discredited, clientelist, old internal politicians and the "excesses" of the external nationalist movement. UDF sought to project itself as a realistic third force that could form a government—although privately it would acknowledge that its hope was to be the swing party holding the balance in a hung assembly (interviews with Erica and Dawed Beukes, 25 October, 1989; and Eric Biwa, 15 November 1989). UDF projected an image as a party of substance by taking offices in prestigious buildings and by similar giveaways of T-shirts, food, and music at their rallies to those of DTA.

NNF similarly attacked SWAPO in its campaigning as well as DTA and even UDF for their history of collaboration with the South African government. NNF campaigned on two issues largely ignored by the other parties: women's rights and land reform. However, after the election Dr. Abrahams of NNF expressed the view that campaigning on women's rights had actually lost NNF votes in Hereroland and perhaps elsewhere, and although the land question seemed to arouse interest at rallies, it did not seem to yield votes (interview, 12 December 1989). This lack of success in winning votes may have been because of the ideological mix in this coalition being reflected in confused messages—women and land being stressed by the radical groups and other more conventional issues by other elements.

## Party Organization

Of necessity, rallies played an important role in getting a party's message across to people, given the illiteracy and the difficult logistics of campaigning in distant communities. But behind these all-too-visible measures of parties' effectiveness in reaching the population, and making these public shows of strength possible, was the more humdrum business of setting up party machines. The main parties took over large multistory buildings in Windhoek to set up headquarters and sought to open premises and have full-time office and organizing personnel and committees operating in towns and districts throughout the country. These bodies set about drawing up manifestoes and lists of candidates; printing materials; organizing big rallies, demonstrations, and small gatherings; and using a variety of means to promote voter education about the complicated mechanisms of actual voting as well as their party program.

*SWAPO's Organization*

SWAPO had virtually no offices and barely any local formal structure before 1989 (especially in Hereroland, Kaokoland, and parts of the south). A SWAPO organizer described the structure that SWAPO had sought to set up in the early registration period as follows:

> In each big town SWAPO has a main office with sub-centres in small places. The field-workers go out into the townships, the farms and the remote areas that may be 100km. from the main centres, house by house, asking if all the people have registered, telling them why registration is important, all these things. If the field-workers see that some people have not registered they encourage them to do so, they make notes and after a week they go back and ask them whether they have registered and any problems they have. (Student fieldworker, talking to *Action on Namibia*, October 1989)

How extensive this door-to-door canvassing was varied between towns, but it was widespread in the north and Windhoek. The same student talked about the serious preparation that went into the rallies themselves: "SWAPO had two big rallies in Keetmanshoop when I was there. First, there would be a seminar, the day before the main rally, with topics on what fieldworkers should do and on the ex-detainee question which was very high on the agenda. Then the day afterwards there would be the public rally with SWAPO leaders" (*Action on Namibia*, October 1989).

As SWAPO was building up this extensive network almost from scratch, much of the administrative work often had to be taken up by returned exiles. This sometimes caused problems in local campaigns when they did not know the language or the current local context, and occasionally there was the feeling that they had been imposed over the heads of people who had been struggling to maintain a local organization. But in Kavango a young, local activist (interview, Rundu, 2 November 1989) suggested that this was not a serious problem compared to the gap between the regions and the national leadership. Certainly, the local educated youth who had become involved in SWAPO there recently were singled out for their excellent organizing role by one CIMS observer. Clearly, a top-down directed campaign in that ED was perhaps indicative of the way SWAPO had been organized in exile and in the north, but perhaps not in the rest of the country.

SWAPO worked harder at voter education than the other parties. The decision to spend a great amount of resources on this, including the last-minute printing of hundreds of thousands of blank ballot papers in South Africa (thanks to the good offices of the Congress of South African Trades Unions), was taken when mock voting trials, even though by a group of SWAPO activists in Windhoek in October shortly after the publication of the electoral regulations, revealed a high proportion of misunderstanding of symbols and procedures: 15 percent produced mistaken ballots (interview, P. Manning, 9 June 1990).

*DTA's Organization*

DTA had well-established local party structures in much of the country and was able to mobilize a considerable political machine. Its lavish funding made possible a vigorous campaign with no stinting on offices, vehicles, publications, and free goods. DTA used rallies for the same reasons as SWAPO, to reach scattered illiterate populations. But because the press publication of the numbers attending played a similar role as a measure of popularity to that of opinion polls in other countries' elections, it became important to get a lot of people there. DTA made sure of this by providing free food and music for the occasion as well as clothing; it also bused in supporters from far afield.

Another aspect of DTA's campaign was to disrupt SWAPO rallies and public displays of SWAPO support. This is how one SWAPO activist reported on a fairly typical occurrence in Keetmanshoop:

> Before the 4 November rally in Tseiblaagte Sports Ground, a lot of the DTA supporters had brought whips and various weapons. The rally was extremely hot and yet everybody came. There were children and old people, people who had made outfits specially for the occasion. During the rally the DTA sent over a low-flying aircraft to stop the people hearing Nujoma. SWAPOL [the police] were actually sitting in trucks with SWAPO members, handling security. A year ago nobody could ever have imagined that . . . there were at least 5,000 people at our rally. (*Action on Namibia,* January 1990)

DTA's strategy in the north certainly seemed to put emphasis on thuggery through the paramilitary hierarchy that had been incorporated into the party structure. Elsewhere the party relied more on patronage; it relied on white employers, especially but not only farmers, to persuade their workers. Often it was unlikely that farmworkers would have voted at all unless the farmers had brought them to the voting stations. In the former reserves it was patronage through the bantustan officials and their local DTA-affiliate party structure—the dependence on jobs and other resources. The alliance did provide voter education by handing out slips marked in the right place for DTA and by organizing chanting on the way to voting.

The routinely thuggish aspect of DTA's campaigning (also discussed in Chapter 5) was a reflection of the personnel DTA recruited to augment the inherited networks, a large number of whom were recently demobilized, or even still existing, members of the security forces. Indeed, where they ended and DTA began was never clear. DTA justified their recruitment by comparing it to ex-PLAN fighters being used by SWAPO. Thus, one of the DTA leaders in Rundu, who later appeared on the DTA list for the Constituent Assembly, was an ex-major in one of the ethnic battalions. In the same area, DTA organizers seen by us in the party's headquarters in Rundu instructing groups of party workers on the eve of poll wore T-shirts emblazoned "Koevoet Kavango" and still packed pistols. However, these new officials' promotion of intimidatory tactics meant that they often simply took over the direction of campaigning, which put them at loggerheads with the inherited hierarchies of chiefs and notables. The networks and tactics that these latter used had much more to do with manipulation of status (if they retained any), jobs, and favors.

However, DTA's experience from previous elections, the benefit of building on existing structures fully resourced, and the role of back-room logistical planners from the white community or security forces did enable it to achieve considerable organizational effectiveness in the routine tasks of electioneering. Thus, the infiltrators of the SAMI operation (*Geheim*, September 1989) quote one regional director of DTA, a white farmer, to the effect that he employed sixty-two organizers at R 500 a month each—a substantial wage. They claimed to have seen a large-scale map in his office with colored pins showing the political affiliation of every household in the ED.

*Other Parties' Organization*

Those who had Namib Foundation money, such as FCN and NPF, tended to spend it on the same kind of symbols and giveaways (T-shirts, flags, hats, hospitality, and glossy manifestoes) as DTA, even if on a more modest scale, plus some minimum of office and vehicle infrastructure, in an attempt to attract votes with the minimum of organization. UDF spent Namib money on publicity material and entertainment at rallies but also acquired some properties and sought to build on some of the structure of local parties, especially in Damaraland (Damara Raad) and the south (PUM). NNF, in contrast, did not have extensive party structures or local notables among its founders. NNF considered that a lack of funds was a major factor in its failure to win votes: "People did not want to vote for a party which could not even raise finances for their own election campaign" (interview, K. Abrahams, December 1989). It intends in future to mobilize only for local elections.

## The Detainees Issue

A major and contentious issue that preoccupied parties and was widely and often vitriolically debated in public gatherings and the media during the election campaign was the plight of Namibians imprisoned and often tortured by SWAPO in camps in Angola and Zambia. The issue of the "detainees" simply would not go away even after the election. A case before the Windhoek Supreme Court in the week after voting accused SWAPO of still holding five named detainees "unlawfully" in Angola (*The Namibian*, 17 November 1989). A debate in the National Assembly pushed SWAPO's information minister into proposing a multiparty committee to look into the questions of missing Namibians (*Times of Namibia,* 31 May and 1 June 1990).

The issue of the detainees assumed a greater significance than merely a stick with which to beat SWAPO as it became a vehicle for the articulation of ethnic politics: it was argued that the majority of those detained and those who had still not been repatriated, were non-Owambo especially from coloured, Damara, Nama, and other communities in the south; and it was in these areas that the issue had its main effect. The furor over the treatment of detainees was intense, no doubt orchestrated and fueled by the hostility of the media toward SWAPO. Yet in order to assess what kind of effect the issue had on SWAPO's electoral performance and on ethnicity, we need first to explore what exactly SWAPO was accused of and to evaluate what the evidence indicates about SWAPO's abuse of the human rights of those it detained and imprisoned.

According to the terms of the UN plan for Namibia's independence, all political prisoners were to be released before the start of the electoral campaign on 1 July 1989. South African authorities had reportedly released their detainees by June 1989, and in May SWAPO announced the release of its prisoners held in military bases in Angola (Amnesty International, *Namibia, April to August 1989,* 4 August 1989; NCC Document 1989: 3–5).

The exact figures of those detained by SWAPO and how many were classed as spies became matters of contention. *The Times of Namibia* noted on 31 May 1989 that of the 201 people SWAPO released in that month, 100 had been detained as South African spies, and many complained of having been tortured. In September 1989, however, NCC in London released a more detailed breakdown of those thought to have been detained by SWAPO. In July 1989 SWAPO released 153 non-SWAPO men, women, and children whom the organization had held in detention camps in Lubango, Angola. In August the same year the SWAPO leadership claimed that it had released all those previously detained, including those who were members of SWAPO. It had released 199 on 24 May, of which 153 were known to have returned to Namibia under UNHCR auspices (NCC

Documents, 1989: 5). An additional 16 returned on 9 August; they were apparently not part of the 199 but of another group of 84 released in May "but who were prevented from leaving Angola." That comment fueled speculation that there were further people still held in Angola and Zambia. However, about 340 did seemingly return anonymously with the SWAPO repatriation program run by UNHCR.

SWAPO thus stood accused of imprisoning as many as two thousand people, usually on charges of spying or of being South African agents, in the ten-year period 1980–1990. It was also alleged during the election campaign that between five hundred and one thousand were still being detained or may have died in detention resulting from execution, mistreatment, torture, and poor living conditions—usually a dirty, overcrowded hole in the ground (*Times of Namibia*, 31 May 1989; Balch and Scholten, 1990: 22). It was still claimed at the end of 1989 that five hundred detainees had not been repatriated (*Times of Namibia*, 8 December 1989 and 30 January 1990), despite SWAPO denials and the report of a special UN mission in October 1989 that no prisoners remained in detention.

The past treatment and present fate of SWAPO detainees became a significant issue in the election in several ways. It attracted international as well as local media coverage, which undermined somewhat SWAPO's status in the outside world, recognized as it had been by much of the international community as the sole embodiment of the Namibian people. It certainly led to severe local and international criticism of SWAPO and questions about the party's funding. Church groups were clearly embarrassed: the September synod of the Evangelical Lutheran Church in Namibia, for example, condemned the torture of former SWAPO detainees (*Africa Today*, third and fourth quarters, 1989: 108; letter from Bishop Dumeni to *Times of Namibia*, 13 October 1989). Green Party representatives in the West German Bundestag visiting Namibia in August with an official team of Bundestag members also deplored human rights violations in SWAPO camps and said the admissions that had been made were insufficient to allay widespread fears about the conduct of SWAPO in exile (*Financial Mail*, 26 August 1989); the Greens did in fact withdraw from continued financial support.

This issue also fostered the mobilization of relatives of detainees and their communities against SWAPO and made viable a political movement opposed to SWAPO that could avoid the collaborationist label. In July 1989 former political detainees formed PCC, an allegedly nonpolitical organization, to prevent SWAPO coming to power by bringing together "all democratic and peace-loving forces against tyranny" (*Windhoek Adviser*, 7 July 1989; *Times of Namibia*, 21 July 1989), and also the Parents' Committee of Namibia, an organization of parents of detainees. These two groups mobilized anti-SWAPO feelings especially in areas where most detainees seem to have originated (interview, UNTAG

Divisional Office, Khomasdal, 25 October 1989). PCC, for instance, drew its initial, and probably sole, support in Windhoek from the coloured township in Khomasdal, and the Parents' Committee was also most active in Windhoek, the south of the country, and Damaraland. The two groupings belied their nonpolitical claims by being involved in the formation of the Patriotic Unity Movement party, which affiliated to the UDF coalition.

UDF was the most vociferous of the electoral groups in its attack on SWAPO's human rights record as reflected in its treatment of detainees. The detainees became a major issue in Damaraland, where UDF had its main support base, because of the contention that Damara-speaking people had suffered most from the nonrepatriation of detainees. Just how effective this issue was, however, in accounting for the UDF majority vote in Damaraland (7,838 against SWAPO's 4,204) is debatable. Wellmer (1990) suggests that in the south generally the detainees issue caused a shift of support from SWAPO to other parties, of which UDF was only one. Nevertheless, it was an issue that did lend itself to the language of some of UDF's ethnic interest campaigning.

Within UDF, the detainees issue was particularly championed by Erica Beukes, one of the leaders of WRP, whose brother never returned from the camps. She led two delegations to the Tintenpalast, one immediately following the UN mission's report and one after the election, that directly challenged SWAPO president Sam Nujoma to "tell us what happened to our people" and demanded the release of people still alleged to be in detention (interview, Erica Beukes, *Windhoek Observer,* 25 October 1989). Another key voice in the assembly was that of Eric Biwa, himself a detainee.

From the moment in May 1989 when the detainees became a potential election issue, SWAPO was grudgingly on the defensive (*Times of Namibia,* 31 May 1989). In a hostile political environment where SWAPO had for decades been painted by the media as little more than a bunch of terrorists, it proved increasingly difficult for the movement to clear itself. But the detainees issue raised serious questions for more sympathetic local and international audiences about SWAPO's style of leadership, internal politics, and organization. Few commentators, however, noted that it was probably for precisely these reasons that SWAPO had tried to come clean on the detainees more than three years earlier (*New Statesman,* 28 February 1986). At a London press briefing in February 1986, SWAPO's international relations secretary, Theo-Ben Gurirab, and information secretary, Hidipo Hamutenya, showed videocassette "confessions" of some of the one hundred men held in SWAPO's Angolan camps admitting to spying for South Africa, including one that was later used in the election campaign and featured Riundja Kaakunga, who was to become the chair of PCC. SWAPO argued that its organization had been infiltrated by a South African spy ring of young Namibians. The spy ring had even allegedly penetrated SWAPO's

Central Committee, on which it reputedly had four members. Gurirab hoped that by breaking the news, SWAPO could preempt a "right wing campaign to deglamourise" the organization.

Yet even at that stage SWAPO seemed set on a course of action likely to involve false arrests and also generate fears of general infiltration that were not based on any reality. SWAPO's tactics for identifying supposed South African espionage recruits seem to have involved casting the net widely and then trying to induce a confession. Moreover, it was alleged that surprisingly, and perhaps suspiciously, little effort was made to debrief those interrogated beyond getting an admission of guilt (Brown, 1989). In such a climate it was probable that when resistance ran out detainees just pleaded guilty to charges that seemed to have been invented (although Mistake himself refused to go on video). So it was almost inevitable that the process would lead to brutalities with little guarantee that the right culprits had been caught. This method of demonstrating the infiltration of its ranks by video confessions smacked of show trials which, easily could, and probably did, get used by SWAPO cadres wanting to conduct internal party or personal vendettas.

At least initially SWAPO's style in responding to allegations of poor treatment of detainees was often very brusque: "Well what do you expect us to do with South African spies? Kiss them?" (*Financial Mail,* 26 August 1989). When it became clear that the issue was going to haunt the party throughout the election campaign, the response became more considered. In July and August 1989 SWAPO admitted that it had tortured its political prisoners (*Times of Namibia,* 10 July 1989; *The Independent,* 24 August 1989). And in a detailed interview with a German newspaper, Ben Gurirab finally admitted that not all the detainees were South African spies (*Frankfurter Rundschau,* 18 October 1989). Some were confirmed as spies, others remained suspects, and some were found innocent and released. He said that it was a "troubling finding" that some had been tortured and physically harmed, one "that we found despicable, SWAPO could not condone, could never have authorised"; where this had happened, he offered a personal apology. That, however, was the extent of any concessions. He refused the prospect of a commission of inquiry, saying SWAPO had its own adequate structures to investigate the accusations and adding, "It might not satisfy outside observers because they don't know what is going on between us, the leaders, and the Namibian communities." SWAPO was nevertheless quick to accept the findings of the UN mission in October 1989. Yet SWAPO's other senior leaders were conspicuous in their silence and lack of public remorse of what unraveled daily during the campaign, serving as an ongoing indictment of the party's brutal treatment of actual and suspected spies. SWAPO's actions were gleefully picked up on by opponents, many of which did not have clean hands themselves.

The publication of Gurirab's interview with the German press almost coincided with that of the report of the UN mission on detainees. Set up in accordance with the settlement proposal and following the SWAPO leadership's invitation to the UN and human rights bodies to check detention centers, the UN established a mission on detainees to visit SWAPO camps in Angola and Zambia from 2 to 21 September 1989. Its main purpose was to "ascertain whether any Namibians were still detained by SWAPO . . . and if so, to ensure that appropriate arrangements for their release and voluntary repatriation were promptly made" (UN Mission, 1989: 1). Before the mission set off, it obtained a consolidated list of names of people who had allegedly been detained by SWAPO. The list contained some eleven hundred names and was supplied by Amnesty International, the Parents' Committee, PCC, SWAPO-D, and the Namibian International Human Rights Organization. The mission was hampered in its work by poor transport facilities, which limited the extent of its findings, but it did visit a total of twenty-two locations in Angola and eight in Zambia. Some SWAPO camps in southeast Angola were not visited. This fact and the UN's refusal to take any ex-detainees on the search cast doubt on the exercise in the eyes of SWAPO's critics. The mission also noted that "the information available to the mission about the persons allegedly detained varied considerably in quantity and quality" (p. 6) and that there were obvious difficulties caused by "variations encountered in the spelling of names and from the use of aliases, nicknames and *noms de guerre*" (p. 7).

Despite these constraints, the mission unanimously concluded that there "were no detainees in any of the alleged detention centres" (p. 8) and, more significantly, that "the majority of persons allegedly detained or missing have been repatriated or accounted for" (p. 9). The mission did conclude that there were 315 persons whose "present status is unknown and require[d] further investigation" (p. 9). The mission confirmed that six of the locations outside Lubango "appeared to be the prisons where detainees were held" (p. 8). It also noted general concern widely expressed by people it had questioned that a "similar exercise should have been or should be undertaken to determine the number and whereabouts of Namibians allegedly detained, killed or missing *inside* Namibia during the period under investigation i.e. by South Africa" (p. 8; emphasis added); little seems to have come from this.

Further checks on those missing or dead against voter registration records in Namibia uncovered many ex-detainees returning unnoticed. In the Secretary-General's report dated 3 November 1989 (S/20943) the UN mission's findings were then revised downward. The actual figures as of 31 October 1989, compared with the mission's original figures of 11 October (in brackets), were:

- 517 persons released and/or repatriated (484)
- 57 persons reportedly not detained, including SWAPO officials (71)
- 123 persons reported dead (115)
- 52 persons who could not be identified owing to insufficient information (52)
- 263 persons with present status unknown and requiring further information (315)

The mission's report did little to satisfy SWAPO's critics, although it may have placated some skeptics among party members, supporters, or sympathizers. Both UDF and NNF condemned the report. NNF president Vekuii Rukoro saw it as an "insult to the people of Namibia" that "parents are [still] being kept in the dark as to the whereabouts of their children" and argued that the UNSGSR should include former detainees and other "appropriate observers" in another fact-finding mission (*Windhoek Observer*, 21 October 1989). UDF extended its criticism of the report with a rally of some five hundred demonstrators outside the Tintenpalast. UDF accused the UN of taking sides with SWAPO and covering up the issue of the detainees with an inconclusive report. Justus Garoeb, UDF president, said it was "highly perfunctory, un-professional, clearly deceptive and deliberately misleading" (*Windhoek Observer*, 21 October 1989).

It is not surprising that the UN report did not satisfy SWAPO's fiercest critics, including the government of Ambassador Clarke (from Nigeria), who led the mission. The UN was still struggling with its reputation of supporting SWAPO even though that formal relationship had ended with the implementation of the settlement plan. Moreover, the mission to the camps in Angola and Zambia did not visit all sites indicated by former detainees and at best could only try to reconstruct events from observations after repatriation had taken place. SWAPO's critics simply argued that any remaining detainees had been taken elsewhere and that the mission's findings that "some of the buildings used for detention purposes were constructed above the ground, while others were half or fully sunken below the ground" (UN Mission, 1989: 8) confirmed the harsh conditions. Many in the UDF, PCC, and PC said they would never forgive the SWAPO leadership and security apparatus for the extensive use of detention and torture, which was still being documented toward the end of the election campaign (*The Independent*, 18 September 1989; *Windhoek Observer*, 8 July and 21 October 1989). Certainly this vehemence made the three groups unlikely to ally with SWAPO (we consider how it affected the Constituent Assembly's deliberations in Chapter 9). Two final questions do need to be addressed here: Why were the detentions as extensive as they were? And what was the effect on the election campaign of the revelations about what went on in SWAPO's camps between 1980 and 1989?

Four interrelated themes emerge when assessing why SWAPO

detained so many Namibians under the charge of spying; the UN mission confirmation of 960 detainees suggests that they represented perhaps 5 percent of PLAN and SWAPO cadres. The first and perhaps most influential factor in initiating the hunt for spies by SWAPO security officers related to the character of the armed struggle against South African occupation. As already noted, SWAPO was able to mount more concerted guerrilla attacks into Namibia and to open up Ovamboland (Katjavivi, 1988: 84–91) only after the downfall of the Portuguese colonial regime in Angola in 1974–1975. The subsequent increase in military activity intensified official recruitment of Namibians into SADF and later SWATF and special police units operating on the border with Angola. This intensification in turn accelerated South African counterinsurgency attacks against SWAPO within Namibia but also with UNITA inside Angola. It became more difficult for SWAPO to penetrate and identify sympathetic areas of support in northern Namibia. There resulted a massive increase in the militarization of Namibia, from an estimated fifteen thousand SADF troops and counterinsurgency police in 1974 to eighty thousand, excluding police, in 1980 (p. 88). Most of this increase was concentrated in Ovamboland.

In May 1978 SWAPO received a major blow. Its main center at Kassinga in Angola was attacked by South African ground and air forces (Katjavivi, 1988; IDAF, 1982; Konig, 1983). The combination of these factors—the increased militarization of the war, the difficulties this posed for SWAPO infiltrating Namibia, and the savagery of a major attack on a base 150 miles north of the Namibia-Angola border (Herbstein and Evenson, 1989)—fueled fears that the organization might at worst be penetrated, or at best be susceptible to infiltration, by South African spies. These fears tended to surround this issue with a certain panic, which was further fueled as the number of dead increased in later attacks in Angola.

A second factor was the tensions between the leadership old guard and new well-educated recruits, a feature also of other Southern African movements (Cliffe, 1980). SWAPO leaders seem to have been wary of the increased criticism they faced from young intellectuals in the movement who were recruited from the mid-1970s on (*Windhoek Observer,* 7 July 1989; *New Statesman,* 28 February, 1986). The case of Johannes Gaomab, nicknamed "Mistake," a deputy commander in PLAN, is instructive in highlighting this source of conflict (Brown, 1989). For Gaomab, June 1982 seems to have marked a watershed. He was a much respected commander, and yet he was increasingly asked to pursue what seemed to him to be suicide missions. He was uneasy. He noted that the SWAPO leadership "were suspicious of all outsiders" (*The Independent,* 29 September 1989), but he feared that South Africa was obtaining key information from SWAPO's general command; SADF always seemed to know the location of fighters.

After a political seminar held in August 1982 where such grievances were voiced, eleven of those who voiced them were detained. A key person who sought to defuse the fear of "outsiders" and "young educated Turks" rising too quickly within SWAPO was the minister of defense at the time, Peter Nanyemba. He tried to give more prominence to educated cadres within PLAN, but he was killed, with his assistant, in a car crash in southern Angola in April 1983. With his death, the educated recruits to SWAPO lost a valuable supporter and one who was generally trying to broaden the social base of the movement. Nanyemba was replaced by the veteran Peter Mueshihange, who had far less sympathy with the aspirations of the educated "upstarts." With the appointment of Mueshihange, the way was more clear for the uneducated and militarily inexperienced, personified by Hawala (Auala) Saloman—to be nicknamed by the detainees the "butcher of Lubango." In March 1984 Mistake was arrested under suspicion of being a spy. After months of interrogation and torture, he was prevailed upon by his fellow inmates to confess. Stubbornness would surely lead to death.

The case of Mistake is interesting for several reasons. First, if as testimonies by other detainees seem to bear out, these witch trial methods were typical of all investigations, they were hardly likely to reveal the actual spies. Just as possibly they could be a means of handling internal conflicts, personal jealousies, and so on; would encourage tribalism, nepotism, and finger pointing; and would harm morale. Second, unlike most other released detainees, Mistake says he is not bitter (although he did go on to coordinate the work of the Namibian International Human Rights Organization): he commented that "it is not a question of destroying SWAPO, it is a question of ridding ourselves of pollution" (*The Independent*, 29 September 1989).

That pollution is the third of the reasons cited to explain why the detentions were so extensive. It is put down to the emergence of a "security clique" within SWAPO, and especially PLAN, and its being allowed to run rampant. That clique, centered in the Lubango and Cunene provinces of Angola and typified by the thuggery of Auala, kept the majority of SWAPO leadership in the dark, it is argued. (A detailed list of what PCC called SWAPO's Gestapo can be found in the *Times of Namibia*, 21 July 1989. The only senior officeholders included in this list are Mueshihange, Auala, and Maxton Joseph, transport secretary.) Most of the leaders were based in Luanda and Lusaka and seem to have seldom visited the camps, although the detainees do testify to visits from Nujoma and other senior officials.

Some detainees and other commentators suggest that the brutality of the uneducated, often combat-inexperienced PLAN commanders in charge of camps in Angola was not a mere result of the mindless paranoia of a security wing that had become unanswerable. Rather, this brutality was a reflection of a concerted policy by the leadership, of which the Angolan and Cuban authorities must have been aware (interview with UNHCR representative, Lubango, Angola, December 1989). It was also seen as in turn an element in jockeying for prominence in the SWAPO leadership, perhaps particularly by a core of the leadership from Ovamboland. Hidipo Hamutenya is cited as one person behind such security and certainly seems to have been a frequent visitor to the camps; he was the one who presented the videotaped confessions to the outside world. However, our UNHCR interviewee suggested that Hamutenya was unlikely to have been the éminence grise behind this. Many observers do emphasize, however, that many of the detainees were not from the Kwanyama ethnic group to which most of the SWAPO military high command belong. Historically the Kwanyama and other Owambo have been the most underprivileged (and uneducated) Namibians, and it seems possible that the purges within SWAPO represented attempts by members of these groups to ensure their political dominance within the organization as well as evidence of their insecurity in the face of educated youth who spoke a different language (interview with UNHCR official, December 1989; *The Independent,* 29 October 1989; *Africa Confidential,* 26 January 1990). This theme of ethnicity, as explanation of some of the regional patterns of the election results, is one to which we return in the following chapter.

## Candidates, Cadres, and Their Social Characteristics

In elections that have single-member constituencies, the standing of the competing candidates as individuals may be a factor that enhances or diminishes the vote they receive because of their party label. However, in a proportional representation system like that in Namibia, with single national party lists of seventy-two candidates, the influence on voter choice of any personalities, whether in terms of their overall reputation or local following, is likely to be negligible. The image of national party leaders may be a partial exception to this rule, although in Namibia such influences were probably muted. Sam Nujoma, SWAPO president, remained a slightly shadowy figure, having been in exile for almost thirty years (and where his image was never as charismatic as other liberation leaders, such as Samora Machal of Mozambique); returning less than two months before voting, he had only a limited chance to stamp his personality and style on the campaign. For DTA, Mishake Muyongo had taken over as president just before the election, having only returned to Namibia from twenty years' exile in 1985; he had the reputation of a local (Caprivi), rather than national, politician and so offered little, if any, major presence. Dirk Mudge, officially the chair, remained the major spokesperson and strategist but could not be used as an image to appeal to African voters.

If the particular characteristics of candidates are of little significance in determining voting, it is still interesting to compare their general characteristics, for even if differences between the main panels were not part of voter calculations, these profiles reveal something of the background of those who subsequently came to power.

## SWAPO Personnel

Of the forty-one SWAPO candidates who got elected to the CA, nineteen had been founding members of the party in the early 1960s; of the rest, twelve had joined the organization in the 1970s, most of these younger people now in their forties, and only one had joined later (a young, white human rights lawyer). Five were not party members; three of them were white nominees (two of whom were theologians), and the other two non-members were also from the church. Of the founding generation, all nineteen sooner or later went into exile, in two cases only after long periods of detention on Robben Island in South Africa; eight of them obtained university education while away. Only four of them could claim any direct experience of guerrilla fighting. We have biographical data (from our own candidates' survey and the valuable reference work by Putz, von Egidy, and Caplan, 1990) on only fourteen of the younger generation: nine of these remained in the country in the internal wing of SWAPO throughout the 1980s; the other five went into exile, got university or postgraduate education, and became key members of the external SWAPO's emerging bureaucracy. Thus, out of all the SWAPO candidates, seventeen were party workers in exile; the data available on the rest give their livelihoods as teachers (seven), professionals (six), clergy (six), businessperson (one), and hunter/farmer (one). Although some of the founders had started their working lives as dockers, office workers, or even migrant workers and three still had trade union involvement, none could be described as workers. The heavy preponderance was of party functionaries and middle-class intellectuals. Only two were seriously engaged in business: Of thirteen who gave us information on their property in rural areas, only two had land, although five (including two exiles) had livestock. So most seem to have had little of any remaining "peasant" base, nor had they acquired commercial farms by the time of the election. Only four of SWAPO's slate were women.

## DTA Personnel

DTA's list reflected the party's history and structure as a coalition. The first thirteen candidates on the national list were all leaders, presidents, or chairs of the local or ethnic parties that made up the alliance. The remaining eight who were returned to the CA were the second-level leaders of these groups. Almost all of them had been involved in DTA since its founding in 1977. Only one woman was included.

In terms of their background, they represented the aspiring petty bourgeoisie rather than those who had already made it: only two were businesspeople, although five were farmers, some of them no doubt substantial. There were eight from the professions, most of them teachers. Only two listed headman or chief as their main source of livelihood, but several more had chiefly status. Seven of them had had university education, and all but four had had secondary schooling. One of the successful candidates had been an officer in the security forces, although many such elements could be found among the main leaders at district and local level.

## Minority Party Personnel

Of the ten assembly members from the minor parties, the three ACN were representatives of the white farming/business community, two Afrikaans speaking, one German speaking. The other seven included four who were professionally engaged in politics, one lawyer, one teacher, and one builder. None were women.

## Political Cadres: Interests and Aspirations

The candidates are just the most visible part of a larger political class. A count of the national officials listed in the invaluable reference work (Putz, von Egidy, and Caplan, 1990) on the more than forty political parties and movements reveals more than 450 such political cadres. As a ratio of Namibia's tiny population of those of the requisite age group and background, this is a very high proportion. Given that most are male, and some schooling would be considered a prerequisite, perhaps 1 out of every 50 educated adult males older than thirty will be an aspiring politician. Although this larger group probably reflect similar employment and educational backgrounds as the candidates and will equally show vast underrepresentation of workers, peasants and/or migrants, or women, the social context from which they emerge may not be so significant in assessing their likely political stances. It may be not the interests they bring to politics but the interest they hope to accumulate through politics that is the big motivation for those who aspire to political careers.

## Conclusion

The review of party programs as revealed in their manifestoes showed a perhaps surprising degree of consensus on a range of issues about Namibia's future political shape and about its economic and social development. All parties were committed to a multiparty representative system of cabinet government, and all promised more services in education, health, and so on as well as hard work. Beyond that, SWAPO articulated a less radical position on transforming inherited economic and social structures than might have been expected from some of its statements in exile, and, most significantly, did not campaign extensively on the land issue. That did not, however, exempt SWAPO from scares being generated by its opponents that land was going to be taken away from people—not only whites but also Herero and other minorities and even middle peasants. The question of land might have been predicted to be one of the basic issues of contention in any future constitution, as it certainly was over Zimbabwe, where the Lancaster House Constitutional Conference was deadlocked for several days by how much freedom or restriction there would be on government's powers to acquire land for redistribution. A general answer to this issue that provided some guarantees to existing property owners had been conceded in the constitutional principles that South Africa had insisted upon during the long negotiations. Nevertheless, it might have been expected that SWAPO would use any controlling majority, perhaps with other nationalist parties, to strengthen government's hand in this respect and that DTA and other collaborationist parties would seek more than one-third vote to block such clauses. In the event, in the party programs and their campaigning and in the CA, land was insignificant as a bone of contention. At the opposite pole, DTA did not campaign, as might have been predicted (and as the white party of ACN and the Rehoboth separatist FCN did), for any specially entrenched group rights, either by means of special political representation other than one person, one vote; residence; or communities controlling their own services, such as education.

If differences in programs did not stand out, what then was at issue in the election? Subjectively, what other bases of appeal did the parties make, and could they have been the basis for voting decisions? Objectively, what do the programs and the campaign tell us about the difference the results could make? Our survey of campaigning suggests that there were major differences in the image that the main parties sought to portray and may well have conjured up in the minds of voters. SWAPO sought to assert its position as the single authentic voice of the Namibian people struggling for national liberation against South African rule. It did so in a manner that generally avoided being strident and attempted to modify its pitch so as to appeal as a truly national, not Owambo, movement and to present an image of undogmatic, sweetly reasonable reconciliation, which, among other things, was SWAPO's technique for trying to defuse the harm of the detainee issue. Against that, DTA and other parties sought to undermine SWAPO, most of them, with the partial exception of UDF and NNF, concentrating more on offering such criticism than on projecting their own positive image. These parties intimated that SWAPO had some *hidden* agenda involving political repression and one-partyism (using the detainee issue again) or some radical social and economic program. DTA's actual strategy was forthrightly summarized by Dirk Mudge (*Financial Mail,* 20 October 1989) as promoting two outcomes: "democracy," not a one-party state and a mixed or market-oriented economy, not socialism. Beyond that,

DTA sought to put forward an image that was not at all precise about policy or issues (thereby saving DTA from having to answer charges about its years of sharing in government) but that was still one of a movement in power. The razzmatazz of DTA's loud campaigning emphasized its resources; its self-confidence and appeals to status—and its strong-arm methods—conjured an image of a party used to power.

## Notes

1. The promotion of a third force has become a classical measure of containing a national liberation movement ever since Harvard political scientist and U.S. adviser Samuel Huntington (1968) criticized U.S. policy in South Vietnam as one that polarized political opinion between collaborators and supporters of the liberation movement. South African repression in Namibia had certainly done that, and RSA's efforts to promote a third force were certainly belated—but not completely unsuccessful.

2. One student supporter of SWAPO talked about "a SWAPO barbecue, where this DTA guy with a DTA cap and a DTA T-shirt, had his revolver and he was just looking for any excuse to fire it" (*Action on Namibia,* October 1989). An eve-of-poll SWAPO rally at Keetmanshoop on 4 November that reported DTA supporters with *sjambok* and other weapons was fairly standard (*Action on Namibia,* January 1990).

# PART 3

# 8
# Results and Explanations

## The Results

When the final results were announced on 14 November 1989, SWAPO had obtained a comfortable majority (57.3 percent) of the valid votes cast, which would entitle it to forty-one out of the Constituent Assembly's total of seventy-two seats. This was, however, short of the two-thirds majority that would have given SWAPO control of the CA. The overall results for each party, the total votes nationally, and the seats won are presented in Table 8.1.

**Table 8.1  1989 Constituent Assembly National Results: Total Votes and Seats for Each Party**

| Party | Valid Votes[a] | % Votes | CA Seats |
|-------|------------|---------|----------|
| ACN | 23,728 | 3.5 | 3 |
| CDA | 2,495 | 0.4 | 0 |
| DTA | 191,532 | 28.6 | 21 |
| FCN | 10,452 | 1.6 | 1 |
| NNDP | 984 | 0.1 | 0 |
| NNF | 5,344 | 0.8 | 1 |
| NPF | 10,693 | 1.6 | 1 |
| SWAPO-D | 3,161 | 0.5 | 0 |
| SWAPO | 384,567 | 57.3 | 41 |
| UDF | 37,874 | 5.6 | 4 |
| TOTAL | 670,830 | 100.0 | 72 |

*Note:* a. This total does not include rejected votes.

SWAPO was the winning party in only eight of the twenty-three electoral districts, but these were the bigger districts, which included 68 percent of the registered voters. Table 8.2 gives some details for each ED, and Appendix E gives all returns. DTA was the only other sizable party, with 28.6 percent of the popular vote, entitling it to twenty-one seats—three short of the one-third of CA votes it would have required for an automatic

**Table 8.2  Percentage Vote for Main Parties by Electoral District**

| Electoral District | Total Votes Cast[a] | SWAPO Vote % | DTA Vote % | Other Party Votes > 4.5% | | | |
|---|---|---|---|---|---|---|---|
| Ovamboland | 248,171 | 92.0 | 4.4 | | | | |
| Lüderitz | 11,278 | 69.0 | 19.0 | 4.6 | ACN | | |
| Swakopmund | 24,083 | 59.0 | 24.8 | 7.3 | UDF | | |
| Tsumeb | 13,872 | 52.9 | 29.4 | | | | |
| Kavango | 61,426 | 50.0 | 40.4 | | | | |
| Windhoek | 97,134 | 45.9 | 36.0 | 7.2 | UDF | 4.9 | ACN |
| Caprivi | 27,006 | 39.6 | 52.4 | | | | |
| Okahandja | 10,380 | 35.9 | 41.3 | 11.0 | UDF | 6.5 | ANC |
| Karibib | 6,582 | 34.5 | 30.6 | 23.6 | UDF | 6.3 | ANC |
| Maltahöhe | 2,578 | 33.8 | 26.6 | 15.5 | ANC | 15.3 | UDF |
| Grootfontein | 19,602 | 33.7 | 46.3 | 8.4 | ACN | 6.9 | UDF |
| Otjiwarongo | 12,318 | 33.0 | 42.8 | 15.1 | UDF | 5.7 | ACN |
| Keetmanshoop | 19,269 | 30.0 | 48.8 | 8.0 | UDF | 7.7 | ACN |
| Damaraland | 15,225 | 27.9 | 17.1 | 52.0 | UDF | | |
| Omaruru | 5,772 | 22.5 | 52.1 | 10.4 | UDF | 5.6 | NPF |
| Mariental | 14,082 | 21.7 | 55.1 | 10.5 | ACN | 7.4 | UDF |
| Outjo | 6,904 | 17.8 | 45.6 | 21.9 | UDF | 11.3 | ACN |
| Rehoboth | 17,356 | 17.6 | 45.3 | 29.3 | FCN | | |
| Hereroland | 15,605 | 15.3 | 64.2 | 12.6 | NPF | 1.2 | NNF |
| Gobabis | 18,111 | 13.9 | 65.9 | 10.9 | ACN | | |
| Karasburg | 18,813 | 12.7 | 53.9 | 27.8 | ACN | | |
| Kaokoland | 12,794 | 10.7 | 65.5 | 19.9 | NPF | | |
| Bethanie | 2,337 | 20.1 | 57.3 | 13.1 | ACN | | |

*Note:* a. These totals include rejected votes as well as valid ones.

blocking one-third of its own. UDF, with 5.6 percent of the vote and its strong local support around Damaraland, and ACN, with 3.5 percent, were the only other parties to win more than one seat. Three other parties with a little more than, or in one case (NNF) less than, 1 percent each got a single CA seat.

In the analysis that follows, we try to offer some possible explanations for SWAPO's overall, although not overwhelming, victory and for the considerable regional variation in party support. In so doing, we use the EDs as the point of departure because these are the only subnational units for which electoral results were announced. But it would be misleading to use EDs as the sole unit of analysis as they vary so considerably in size, from Ovamboland in the north, whose quarter-million voters was a hundred times bigger than the tiny constituency in Bethanie in the far south. (For more details of EDs, see Appendix F.)

The different social and regional voting patterns can be seen more starkly if we classify the results into three more nearly equal divisions of the country along the lines indicated in Table 8.3.

**Table 8.3  Proportions of Votes in Regions of Differing SWAPO Strength**

| Type of Regional Result | No. of EDs | % of Total Votes Cast | SWAPO Vote (%) | DTA Vote (%) |
|---|---|---|---|---|
| SWAPO overwhelming (Ovamboland) | 1 | 36.5 | 92.3 | 4.4 |
| SWAPO plurality[a] | 7 | 31.9 | 49.4 | 34.2 |
| SWAPO minority[b] | 15 | 31.7 | 24.0 | 48.4 |

*Notes:* a. Karibib, Kavango, Lüderitz, Maltahöhe, Swakopmund, Tsumeb, and Windhoek.
b. Bethanie, Caprivi, Damara, Gobabis, Grootfontein, Hereroland, Kaokoland, Karasburg, Keetmanshoop, Mariental, Okahandja, Omaruru, Otjiwarongo, Rehoboth, and Outjo.

Ovamboland is a case apart, deserving separate consideration because of its size alone and because the result was so radically different from everywhere else. It showed such a majority (92 percent) of support for SWAPO that it can be considered a virtual one-party state—a pattern that is familiar in the monopoly that other ruling parties in the Southern African region enjoy in their heartlands (BDP in the central district of Botswana; ZANU-PF in the Shona-speaking provinces of Zimbabwe).

At the opposite end of the spectrum there was a range of many, mostly small EDs (the last category in Table 8.3), in all of which SWAPO's vote was 30 percent or less and in which DTA was overall the largest party. Even here what has to be recognized, and accounted for in explanations, is that the support for the main opposition is nothing as clear-cut as the more than 80 percent of the vote that Nkomo's ZAPU got in Matabeleland in Zimbabwe; over them all, DTA got only a bare majority, 50.3 percent. It is nevertheless the case that in the twenty-two EDs outside Ovamboland, which single CA delivered 70 percent of SWAPO's total vote, DTA received more votes than SWAPO: 180,787 to 158,946.

## Seeking Explanations

In prediction and explanation of the Namibian election results there has been much recourse to simple explanations in terms of ethnicity: "Of course, SWAPO is an Ovambo party," "The Herero will vote for the DTA,"

"Justus Garoeb can count on the Damara vote," "The Bushmen voted for the DTA." And this was certainly the basis for most preelection predictions by commentators and participants and indeed was probably the basis on which the parties, and before 1989 RSA and WCG, based their calculations and strategies. But as our three-way categorization in Table 8.3 immediately begins to make clear, what is striking is that, Ovamboland apart, the returns indicate mixed party support in most regions. Although party support varied regionally, there is only a very partial correlation of party support with the ethnic makeup of the local electorate.

There is a further problem in the identification of voting patterns with ethnicity: lack of evidence. Ethnicity (whether self-identified or not) was obviously not recorded with vote, and there were almost no surveys. Thus, it is impossible to make accurate calculations of which people voted for which party. It is only possible to compare the overall voting proportions for an ED with the aggregate ethnic or other demographic makeup of the population of that area. The only source of these latter data is the 1981 census. These data are thought to be quite inaccurate (as information was simply taken from local official records rather than from household inquiries) but, as discussed in Chapter 4, they stand as the solitary source of national demographic data. Analysis using the *proportions* of different social categories of the population within regions hopefully cuts down the errors of using absolute numbers, and even though census districts were slightly different from electoral districts, it is possible to deduce social profiles of areas based on ethnic classification and occupation. The census does underline the fact that the ethnic makeup of most districts is mixed, especially in towns and in areas of commercial farming. As few districts are ethnically homogeneous, a simple ethnic bloc analysis is not possible for an ED as a whole.

Nor does the evidence exist to see whether party support in EDs with localities occupied by distinct ethnic groups (for instance, the three tribes in different parts of Caprivi, the small Herero reserves included in Damaraland or Gobabis, or the Nama area that became part of Keetmanshoop) does correlate with these distinct areas. Counting was done separately for each polling station, but those figures that would have made possible such calculation were never released. We did, however, manage to obtain some of these results, from twenty-nine polling stations out of an estimated seventy, in Kavango. Although that ED was one of the most ethnically homogeneous (more than 80 percent Kavango), it might have been expected to reveal another kind of ethnicity, that of a clan or chiefdom, or at least the influence of patronage. The district is made up of four chiefdoms, and it was widely expected that the westernmost of these, Kwangali, whose chief was thought to be pro-SWAPO, would vote SWAPO and that the other areas would be DTA strongholds. The available figures for the polling stations, while showing some geographical distinction in voting (roughly 60 percent SWAPO west of Rundu Town, a little more 50 percent around the town, and about 40 percent immediately to the east), the differences are only marginal. Both parties commanded significant support across all the polling stations, with only one exception (the smallest) with an overwhelming vote for one party.

Using the census data to interpret ethnic analyses of voting patterns is, however, more reliable than trying to uncover divisions along gender lines. Although in some parts of the country we might expect considerable demographic imbalances in terms of gender as a result of male labor migration from rural areas, and therefore it would be desirable to examine the results with this in mind, we cannot do so from the census report because any imbalance between the presence of adult men and women is masked by the presence of children in the totals. (Children are likely to belong to the same ethnic group as their parents and so do not distort the ethnic percentages to the same extent as those of gender.)

To the extent that there is any correlation between an area and party support, as in Ovamboland, applying the simple label *ethnicity* to the voting pattern is not in itself an explanation: it is the correlation that itself needs to be explained. If the majority of Herero voted for DTA, or the Owambo overwhelmingly for SWAPO, why was that so? To put it down to some automatic ethnic identity is to offer what has to be explained as itself the cause.

In part ethnic voting patterns could be seen as a legacy of political practices and structures already established by the South African administration, which created tribal structures, set up second-tier authorities, and supported the tribal DTA alliance (see Chapter 2). As a consequence, "open" politics in Namibia over the previous twenty years had centered around patron-client relationships channeling often misappropriated funds from the second-tier authorities (Thirion, 1985). As was seen in Chapter 2, elections held during the colonial period were accompanied by intimidation and patronage channeled through the same ethnic structures of authority. Many observers supposed that the use of similar techniques in the independence elections would promote results reflecting the party political allegiances of ethnic leaders, and so prediction and, to some extent, analysis after the event took the form of "reading off" regional results from the political hues of socially dominant individuals and groups, whether chiefs, well-known political leaders, or employers.

A further complication in trying to estimate any ethnic factor is that it figured differentially in the public stances of the main contenders. DTA's constituent elements and other, small parties did make explicit calls to a local ethnic identity and certainly built more systematically on patronage networks than SWAPO, which had always articulated a conscious, pan-Namibian nationalism and condemned tribalism. Both main contenders had a broad leadership covering all ethnic groups, but DTA had built up its leaders by an alliance of tribal barons, whereas SWAPO's leaders came from all areas and tried, at least in their public stance, to transcend an ethnic identity. The matter of the role of ethnicity in Namibian nationalism was thus one of those items of difference about alternative futures at issue between the two sides (Dollie, 1989). A further implication of this particular area of contestation is that the extent to which party support followed any discernible ethnic pattern would be a measure of the success of the DTA/RSA conception of nationalism as opposed to SWAPO's "nation-statism." It is thus ironic that the only clear-cut such pattern was the overwhelming Owambo support for SWAPO.

Where intimidation and patronage or some other mechanism for exerting ethnic bloc voting (whether as a deterrent against voting or an encouragement to vote a certain way) was thought to have been minimal in its occurrence and effect, some other sets of explanation have to be found for the preponderance of ethnic groups voting en bloc for one or other party. One possible answer may simply be that ethnicity roughly coincides with some other category, such as class: for example, those Owambo people resident in the southern and central parts of Namibia constitute a large proportion of the industrial working class, and it may be that the explanation for their voting for SWAPO in those areas is because of their shared interests as workers rather than as Owambo per se.

Another standard approach to analyzing election results is to look for correlations between political consciousness and actual voting behavior, on the one hand, and the social and economic profile of the electorate (rather than its ethnic or demographic composition), on the other hand. We have already discussed the difficulties in establishing anything other than quite superficial social profiles of EDs, and estimations of political consciousness remain very speculative, but even after the event these are difficult to interweave with actual voting patterns. In other circumstances opinion polls would be conducted during election campaigns and exit polls during voting. We concluded that both these methods were impractical and unreliable for this election: impractical in that the atmosphere of intimidation and fear, especially in the north of the country, was not conducive to conducting opinion polls and unreliable in that for the same reasons people would be unlikely to give straight answers that they perceived as unexpected or undesirable to the enumerator. Thus, we have to try an analysis by deduction—which at least eliminates those hypotheses that do *not* fit the facts and identifies those that it remains possible to square with the facts—and then speculate as to what were the likely reasons for such patterns. Perhaps it is true to say that one can never really be sure why any one person votes in a certain way, but under circumstances that would have allowed surveys, one could have deduced what issues were probably important to voters. We attempt a rough approximation of the factors that could have determined outcomes for each region in Appendix E. Here we limit analysis to examining the vote for each party to determine what has to be explained and to offer some possible explanatory hypotheses.

## The Bases of Party Support

In thus reviewing the detailed geographical spread of results for each party, we deal with them in groups. There are four: (1) those that failed to win a CA seat (CDA, NNDP, and SWAPO-D), those that won only one seat (FCN, NNF, and NPF), those that won a handful (UDF and ACN), and the main contenders (DTA and SWAPO).

### The Failures

Three parties—SWAPO-D (3,161), CDA (2,495), and NNDP (984)—among them got less than 1 percent of the national vote and can be dealt with summarily. None of the three could command even any small pockets of local support. As can be seen from detailed figures in Appendix E, only in one ED did any of these parties manage to acquire slightly more than 1 percent of the vote—CDA had 1.4 percent in tiny Bethanie. Clearly, then, their positions, their leaders, and their organizations had no basis for appeal to voters, for ethnic or other identity with them, or for even the prospect of patronage. What has to be explained is not the votes they received but why they were so unsuccessful.

It is perhaps relevant to note they were, apart from SWAPO, the only three single parties, rather than alliances, to contest the elections. Moreover, each of them could be seen as something of a vehicle for a personality with long political credentials (see Chapter 7). Andreas Shipanga (SWAPO-D) and Paul Helmuth (NNDP) had been involved in the early days of SWAPO and then had left the organization to return to Namibia. Both had eventually taken part in the transitional interim government but had not built up any local political base through the ethnic administrations. Peter Kalangula of CDA had such a base in the Ovamboland administration, which he led in the 1980s. Having split from DTA and distanced himself from government policies, this was not enough for him to retain even token support in the wake of the near monopoly of support for SWAPO in Ovamboland. The strength of this avalanche also left Shipanga, himself from the area, with only a handful of votes scattered throughout the country.

### The Single-Seat Parties

Three fronts—FCN, NPF, and NNF—managed to secure one CA seat, the latter only by benefit of the remainder formula (see Appendix C), which pulled it over the minimum, despite its total being below the quota for a seat. Between them they polled only 26,489 votes, 4 percent of the total, so any explanation does not have to uncover major bases of support. In regional and perhaps social terms, the pattern of such support as they did enjoy differed. FCN and NPF both received a significant minority of their votes in one area of the country, whereas NNF picked up a few votes across most of the country with no area significant. Each of the three parties got a share of the vote in a big ED such as Windhoek at least as big as their national share, but they got a negligible proportion in the heavily populated three northern EDs. The details of their votes and the percentage for each ED are given in Appendix E, but the specific patterns of their support can be summarized as follows:

1. FCN had espoused some devolution of central powers and espoused some group rights and had brought together groups from several areas (see Chapter 7). In the event, it secured almost half of its 10,542 from Rehoboth, where it polled almost 30 percent of all votes. Only in four other small EDs toward the south of the country did it manage to secure 2 percent of the vote or more. Its significance was thus confined principally to the Rehoboth Baster, where it was still simply the main opposition party among them. Issues of decentralized or federal structures clearly did not appeal to any significant numbers of black voters. (For the significance of the issues among white voters, see the analysis of ACN later in this chapter.)

2. NFP got significant shares of the total vote in only two, both Herero-speaking EDs, Hereroland (12.6 percent), where it had third place, and Kaokoland (19.9 percent), where it beat SWAPO into third place (see Table 8.2). These two districts contributed 41.3 percent of the front's national vote, so to that extent it could be said to have gleaned support far more from Herero speakers than others. However, in no sense was NPF a Herero party: it gained only minority support in those areas and did manage to get a few hundred votes from each of a number of EDs, mainly in the center and east of the country and in Windhoek. This broader sprinkling of support was what gave NFP a seat and could be explained in terms of Herero speakers in these other areas or a legacy of old SWANU support.

3. NNF was also expected to get support in Hereroland, but although its share there (4.6 percent) was higher than in other EDs, it received small proportions of 1–2 percent of the vote throughout much of the country but was never even in third place in any ED. If anything, NNF had slightly higher shares in towns, including Windhoek. This would be consistent with the inclusion in this alliance of some sophisticated, left political groups of teachers and professionals.

*The Handful-of-Seats Parties*

*UDF.* UDF's most obvious success was in Damaraland, where it gained an absolute majority of all votes—the only case where a minor party got more than 50 percent in any ED. This vote confirmed the local strength of its main constituent party, the Damara Council, and on its own that area guaranteed one seat in the CA. However, the ED included Arandis, the dormitory township for the Rossing uranium mine. The UNTAG office and senior local officials of both UDF and SWAPO (interviews, 1 and 2 November 1989) all agreed that UDF had made very few inroads there into what they all anticipated was SWAPO's overwhelming support among the estimated forty-five hundred registered mineworkers and their families, who were assumed to be mainly Owambo (although the 1981 census suggests that there were then as many Damara, but there could have been significant changes in the intervening years because in the 1980s the workers there were settled and made nonmigrants). There is another significant non-Damara minority (12 percent in 1981) in the district, in a Herero-speaking enclave—perhaps the source of DTA's small share, although we have no circumstantial evidence for this ethnic assumption. If that was the case, then UDF must have commanded a very high proportion of the two-thirds of the ED population who were Damara. Damaraland still provided only 20.7 percent of the total UDF vote and guaranteed only one seat in the CA, so without significant support elsewhere, the party would not have won its further three seats.

Some of the rest of UDF's support was regional: in five EDs close to Damaraland (Karibib, Okahandja, Omaruru, Otjiwarongo, and Outjo), UDF's share of the vote was between 10 percent and 24 percent, and these small EDs provided it with 17.4 percent of its total vote, almost enough for another seat. It seems likely that the vote in these areas in the center of the country came from Damara people, although in each of these other EDs, the UDF share of the poll was about half the percentage of Damara people recorded as resident in the 1981 census.

The significant vote UDF received in other parts of the country, notably in Windhoek and other towns and even in Ovamboland, where it was the only minor party to gain a significant vote, is more difficult to correlate with the ethnic composition of the population. UDF's share of the vote in these areas could correspond to the proportion of Damara speakers (although the party's share was always significantly lower than their proportion of population) or represent small minorities backing the groups raising the SWAPO detainees issue or those socialists mobilized by the explicitly left-wing parties within UDF.

*ACN.* The ACN alliance stood on a platform of preserving the rights of the white communities and of "maintaining standards." The presumption must be that its 23,728 votes came overwhelmingly from whites. This is seemingly confirmed by the fact that it got less than 1 percent of the votes in all those EDs made up of reserves. Its highest share of the vote by far was in Karasburg, the border ED where so many South Africans voted. There was an apparent geographical pattern to ACN support between north and south. In the EDs in the northern towns, farms, and mining areas, ACN's share of the vote was in almost all cases considerably less than 10 percent, a figure that represents, on the basis of the 1981 census figures, usually about one-fifth to one-quarter of the proportion of the estimated white voters in the total electorate. In the farming EDs of the south, including Gobabis, in contrast, the ACN share was more than 10 percent, which represented a higher proportion of the white electorate, in these areas more than one-half. These figures are only indicative because the white population has been falling as a share since 1981, but there does seem to be some basis for concluding that southern white voters were more inclined than those in the north to vote ACN—or else they more successfully pressured their farm laborers to do so.

*The Main Contenders*

*SWAPO.* SWAPO's strength was overwhelmingly in Ovamboland, which alone contributed 57.8 percent of its vote and where its appeal successfully reached all areas, social strata, and classes. Kavango was another area of large support, where SWAPO got more than 50 percent. But SWAPO's more mixed success there perhaps reflected a rather more complex political history during the colonial period and the war. SWAPO also got majority support in centers of organized labor, the mines, and the major towns. Counting these latter workers and migrants, a very large proportion of Owambo obviously did vote for SWAPO, but over the whole country significant proportions of people of other ethnic groups did, too. SWAPO's appeal was, however, much less nationwide than it had anticipated.

What first has to be explained is the extent of this SWAPO vote in Ovamboland and among Owambo. Why did no significant section of the population vote against the party? Clearly its origins among Owambo and among migrant workers were not seriously challenged. The area's proximity to the fighting throughout the 1970s and 1980s and its supply of recruits from among peasants, workers, and school students reinforced these linkages with the movement. Support for the party even before 1989 seems to have been strong among educated youth, teachers, and the churches. The possible identification of these and other professionals with either the Bantu administration or the transitional government may have been reduced because the provision of instruction in English in the region's schools, unlike other areas, may have excluded them from preferment in local and national administrations that used Afrikaans. It is also evident that the several large entrepreneurs and many hundreds of small traders, shopkeepers, and barkeepers also backed the party, even though they had prospered from a local economy fueled by the presence of SADF, SWATF, and counterinsurgents. Moreover, it is clear that the party must even have got the votes of some of those who were directly benefiting from the exist-

ing structures—members of ethnic battalions and Koevoet, local administration employees, and their dependents.

An ethnic explanation has been put forward to explain not only the
Owambo result but also SWAPO's getting more than 50 percent in the
main towns Lüderitz, Swakopmund (including people from Walvis Bay),
and Tsumeb and almost 46 percent in Windhoek. No survey data allow us
to say whether Owambo migrants and workers voted SWAPO in the same
large proportion. But a comparison of proportions of votes with the census
population in these EDs suggests that workers in the mines and in fishing
from other ethnic backgrounds also gave strong support to SWAPO.
Subjective evidence suggests how the mechanisms of this tendency for
class identification with SWAPO may have worked themselves out. In
Arandis, the miners' township for Rossing Uranium and part of
Damaraland ED, a leader of the Mineworkers Union (interview, Arandis, 1
November 1989) explained how the local branch had debated which party
to back. Some consideration was given to smaller parties (NPF, NNF, and
WRP) with a progressive, proworkers platform, but their records were not
considered to be strong enough to provide a solid alternative to SWAPO,
which was seen as likely to deliver most for workers in future. As a reaction, some seventy-five members, mostly Damara, he said, resigned from
the union. This is some indicative evidence, then, of a workers' bloc vote
for SWAPO marginally qualified by ethnic loyalties.

Kavango was the other large area where SWAPO won 50 percent. Its
involvement in the war after the 1970s was not as direct as in Ovamboland,
but its support among youth, teaching, and church seemed to have been a
partially effective counter to the patronage politics and widespread intimidation by Koevoet. In Caprivi, another border reserve, against the predictions, SWAPO also got a significant share, even though this was the DTA
president's home base. Elsewhere in the country, SWAPO was not majority
party, but everywhere it got significant proportions. In the central, commercial farming areas, it got roughly one-third of the vote and in some of them
was indeed the largest single party. But it got less than one-quarter in the
south and in the Herero-speaking areas.

These proportions in the south and center certainly undercut SWAPO's
claim to represent the nation and were a poorer result than SWAPO expected. Thus, for instance, a party organizer in Keetmanshoop reckoned that
SWAPO would get two-thirds of the vote—"despite the detainees issue"
(interview, 28 October 1989). There are two kinds of explanation for the
performance in these areas. Apologists stress the lack of any preexisting
party infrastructure and the difficulty in a short period of building it up sufficiently to challenge built-in patron-client patterns. An alternative perspective (e.g., Susan Brown, personal communication, June 1990) suggests that
SWAPO actually *lost* popular support in the months leading up to the elec-

tions. If valid, such an actual trend would undermine the first explanation. Of course, statistical evidence of any such trend is not available, but there are some straws in the wind that do indicate a swing away from SWAPO in 1989. Some commentators point to a below-par attendance by some Nama in 1989 at the annual memorial of the struggle against the Germans led by the ancestor of SWAPO's internal leader, Henrik Witbooi. He himself (interview, 28 October 1989) thought that, while justifying detention as necessary in war, the issue and the way it was taken advantage of in ethnic terms by opposition parties would cost SWAPO what he otherwise estimated would have been a two-thirds majority nationally.

Another contributory factor that might explain why SWAPO managed to get only a significant minority in many central and southern areas was hinted at by one of the party's regional election directors, who admitted (interview, 23 October 1989) that SWAPO had "little to offer the poorest" of the rural population in Hereroland. This statement not only implied SWAPO's support was among the town population, those who were schooled and professionals, but also pointed to a policy failure of being unable to articulate a land or resource distribution or other income-generating formula that would benefit farm laborers and peasants.

*DTA.* DTA scored highest in the south of the country, in other farming areas, and in Hereroland and Kaokoland. But nowhere did DTA reach as much as 66 percent of the vote; in all areas its vote was shared. It is equally true that in only three EDs, two of them being Lüderitz and Damaraland, did it get less than one-quarter of the vote. One set of explanations is that DTA's support built upon the patronage of local affiliated parties that had access to the resources of second-tier administrations, plus the backing of a majority of whites, farmworkers, and residents from Angola and South Africa. But it also has to be recognized that DTA's support extended beyond these elements with a direct interest in the status quo. It is hard to calculate numbers, but the manipulation of the detainee issue probably did lead many to calculate that DTA was the only viable alternative to dominance by a single party with a questionable record of repression. The alliance may also have benefited from its image as a party of resources that could deliver.

DTA's one great failure was in Ovamboland. Its own estimates of support there were modest enough (Basson suggested 7 percent), but it gained only 4.4 percent. An estimate of those employed in the administration there (although many were teachers) plus ethnic battalion and Koevoet personnel, let alone their adult dependents, was far more (perhaps fifteen thousand) than the vote of a little more than ten thousand that DTA received. Moreover, these figures suggest that the widespread campaign there of intimidation must have failed to deliver votes, even if it prevented registration, and may have been counterproductive. However, the same conclusion cannot be assumed for Kavango and other areas where intimidation was common.

## Conclusion: Implications for the Future of Parties

One lesson that can be taken from an analysis of the election successes and failures is that in future Namibian elections any party that simply seeks to build support by appeals through community leaders or appeals to ethnic labels is unlikely to be sufficiently successful. The electorate in 1989 demonstrated a greater degree of political sophistication in using democratic procedures. Given the limited explanation of simple ethnic or local community loyalty or patronage, it is hard to escape the conclusion that significant numbers of Namibians came to differing conclusions about the parties and what they stood for and made fine distinctions on some of the issues presented to them. Class, too, can offer only some partial explanations, particularly among workers, but their identification with SWAPO may not be everlasting (see Chapter 9).

What appealed to the electorate about the different parties' programs varied in different regions, as did the programs themselves to some extent. If actual political demands and perceptions vary regionally, as is implied here, the possibility of a truly national party representing the electorate uniformly over the whole country (which is what SWAPO had previously claimed to be) is undermined. This is not unusual in a democracy (examples can be cited in Europe as well as the Third World). Ruling parties may then calculate the cost of losing regional support as a result of the adoption of a certain policy mix in terms of absolute numbers of voters rather than regional balance per se. Thus, in the future SWAPO will have to reorient itself to generate a more widespread appeal while also meeting the demands of its supporters in Ovamboland and among workers. DTA will have to go beyond an alliance of patrons, in a context where it cannot dispense local authority largesse, and develop policy positions and direct appeals to the interests of some voters.

# 9

# The Transition to Independence

The elections to the Constituent Assembly and its deliberations settled two dimensions of the formal business of the transition from South African rule: they defined the institutional structures that would provide the legal basis of the new state, and they constituted the new parliament and installed the majority party, SWAPO, as the new government. The story of how the CA conducted its deliberations and their outcome are discussed at some length in the next section. However, there were many other matters of transition set in motion in the period from November 1989 to independence day, 21 March 1990, even if they were not irrevocably settled during the life of CA. These included the formation of the broader governmental structures, not only the appointment of ministers and composition of the cabinet but also the whole makeup of the civil service, and the reconstitution of security forces after the long war.

The short-term dynamics within the whole body politic—its mood, aspirations, and actions—at the moment when the dust of fighting and of tough electioneering began to settle and the handling of the sensitive issues of security and public confidence by the new authorities were a second, critical dimension to the transition. A third and related area of significant evolution was the process of defining the policies and programs of the new order. In one sense SWAPO had begun the definition of its own stance in the preparation of policy documents, often through the UN Institute for Namibia, that took place in exile beginning in the late 1970s; SWAPO then actively reshaped its platform (details of which were provided in Chapter 7) during 1989 as it made a bid for support not only from the electorate but also from international opinion, particularly Western governments, prospective aid donors, and international business. This task of definition intensified during the CA period once it became clear SWAPO would be in power and of course continued into the first months of the newly independent state. But policies were shaped not just by SWAPO's pronouncements but also by initiatives, some of them intended to be preemptive, by the outgoing administration; other entrenched interests, especially among whites; and pressure groups.

The election results sparked off another new process: the reshaping of the political parties themselves. SWAPO had only been able hurriedly and incompletely to transform itself from a largely exile movement of struggle into a political party. How would it continue this task, and how would it react to finding that it had overwhelming support in only one area of the country? And what would the other parties do? Would DTA be able to build on its significant minority vote and on its position as the official opposition, and would it change its traditional patronage basis to do so? Would the myriad small parties and the tactical alliances built up quickly for the election and artificially sustained by outside money have a continued viable existence? What patterns of fission and fusion would get under way?

A final dimension of this reshaping concerned Namibia's relations with the surrounding countries. Just as Namibia's fate over the previous two decades had been shaped, as we argued in Chapter 3, by forces at work and evolutions occurring in South Africa and the conflicts in Angola, and less directly by African governments, so the transition in Namibia allowed new relationships in Southern Africa to be drawn. How would an independent Namibia attempt to redefine its economic and political links with South Africa, and to what extent would there be options given the extreme economic dependence? How would Namibia's position and its internal dynamic be influenced by the process of democratizing apartheid going on in South Africa? Namibia was linked with South Africa in many ways, most obviously in terms of a common currency and involvement in a common market, but now the prospect was held out of a reorientation through involvement with the independent countries of the Southern African Development Coordination Conference. What difference would this opportunity make to Namibia (see Oden, 1991)? And, more generally, how would Namibia's changed situation affect other relationships in the region? Would it herald an overall peace? Would it facilitate an overall rapprochement with South Africa?

Discussion of the new prospects for an independent Namibia in its dealings with its neighbors is but one aspect of the changing regional relationships. There were new options, perhaps, for some of these surrounding countries. Would Angola, whose people had borne so much, in part in the cause of Namibia's freedom, now attain peace at last? Would South Africa's withdrawal from Namibia back into its own borders herald the end of the republic's tactics of destabilization toward the region as a whole? Most crucially, what would Namibia's independence mean for the struggle for freedom inside South Africa? Would it give heart to the forces of black liberation? From the ruling National Party's perspective, did its tactics in Namibia offer a blueprint for managing the transfer of power inside South Africa itself?

These several questions about government structures, the political climate in the transition, the definition of policies, the flux within and between parties, and the broader regional patterns were certainly posed during the months up to independence, even though they were by no means settled. We do not seek to extend the story much into this new, postinde-pendence era, but it still seems worthwhile to outline the early stages of the processes at work, if only to isolate what will be at issue as these arenas of flux and struggle are shaped in the years ahead.

## The Constituent Assembly

### The Formation of the Constitutent Assembly

The attempts by the AG to make CA subordinate to him were noted in Chapter 6. He only agreed to the UNSGSR's insistence that the UN plan intended that CA have complete freedom "to formulate and adopt a consti-tution" on the day before elections. But this freedom meant that there was no specified formula for the CA's procedures and method of ratification, except for the accepted principle that a two-thirds majority be necessary. When the Constituent Assembly met for the first time on 21 November 1989, SWAPO was in the driver's seat even without the forty-eight seats needed to vote its own constitution, for it was agreed that only the final vote on the draft constitution as a whole would require two-thirds. Each separate article and clause, however, and decisions about procedures could be passed by a simple majority vote. Hage Geingob of SWAPO was elected chair by a vote of forty seven to twenty-four (with one abstention), and SWAPO's Sephaniah Kameeta opened the first session with a prayer. But even with this auspicious start, there was much speculation about what would happen. SWAPO alone could not write its own constitution, so what coalitions and alliances would be forged? Would the parties opposing SWAPO make common cause? Would they adopt delaying tactics? Or would they prove accommodating in order to hasten the independence process? Would there be a blocking one-third by DTA and ACN arguably representing white interests, with twenty-four votes between them and only one more needed to effectively have a veto? And what kinds of deals would be struck over what kinds of issues? Would the smaller parties use their weight to bargain for specific concessions? Would the entrenched protec-tion of property rights, especially land, become a contentious issue, as in Zimbabwe? What about provision for human rights and political pluralism? Would there be a rearguard action over group rights?

One potential issue was whether all CA members would feel bound by the 1982 constitutional principles that had been brokered by WCG, for many could claim they had not been a party to them and that anyway these principles restricted the sovereignty of CA and of the Namibian people. However, this would have been difficult as they were formally communi-cated to CA by the UNSGSR. At the outset SWAPO took a conciliatory tone, however: Theo-Ben Gurirab formally proposed the incorporation of the 1982 constitutional principles, a proposal that was adopted to resounding applause. These 1982 principles laid down ground rules for a multiparty democracy with regular elections by secret ballot, an independent judiciary, and a declaration of fundamental human rights, including recognition of property rights. The reassertion of these principles laid to rest the specter of a one-party state that had worried some of SWAPO's opponents.

In general, agreement came about quickly, and there was little sign of old animosities. All parties seemed more anxious to get on with the business of running their own country without the South Africans than giving lengthy consideration to the principles that would govern political life in the long run. SWAPO in particular seemed extremely impatient to complete the transition and take up the reins of power; one comment from a senior official in an interview (January 1989) suggested SWAPO senior officials were keen to secure a salary source. The widespread knowledge of this impatience reduced their bargaining strength in CA and its standing committee proceedings.

The daily drama of the Constituent Assembly kept observers in the public gallery riveted, watching the drama unfolding between the SWAPO veterans and those they had termed *South African puppets*. SWAPO supporters were delighted to see their leaders in power, with a front row of founding members: Sam Nujoma himself, then Hendrik Witbooi, David Merero, Herman Toivo Ya Toivo, Peter Mueshihange, Moses Garoeb, Lukas Pohamba. Most of this senior leadership sat quietly, leaving others to do the talking. The lawyers, Tjiriange and Hartmut Ruppel, were frequently on their feet, as might be expected, and younger, academically trained politicians such as Hamutenya and Gurirab made substantial contributions. Nahas Angula, nominated minister of education, was keen to get things moving, impatient with the "speechifiers" and often making points of order. Four of the five women members were SWAPO representatives, but only two took part in debate: Pendukene Ithana and Dr. Libertine Amathila, who did both make several contributions.

On the DTA side, Barney Barnes, who had caused trouble at Lüderitz during the election campaigning by making inflammatory speeches, seemed determined to remain in the limelight and often rose to his feet to reprimand SWAPO members for not observing petty rules, such as bowing to the chair on leaving the room or wearing appropriate dress. Next to him in the back row were three silent chiefs: Kgosimang of the Tswana, Majavero from Kavango, and Kashe of the Bushman Alliance. In the front row, too, there were silent tribal leaders, token representatives of the alliance, and it was Dirk Mudge who was the chief DTA spokesperson, frequently on his feet to ask for clarification, to make points of order, and to point out errors in the draft. Mishake Muyongo, who had become president of the DTA just before the election, sat impassively next to Mudge without speaking, except to make the set speeches required at key stages: introducing the DTA constitution, asking for a public debate on constitutional principles, and finally accepting the constitution formally. The old, longtime exile politician Fanuel Kozonguizi of NUDO, part of DTA, amazed everyone by recounting the story of his life when he was supposedly discussing the preamble to the constitution, claiming to be better acquainted with SWAPO than with members of his own party. He even called into question the advantages of democracy and suggested that there was nothing wrong with a one-party state. SWANU president Moses Katjiuongua was determined to make the presence of NPF felt, even though he was its only representative, and he was constantly on his feet for one reason or another, making suggestions, objections, or observations. Vekuii Rukoro of NNF was also the only representative of his party; as the only non-SWAPO lawyer in the assembly he made significant contributions on many occasions. SWAPO later offered him the post of deputy minister of justice, which he accepted.

All seven parties represented in the Constituent Assembly formally presented constitutions, but there was no public debate on constitutional principles, as proposed and argued for on the first day by the DTA vice-president, Mishake Muyongo. The task of sorting out areas of agreement and disagreement in these various drafts was given to the Standing Committee on Rules and Orders, composed of representatives from all the parties, which met constantly and in camera during December and early January. Thus, although the meetings of the Constituent Assembly were public, the real work of the assembly, the actual drafting of the constitution, was done in committee, so that the public could only guess at the nature of discussions leading to the final draft or rely on secondhand accounts gained from committee members. The minutes of the committee were available to the party representatives but not to all party members, and they were considered to be too confidential even to be given to the lawyers appointed to advise on the draft constitution (minutes, 18 December 1989). (However, this book has been valuably informed by access to these minutes from one of the parties anxious for the record to be available to posterity.)

The *Windhoek Observer* echoed other media in drawing attention to the secret nature of the constitutional negotiations, taking place "behind closed doors" instead of being publicly debated, and suggested that keeping negotiations secret "seems to be in the interests of the political parties who would rather not be seen 'wheeling and dealing' with the interests of their voters" (*Windhoek Observer,* 16 December 1989). In particular, the *Observer* saw such secrecy as being in SWAPO's interests. *The Namibian,* generally pro-SWAPO, also commented on the secret proceedings of the committee and in January leaked a copy of the draft constitution, to the annoyance and consternation of committee members (*The Namibian,* 9 January 1990).

*The Standing Committee*

The Standing Committee on Rules and Orders unanimously agreed to use SWAPO's constitutional proposals as the "working document" and "basis for deliberations," although other constitutions were considered during debates, particularly in areas where the SWAPO constitution was thought lacking, as in the provision for a second legislative chamber. It was decided to call upon South African lawyers to assist in the drawing up of the draft constitution over the Christmas recess and to give advice in the final stages of discussion over legal terminology and constitutional practice. Lawyers from Zimbabwe were standing by ready to offer their services, and so were lawyers from Germany and the United States. Existing Namibian law was based on Roman-Dutch law, in which the South African lawyers were experts, went the justification, but there was clearly an argument for calling upon lawyers conversant internationally with constitutional law and practice. It has been suggested that SWAPO was wary of advice from Zimbabwe, but in many ways SWAPO was being forced back on South African goodwill because of uncertainty about aid from abroad, which it was feared would go to Eastern Europe rather than Namibia. F. W. de Klerk's release of Mandela and reformist promises also made it possible for SWAPO to take a less hard-line attitude toward South Africa. In fact, Pienaar was expecting to be asked to draft the final document, but this suggestion was firmly rejected, the final drafting being in the hands of Advocate Chakalson representing SWAPO, Advocate Wiechers representing DTA, and Advocate Erasmus representing all the other parties together. This turn to South Africa can also be seen as a sign that SWAPO wished to maintain links with progressive groups in South Africa, seeing Namibia's future as firmly linked with that of South Africa.

The minutes of the standing committee make interesting reading. The outcome of the debates there resulted in significant changes from the SWAPO draft of 4 December, changes made with unanimous agreement:

1. There would be a list system of voting in future elections, as in the independence elections. SWAPO had wanted single-member constituencies. There was no argument over this because on the first day of discussion Hidipo Hamutenya announced, "We are not fighting on the question of proportional representation. We are prepared to agree to your proposals" (minutes, 8 December 1989). The list system had in any case been to SWAPO's advantage: if there had been a winner-take-all constituency system, then DTA could have won more seats in the election. Of course, we can assume that SWAPO would have radically changed the constituencies from the present EDs, for it was absurd that the whole of Owambo should have been taken as one electoral district. However, it was clear that SWAPO was pre-

pared to begin by appearing to make some kind of concession on this matter, no doubt in the expectation of thereby gaining some reciprocal concession on a matter of more importance. But whether to SWAPO's advantage or not, another possible effect of this decision on future patterns of Namibian politics can be discerned. Not only would a PR system allow votes for SWAPO, or any other party, in areas where it had only a minority to count toward its aggregate national representation; this system would also arguably remove some of the preconditions that would generate a regional, clientelist type of politicking between and even within parties. National leaderships would not be so dependent on local barons who could deliver the vote in their constituencies.

2. The Bill of Fundamental Human Rights had been expanded and tightened, but there was still provision for preventive detention. Indeed, this was not a matter for any significant discussion by any party during the meetings of the standing committee. However, groups both inside Namibia and internationally made representation to the committee and to the chair of the Constituent Assembly on this matter.

3. The death penalty would be abolished.

4. The role of the executive president would be limited and constrained. This had been debated at length in the standing committee, Mudge declaring at the beginning of discussion, "If we didn't have any reservations before, Mr Botha gave us all reason to be concerned about an executive president" (minutes, 8 December 1989). SWAPO, however, with Sam Nujomo in mind as first president, saw the role of president in an idealized way: "For us the President of the Republic should be seen as a father figure, as a symbol of the authority of the nation and that is why we go ahead and provide that he be elected by all those who are qualified to participate in the vote" (minutes, 8 December 1989). SWAPO broadly got its way on this matter despite DTA opposition to an executive presidency; the only concession made was to limit a future president to two terms.

5. Government ministers would be appointed from among members of the National Assembly.

6. Trade union rights would be included, but not in the Bill of Fundamental Human Rights as the trade unions had wanted.

7. SWAPO had agreed to the establishment of a second chamber with power to review and delay legislation as part of a trade-off whereby its proposal for an executive presidency (opposed by DTA) was accepted. Members of this National Council would be chosen by representatives at regional and local levels. There had been hard bargaining over this issue in the standing committee, which nearly brought proceedings to a standstill, some SWAPO members adamantly refusing to give way. In the end reconciliatory moves were made by Theo-Ben Gurirab and Hidipo Hamutenya, which brought acceptance of the second chamber in principle before the Christmas recess (minutes, 18 and 19 December 1989).

It was interesting to see that DTA, although anxious to be seen as the official opposition, was not interested in blocking SWAPO's every move. Dirk Mudge declared clearly, "As I see it we will not have any difficulty in agreeing on a constitution, but . . . we might disagree more when we come to government policy" (minutes, 8 December 1989). On some key issues, such as preventive detention, the DTA leadership did not speak out; neither did the small parties, such as UDF and NNF. SWAPO's lawyer, Ruppel, exclaimed in astonishment during one of the early sessions at which it had been agreed to marry the DTA and SWAPO clauses concerning the right to a fair trial: "Marry to DTA ! Who would have thought that we would marry the DTA!" (minutes, 8 December 1989).

When the Constituent Assembly met again on 25 January 1990 to receive the draft constitution and to proceed to public debate at last, considerable agreement had been reached. Some matters continued to be wrangled over in public, particularly the question of presidential powers, and other matters assumed an importance that had not surfaced in the meeting of the committee, especially the crucial matter of preventive detention. We now consider some of the issues and debates that proved controversial in more detail, as they were debated and discussed in both the standing committee and in the public arena of the Constituent Assembly.

*Issues and Debates*

*Land and Property Rights.*  In the preelection period white farmers had been worried that they would lose their farms or at the very least be required to give up some of their land, but SWAPO showed no sign of being interested in any kind of major land redistribution, as has already been noted (Chapter 2). SWAPO did say, however, that absentee landlords would not be tolerated. But of course there was a latent fear that SWAPO would pursue the land issue now that the election was over. The only party that campaigned systematically on the land issue was NNF, and its showing in the election was very disappointing, although it claimed that during campaigning there had been great interest in the land issue.

On the eve of the election "there was a massive flight of capital" from Namibia (local banker, quoted in *The Namibian*, 20 December 1989), and it was estimated that at least R 70 million were switched out of the country. Most of that trickled back after the election result was known and it was clear that SWAPO did not have carte blanche but would have to make compromises to get the two-thirds majority needed to pass the constitution. Nevertheless, this capital flow underlined the short-term context within which the issue of property would have to be faced. Abel Gower, director of Consolidated Diamond Mines, put the problem that businesspeople were asking themselves succinctly: "The key question is how SWAPO will balance its ideological stance against the need for a prosperous country" (*The Namibian*, 20 December 1989).

It was soon clear that SWAPO did not intend to do anything in a hurry that would frighten white farmers and business interests out of the country, although there were indications that the heavy subsidies to white farmers would cease. On 21 November Ben Amathila stated clearly, "We do not intend to interfere with land ownership as set out at present" (*The Namibian*, 21 November 1989).

It was interesting that land and property rights were never the subject of public debate, as if there was common agreement by all political parties to avoid this sensitive issue. However, in the closed meeting of the standing committee this matter was discussed heatedly and frankly, although it seems to have been tacitly agreed that such issues were not to be taken into the public arena. Mudge, on behalf of DTA (and more specifically white property owners), felt confident enough to declare his hand in one of the opening sessions and say to SWAPO members, "If you want more of the presently white-owned farms to be bought by black people: in principle, no problem. You can have my farm, you must only pay my price" (minutes, 11 December 1989). Gurirab, on behalf of SWAPO, had, however, conceded much of the matter when on the first day he had remarked almost casually, "Your property is your property."

*Fundamental Human Rights.*  The detainee issue at first threatened to disrupt the proceedings of the Constituent Assembly, when Erica Beukes and other members of the Parents' Committee demonstrated outside the Tintenpalast on the morning of the assembly's opening session, hurling insults at the SWAPO leadership. Moreover, on that first day Justus Garoeb of UDF claimed that the elections were not free and fair because hundreds of Namibians still detained by SWAPO had not participated in the electoral process. He suggested that the assembly should take upon itself all the unresolved problems of the election, such as the fate of those Namibians denied participation. However, this plea seems to have been little more than a token protest to placate the ex-detainee PUM element of the UDF alliance. Garoeb went on to say that the UDF would be cooperative in a "spirit of reconciliation." Although Eric Biwa of PUM later attempted to raise the detainee issue in the assembly, he did not table a formal motion and was not able to catch the chairperson's eye (interview, 16 December 1989). Yet although the detainees issue was never directly raised, the question of human rights was a recurring theme of constitutional debate, both in the standing committee and in the public debate of the assembly itself, and so the detainee issue was an underlying current to the whole proceedings.

Although the standing committee seemed unconcerned about preventive detention, one of the most important debates in the public discussion of the Constituent Assembly itself was over the question of fundamental human rights and in particular the clauses on preventive detention. These clauses were deleted from the committee's draft constitution in the most significant shift during the whole public debate. The deletion of these clauses came about, however, not as the result of pressure from DTA but as a result of a combination of pressures inside Namibia and from international agencies such as Amnesty International, which wrote a key letter to Hage Geingob on human rights issues. Some DTA elements spoke out on the issue of fundamental human rights, in particular Kautire Kaura, and so did the small parties: Vekuii Rukoro of NNF and Moses Katjiuongua of NPF. At the same time, elements within SWAPO itself were not happy about preventive detention clauses, and CCN commented critically on the draft constitution when it was debated in the Constituent Assembly in January, pointing out that some basic human rights included in the Universal Declaration of Human Rights were omitted from the fundamental rights in the draft constitution: freedom of the press, the right to leave Namibia and to return, freedom of thought, conscience, and religion. CCN also criticized the provisions for a state of emergency, such as the abrogation of rights during such a period, declaring that these were rights so fundamental that even during an emergency they should not be violated or suspended: the right to life; the right not to be subjected to torture or to cruel, inhuman, and degrading treatment or punishment; the right not to be held in slavery; the right to freedom of thought, conscience, and religion. CCN asked SWAPO to consider past experience in Namibia and in South Africa, where loose provisions for preventive detention have proved to be an invitation to torture and abuse of prisoners. Preventive detention violates the right to be presumed innocent until proved guilty and the right to liberty, and CCN therefore asked for it to be made difficult for the state to hold someone in detention without being charged and tried. CCN also argued against the article in the draft allowing for a constitutional decision of the Supreme Court to be reversed "by a statute lawfully enacted," arguing that the legislature would be able to overrule the courts, thus defeating the separation of powers and the independence of the judiciary.

During the final public debate on the constitution, Katjiuongua asked for the scrapping of the clauses allowing for preventive detention and Rukoro of NNF supported him, saying that the provisions of Article 11 represented a "black spot" in an "otherwise impeccable document" and that the provisions for emergency powers were sufficient to deal with any eventuality as they also provided for preventive detention but subject to parliamentary review and approval by a two-thirds majority. He reminded the house of the recent use of preventive detention by the South African authorities and maintained that "we cannot encourage people to forget the past if we write it into our constitution." (All quotes in the rest of this section are our detailed notes from observation of all proceedings of the full Assembly.) Biwa of UDF also supported Rukoro, saying that he had prepared a statement but that Rukoro had already put the case against preventive detention clearly.

DTA and SWAPO both initially supported the clauses on preventive detention, and it was interesting to see these opponents on the same side over this crucial issue. Kozonguizi tried to justify this by saying that in the past preventive detention had been wrong because it had been used by an illegal regime but that the future was different because preventive detention would be used to protect the elected government of an independent state. Mudge frankly said he had supported preventive detention when he had been a member of the interim government's cabinet, and he still supported it. At that time it had been used against SWAPO members who constituted a threat to the state, "but the wheel turns." He continued, "I hope members of the other side will have more understanding of the method now. This is the way we all learn."

SWAPO maintained that preventive detention was necessary in a situation where destabilization of the state was a possibility and referred to these clauses as a "necessary evil." Tjitendero supported Konzonguizi in that he thought preventive detention was different under an elected government and considered that emergency powers were not adequate because a country could not live in a permanent state of emergency. He supported preventive detention, "although all of us suffered under laws known as detention without trial in the past."

Ruppel similarly said that preventive detention was a painful matter but that realism was necessary even if it was painful: "I know what it feels like to be detained without knowing when you will be released." Maxuilili, who had himself suffered detention, torture, and twenty years of banning orders in Walvis Bay, also spoke in favor of preventive detention, saying that to scrap these provisions would be to invite lawlessness: "We must be careful not to make the incoming government seem too much like a nice boy." Eventually, however, the preventive detention clauses were withdrawn from the constitution, to resounding applause from public and press galleries.

*The Power of the President.*  This was a key issue in the discussions of standing committee spreading over several sessions, even though there was always an air of reconciliation. When there were inquiries whether the executive president represented a "bottom line" for SWAPO, Hamutenya was quick to respond soothingly that it was not a question of bottom lines but of "give and take" (minutes, 8 December 1989).

Mudge objected to the wide range of presidential powers of appointment, in particular appointing an extra six persons to the National Assembly, which he thought ran "contrary to the democratic principle" (minutes, 14 December 1989) and giving the president "complete power regarding the appointment of judges" and therefore "direct authority on the judiciary" (minutes, 14 December 1989). He also objected to Article 48 (2), which said that "the President may decline to sign any law passed by the National Assembly," and to the president's power to dissolve the National Assembly. He summarized his objections in the following terms: "We don't want to remove presidents, we want to keep them, but we don't want them to find themselves in a position where they can abuse power. The proposals in this working document concerning the president are also, as we see it, politically unwise and practically impossible" (minutes, 11 December 1989).

Mudge considered that the direct election of the president would emphasize ethnic divisions: "Politically, the proposal for a directly elected president is unsound and dangerous, because it denies the existence of a multiparty system." Mudge put forward arguments in favor of a parliamentary head of state and a separation of powers: "A parliamentary head of state who is mandated by a parliament becomes a symbol of unity and conciliation, since in the exercise of his executive powers he needs to follow the wishes of the representatives of the people" (minutes, 14 December 1989). Thus, DTA was in favor of an executive president but not of a directly elected president: "We don't want a ceremonial head of state. . . . We want somebody who has power, but the power must ultimately rest with the people and not with the individual."

Katjiuongua was similarly in favor of an executive president but was "a strong proponent and supporter of the separation of powers" (minutes, 14 December 1989). However, Katjiuongua also linked the role of the cabinet and the presidency to the question of bicameralism "We must link the method of electing the president to his role in the system of government we are going to have" (minutes, 14 December 1989).

Tjitendero summarized four areas of disagreement: the method in which the president is elected, the powers of the president, the functions of the president, and the tenure of the president (p. 36). However, the differences were not irreconcilable, as Rukoro soon pointed out: everybody was agreed about the necessity for the separation of powers and the need for checks and balances, so that the question really turned on how that was to be done—the mechanisms of control. Biwa was concerned about the relationship between the cabinet and the legislature and the capability of the legislature to censure cabinet decisions. He also considered that a directly elected president was not more democratic than one elected via the democratically elected legislature.

During the discussion of presidential power, the thorny question of bicameralism began to appear, and it was this question that divided the committee most severely, even at this stage of discussion. Rukoro pointed out that a complete separation of powers was never in practice possible.

It was interesting that the clause allowing the president to nominate six members to the National Assembly, but without voting powers, divided committee members across party lines. Mudge declared that DTA "felt strongly that it goes against the principle of democracy" to appoint people to legislative bodies, a line he maintained in the public debate later. However, Hamutenya said that "it was also a bone of contention within the SWAPO caucus itself before" and that "SWAPO had no strong line on this" (minutes, 15 December 1989). Later he admitted that "I have a problem with this clause myself, if it was left to me I would do without it." However, Gurirab argued that this was not a clause interfering with democracy, as the members would have no vote, and he considered that such members would enrich the assembly. Rukoro was in favor of retaining this clause, and even ACN was happy. As Geingob put the matter in summary, "The majority wants it to be included. Only Mr Mudge and Mr Hamutenya have contrary views." There was also some discussion of the circumstances under which the president could dissolve the legislature. However, the question of the executive president was in the end ceded without any difficulty, although the question of the election of the president became a matter for considerable discussion, SWAPO insisting on the direct election of the president by the people and DTA and NPF wanting the president to be chosen by the legislature.

Discussion concerning the power of the president continued up to and including the final debate in CA, when it was again examined at length. Biwa was still concerned about presidential accountability. Was the president only to attend the annual presentation of the budget? Could the president be called to parliament on other occasions when his presence was deemed necessary to answer pressing questions? As the clause stood in the draft constitution, presidential access was too limited. As a result of Biwa's intervention, an amendment was made to Article 32, subparagraph 2, to read, "The President shall address Parliament when Parliament so wishes." Mudge questioned the presidential power to call the National Assembly together and to prorogue sessions. Was this merely a presidential privilege? Barney Barnes thought that this presidential privilege ran contrary to the separation of powers, with the president empowered to intervene directly in legislative affairs. This, however, remained unchanged.

Changes were made after Katjiuongua's suggestion, supported by Mudge, that the president should announce a "state of national defence" rather than declare war. The assembly made it obligatory for the president to seek parliamentary approval for a declaration of war: he would now be able to declare martial law and a state of national defense on the understanding that he informed parliament in reasonable time for its approval by two-thirds majority of the National Assembly or a simple majority of both houses.

There was also discussion about various presidential appointments, in particular the right to appoint the chief of the defense, the auditor-general, the inspector general of police, the attorney-general, and the deputy governor of the central bank. Katjioungua said that during the infancy of a democracy, these appointments entrusted too much power in the hands of the president. Hamutenya was conciliatory: the need to consult over these appointments was important, especially as SWAPO recognized the importance of a division of powers. Leaving these appointments in the hands of the president might create the impression that the executive was interfering in the affairs of the judiciary, for example. He therefore proposed that the Judicial Service Commission be consulted in the appointment of the chiefs of defense and police and that party leaders also be involved in the election, especially at the beginning. Staby said that it was important to distinguish between political and nonpolitical appointments, such as civil service appointments, which ought not to be partisan. He considered that the Civil Service Commission could be useful, involving not only consultation but also control of appointments and the creation of mechanisms of control.

De Wet (ACN) came up with a compromise solution to the doubts about appointments, suggesting a strict distinction between political and nonpolitical appointments. The former were to be the prerogative of the president, whereas there would be a two-tier mechanism to deal with the latter, with the president making them on the recommendation of the Civil Service Commission (for civil servants, including permanent secretaries), the Judicial Service Commission (legal officers), or a security service commission (for chiefs of police and defense). These commissions would themselves be appointed by the president with the approval of the National Assembly. The president would appoint without consultation only the obviously political appointments—the prime minister and cabinet ministers—but he might also include the attorney-general and director of planning in the cabinet, making these appointments potentially political.

There was considerable wrangling about the office of attorney-general. The new post of prosecutor-general effectively took over many of the tasks of the previous attorney-general, the existing holder of which would now fill this new post. Ruppel became SWAPO's nominee for attorney-general and would thus be a political appointment, as adviser to the president.

On 1 February the Constituent Assembly was in debate for three hours over the question of the president's right to call a referendum in the event of deadlock between the two houses over a constitutional amendment. According to Article 127, an amendment would be valid only if there were "at least two thirds of the National Assembly" plus a majority in the second chamber in support. The draft said that if such a majority decision could not be reached, "the president may by proclamation make the proposed constitutional amendments the subject of a national referendum." Kaura wanted the bill of rights entrenched, expressing concern that a two-thirds majority could take away his "right to life." There was lengthy discussion of this issue.

On the next morning, Nahas Angula proposed an amendment to Article

37 allowing the president to look outside the legislature when selecting deputy ministers. He described this as a "minor matter," and said that the president should not be restricted to the legislature and the six nominated members already agreed. This provoked an outcry. Barnes said DTA already regarded the six nominees as a compromise and was not prepared to make further concessions over this matter. He pointed out that DTA had been called puppets in the past because it had been appointed and not elected; it was not in the interests of the country to continue such a practice, and to support Angula would be contrary to the 1982 constitutional principles. Hamutenya pointed out that there was a contradiction in insisting upon a second house with special expertise and then insisting that there was enough expertise in the National Assembly to form a cabinet; indeed, if people could be drawn from the second house that would solve the problem, but there would be no need for special provisions until that house came into existence. The matter was left there, and this was the last major debate during the constitutional proceedings.

*Trade Union Rights.* The National Union of Namibian Workers was critical of the secrecy over the constitutional negotiations and called upon "the Standing Committee to open the proposed draft constitution to the public for comments and debate before it is finally accepted" (*The Namibian,* 11 January 1990). This never happened. This criticism of the secrecy of the standing committee gave rise to speculation about the relationship between SWAPO and the unions in the postelection period. A South African newspaper reported that Geingob had given instructions to the unions not to criticize SWAPO in public and stated that Marko Hausiku had lectured them about their role in the election campaign. The unions, however, strenuously denied that there was any conflict between them and SWAPO, pointing out that they had made a significant contribution to the SWAPO victory and that they considered that the lack of a two-thirds majority for SWAPO was a serious impediment to true independence. However, an interview with Ben Ulenga made clear that the unions wished to maintain their independence; they were not affiliated to SWAPO and believed that their funding should be as independent of the government as possible. They did not intend to take part in the SWAPO government, although union representatives in the National Assembly would continue to take care of their members' interests, in particular pushing for immediate implementation of labor and industrial relations legislation (*The Namibian,* 4 December 1989).

Trade union rights were not mentioned in the first SWAPO draft (although there had been an earlier SWAPO draft in private circulation that had spelled out trade union rights). NUNW therefore handed in suggestions to SWAPO at various stages of the drafting process; and after the constitutional draft had been rewritten by the lawyers for presentation to the full assembly, NUNW noted that a number of workers rights and freedoms had been included, but only under the articles on "Principles of State Policy." NUNW therefore issued an open letter to the assembly demanding that fifteen basic rights should be included as fundamental freedoms, not simply under the "Principles of State Policy"; NUNW argued that these basic rights should be entrenched so that they would be respected by all governments at all times, whatever their political persuasion. The rights specified included the right to a living wage; the right to a forty-hour week in safe and hygienic working conditions; the right to rest, leisure, paid holidays, maternity leave, family leave, and sick leave; the right to proper training; the right to work; and the right to water. The right to form and to join trade unions was guaranteed in the final draft constitution, but the right to strike could be suspended during an emergency as it was not entrenched among the fundamental human rights as the unions had requested. In the final constitution the "right to withhold labour without being exposed to criminal penalties" was guaranteed.

*Group Rights.*   Group rights were a major area for discussion during the meetings of the standing committee. When it was discovered that the administration for whites was trying to push through a scheme for selling off schools very cheaply to private buyers, usually (white) parents, several parties spoke out against the scheme, and members of the committee spent a considerable amount of time discussing this issue and preparing a public statement censuring such moves before independence, even though such concerns were not strictly part of the constitution-writing mandate (minutes, 18 December 1989).

The committee received a letter from the Namibian Chiefs' Council asking it to recognize the powers of traditional leaders and the importance of tribal lands in the constitution. This was never a matter for serious debate in the committee itself, although Katjiuongua tried from time to time to raise the issues.

During public debate only ACN raised the question of group rights, but without support from other parties. Despite strong argument from DTA's Kautire Kaura, supported by Hendrik Witbooi of SWAPO, himself a traditional leader, it was decided that traditional courts would not be enshrined in the constitution. Article 105, concerning chairpersons/governors of regional management committees, brought Sam Nujoma to his feet for the first time during public debate, speaking out against apartheid policies and bantustans and declaring that SWAPO's aim was to create a strong central government, with regional governors appointed from Windhoek.

It was clear that group rights were not a serious consideration. The establishment of a second chamber had been agreed to reluctantly by SWAPO, which did not want to cede any power to tribal leaders and local government.

*Constitution-Making: A Summary*

The constitution was rushed through by all parties, eager to seize the reins of power. For SWAPO, independence was urgent because the coffers were empty and party members were in limbo, without income or occupation, waiting to know what they would be offered in the new government. After the excitement of the campaigning period, hundreds of SWAPO cadres suddenly had nothing to do except wait patiently for independence—and jobs. These short-run preoccupations seemed to have reinforced SWAPO willingness to accept any substantive changes, or did SWAPO feel constitutional change might be possible later? The constitution finally came to be accepted by almost all parties, an outcome that had seemed very unlikely at the outset. There was congratulation on all sides for the liberal nature of the final constitution, without the clauses on preventive detention, except in a state of emergency and with parliamentary permission, and exclusion of the death penalty. There were a few grumblings about the dangers of a "toothless" constitution, but overall there was an atmosphere of approval, both from the Namibian people and from international observers.

There were criticisms. Some said the constitution was a document drawn up as much for international approval as for the approval of the Namibian people. Indeed, the lack of consultation of the Namibian people by the Constituent Assembly was a matter for heated criticism, especially from the press and from the trade unions. Like popular parties elsewhere in developed and developing countries alike, SWAPO, once elected, did not see as part of its role consultation or education, even of its own supporters.

When the constitution was finally agreed, SWAPO had removed the clauses on preventive detention, and the role of the executive president had been considerably modified. The president was to be elected by direct voting by the people but could remain in office only for two terms of five years. SWAPO had been forced during the meetings of the standing committee to give way over the question of the second legislative chamber and to agree to an electoral system on the proportional representation pattern used during the independence elections, and this remained unchanged in the final draft.

The question of presidential powers and of preventive detention had in the end been settled amicably, but it seemed that the pressure to remove the preventive detention clauses came as much from groups represented inside SWAPO, such as the churches and the trade unions, and from international human rights groups as it did from other parties. Opposition to preventive detention was voiced by Rukoro of NNF and Katjiuongua of NPF, but not by DTA, although it was Kaura of DTA who was vocal on the question of the entrenchment of the Bill of Fundamental Human Rights when it came to the rules for the amendment of the constitution. Surprisingly, UDF kept

a low profile on this issue, even though Biwa of PUM was the UDF representative on the standing committee.

That aspect of the Bill of Fundamental Human Rights that gave guarantees to existing property owners received surprisingly little attention,
perhaps because all parties accepted the property-protecting provisions in
the 1982 constitutional principles. Neither SWAPO nor NNF, which had
specifically campaigned on land, made an issue of it, but equally DTA and
ACN, which might have been expected to get property rights more deeply
entrenched, clearly thought that the prevailing economic climate and reconciliation policies were enough of a guarantee without clauses as restrictive
of land acquisition as in Zimbabwe's 1980 constitution.

There were a number of events in the postelection period that indicated
that all groups were not happy with the Constituent Assembly and with the
constitutional proposals. There were, for example, a number of women's
meetings, in Katutura and in Khomasdal, where women voiced their dissatisfaction with the small number of women in the Constituent Assembly
(only five) and with the scant attention given to women's issues in the constitution itself. In Rehoboth "Kaptein" Hans Diergaardt, the former authority leader, attempted to preempt the loss of autonomy for the people of
Rehoboth in the new Namibia by staging a referendum. This was ruled
invalid by the new government and ignored, but major protests during the
campaigns for regional and local elections two years later attested to the
depth of feeling by the Baster people.

SWAPO's policy of reconciliation did not, however, meet with universal approval and was said by some observers to be very convenient for the
SWAPO leadership, which wished to let the detainees issue subside into
past history rather than open that particularly unpleasant can of worms.
Others argued that it was a formula that would lead to too many concessions to whites and to property. This dissatisfaction with reconciliation
smouldered away, with rumors of a boycott of the independence celebrations themselves, and eventually led to the boycott of the May Day celebrations when the workers stayed at home in protest against the lack of consultation over the May Day celebrations, and the collaboration of the
leadership in banquets with employers.

## The Restructuring of Government

In the period prior to independence while the constitution was being drawn
up, the administrator-general's civil servants cleared their offices and tried
to negotiate with their new bosses. During the Christmas recess, SWAPO
published its list of ministers, deputy ministers, and permanent secretaries,
giving the first glimpse of what a SWAPO government would look like.
The shift from the existing colonial directorate to sixteen different min-

istries designated by SWAPO necessitated considerable administrative reorganization, including the changeover of permanent secretaries, for SWAPO appointed its own people to head each ministerial department and immediately laid on a training program for these new civil servants.

Of the thirty-two ministerial appointments across sixteen ministries, half were from the external SWAPO leadership. Eleven of the sixteen ministers had been in exile, if Andimba Toivo Ya Toivo is included, and of the remaining five, two were whites: Otto Herrigel (who resigned within two years) and Gert Hanekom, at the key Ministries of Finance and Agriculture. Only three were from the internal leadership: Hendrik Witbooi, SWAPO's vice-president, at the Ministry of Labor; Marko Hausiku, previously SWAPO's Windhoek secretary, at the Ministry of Lands and Resettlement; and Nico Bessinger at the Ministry of Wildlife, Conservation, and Tourism. Many of the appointments were predictably carryovers from SWAPO roles in exile—Theo-Ben Gurirab as minister of foreign affairs, Peter Mueshihange as minister of defense, Lukas Pohamba as head of the Home Office, Nahas Angula as minister of education, Tjiriange as minister of justice, Ben Amathila as minister of trade and industry, and Andimba Toivo Ya Toivo as minister of mines and energy. Peter Tsheehama, formerly senior PLAN commander, did retain the key post of minister of state and security, located in the office of the prime minister, for a time, but the post had been discontinued by 1992. More unexpected was the appointment of Dr. Libertine Amathila to the Ministry of Local Government and Housing; it might have been expected that she would be in the Ministry of Health, for which Dr. Nicky Iyambo became responsible. The only other woman appointed to the government was Pendukene Ithana, deputy minister of wildlife, conservation, and tourism, initially a low-profile post for SWAPO's Women Council secretary, but she was promoted within two years to ministerial rank (youth and sport).

Hidipo Hamutenya, who had previously used the SWAPO Information Office as a power base, was installed at the Ministry of Information and Broadcasting, together with one of the most respected of the internal leadership as deputy, Daniel Tjongerero, and Bob Kandetu, who had coordinated CIMS, as permanent secretary. SWAPO offered two posts to Constituent Assembly members who were not in SWAPO and both accepted: Vekuii Rukoro of NNF as deputy minister of justice and Reggie Diergaardt of UDF as deputy minister of trade and industry (later youth and sport). Hartmut Ruppel was appointed attorney-general, in a post that would have cabinet status, another appointment from the white community. Zed Ngavirue, in the important post of director of national planning, did not have a SWAPO record and had been a director of the Rossing uranium mine; his appointment was a clear sign that it was business as usual in dealing with the economy and mining, in particular. David Meroro, who was a sick man, was not given a ministerial post; it was perhaps intended that he be a member of the second chamber if it came into being. Moses Garoeb retained responsibility for the SWAPO party organization but did not hold a government post.

The announcement of the cabinet was but one step in restructuring the inherited machinery of government. Also announced at the same time were permanent secretaries of the sixteen new ministries, none of them previously members of the Namibian Government Service (NGS), which had been set up in 1981 to begin replacing what had been hitherto been a colonial bureaucracy of officials appointed from South Africa. These new ministerial heads were seen as political appointments, although not all of them had had links with SWAPO. They had little direct experience of the actual working of Namibian government departments, although they did have other experience and qualifications (four had Ph.D.s). They thus became the new accountable authorities put in over the heads of incumbent officials. The political need for such a change was the more glaring given that virtually none of the top-level NGS posts had been occupied by black Namibians. Out of 108 senior posts as heads of departments and their constituent directorates plus the heads and section heads of bodies such as the police, the high court, central personnel, and security, there were 6 vacancies and only 3 names that were obviously those of Namibian Africans—and only 1 woman.

These and other changes were set in motion by a "civil service restructuring team" with a SWAPO minister (Herigel, Finance), a SWAPO CA member (Tjitendero, who had been in charge of SWAPO's teacher training in exile), Deputy Minister Rukoro of NNF, and a DTA CA member (Matjila, who had previously been minister of education)—a forerunner, no doubt, of the Public Service Commission provided for in the new constitution. They obviously sought to insert a change of personnel to include as many black nominations at the top, although two of the new commissioners were white. But they also sought to temper this infusion with some continuity at lower levels and to retain enough personnel to avoid collapse of services.

Nevertheless, one case offers an example of the policy tangles that were potentially involved in the course of ministers taking over from the previous secretaries, who were often on a different wavelength: the incumbent secretary for finance was taken to task for "attempting to preempt" decisions when he expressed his view that Namibia should stay within the monetary and customs area dominated by RSA (*The Namibian*, 19 January 1990).

The indications were that there was no mass exodus or resignations of officials in the weeks leading up to independence (interview with Dr. J. Jones, AG's general secretary for economic affairs, 16 February 1990). One senior official, Gouwyo, who had been head of Central Personnel before the election, attributed this lack of mass resignations to the fact that many of the South African officials had made their choice in 1981 when NGS was set up and those who had stayed on were either Namibian born or bred (he arrived at age two), South Africans who had spent many years here (for him thirty years), or South Africans who had developed a commitment (in some cases one of self-interest—like another interviewed senior official who was hoping his farm would be secure, even though he was an absentee owner living in Windhoek!). Gouwyo cited the stance of the most senior officials against attempts in 1989 to privatize white schools and against the views of the AG as an example of a kind of concern for "national" interests. Indeed, he spoke to us of "in-fighting between officials and the AG" on several matters, such as diamond revenues and fishing rights, wherein the latter saw matters in terms of the South African interest. But officials anxious to stay would play up such divisions and take "patriotic" stances. Nevertheless, in the early months of 1990, there was some insecurity felt by incumbent officials. Their professional body, the Government Senior Staff Association (GSSA), made representations to CA in December 1989 and had a further meeting with prime minister designate in February to clarify their job security in the light of a speech "warning" them they could be replaced—although their right to continue in office until they resigned or were removed lawfully was set out in Article 141 of the constitution. But the fact that they still represented whites and the inherent elitism of GSSA was under attack by junior officials who proposed an alternative, black association.

Altogether there was a major expansion of all branches of the civil service, the police (where recruitment was initiated by the AG in October 1989), and the newly formed national army. As a result of this influence, state employment rose from 30 percent to 50 percent of formal sector jobs (Freeman, 1991). This process also marked the emergence of a new class element of well-paid black Namibian administrators and cast doubt on whether the country could find the resources to pay them without this being at the expense of social services, minimum wages, investment in agriculture and rural development, and other measures that would benefit the masses of the people. A further worry was that this sizable expansion had done little to absorb the thousands of returnees, many of them lacking the formal skills for middle-level civil service jobs. By June 1990, a year after their return, less than 10 percent of those who were potentially economically active had managed to find wage employment (Tapscott, 1990: 38). Particularly disheartening was the role of the many women returnees, some five thousand of them former fighters—and not all of them by any means, as Nujoma depicted them, simply the "cooks" of the liberation movement. Apart from their greater difficulty in getting government or private-sector jobs in fierce competition, they were specifically and completely excluded from the national army.

Another dimension of change in government structures, in addition to the composition of the political leadership and the bureaucracy, was the eventual specification of provisions in the constitution with implications for local government. These were partly contained in the setting up of a second legislative chamber. That was to be called the National Council, as distinct from the National Assembly, which CA turned itself into and which would henceforth be elected by a national PR system. The National Council would comprise two representatives from each of the regional councils, which would in turn be divided into constituencies, the latter perhaps to become the basis for local authorities. What remained was to set up the regions—a task that has taken more than the specified two years. The eventual blueprint amounted to "a redrawing of the country's internal political geography" (Simon, 1993: 7). The bantustans as units were erased; thirteen regions were delineated that encompassed both communal areas and commercial farming areas, including provision that Ovamboland be divided between four regions. These measures potentially removed the patronage base of authorities, implied some political and developmental integration of formerly "white" and "black" areas, and held some promise of providing more services to African areas beyond what had been possible from their tiny tax bases, thereby yielding some redistribution of income and services.

## The Postelection Political Climate

The CA deliberations and the formation of the new government were going on against a background of major political readjustments that could have been destabilizing. SWAPO took over the reins of power but with less than the overwhelming support it had anticipated, without the self-confidence that would have given it, and in the teeth of small but powerful interests in the society—most of the whites, plus local notables in the ethnic administrations—who saw SWAPO as the enemy. Some experienced commentators made the insightful comment that the reaction of the whites to a clear SWAPO victory would have been that much greater because it would have been a surprise to them, as probably 60–70 percent had believed their own propaganda that SWAPO had only minority support. At the same time, SWAPO's own activists had great and immediate expectations. How then to mollify the whites and other opponents while meeting the demands of supporters?

The situation in the immediate aftermath of the voting was the more tense because many of those who had opposed SWAPO had access to the means of violence. Many whites had received training and acted as reservists, especially among the farming community, in addition to those who had been called up in SADF and SWATF. Then their private arsenals had been reinforced in the few weeks before the election in what seemed to be a concerted program through SWAPOL (interviews with UNTAG election officers, Gobabis and Tsumeb, October 1989). In the farming town of Outjo north of Windhoek, the SWAPOL station commander issued a general warning to white residents, which was to apply "before as well as after the elections," that stressed the need for preparedness and "keeping weapons in your house . . . clean, oiled and ready" and that instructed reservists to look out for unprotected homesteads (CIMS, 1990: 207). How far this kind of alert was a defensive response by paranoid white communities or aimed at a preemptive strike or coup is not clear. SWAPO's efforts at reconciliation seemed to defuse these feelings.

A rather different situation prevailed in the various reserves, especially in the north, where there was no significant white minority and where the proponents of the old order included those still on the payroll of the ethnic battalions or Koevoet, for they continued to parade fortnightly for pay until 1 February 1990. In these areas violence erupted immediately after the election; *The Namibian* was already talking about a "DTA backlash" on 16 November. In one of the most reported incidents, a SWAPO member of CA and a prominent businessman were badly beaten in Owambo. UNTAG reported "two weeks of violence in Owambo" following the results but thought it was "at an end" (*The Namibian,* 29 November 1989); but two months later the UNSGSR had to express to the AG an "acute concern about increased lawlessness in the border areas of the North" (*The Namibian,* 24 January 1990). In Caprivi there were reports of arson and of "intimidation mounting" (*The Namibian,* 28 and 29 November 1989). This "lawlessness" was not simply an expression of the frustration of those who had lost power and were, as they clearly were in Owambo, among the beleaguered minority, nor was it just the violence associated with "drinking sprees" following the pay parades, as was reported from Oshakata in Owambo (*The Namibian,* 1 February 1990). Several features point to a more orchestrated dimension to the violence, just as there had been during the election campaigns. First, much of it involved ex-security personnel, who operated not merely as individuals; they were in touch with others, and former commanders, on paydays. Reports from Katima Mulilo in Caprivi refer to a convoy of twenty whites appearing in army-type vehicles (*The Namibian,* 23 February 1990). Second, there was a continuation of the tendency seen earlier for "cultural" and other organized bodies to be formed around ex-security personnel, although apparently not in Owambo. In Kavango "organised gangs were operating even after Independence" (*The Namibian,* 27 April 1990), in Caprivi "a local ex-SWATF organisation . . . [issued] uniforms" (*The Namibian,* 4 December 1990), and ex-members of 701 Battalion formed a cultural group *Kopano Yatou,* although some of them set off to try joining the new Namibian army.

Third, the violence in the north had links with UNITA in Angola, whose demobilization had not been part of the various 1988 accords and which was still receiving U.S. support (*The Guardian,* 1 December 1989). UNITA elements were reportedly coming over the border and joining forces with ex-SWATF to engage in looting and cattle rustling on an alarming scale (*The Namibian,* 26 January 1990). The AG admitted the problem of infiltration (*The Namibian,* 26 January 1990); border patrols by SWAPOL were increased, and a Malaysian battalion of UNTAG was sent to the border around Kavango (*The Namibian,* 1 February 1990). But ex-SWATF elements were also flocking to UNITA colors, especially after their last payday; some three to four thousand, according to one report, disappeared from Owambo across the border, where there was reputedly a base for ex-Koevoet and ex-101 Battalion personnel.

The disruptive activities of these DTA supporters in the north were amplified by the unstable social and economic climate that faced the people, including the many returnees, thirty-one thousand of whom settled in Owambo. That area had previously benefited from the jobs and extra income generated by the security forces and then the UNTAG presence, but the circumstances had ended, and the payment of salaries to local ex-SWATF was about to be terminated. Unemployment was mounting, so returnees, who had received only rations and no cash income, found themselves in desperate circumstances—with only the promise, for some, of being absorbed into the new army or elsewhere in government. The climate of violence and the impatience and desperation of returnees may well have been reasons SWAPO in particular was anxious to complete the business of CA and may explain its readiness to compromise.

One effect of the violence and declining economy was a massive exodus to the towns to the south now that there were no longer institutional impediments to movement: thirty thousand reportedly moved from Owambo to Katutura between the elections and independence in March 1990. What these circumstances meant in personal terms is illustrated by the fate of one family: a daughter returned to the family home having been a PLAN fighter but as a woman was not eligible for the new army, so she was unemployed. She became more despondent when the family blamed her for the redundancy of her two brothers, who had lived reasonably well as members of the security forces. She committed suicide (Chris Tapscott, personal communication Windhoek).

Efforts were made immediately after the election, in accordance with SWAPO's policy of reconciliation, to ease the tensions in the north. Talks were initiated in Owambo to get SWAPO and SWAPOL and ex-Koevoet representatives to agree to end the violence; the talks "ended in acrimony" (*The Namibian,* 31 January 1990). But a month later the work of this "peace committee" was seen as beginning to succeed (*The Namibian,* 21 February 1990). At an earlier meeting, on 29 November 1989, Nico Smith of DTA had "admitted that many DTA supporters were involved in cases of intimidation, and these included Koevoet members . . . [but] vehemently denied that any intimidation was centrally organised from the DTA office and that no DTA leader knew about these incidents beforehand" (CIMS, 1990: 120). Interestingly, he also wished that "the CA [would speed] up the writing of the constitution . . . because the situation was fragile." SWAPO had also had a meeting with the former head of Koevoet, Hans Dreyer, in a bid to demobilize ex-Koevoet.

Such initiatives were part of the general overtures to whites, to ex-security personnel and to political opponents so that they did not fear for their future under a new SWAPO-led government. These were part of the reconciliation strategy that had been adopted by the party's Central Committee in February and articulated by SWAPO leaders on their return at the start of the election campaign and in a pamphlet they produced in July 1989, "Healing the Wounds of War." These sentiments were even more strongly emphasized by Sam Nujoma at speeches where the election results were announced and by Hage Geingob at the opening of CA. The strategy referred to the healing of divisions between tribes and within communities and families as well as between white and black. It also, magnanimously, implied forgiveness of those who had committed the many atrocities in the war and craved similar forgiveness from the detainees and their families—although this last hope was sorely taxed when SWAPO's Hawala (Auala) Saloman, who was widely held responsible for much of the torture and detention, was made commander of the defense forces. These messages did go some way to easing the worries of the majority of whites and probably helped, as they were intended to (following advice from Zimbabwe and the negative examples of Angola and Mozambique), to slow down any tendency of a mass, sudden exodus to South Africa. Some did leave: from remote communities—one-third of the 350 whites in Katima Mulilo—and also from some mines. A high percentage of whites were reported as leaving Tsumeb at the end of November (*The Namibian,* 29 November 1989), but the president of the South West African Agricultural Union said on 28 November 1989 that "only a handful of farmers left the country—more for emotive reasons not national reasons. . . . [For] independent Namibia has a lot of [economic] advantages" (CIMS, 1990: 407). There had been a significant emigration earlier in the 1980s—the white population had fallen from 120,000 to 80,000, according to the head of the administration for whites (CIMS, 1990: 397). But apart from officials and security personnel going back to South Africa, other whites were not so tempted, given trends in South Africa, or their fears were assuaged by reconciliation.

Following independence the potential for violence and the overt tensions had diminished, but continued acts of sabotage by white right-wing extremists, such as firebombings, destruction of public property, and smear campaigns against government leaders, did continue. At the same time, the concessions made to commercial farmers, businesspeople, and professionals as well as the retention of other white social privileges came under attack and even led to popular protests. Several editorials in *The Namibian* voiced this growing concern that too much had been conceded under the banner of reconciliation (e.g., 12 April 1990). And in the subsequent two years, the mood of frustration with an increasingly perceived failure to modify inherited economic and social inequalities became more apparent. These were fueled by perceptions that the new leaders were clearly benefiting from the new political scene. There was considerable political fallout when the president took delivery of an executive jet for his personal use at the very moment in mid-1992 when the appeals for victims of drought were at their height.

## The Realignment and Reshaping of the Political Parties

Meanwhile, after the election the various political alliances of the opposition fronts began to crumble, and there were splits in the parties. In ACN there was doubt whether Jan de Wet could continue as a member of the Constituent Assembly after his resignation from the National Party: he maintained that the Namibian organization was separate from the South African organization and that as leader of the ACN alliance he was entitled to remain in office. An attempt to involve Hage Geingob in the dispute failed as Geingob maintained it was not part of the CA chair's task to intervene in disputes within the parties. In the end de Wet remained in office, only to resign "for family reasons" in mid-1992. FCN seemed to have a difference of opinion with its sole representative, Mburumba Kerina, directing him to reject the constitution as it did not meet with FCN's federal demands, among other things. Rebellion broke out in Rehoboth on the eve of independence, led by veteran leader of the FCN Hans Diergaardt, and had to be dealt with by the AG as a matter of urgency. In the middle of February, WRP left the ranks of the UDF alliance over the detainee issue and in particular over Reggie Diergaardt's acceptance of a ministerial post in the SWAPO government. WRP maintained that in early 1989 it had at first wanted to join an alliance with SWAPO but on the condition that the detainee issue be resolved; SWAPO had not responded, and WRP had then approached NNF before finally accepting overtures made by UDF.

Dirk Mudge sought to maneuver toward transforming the DTA alliance into a single party (*The Namibian,* 16 March 1990), hopefully with other small parties, in order to build a united but also more credible and more centrally organized opposition, dispensing in the process with the tribal leaders whose clientelist support had been useful but who had neither the experience of politics nor the ability to provide any kind of viable opposition. Chief Riruako resigned from the DTA vice-presidency, taking the NUDO element of DTA with him (see Chapters 2 and 7), although NUDO had in the past been DTA's most substantial support. It seems Mudge and

DTA did not get far in attracting some of the other small parties into his alliance with the offer of seats in the assembly or in dispensing with the tribal leaders. Most parties and coalitions were prepared to listen to overtures without committing themselves; the only positive, overt response came from some factions of NNF, whose intellectually influential radical leaders, Kenneth and Ottilie Abrahams, argued that SWAPO had become so resistant to opening the detainee issue and more generally to intraparty democracy that they wanted to throw their weight behind an effective, even if ideologically disparate, opposition (*The Namibian,* 4 June 1990). Their initiative and Rukoro's acceptance of a government post had in turn divided NNF.

SWAPO was itself making approaches to some of the other political groups and individuals, not leaving DTA to absorb them all. As well as offering government positions to people such as Rukoro of NNF and Diergaardt of UDF; less partisan individuals such as Dr. Zed Ngavirue, a former SWANU activist who had become chair of Rossing Uranium and who was made director-general of the National Planning Commission; and some whites, overtures were made to other political groups and influentials of different ethnic groups. But this very process of trying to weld alliances and incorporate existing notables was a strategy different from what SWAPO seemed to have envisaged for itself during the years of exile. Believing no doubt its own propaganda about being the "sole and authentic representative of the [whole] people," SWAPO seemed to have assumed either that it would be in the position that TANU in Tanzania and FRELIMO in Mozambique found themselves in after independence of being the sole de facto movement, or that it would mimic ZANU's position in Zimbabwe, where it could claim the support of four out of five people and all but a few areas. The choice then would not be just one of confirming a single-party state, but also one of determining the future character of a movement whose purposes would no longer be those of conducting a struggle and winning diplomatic support. What would be the role of the party as distinct from the state—an ideological vanguard and final arbiter of policy, such as FRELIMO and MPLA were; a national front embracing all tendencies and classes, such TANU, later CCM, was; or simply an adjunct of the state that was the funnel for political recruitment, such as KANU in Kenya or UNIP in Zambia was? And what then would be the basis for party membership or the role of interest groups in relation to it?

FRELIMO and MPLA certainly offered one model of party transition. Each transformed a national front geared to armed struggle and the mobilization of mass support for that struggle into a vanguard party with a specific, Marxist-Leninist ideology and commitment to revolutionary change in social and economic structures; a stated emphasis (in theory, anyway) on worker and peasant members; the scrutiny of members, all of whom had to reapply; and a role for the party's higher echelons as the final policymakers. In both Angola and Mozambique the widespread and informal organs of *poder popular* (people's power) that mushroomed in the months before and after independence wilted in the process of this party formation. SWAPO seemed to have had only the vaguest formulation of a possible transition worked out. The UN Institute for Namibia (UNIN, 1986: 610) publication that carried some semiofficial working out of future policies does partially reflect the foregoing model in talking about SWAPO "uniting *all* Namibian people . . . into a *vanguard* party, capable of safeguarding national independence and of building a non-exploitative society based on the ideals of and principles of scientific socialism." As Cole (1990) perceptively points out, uniting all Namibian people into a vanguard party is a contradiction in terms, evidence that SWAPO's ideologues had only a vague understanding of the scientific socialism they were talking about. Other statements in the same volume do stress the participation of "the masses of people at different levels in the decisionmaking process . . . [and] initiating, planning and controlling a large part of their social and economic betterment" (UNIN, 1986: 745)—statements that belie the centralist implications of vanguardism but that do not specify any concrete modalities that would give expression to this participation. However, the outcome of party politics and party government relations that seemed to be emerging in Namibia in the two years after independence was a political system closer to the one-and-a-bit party system of Botswana (another sparsely populated, mineral-based country) than to other neighbors. This was a system in which there were the trappings of multipartyism, periodic electoral competition, but no real challenge to the continued dominance of the ruling party.

   In the event, the political realities and the main structures that SWAPO found on the return of its leaders were such that theorizing about vanguards and one-party states was not appropriate. The immediate imperative during the election was, as was evident in Chapter 7, to build up party organization structures and a capability to get people's votes. There was therefore during the election campaign a process of transformation already under way, of building on, transforming, or replacing the branches that had been allowed to exist under South African rule and merging activists from the churches, trade unions, and student movement, many of them young people in their twenties or teens who had breathed life into popular, formal protest from the mid-1980s, together with the several generations of returned leaders, fighters, and educated professionals. Despite some internal tensions, some effective structures had come into existence in the northern provinces, in Windhoek, and in some of the mining enclaves, but the kind of mass support that could be the basis of any type of one-partyism came into existence only in Owambo.

   The questions that SWAPO faced as a party were in some sense regionally specific. In Ovamboland the questions were whether and how to win over the dissenting one-tenth of the population, consolidate one-partyism, and recast the role of the party within the district. Would the party be simply a machine kept oiled to win the local or next general elections, or would it be a mobilizing force for local development initiatives, for participation, or for politicization? The tiny proportion of SWAPO opponents in the area remained highly visible and vocal in the months after the election, but a watershed came with the final monthly pay parade of the ex-Koevoet and ex-SWATF elements that made up many of their number in February 1990. Strong-arm methods, especially against returnees, were already giving way to banditry and cattle rustling, often from across the Angolan border. Beyond establishing a peace committee to try reconciling such elements, SWAPO's activities seemed to have been confined to speeches by leaders telling the people to stay loyal. Crucial in the long term would be the fate of the local economy, based as its relative prosperity in the 1980s had been on a "bottle store bourgeoisie" catering to SADF, SWATF, and then UNTAG. This was an economy where turnover of the formal business sector declined by one-third in the five months after independence, twenty-five thousand workers lost their jobs (*Southscan,* 14 September 1990), and there were other factors affecting the livelihood of migrant workers and peasants.

In Kavango, Windhoek, and other towns/mining areas where SWAPO had effective organized branches and had won a majority of the votes but where it was simply the most popular among several parties, what was at issue was whether SWAPO could make inroads into the support of other parties. In doing this, it might count on actions and initiatives by the SWAPO government that would appeal to the interests of certain classes, or to the area as a whole, on winning over and incorporating leaders of other parties and local notables with their supporters by patronage. Such efforts were made, especially the latter. There was perhaps a greater imperative in such areas on maintaining and building further the local party structures, but only limited effort went into that kind of initiative following the election.

In the many districts where SWAPO had only minority support, it faced a real dilemma in how to proceed. In some areas and among some groups, reputedly such as the Herero, influential, educated members of the SWAPO leadership who were now in the new government did attempt to convert other Herero by meetings and appeals. They were attempting to take advantage of the apparent discontent in NUDO, one of DTA's main affiliates, whose members claimed that it delivered 60–70 percent of DTA's vote but was rewarded with only two members in CA. Other public meetings addressed by SWAPO leaders, not always from the locality, were held up and down the country during the period of CA, but these seem to have taken the form of rallies with the speaker making rhetorical appeals reminiscent of the election campaign rather than taking the opportunity to educate people (let alone consult them) about the form the constitution might take (see reports in *The Namibian,* 31 January and 6 February 1990). In another reported meeting in the south in mid-1990, SWAPO leaders seemed not only to have been dismayed by a small and indifferent audience but also to have responded by hectoring those people who were there for the "failings" of those who didn't attend (Colin Leys, personal communication).

In general SWAPO seemed to have put more reliance on winning over local leaders or small local parties by inducements to influential individuals to join the government, if not the party. This was a tactic of broadening the front by federal alliances of the sort that DTA had built up and that SWAPO had refused to cement when Garoeb wanted to bring in his Damara Council as a distinct element rather than as individual members. No effort was made to reach the less influential clients among less privileged workers or livestock owners by offering or even just rhetorically discussing radical change in social and economic structures.

But SWAPO's appeal and any organizational strengthening have to be assessed in terms of social groups and classes at the national level, not just in ethnic terms. As with other national movements that have come to power, Zimbabwe's in particular, there was a flow of returning intellectuals trained abroad who had not been especially engaged in the movement's exile networks, as well as other trained people within the country, many of whom now sought office. An editorial in *The Namibian* shortly after the election (17 November 1989) remarked on this phenomenon whereby "all of a sudden, the SWAPO bandwagon began to swell with opportunists and those who had 'always' supported the movement but hadn't been terribly vocal about it." Kenneth Abrahams (1990: 5) of NNF also spells out what he saw as the "SWAPO offer to other parties" in the weeks after the election: "It was seriously asking competent and suitably qualified personnel from other political parties to consider positions in the SWAPO Cabinet, in the civil service, the diplomatic corps and in the parastatals" and even implied that in the context of reconciliation "a refusal could be interpreted as being opposed to the welfare of the nation."

At the other end of the social scale, SWAPO did little to meet the demands of organized workers. Trade union rights were only partially recognized in the constitution, nor were the unions included in discussions. No labor code was drafted until late 1992 (it had been promised in September 1991), and no minimum wage legislation was proposed. SWAPO did, however, try to incorporate trade union leadership: it parachuted in a SWAPO official, John ya-Otto, with only limited trade union experience as head of the National Union of Namibian Workers, brushing aside the claims of the internationally respected general secretary of the mineworkers, Ben Ulenga, who it then sought to sideline as deputy minister for wildlife. Despite this incorporation of leaders, NUNW indicated some hesitancy about affiliating with SWAPO (*The Namibian,* 5 December 1989).

Likewise, little prospect was held out for improving the lot of rural dwellers—for reasons that were in part the result of circumstances. But the resulting popular frustration did not seem to translate itself into political expression. On the first occasion when SWAPO's popular support was tested, in local and regional elections in late 1992, the party seemed to increase the breadth of its support. The organized labor movement was further disappointed by the publication of the long-awaited Labor Act in 1992, which in the event provided little more than the preindependence Wiehahn Commission proposals and seemed to imply the continuation of many discriminatory practices. The frustrated expectations of workers seemed to be matched by those of returnees, many of whom remained unemployed, and by people in rural areas. Their frustrations were creating what many observers felt was a growing popular discontent about the government's failure to address inherited inequalities, worsened by a genuine and growing economic crisis by the end of the honeymoon period in about 1992. Some of the discontent was articulated within the party around the issue of holding a party congress (only one having been held in the past during the long years of exile) with a view to making SWAPO leaders answerable. This was promised at several points in the two years after 1990 but was delayed.

The first test of whether the party realignments and/or the mood of frustrated expectations would be translated into a change in people's party political preferences came at the end of 1992. Elections for the ninety-five constituencies that made up the thirteen new regions were held 30 November–3 December. There was a surprisingly high turnout for essentially local elections, about 70 percent of the number that had voted in 1989. SWAPO won control of all but four of the thirteen regions, DTA won more constituencies in three regions, and one was split between DTA and UDF. No parties other than these three will thus be represented in the National Council. SWAPO also had majorities in thirty-nine of the forty-eight local authorities to have been carved out of the regions by then, with UDF in control of two and DTA in control of seven. These results, on a single-member constituency basis that thus disadvantaged small parties and does not offer a safe basis for predicting National Assembly elections, do, however, suggest a trend toward polarization but also indicate that any popular frustration has not yet been translated into voter opposition to SWAPO.

## Early Policy Initiatives

During the years of exile SWAPO had worked out some policy blueprints: a political program was agreed in 1976; a more detailed set of priorities and policies was worked out in a massive tome produced by UNIN, *Perspectives for National Reconstruction and Development* (UNIN, 1986).

In a dedication to this latter, Sam Nujoma set out the starting point for a SWAPO "political economy of liberation and development" (p. 59) which would seek to "bring about a fundamentally new social order" (p. 5). Elsewhere the document dismissed it as "absurd to assume that the goals of an independent Namibian government would be to run the present economic system somewhat more efficiently with a number of black faces replacing white ones but no basic changes in structure or mode of production or in income distribution" (p. 59). It went on to speak of socialism as the basic goal, which involved "bringing all the major means of production and exchange into the ownership of the people" (p. 60) and making a commitment to planning. Among the specific measures envisioned in the program were a commitment to comprehensive agrarian reform, including the extinguishing of all colonial land rights, land redistribution, the promotion of cooperatives and collectives, and an emphasis on food security; a commitment to limit "parasitic" profitmaking, end the contract labor system, and put in place a nondiscriminatory wage and salary structure; guidelines for the fishing, mining, and manufacturing industries that would increase the retention of their surpluses in the country and contribute to some delinking of the economy from South Africa; and the wider distribution of education, health, and other social services to the African population. But the program also recognized the need for "a transitional period with state, cooperative, joint venture and private ownership" (p. 60). Thus, it would have been mistaken to expect the SWAPO government to embark on an immediate program of social and economic transformation at the instant of transition. However, it is instructive to review that period from late 1989 to mid-1990 to see what foundations or markers were laid for subsequent policies.

We noted in Chapter 7 that SWAPO's election manifesto had already muted the radicalism of the exile documents, playing down mentions of socialism and omitting any mention of nationalization or abolition of colonial property rights, although SWAPO was still significantly more outspoken on agrarian issues and social and economic equality than almost all other parties. The interim SWAPO government was further constrained by two sets of political circumstances. First, it was faced with a by no means insignificant parliamentary opposition that would take particular issue over economic policies that challenged the status quo. In one symptomatic exchange in the National Assembly, Mudge taunted the government to unveil its inarticulated economic strategy and to admit that it had in fact dispensed with the strategies outlined in "the studies that the UN paid for" (*Hansard*, 14 June 1990). Second, the entrenchment of property rights in the constitution, which provisions had already been conceded by SWAPO when it signed the constitutional principles in 1982 constrained any measures to redistribute land or acquire other property. SWAPO's inhibitions in this area were reinforced by its commitment to a policy of reconciliation,

which inevitably meant keeping the white population sweet by not dismantling its considerable privileges.

On the land issue, some tentative steps were taken: an initial study was
quickly commissioned to review the present structure of agriculture and to
assess policy options (Adams and Werner, 1990); a new ministry of lands
was set up, which included a department specifically to deal with land
reform and resettlement. And even if no steps were taken to acquire colonial land rights in general, a special probe was ordered into any land trans-
fers initiated by the second-tier authorities in the last six months of their
lives as some kind of preemptive sale to whites (*The Namibian*, 20 April
1990). Nujoma did still refer to land reform as a policy commitment in a
major interview with the BBC (17 April 1990), but he also added that white
commercial farms would still be encouraged as they were crucial for food
security, although whether they would be in the longer run was open to
debate. Some momentum was maintained through 1990 by preparation for
a public conference on land reform, held in June 1991, which in turn led to
the commissioning of a further study team, which eventually reported in
December 1992.

There was also soft-pedaling about the mines, with every effort being
made to reassure the mining corporations that no short-run nationalization
was intended, although Minister Ya Toivo did say that it was still a long-
term priority (*The Namibian*, 12 April 1990) and that an investment code
would guarantee the repatriation of profits. The government did, however,
begin to enter into negotiations with some of the mining houses to try
retaining more royalties and taxes within the country and sought expert
help in ways of keeping more of the surplus (*The Namibian*, 12 April
1990). Some small initial steps were taken to retain more of the value
added from fishing: a Spanish company was to set up a processing plant at
Lüderitz, and some Soviet interest was expressed.

There were some efforts made straightaway to reallocate services. The
first budget in June 1990 devoted 41 percent of its expenditure to the fields
of health, education, and housing, which represented two- and threefold
increases in the first two categories, respectively. Existing schools were
opened to all, and a commitment to free schooling for the first six years
was announced. Efforts in education were partly a rearguard response to
the departing white administration's attempts in the last months of 1989 to
sell off schools to parents and private trusts at nominal rates; fifteen
schools had been privatized, and the Constituent Assembly sent a delegation to the Ministry of Education to head off this preemptive move.
Struggles between the white community and public authorities over the
control of schools remained prominent through the early 1990s.

The constraining effects of the constitution and the opposition seemed
to have been reinforced by an unwillingness of leaders to translate rhetoric

into practice—whether for a lack of ideological commitment or a rapidly acquired personal interest will only be revealed by subsequent research on the internal workings of SWAPO. But perhaps most limiting were the objective economic constraints that the transitional government faced. At the most general level, events in the USSR and Eastern Europe were making clear the limits of existing socialisms as a model, and the need to curry favor with socialist backers no longer existed. The constraints of the links with South Africa were also becoming fully apparent. The government's sensitivity to what outsiders in the diplomatic, aid, and business communities thought of it was also becoming clearer and was partly a function of the rather dire economic straits in which it found itself. The years of war and of drought in the 1970s and 1980s had taken their toll on production and infrastructure. The fishing industry had greatly shrunk, and mining was faced with declining reserves and production. Several immediate shocks to the country's finances were also experienced. The South African government was in a strong enough position to insist that the new state fully take over responsibility for the foreign debt incurred in colonial times, which amounted to some R 727 million (equivalent to 20 percent of GDP), much of it owed to South Africa. In October 1989 the RSA administration allowed civil servants in Namibia to invest their pension funds in one of three major insurance firms in South Africa, an offer that at that time was difficult for the officials to refuse and that led to a loss of a further capital stock of more than R 400 million. These and other circumstances meant that the incoming government was virtually bankrupt. And there was no lack of influential voices proclaiming the need for a pragmatic approach to economic policy. Harry Oppenheimer of the South African–based Anglo-American Corporation turned up to give a public talk to the Chamber of Mines and to give the message "Avoid socialism" (*The Namibian,* 5 March 1990). Another sign of the times was that SWAPO's own research unit held a seminar on "economic realities" in April 1990 sponsored by Standard Bank. Such pressures would inevitably have been strengthened by Namibia's immediate determination to seek aid.

The first such major effort was the holding of a donors conference in June 1990 in an effort to attract aid, but this had to be held in New York at the headquarters of UNDP, not in Windhoek. The conference sought both short-term budgetary support to meet the shortfall from the withdrawal of South African government budget subventions and long-term development project aid. This also was the first opportunity to present a development strategy and a draft code to protect foreign investors. These documents, which were tabled with virtually no public discussion in Namibia (a point made by the opposition in parliament), certainly downplayed any agenda for socioeconomic transformation. The roundtable resulted in total pledges of U.S. $696 million over three years, somewhat less than the $810 million being sought. Namibia was also accepted into membership of the

International Monetary Fund, the World Bank, and the Lome Convention of the European Community. However, its application for least-developed-country status under the latter two bodies was turned down because average national income per head was greater than $1,000—even though the conditions of the people were scarcely reflected in this figure, which was in turn a result of the skewed income distribution and the huge share of GNP that left the country (see Chapter 2).

## Namibia in the Southern African Region

With the approach of independence, Namibia began to take its first steps as a separate actor on the international scene. But even this initial period began to indicate the options that were available to it and their limited nature. Here we take the opportunity to explore not only Namibia's emerging foreign relations but also what difference the liberation of Africa's last colony made to the international politics of the region.

For a start the country immediately entered into formal relationships that strengthened its links with neighboring African states. It automatically became the tenth member of the Southern African Development Community (SADC, formerly SADCC), which sought to promote regional links and mutual development, especially in transport and trade, but also had among its aims lessening dependence on South Africa. The latter had certainly been one of SWAPO'S stated aims since its inception, although given the extreme degree of economic reliance, this was not so easily accomplished. Namibia also applied to the overlapping Preferential Trade Area of Eastern and Southern African countries.

However, there were few actual infrastructural links and complementarities with neighbors other than South Africa on which Namibia could build any kind of economic cooperation. Trade with any of them has been virtually nil, and transport links are few. There is some potential to seek oil supplies from Angola, but otherwise and despite the close proximity and ethnic similarity of the Owambo, Kavango, and Caprivi peoples with Angolans on the other side of the border, there are few other prospects but the casual trade in livestock and foodstuffs. The productive areas and markets of Namibia's two northern and western neighbors are far distant. From the common border Angola offers no route to the sea or to any other country. Botswana would offer a real alternative transport linkage to other SADC countries, and a rail link has been mooted for some years, but this would be more of a priorty for Botswana. Such a link would give Botswana access to the outside world for its considerable coal reserves, but only if Walvis Bay was under Namibian control, and world coal prices improved, would this be an alternative to South African routes. The Bot-Nam road now under construction could provide Namibia with a market for fish and perhaps consumer goods and trade from Botswana. There is a tentative but very long road link to other countries through Caprivi and southwest Zambia, but it is hard to see what important trade it might bear. Nor are there any significant Namibian products that these Southern African economies buy.

These projects offering links with independent Africa need to be seen in the context of Namibia's primary economic linkages with South Africa. While a colony, Namibia had been automatically a member of the Southern African Customs Union (SACU) with South Africa, Lesotho, Botswana, and Swaziland, whose customs payments were a crucial source of budget revenues, and Namibia shared the rand as its currency. The minister of finance announced in February 1990 that Namibia would stay in SACU and the rand monetary union for at least two years; the establishment of a Namibian dollar, probably tied to the rand, was later held out as something to be introduced in mid-1993. There was a conference on monetary issues in May 1990, but the only comparative expertise sought was that of Lesotho, Botswana, and Swaziland, each of which has its currency tied to the rand in ways that vary in their direct and formal linkages (Harvey and Isaksen, 1990). The customs union and monetary links with South Africa merely formalize a major dependence (see Chapter 2), particularly for imports of food and other consumer essentials, manufactures, and equipment. For some of the former, SADC countries could present a possible but not very accessible alternative, and internal production could reverse recent patterns that have increased reliance on South African sources of supply (for this latter trend, see Simon and Moorsom, 1987: 92–93). But both these factors would require, as these two authors recognize, a fundamental restructuring of the whole economy whereby "production and distribution should be geared first and foremost to the needs of Namibia's population" (p. 99). For manufactured goods and capital equipment for mining and for any new industry, the alternative to South Africa would be increased trade with the Western world and Japan, and Namibia's mineral earnings offer less of a foreign exchange constraint than some other African countries face. More generally, diversification from reliance on South Africa could involve increasing the already large share of Namibia's exports going to the outside world and encouraging multinational corporations and agencies to set up plants and initiate infrastructural and other development projects. Efforts along these lines were certainly fostered in the transitional period and culminated in the donors conference' in New York.

One crucial lever that South Africa still retains over Namibia's trade in both directions, over its customs revenue earnings via SACU, and over attempts to retain more fishing revenues is its continued occupation of Namibia's main port, Walvis Bay (Evans, 1990). In an interview (8 March 1990) John Sunde, the South African chargé d'affaires appointed to Namibia, suggested that this was only temporary, that Walvis Bay would ultimately revert to Namibia, but that right-wing pressure inside RSA meant this "concession" could not be made immediately. It is certainly true that international, regional, and internal developments are making Walvis Bay a lever of declining importance to South Africa. Meanwhile, however, the South Africans gave the appearance of maintaining a presence for a longer period when work began in December 1989 to construct a new military base to accommodate RSA's 61 Mechanized Battalion, a unit that had been withdrawn from Namibia, and to extend other facilities (*The Namibian,* 14 December 1989 and 26 April 1990).

Whether such military preparations indicate that South Africa is seriously contemplating some future destabilization of Namibia, as some have suggested (Manning and Green, 1987), is not clear. Perhaps the need for a capability for military intervention has passed because South Africa seems to have reassessed the SWAPO leadership and concluded that it "can live with SWAPO" (statement by chief of SADF, J. Geldenhuys, *The Namibian,* 16 November 1989). In any event, this military presence inside the territory of Namibia serves as a further lever for South Africa to influence events, while holding out the prospect of leaving Walvis Bay offers South Africa another bargaining counter. By 1992 a "joint administration" had come into being. Using this and other leverage, South Africa was clearly dictating terms to the Namibian government in the transition. The new Namibian authorities were forced to take over all existing loans outstanding to South Africa and outside bodies, and the annuities paid out to retiring officials of the Namibian government were all deposited in accounts in RSA. When the minister of finance, Herrigel, objected to these losses, it was suggested that the South Africa chargé d'affaires would "tell Nujoma to sort him out" (interview with John Sunde, 8 March 1990).

The new SWAPO government tried to distance itself from Pretoria in its rhetoric: Nujoma's first statement after the elections declared that a SWAPO government would not be supporting withdrawal of UN sanctions against South Africa and would not work with the present white regime (*The Namibian,* 17 November 1989). There was no full diplomatic representation following independence. However, at the level of actual decision-making and especially economic policymaking, the links with South Africa were not disturbed, and the latter seemed to be set to exert significant influence. One of the areas where this influence had an impact, albeit a publicly invisible one, was in RSA's enforcement of political conditions, similar to the Nkomati Agreement signed in 1984 with Mozambique, that Namibia would not provide support or sanctuary for ANC—one of the essential preconditions for independence long sought by South Africa (Landis, 1988). Thus, early trends seemed to deny conclusions like that of Simon and Moorsom (1987: 92): "There is little scope for a neo-colonial solution [in Namibia] favourable to South Africa: the choice is between continued occupation, however dressed up, and genuine independence." In the event,

234 THE TRANSITION TO INDEPENDENCE IN NAMIBIA

South Africa's occupation had ended, but no challenges to South African neocolonialism seemed indicated. The Simon and Moorsom calculation was based on an overly optimistic assessment that South Africa's options in Namibia were limited, in large measure because "it lacks a conservative black elite with any substantial political support . . . [and] it is starkly confronted in SWAPO with a broad-based liberation movement with strong roots in the black working class and poor peasantry" (p. 91). In fact, the "collaborationist politicians" commanded something more than "small political followings" (p. 91), so SWAPO was constrained by a significant opposition, by its own readiness to compromise, and by an economic stranglehold and occupation of Walvis Bay.

Precisely how South Africa reaped these benefits from an unpromising situation where it could count on little political support will be instructive for events in South Africa itself. It is these events dictating the manner of apartheid's ultimate demise that will further define the options open to Namibia and to the rest of Southern Africa. Indeed, there are pointers suggesting that the Namibian experience was a learning process and even a laboratory for ruling circles in South Africa in their quest to manage change in the republic itself, that it was "the crucible in which the South African Government forged that counterrevolutionary strategy of ideological and institutional restructuring it now imposes upon the South African state itself" (Gottschalk, 1987: 27).

Not all these policies and tactics have worked, but they have induced a black politics in opposition to the main national liberation movement. The original form of fostering ethnic building blocks went beyond setting up mere bantustan administration to having their leaders spawn patronage networks and political parties of some sort, eventually to be financed massively so that opposition political parties could buy a minimum of support. But what was decisive was that the South African government managed to weld into an alliance these parties of ethnic political groupings with, and indeed under the tactical leadership of, a party for the white minority. This in turn allowed for a constitutional settlement that was not as crude as that in Zimbabwe, where the whites were permitted to elect a separate bloc of seats and a temporary veto over certain kinds of legislation, especially to protect property rights, but thereby remained an isolated force in Zimbabwe politics and only exerted a limited negative influence. In contrast, DTA could orchestrate the main opposition and with its ethnic allies command a substantial say. Also critical at the margins was the promotion of a third force: parties that were opposed to the main national liberation movement but that could not be dismissed as collaborationist. These considerations direct attention in South Africa to any process of the National Party involving itself in an electoral alliance with black parties; and, of course, a different kind of third force has emerged with Inkatha and with the equally clear evidence of it being bankrolled by the state. Crucial to the success of these tactics was the stretching out of this process by interminable delays, and a decade-long transition seems to be one of the lessons de Klerk gleaned from Namibia's experience (see Wood, 1991: 767).

The role of violence in this process also has to be understood. It served to put people in a state of anxiety and probably inhibited people from embracing SWAPO in areas where the party did not already have strong support. Although orchestrated by the white state, this violence was promoted in its most vicious forms only by black ethnic forces, so the violence took on a black-on-black form and thus fueled ethnic and other antagonisms. This clear pattern is now emerging in South Africa. The violence also served to undermine support for SWAPO, although not so much in areas where the party was strong, partly because of the arbitrary nature of the repression (in areas such as Ovamboland, it may ultimately have been counterproductive in terms of winning votes). In the transition period, a decisive card played by the South Africans for all it was worth was provided by revelations about SWAPO's treatment of its detainees, an issue that not only provoked concerns about a SWAPO regime's repressive tendencies and about a one-party state but also fueled the ethnic images of SWAPO as an Owambo party. Already the issue of ANC's treatment of its dissidents has been raised; ANC would be wise to come clean at the outset to limit damage.

Another track in the strategy has been the pulling of SWAPO's radical teeth. This has been partly achieved by limiting SWAPO's future scope, starting in the 1970s with the concessions that the South African state won by its direct involvement in the negotiating process. The Zimbabwe experience at Lancaster House in 1979 suggests that white interests are best served if a constitution is settled through a bargaining process in which they have a say proportional to their actual power rather than through a constitutional assembly or some other process that subject constitution-making to a democractic process in which whites would vote only their relative population weighting. This step of agreeing to the constitution in advance of elections was opposed for Namibia by the UN plan, but the potential gains to the African majority of CA were considerably reduced by South African demands, largely accepted by the West and forced on SWAPO, for the constitutional principles. Certainly beginning in 1990 the South African government sought by offering reforms to entice the radical African nationalist parties into negotiating a constitution prior to any democratic popular vote (Wood, 1991: 786). Perhaps the ANC has confidence in its own program for reform and its own bargaining power and may not trust a popular vote sufficiently; if so, this would be ill-conceived from their point of view.

A further major concession won by the RSA negotiators was a two-thirds majority to ratify the constitution. This requirement then defined the electoral strategy: to obtain at least a blocking alliance led by the white party. The final ingredient that enabled the South Africans to orchestrate the transition was their retaining control over the whole period, especially the elections. They limited the role of any international referee of the decolonization—in Namibia's case, the UN—and did not concede any power-sharing during the transition. They were thus able to spell out the regulations under which elections were held and dictate their conduct, which added up to having a marginal but arguably decisive influence on the results and on who would have power. If applied to the South African case, this strategy implies a real dilemma for ANC: it would not want to concede too much by reducing its political pressure for change through joining a government too soon, but it would make a big mistake if it stood aside throughout the transition, especially with regard to the administration of an election and security, without at least some considerable international over-sight of the process. But this is legally less easy to guarantee in South Africa; and Namibian experience shows that even a large UN presence can be whittled down by the West and even then may not be guarantee enough of a fair outcome.

# APPENDIXES

# Appendix A
## Selected Source Documents
## Relating to the UN Plan for
## Independence in Namibia

### WESTERN SETTLEMENT PLAN

*United Nations Security Council Document, S/12636, 10 April 1978*

Letter 1978 from the Representatives of Canada, France, Germany, Federal Republic of Germany, the United Kingdom of Great Britain and Northern Ireland and United States of America Addressed to the President of the Security Council.

On instruction from our Governments we have the honour to transmit to you a proposal for the settlement of the Namibian situation and to request that it be circulated as a document of the Security Council.

The objective of our proposal is the independence of Namibia in accordance with resolution 385 (1976), adopted unanimously by the Security Council on 30 January 1976. We are continuing to work towards the implementation of the proposal.

*(Signed by the Permanent Representatives to the United Nations:)*
*William H. BARTON for Canada*
*M. Jacques LEPRETTE for France*
*Rudiger von WECHMAR for the Federal Republic of Germany*
*James MURRAY (Deputy) for the United Kingdom of Great Britain*
*& Northern Ireland*
*Andrew YOUNG for the United States of America*

### Proposal for a Settlement of the Namibian Situation

*I. Introduction*

1. Bearing in mind their responsibilities as members of the Security Council of the United Nations, the Governments of Canada, France, the Federal Republic of Germany, the United Kingdom, and the United States

have consulted with the various parties involved with the Namibian situation with a view to encouraging agreement on the transfer of authority in Namibia to an independent government in accordance with resolution 385 (1976), adopted unanimously by the Security Council on 30 January 1976.

2. To this end, our Governments have drawn up a proposal for the settlement of the Namibian question designed to bring about a transition to independence during 1978 within a framework acceptable to the people of Namibia and thus to the international community. While the proposal addresses itself to all elements of resolution 385 (1976), the key to an internationally acceptable transition to independence is free elections for the whole of Namibia as one political entity with an appropriate United Nations role in accordance with resolution 385 (1976). A resolution will be required in the Security Council requesting the Secretary-General to appoint a United Nations Special Representative whose central task will be to make sure that conditions are established which will allow free and fair elections and an impartial electoral process. The Special Representative will be assisted by a United Nations Transition Assistance Group.

3. The purpose of the electoral process is to elect representatives to a Namibia Constituent Assembly which will draw up and adopt the Constitution for an independent and sovereign Namibia. Authority would then be assumed during 1978 by the Government of Namibia.

4. A more detailed description of the proposal is contained below. Our Governments believe that this proposal provides an effective basis for implementing resolution 385 (1976) while taking adequate account of the interests of all parties involved. In carrying out his responsibilities the Special Representative will work together with the official appointed by South Africa (the Administrator-General) to ensure the orderly transition to independence. This working arrangement shall in no way constitute recognition of the legality of the South African presence in and administration of Namibia.

## II. The Electoral Process

5. In accordance with Security Council resolution 385 (1976), free elections will be held, for the whole of Namibia as one political entity, to enable the people of Namibia to freely and fairly determine their own future. The elections will be under the supervision and control of the United Nations in that, as a condition to the conduct of the electoral process, the elections themselves, and the certification of their results, the United Nations Special Representative will have to satisfy himself at each stage as to the fairness and appropriateness of all measures affecting the political process at all levels of administration before such measures take effect. Moreover the Special Representative may himself make proposals in regard to any aspect of the political process. He will have at his disposal a

substantial civilian section of the United Nations Transition Assistance Group, sufficient to carry out his duties satisfactorily. He will report to the Secretary-General of the United Nations, keeping him informed and making such recommendations as he considers necessary with respect to the discharge of his responsibilities. The Secretary-General, in accordance with the mandate entrusted to him by the Security Council, will keep the Council informed.

6. Elections will be held to select a Constituent Assembly which will adopt a Constitution for an independent Namibia. The Constitution will determine the organization and powers of all levels of government. Every adult Namibian will be eligible, without discrimination or fear of intimidation from any source, to vote, campaign and stand for election to the Constituent Assembly. Voting will be by secret ballot, with provisions made for those who cannot read or write. The date for the beginning of the electoral campaign, the date of elections, the electoral system, the preparation of voters rolls, and other aspects of electoral procedures will be promptly decided upon so as to give all political parties and interested persons, without regard to their political views, a full and fair opportunity to organize and participate in the electoral process. Full freedom of speech, assembly, movement and press shall be guaranteed. The official electoral campaign shall commence only after the United Nations Special Representative has satisfied himself as to the fairness and appropriateness of the electoral procedures. The implementation of the electoral process, including the proper registration of voters and the proper and timely tabulation and publication of voting results will also have to be conducted to the satisfaction of the Special Representative.

7. The following requirements will be fulfilled to the satisfaction of the United Nations Special Representative in order to meet the objective of free and fair election.

A. Prior to the beginning of the electoral campaign, the Administrator-General will repeal all remaining discriminatory or restrictive laws, regulations, or administrative measures which might abridge or inhibit that objective.

B. The Administrator-General shall make arrangements for the release, prior to the beginning of the electoral campaign, of all Namibian political prisoners or political detainees held by the South African authorities so that they can participate fully and freely in that process, without risk of arrest, detention, intimidation or imprisonment. Any disputes concerning the release of political prisoners or political detainees shall be resolved to the satisfaction of the Special Representative acting on the independent advice of a jurist of international standing who shall be designated by the Secretary-General to be legal adviser to the Special Representative.

C. All Namibian refugees or Namibians detained or otherwise outside

the territory of Namibia will be permitted to return peacefully and participate fully and freely in the electoral process without risk of arrest, detention, intimidation or imprisonment. Suitable entry points will be designated
for these purposes.

D. The Special Representative with the assistance of the United
Nations High Commissioner for Refugees and other appropriate international bodies will ensure that Namibians remaining outside of Namibia are
given a free and voluntary choice whether to return. Provision will be made
to attest to the voluntary nature of decisions made by Namibians who elect
not to return to Namibia.

8. A comprehensive cessation of all hostile acts shall be observed by
all parties in order to ensure that the electoral process will be free from
interference and intimidation. The annex describes provisions for the
implementation of the cessation of all hostile acts, military arrangements
concerning the United Nations Transition Assistance Group, the withdrawal of South African forces, and arrangements with respect to other organized forces in Namibia, and with respect to the forces of SWAPO. These
provisions call for:

A. A cessation of all hostile acts by all parties and the restriction of
South African and SWAPO armed forces to base.

B. Thereafter a phased withdrawal from Namibia of all but 1500 South
African troops within 12 weeks and prior to the official start of the political
campaign. The remaining South African force would be restricted to
Grootfontein or Oshivello or both and would be withdrawn after the certification of the election.

C. The demobilization of the citizen forces, commandos, and ethnic
forces, and the dismantling of their command structures.

D. Provision will be made for SWAPO personnel outside of the territory to return peacefully to Namibia through designated entry points to participate freely in the political process.

E. A military section of the United Nations Transition Assistance
Group to make sure that the provisions of the agreed solution will be
observed by all parties. In establishing the military section of UNTAG, the
Secretary-General will keep in mind functional and logistical requirements.
The Five Governments, as members of the Security Council, will support
the Secretary-General's judgement in his discharge of this responsibility.
The Secretary-General will, in the normal manner, include in his consultations all those concerned with the implementation of the agreement. The
Special Representative will be required to satisfy himself as to the implementation of all these arrangements and will keep the Secretary-General
informed of developments in this regard.

9. Primary responsibility for maintaining law and order in Namibia
during the transition period shall rest with the existing police forces. The

Administrator-General to the satisfaction of the United Nations Special Representative shall ensure the good conduct of the police forces and shall take the necessary action to ensure their suitability for continued employment during the transition period. The Special Representative shall make arrangements when appropriate for United Nations personnel to accompany the police forces in the discharge of their duties. The police forces would be limited to the carrying of small arms in the normal performance of their duties.

10. The United Nations Special Representative will take steps to guarantee against the possibility of intimidation or interference with the electoral process from whatever quarter.

11. Immediately after the certification of election results, the Constituent Assembly will meet to draw up and adopt a Constitution for an independent Namibia. It will conclude its work as soon as possible so as to permit whatever additional steps may be necessary prior to the installation of an independent Government of Namibia during 1978.

12. Neighboring countries shall be requested to ensure to the best of their abilities that the provisions of the transitional arrangements, and the outcome of the election, are respected. They shall also be requested to afford the necessary facilities to the United Nations Special Representative and all United Nations personnel to carry out their assigned functions and to facilitate such measures as may be desirable for ensuring tranquillity in the border areas.

## THE UN PLAN

*United Nations Security Council Resolution 435 (1978)*

Adopted by the Security Council at its 2087th meeting on September 1978

### The Security Council

RECALLING its resolutions 385 (1976) and 431 (1978), and 432 (1978),

HAVING CONSIDERED the report submitted by the Secretary-General pursuant to paragraph 2 of resolution 431 (1978) (S/12827) and his explanatory statement made in the Security Council on 29 September 1978 (S/12869),

TAKING NOTE ALSO of the letter dated 8 September 1978 from the President of the South West Africa People's Organization (SWAPO) addressed to the Secretary-General (S/12841),

REAFFIRMING the legal responsibility of the United Nations over Namibia,

1. APPROVES the report of the Secretary-General (S/12827) for the implementation of the proposal for a settlement of the Namibian situation (S/12636) and his explanatory statement (S/12869);

2. REITERATES that its objective is the withdrawal of South Africa's illegal administration of Namibia and the transfer of power to the people of Namibia with assistance of the United Nations in accordance with resolution 385 (1976);

3. DECIDES to establish under its authority a United Nations Transition Assistance Group (UNTAG) in accordance with the abovementioned report of the Secretary-General for a period of up to 12 months in order to assist his Special Representative to carry out the mandate conferred upon him by paragraph 1 of Security Council resolution 431 (1978) namely, to ensure the early independence of Namibia through free and fair elections under the supervision and control of the United Nations;

4. WELCOMES SWAPO's preparedness to co-operate in the implementation of the Secretary-General's report, including its expressed readiness to sign and observe the cease-fire provisions as manifested in the letter from the President of SWAPO dated 8 September 1978 (S/12841);

5. CALLS on South Africa forthwith to co-operate with the Secretary-General, in the implementation of this resolution;

6. DECLARES that all unilateral measures taken by the illegal Administration in Namibia in relation to the electoral process, including unilateral registration of voters, or transfer power, in contravention of Security Council resolutions 385 (1976), 431 (1978) and this resolution are NULL and VOID;

7. REQUESTS the Secretary-General to report to the Security Council not later than 23 October 1978 on the implementation of this resolution;

* * *

## "CONSTITUTIONAL PRINCIPLES"

*United Nations Security Council Resolution 435*
*as Supplemented (S/15287, 1982).*

Letter Dated 12 July 1982 from the Representatives of Canada, France, Federal Republic of Germany, the United Kingdom of Great Britain and Northern Ireland and the United States of America Addressed to the Secretary-General.

On instructions from our Governments we have the honour to transmit to you the text of Principles concerning the Constituent Assembly and the Constitution for an independent Namibia put forward by our Governments to the parties concerned in the negotiations for the implementation on the proposal for a settlement of the Namibian situation (S/12636) in accordance with Security Council resolution 435 (1978) adopted on 29 September 1978.

We have pleasure in informing you that all parties to the negotiations now accept these Principles. Our Governments believe that a decision on the method to be employed to elect the Constituent Assembly should be made in accordance with the provision of Security Council resolution 435 (1978). All parties are agreed that this issue must be settled in accordance with the terms of Security Council resolution 435 (1978) and that the issue must not cause delay in the implementation of 435 (1978). In this regard, our Governments are in consultation with all parties.

Principles concerning the Constituent Assembly and the Constitution for an independent Namibia (S/15287)

## Constituent Assembly

In accordance with United Nations Security Council Resolution 435 (1978), elections will be held to select a Constituent Assembly which will adopt a Constitution for an independent Namibia. The Constitution will determine the organization and powers of all levels of government.

• Every adult Namibian will be eligible, without discrimination or fear of intimidation from any source, to vote, campaign and stand for election to the Constituent Assembly.

• Voting will be by secret ballot, with provisions made for those who cannot read or write.

• The date for the beginning of the electoral campaign, the date of elections, the electoral system, the preparation of voters rolls and other aspects of electoral procedures will be promptly decided upon so as to give all political parties and interested persons, without regard to their political views, a full and fair opportunity to organize and participate in the electoral process.

• Full freedom of speech, assembly, movement and press shall be guaranteed.

• The electoral system will seek to ensure fair representation in the Constituent Assembly to different political parties which gain substantial support in the election.

The Constituent Assembly will formulate the Constitution for an independent Namibia in accordance with the principles in Part B below and will adopt the Constitution as a whole by a two-thirds majority of its total membership.

## Principles for a Constitution for an Independent Namibia

1. Namibia will be a unitary, sovereign and democratic state.

2. The Constitution will be the supreme law of the state. It may be amended only by designated process involving the legislature and/or votes cast in a popular referendum.

3. The Constitution will determine the organization and powers of all levels of government. It will provide for a system of government with three branches: an elected executive branch which will be responsible to the legislative branch; a legislative branch to be elected by universal and equal suffrage which will be responsible for the passage of all laws; and an independent judicial branch which will be responsible for the interpretation of the Constitution and for ensuring its supremacy and the authority of the law. The executive and legislative branches will be constituted by periodic and genuine elections which will be held by secret vote.

4. The electoral system will be consistent with the principles in A.1. above.

5. There will be a declaration of fundamental rights, which will include the rights to life, personal liberty and freedom of movement; to freedom of conscience; to freedom of expression, including freedom of speech and a free press; to freedom of assembly and association, including political parties and trade unions; to due process and equality before the law; to protection from arbitrary deprivation of private property without just compensation; and to freedom from racial, ethnic, religious or sexual discrimination. The declaration of rights will be consistent with the provisions of the Universal Declaration of Human Rights. Aggrieved individuals will be entitled to have the courts adjudicate and enforce these rights.

6. It will be forbidden to create criminal offences with retrospective effect or to provide for increased penalties with retrospective effect.

7. Provision will be made for the balanced structuring of the public service, the police service and the defence services and for equal access by all to recruitment of these services. The fair administration of personnel policy in relation to these services will be assured by appropriate independent bodies.

8. Provision will be made for the establishment of elected councils for local and/or regional administration.

* * *

## OTHER UN DOCUMENTS THAT
## FURTHER ELABORATE THE UN PLAN

- UN Security Council resolutions on Namibia
  UNSCR 385, 30 January 1976

UNSCR 431 and 432, 27 July 1978
UNSCR 439, 13 November 1978
UNSCR 532, 31 May 1983
UNSCR 539 and 566, 19 June 1985
UNSCR 601, 30 October 1987
UNSCR 629, 16 January 1989
UNSCR 632, 16 February 1989

- Reports and explanatory statements by the Secretary-General
S/12827, 29 August 1978
S/12869, 28 September 1978
S/15776, 19 May 1983
S/17658, 26 November 1985
S/20412, 23 January 1989
S/20457, 9 February 1989
S/20479, 21 February 1989

### OTHER INTERNATIONAL AGREEMENTS THAT
### HAD A BEARING ON EVENTS IN NAMIBIA INCLUDE:

- Protocols of Geneva and Brazzaville and the Tripartite Agreement, 1988—all signed by Cuba, Angola, and South Africa
- Annexure on the Joint Commission (among Angola, Cuba, and South Africa)
- Mount Etjo Declaration, May 1989—reaffirming the cease-fire in Namibia

# Appendix B
## Population, Estimated Eligible Voters, and Registered Voters

**Table B.1  Population and Estimated Voters per Electoral District**

| Electoral Districts | Total Population 1981 Census | Total Population 1989 (Est.) | Estimated Population, Age 18+[a] | Estimated Population 18% + 5%[b] |
|---|---|---|---|---|
| Bethanie | 2,808 | 3,502 | 1,975 | 2,074 |
| Caprivi | 40,376 | 50,349 | 21,994 | 23,093 |
| Damaraland | 24,214 | 30,195 | 14,818 | 15,559 |
| Gobabis | 22,079 | 27,533 | 14,228 | 14,939 |
| Grootfontein | 21,989 | 27,420 | 15,207 | 15,967 |
| Hereroland | 34,329 | 42,808 | 18,513 | 19,438 |
| Kaokoland | 16,637 | 20,746 | 11,622 | 12,203 |
| Karasburg | 9,502 | 11,849 | 6,611 | 6,942 |
| Karibib | 8,953 | 11,164 | 5,429 | 5,700 |
| Kavango | 105,690 | 131,795 | 58,214 | 61,125 |
| Keetmanshoop | 17,608 | 21,957 | 11,908 | 12,504 |
| Lüderitz | 14,314 | 17,850 | 13,254 | 13,917 |
| Maltahöhe | 4,751 | 5,924 | 3,442 | 3,615 |
| Mariental | 20,578 | 25,661 | 13,536 | 14,212 |
| Namaland[c] | 12,766 | 15,919 | 8,131 | 8,538 |
| Okahandja | 13,336 | 16,630 | 9,498 | 9,973 |
| Omaruru | 5,498 | 6,856 | 3,835 | 4,027 |
| Otjiwarongo | 16,126 | 20,109 | 11,996 | 12,595 |
| Outjo | 8,866 | 11,056 | 5,951 | 6,249 |
| Owambo | 452,036 | 563,689 | 267,082 | 280,436 |
| Rehoboth | 27,664 | 34,497 | 16,070 | 16,873 |
| Swakopmund | 15,473 | 19,295 | 13,330 | 13,996 |
| Tsumeb | 19,447 | 24,250 | 15,323 | 16,089 |
| Windhoek | 110,644 | 137,973 | 83,421 | 87,592 |
| Not allocated | 7,512 | 9,367 | 7,182 | 7,541 |
| Total | 1,033,196 | 1,288,394 | 652,645 | 685,192 |

*Source:* UNTAG
*Notes:* a. 1981 census statistics are multiplied by a factor of 1.247 to update figures for 1989.
b. Add 5% to allow for possible undercount in 1989 census.
c. Namaland became part of Keetsmanshoop ED for election in 1989.

**Table B.2  Registered Voters and Estimated Eligible Voters in Each Electoral District**

| Electoral District[a] | Estimated Eligible Voters[b] | Registered Voters | % Registered[c] |
|---|---|---|---|
| Ovamboland | 280,436 | 248,272 | 88.5 |
| Lüderitz | 13,917 | 10,740 | 77.2 |
| Swakopmund | 13,996 | 25,363 | 181.2 |
| Tsumeb | 16,089 | 14,651 | 91.1 |
| Kavango | 61,125 | 64,156 | 105.0 |
| EDs with SWAPO majority | 385,563 | 363,182 | 94.2 |
| | | | |
| Windhoek | 87,592 | 105,382 | 120.3 |
| Caprivi | 21,267 | 28,096 | 132.1 |
| Okahandja | 9,973 | 11,233 | 112.6 |
| Karibib | 5,700 | 6,955 | 122.0 |
| Maltahohe | 3,615 | 2,635 | 72.9 |
| Grootfontein | 17,793 | 20,510 | 115.3 |
| Otjiwarongo | 12,595 | 13,287 | 105.5 |
| Keetmanshoop | 21,042 | 20,039 | 95.2 |
| Damaraland | 15,559 | 15,127 | 97.2 |
| Omaruru | 4,027 | 6,008 | 149.2 |
| Mariental | 14,212 | 14,630 | 102.9 |
| Bethanie | 2,074 | 2,464 | 118.8 |
| Outjo | 6,249 | 7,219 | 115.5 |
| Rehoboth | 16,873 | 17,346 | 102.8 |
| Hereroland | 16,892 | 16,317 | 96.6 |
| Gobabis | 17,485 | 19,250 | 110.1 |
| Karasburg | 6,942 | 18,257 | 263.0 |
| Kaokoland | 12,203 | 13,546 | 111.0 |
| EDs SWAPO < 50% | 292,093 | 338,301 | 115.8 |
| | | | |
| Total | 677,656[d] | 701,483 | 103.5 |

*Notes:* a. The Electoral Districts are listed in descending order of % vote for SWAPO.
b. The higher estimate made by AG's office on basis of 2.9% annual growth on 1981 Census plus 5% (see last Column of Table B.1)
c. Column 3 represents Column 2 as % of Column 1.
d. The UNTAG estimates total (see Table B.1) includes 7,541 extra estimated people of voting age not allocated to an ED.

# Appendix C
## Namibia's System of
## Proportional Representation

Namibia's election was conducted under a system of proportional representation. Systems of proportional representation are designed to produce elected assemblies in which the share of the popular vote received by each competing party is reflected in the share of the seats won by that party in the assembly. Systems of proportional representation are different from systems of first past the post. In the latter system, the assembly is made up of candidates elected in single-member constituencies. This can produce unrepresentative patterns. In a case of two parties competing, party A may receive 51 percent of the votes in each constituency and hence win every seat in the assembly on the basis of a little more than half the vote, while the 49 percent of electors voting for party B would be left unrepresented.

There are a number of types of proportional representation, but common to each is a modification of the single-member constituency as the basis for which the preferences of all the electors may be registered. The basis of the system used in the Namibian elections was that the country became, in effect, a single constituency. The number of votes required by a party to receive a seat, the quota, was established through the following calculation: the quota is equal to the total votes recorded divided by the number of seats.

Since 72 seats were contested in the election, the calculation of the quota gives the actual number of votes that represent 1/72nd of the total. With 72 seats to be elected, for each 72nd of the vote received, a party wins one seat. Since 670,830 total votes were recorded, the quota in the election was 9,318 votes.

Individual candidates are drawn from an ordered list presented by each of the parties before the election. Thus, if one party receives a vote equal to three times the quota, its first, second, and third listed candidates would be elected. Most seats will be directly allocated by this procedure of dividing the total votes of a party by the quota of votes required to win one seat. However, since the votes received by each party are unlikely to be perfectly divisible by the quota, there will still be a number of unallocated seats.

**Table C.1  Illustrations of Namibia's Voting System**

| Party | Votes | Seats | Remainder | Extra Seats | Total Seats |
|---|---|---|---|---|---|
| ACN | 23,728 | 2 | 5,092 | 1 | 3 |
| CDA | 2,495 | 0 | 2,495 | 0 | 0 |
| DTA | 191,532 | 20 | 5,172 | 1 | 21 |
| FLN | 10,452 | 1 | 1,134 | 0 | 1 |
| NNDP | 984 | 0 | 984 | 0 | 0 |
| NNF | 5,344 | 0 | 5,344 | 1 | 1 |
| NPF | 10,693 | 1 | 1,375 | 0 | 1 |
| SWAPO-D | 3,161 | 0 | 3,161 | 0 | 0 |
| SWAPO | 384,567 | 41 | 2,529 | 0 | 41 |
| UDF | 37,874 | 4 | 602 | 0 | 4 |
| Total | 670,830 | 69 | | 3 | 72 |
| Quota | 9,318 | | | | |

There are a number of methods for the allocation of remaining seats. The method chosen for Namibia was that of the largest remainder, in which the unallocated seats were distributed to the parties that had the largest remainder of votes following the division of their total vote into the quota. Therefore, the 3 seats remaining unallocated were distributed, in order, to ACN, DTA, and NNF.

Some states operate a "threshold" in their system of proportional representation, in which a party must receive a minimum share of the vote, often around 4 percent or 5 percent, in order to receive any representation in the assembly at all. The electoral system enacted in Namibia did not operate a threshold. Since the quota represented 1.39 percent of the vote, any party achieving that level of support would be guaranteed a seat. Indeed, the effect of this arrangement, together with the system of the largest remainder, was that a party could gain a representation with an even lower share than this. The method of proportional representation operated in Namibia, therefore, was particularly advantageous to small political parties, which would have been excluded from assemblies elected under most other arrangements.

In a simulation exercise we performed on the basis of a first-past-the-post system of elections, results were estimated as:

| | |
|---|---|
| SWAPO | 44 seats |
| DTA | 25 seats |
| UDF | 2 seats |
| ACN | 1 seat |
| ACNFCN | 1 seat |

Based on these estimates, the operation of such a system would have benefited the largest parties (SWAPO and DTA) at the expense of the smaller
parties. While SWAPO would have increased its dominance of the
Constitution Assembly (from 57 percent to 61 percent of the assembly
vote), these results would have proportionally benefited DTA (increasing
its share of assembly votes by 19 percent against an increase for SWAPO
of 7 percent) and would still have left SWAPO short of the majority
required for amending the constitution on its own.

**Figure D.1 The Structure of UNTAG**

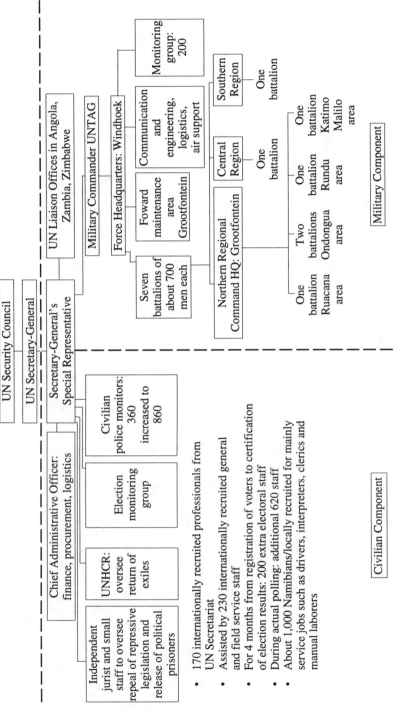

*Source:* Adapted mainly from documentation of the preimplementation meeting, Geneva, 1981.

**Table E.1  Votes Cast by Electoral District for Each Party in Constituent Assembly Elections**

| | Estimated Eligible Voters[a] | Registered Voters | Votes Cast | Valid Votes | ANC | CDA | DTA | FCN | NNDP | NNF | NPF | SWAPO-D | SWAPO | UDF |
|---|---|---|---|---|---|---|---|---|---|---|---|---|---|---|
| Bethanie | 2,074 | 2,464 | 2,337 | 2,293 | 301 | 32 | 1,314 | 55 | 4 | 8 | 15 | 16 | 461 | 87 |
| Caprivi | 23,093 | 28,096 | 27,006 | 26,333 | 104 | 168 | 13,786 | 436 | 44 | 44 | 687 | 93 | 10,415 | 556 |
| Damaraland | 15,559 | 15,127 | 15,215 | 15,063 | 175 | 28 | 2,579 | 34 | 9 | 109 | 62 | 25 | 4,204 | 7,838 |
| Gobabis | 14,939 | 19,250 | 18,111 | 17,732 | 1,940 | 158 | 11,684 | 173 | 50 | 391 | 377 | 59 | 2,458 | 442 |
| Grootfontein | 15,967 | 20,510 | 19,602 | 19,036 | 1,606 | 115 | 8,818 | 236 | 32 | 66 | 376 | 51 | 6,417 | 1,319 |
| Hereroland | 16,892 | 16,317 | 15,605 | 15,396 | 68 | 89 | 9,880 | 193 | 33 | 705 | 1,935 | 40 | 2,353 | 100 |
| Kaokoland | 12,203 | 13,546 | 12,794 | 12,478 | 64 | 91 | 8,180 | 120 | 70 | 48 | 2,480 | 24 | 1,330 | 71 |
| Karasburg | 6,942 | 18,257 | 18,813 | 18,687 | 4,820 | 54 | 10,068 | 367 | 30 | 40 | 152 | 39 | 2,378 | 739 |
| Karibib | 5,700 | 6,955 | 6,582 | 6,496 | 406 | 24 | 1,989 | 67 | 2 | 56 | 161 | 14 | 2,244 | 1,533 |
| Kavango | 61,125 | 64,156 | 61,426 | 59,431 | 527 | 449 | 24,817 | 401 | 179 | 151 | 497 | 319 | 30,755 | 1,336 |
| Keetmanshoop | 21,042 | 20,039 | 19,269 | 18,968 | 1,458 | 100 | 9,249 | 335 | 58 | 432 | 209 | 113 | 5,496 | 1,518 |
| Lüderitz | 13,917 | 10,740 | 11,278 | 11,233 | 521 | 17 | 2,138 | 89 | 14 | 218 | 67 | 26 | 7,753 | 390 |
| Maltahöhe | 3,615 | 2,635 | 2,578 | 2,507 | 388 | 15 | 668 | 161 | 13 | 8 | 14 | 9 | 848 | 383 |
| Mariental | 14,212 | 14,630 | 14,082 | 13,913 | 1,476 | 85 | 7,665 | 403 | 26 | 77 | 101 | 29 | 3,024 | 1,036 |
| Okahandja | 9,973 | 11,233 | 10,380 | 10,350 | 672 | 42 | 4,273 | 56 | 9 | 81 | 334 | 23 | 3,718 | 1,142 |
| Omaruru | 4,027 | 6,008 | 5,772 | 5,683 | 213 | 40 | 2,959 | 48 | 5 | 206 | 318 | 24 | 1,281 | 589 |
| Otjiwarongo | 12,595 | 13,287 | 12,318 | 12,176 | 699 | 49 | 5,213 | 81 | 12 | 134 | 114 | 19 | 4,020 | 1,835 |
| Outjo | 6,249 | 7,219 | 6,904 | 6,741 | 765 | 37 | 3,072 | 88 | 3 | 31 | 52 | 13 | 1,197 | 1,483 |
| Ovamboland | 280,436 | 248,272 | 248,171 | 245,157 | 465 | 489 | 10,745 | 150 | 214 | 95 | 505 | 1,706 | 225,621 | 5,167 |
| Rehoboth | 16,873 | 17,346 | 17,356 | 17,105 | 127 | 66 | 7,746 | 5,010 | 84 | 304 | 243 | 48 | 3,015 | 462 |
| Swakopmund | 13,996 | 25,363 | 24,083 | 23,943 | 1,271 | 32 | 5,931 | 395 | 5 | 241 | 145 | 64 | 14,123 | 1,736 |
| Tsumeb | 16,089 | 14,651 | 13,872 | 13,724 | 922 | 36 | 4,028 | 96 | 11 | 46 | 72 | 57 | 7,254 | 1,202 |
| Windhoek | 87,592 | 105,382 | 97,134 | 96,385 | 4,749 | 279 | 34,730 | 1,458 | 77 | 1,853 | 1,777 | 350 | 44,202 | 6,910 |
| Total | 685,917[b] | 701,483 | 680,688 | 670,830 | 23,728 | 2,495 | 191,532 | 10,452 | 986 | 5,366 | 10,693 | 3,161 | 386,567 | 37,874 |

*Note*: a. The higher estimate of 1989 population of voter age (see Table B.1)
b. Includes 7,541 estimated voters not allocated to any ED.

**Table E.2  Percentage Vote for Each Party by Electoral District**

| | ACN | CDA | DTA | FCN | NNDP | NNF | NPF | SWAPO-D | SWAPO | UDF |
|---|---|---|---|---|---|---|---|---|---|---|
| Bethanie | 13 | 1 | 57 | 2 | 0 | 0 | 1 | 1 | 20 | 4 |
| Caprivi | 0 | 1 | 52 | 2 | 0 | 0 | 3 | 0 | 40 | 2 |
| Damaraland | 1 | 0 | 17 | 0 | 0 | 1 | 0 | 0 | 28 | 52 |
| Gobabis | 11 | 1 | 66 | 1 | 0 | 2 | 2 | 0 | 14 | 2 |
| Grootfontein | 8 | 1 | 46 | 1 | 0 | 0 | 2 | 0 | 34 | 7 |
| Hereroland | 0 | 1 | 64 | 1 | 0 | 5 | 13 | 0 | 15 | 1 |
| Kaokoland | 1 | 1 | 66 | 1 | 1 | 0 | 20 | 0 | 11 | 1 |
| Karasburg | 26 | 0 | 54 | 2 | 0 | 1 | 1 | 0 | 13 | 4 |
| Karibib | 6 | 0 | 31 | 1 | 0 | 0 | 2 | 0 | 35 | 24 |
| Kavango | 1 | 1 | 42 | 1 | 0 | 0 | 1 | 1 | 52 | 2 |
| Keetmanshoop | 8 | 1 | 49 | 2 | 0 | 2 | 1 | 1 | 29 | 8 |
| Lüderitz | 5 | 0 | 19 | 1 | 0 | 2 | 1 | 0 | 69 | 3 |
| Maltahöhe | 15 | 1 | 27 | 6 | 1 | 0 | 1 | 0 | 34 | 15 |
| Mariental | 11 | 1 | 55 | 3 | 0 | 1 | 1 | 0 | 22 | 7 |
| Okahandja | 6 | 0 | 41 | 1 | 0 | 1 | 3 | 0 | 36 | 11 |
| Omaruru | 4 | 1 | 52 | 1 | 0 | 4 | 6 | 0 | 23 | 10 |
| Otjiwarongo | 6 | 0 | 43 | 1 | 0 | 1 | 1 | 0 | 33 | 15 |
| Outjo | 11 | 1 | 46 | 1 | 0 | 0 | 1 | 0 | 18 | 22 |
| Ovamboland | 0 | 0 | 4 | 0 | 0 | 0 | 0 | 1 | 92 | 2 |
| Rehoboth | 1 | 0 | 45 | 29 | 0 | 2 | 1 | 0 | 18 | 3 |
| Swakopmund | 5 | 0 | 25 | 2 | 0 | 1 | 1 | 0 | 59 | 7 |
| Tsumeb | 7 | 0 | 29 | 1 | 0 | 0 | 1 | 0 | 53 | 9 |
| Windhoek | 5 | 0 | 36 | 2 | 0 | 2 | 2 | 0 | 46 | 7 |
| Percent of Total Votes | 3.5 | 0.4 | 28.6 | 1.6 | 0.1 | 0.8 | 1.6 | 0.5 | 57.3 | 5.6 |

# Appendix F
## Regional Analyses
## of Election Results

This discussion groups together EDs into regional sections rather than dealing with all of them in turn. It offers some sketch of the demographic and political-economic character and some hypotheses as to the factors likely to have affected voting.

### The North

All the northern border districts (in descending order of size: Ovamboland, Kavango, Caprivi, Kaokoland) were distinct from the rest of the country in that they were north of the police zone, they were labor reserves (see Chapter 2), and they bore most of the brunt of the war. They were also each dominated by one ethnic group, and the three most populous not only made up almost half the electorate but also had very concentrated populations, unlike the rest of the country.

### Ovamboland

Ovamboland was the single most crucial ED; it contained one-third of the registered voters. There was a remarkable turnout of 98.39 percent here, and the percentage of tendered votes was the lowest of any electoral district (5.8 percent), suggesting most people were registered locally. SWAPO's overwhelming majority (92.3 percent) and the high turnout show that the Owambo people voted for SWAPO across all areas, classes, and strata. Such consensual voting occurred only in this part of the country.

SWAPO certainly insisted that a "vote for SWAPO is a vote for peace" in its campaigns in the north—a message that must have had a powerful pull in war-torn Kavango and Caprivi as well as Owambo. The message was also pushed home by the sons and daughters of Owambo families, who had provided the bulk of PLAN fighters and came back to the north to campaign for SWAPO. SWAPO also had an organizational structure in Ovamboland that was set up during the war and therefore became fully functional once the election process started. The organization was built up from cells consisting of a group of homesteads and was used by SWAPO to facilitate the registration process, voter education, and the getting of people to the polls (interview with SWAPO organizer, October 1989).

Central to the experience of people in the Owambo region was the contract labor system, described in Chapter 2. SWAPO was formed specifically to resist this system, and to that extent was in fact a workers' party. But SWAPO voters must have included people of all economic strata, not just migrants and their rural families. Teachers and educated youth played an important part in SWAPO's mobilization during the campaign and voting periods, and the school boycotts of the previous year could be taken as evidence of the support among this group for SWAPO long before the election. But SWAPO also succeeded in getting support from some wealthy businesspeople, who provided finance and transport, as well as smaller traders.

One assumption had been that all those people who had worked for the previous administration and had been on the payroll in some form or other, plus their dependents, would support DTA. In other words, a form of patronage similar to that operating in previous elections would ensure that those who had a stake in the system would see their interests as being represented by DTA. In order to establish whether this was true of all such people, we have to make some calculations about their number. The number of security personnel for the whole of the north (Owambo, Caprivi, and Kavango) has been estimated at ten thousand (IDAF, 1983), and if the regional figures are proportionate to local populations as suggested by the registered voters, the figure for Owambo would be more than seven thousand. In addition, there were more than eight thousand employees of the second-tier authority in Owambo, bringing to fifteen thousand the people who were part of the existing system as well as a growing number of shopkeepers, traders, and other businesspeople who had shared in the prosperity brought by an occupying army. The 10,745 DTA votes may well have come from these people, but they and their dependents totaled far more than the DTA vote or even the total non-SWAPO vote (19,536). What is evident from these figures is that many people in more prosperous classes, including those who were in the pay of the state or a dependent of someone who was, must have voted for SWAPO.

It was assumed by many observers (as well as SWAPO) that the various forms of intimidation that took place in Ovamboland (outlined in Chapter 6) were intended to increase the DTA vote. As the Koevoet/DTA intimidation did not bring about a close vote between the two rival parties, and indeed SWAPO seemingly gained support from voters in all classes, it is possible that intimidation had a countereffect of alerting people to the need to vote if they wanted SWAPO to win and wanted peace.

Evidence does not allow us to conclude to what extent this allegiance was owed to SWAPO because of the specifics of its policies or because of it being regarded in this region as the party that had the ability (military strength) to bring and guarantee peace (like ZANU in Zimbabwe). No other party had that power here, and SWAPO could not guarantee it for other parts of the country. Or, as one of the common explanations would have it, was overwhelming support given here because of SWAPO's history as the significant nationalist party that originated as an Owambo organization in a part of the country where 98.9 percent of the population was Owambo?

### Kavango

To the east of Ovamboland, Kavango also bore the brunt of the violent border war. The population is densely concentrated along the banks of the Okavango River, which defines the national boundary with Angola. Away from the river the land is too arid for cultivation, and from the earliest days of settlement related people have lived on both sides of the river in spite of the political dividing line between the two states drawn in the colonial period. People on the Namibian side in Kavango were moved away from the riverbanks by SADF with the escalation of the war in the late 1970s, as the dense vegetation had previously allowed SWAPO cadres and PLAN guerrillas to move through the area undetected. SADF then discovered that this more dispersed population in the drier areas could well harbor PLAN fighters. People were then herded back to the confines of the river valley in 1982. By this time, SADF had set up bases along the riverbank, enabling it to use Casspirs to mount police actions. SADF also organized such activities through the actions of Koevoet-Kavango, the 202 Battalion, and Ezura, a political "cultural" parastatal body.

The Kavango ED also contained western Caprivi and was the third largest ED (containing 9.1 percent of the registered voters). Conflict over the use of the arid Caprivi area has raged between San groups and the occupants of eastern Caprivi (both of which want to use it for farming and poach animals from it), on the one hand, and the conservation lobby, on the other, although legally it remains a conservation area in which some San people were given permission to reside. Many of these San people were recruited into the army and subsequently lived in the Delta and Omega military bases, where they registered and voted.

Many observers predicted that people in Kavango would vote for DTA as four out of the five chiefs supported DTA and SWAPO organization was much weaker there than in Ovamboland. SWAPO officials and church people in Kavango had, however, predicted a SWAPO victory (interviews with SWAPO officials and Catholic priests, Rundu, October 1989), arguing tribal leadership had been discredited, as it had aided and abetted the colonial state in causing the suffering of local people. The results were very evenly balanced, an important area for DTA, as its Kavango vote constituted 13.1 percent of their total, but it also provided a crucial 8 percent of SWAPO's national vote (equivalent to four seats).

SWAPO organization had begun growing in the mid-1980s, with the school boycotts of 1988 heightening political awareness here, being initiated by teachers, pastors, and young people and coalescing around schools and churches. SWAPO cadres and returnees were thus able to build upon existing political structures in their campaigning, notably to the western side of Kavango. SWAPO support was thought to be strongest in the Kwangali area of western Kavango around Nkurenkuru, known as the "red area." The chief here supported SWAPO, and this was the region in which PLAN guerrillas were active, coming into Kavango from the Owambo region, and engaged in political education as well as in guerrilla activity. But a selection of the returns by polling station (see Chapter 8) showed that such an east-west pattern was by no means clear. Rather, the vote was divided in each polling station in Kavango. Regional variation in the success of either party within Kavango was no more than 30 percent, and there was considerable SWAPO voting even in the far east of Mbukushu, reportedly strong DTA territory.

Violent intimidation was prominent in campaigning in Kavango, as in Owambo. CIMS observers suggested that many people were scared into voting for DTA by intimidatory tactics. If this was indeed the case, then the same kind of intimidation from DTA had a different outcome in Kavango from Ovamboland. An alternative interpretation for Kavango would be that DTA-organized intimidation had the same effect as in Ovamboland and actually strengthened SWAPO's more limited support, which might not have coalesced in the same way in the absence of such intimidation.

The presumption was that voters being brought across the Kavango River from Angola at gunpoint to vote in Kavango, with the connivance of chiefs (Nadel lawyers' report, 8 and 12 November 1989), would support DTA because all those coming from the Angolan side would be close to UNITA (CIMS, 1990: 50). As we do not know the results from the polling station where these people actually voted, it is difficult to assess the numerical effect of their presence. The most serious breaching of electoral regulations with regard to the Angolan voters occurred at the registration stage; it appears that many of those thought to have been brought to vote against their will had in fact been formally registered (see Chapter 6). Even if all the allegations were true and all those from the Angolan side of the border voted for DTA, this would explain only a small part of DTA support, 2–3 percent of the total Kavango vote.

Besides the Angolans and those who may have been coerced or intimidated in some way, support for DTA was also likely to have come from various groups with connections to the military: ex-SWATF 202 Battalion soldiers (who were used as field organizers for DTA), members of Koevoet and their dependents, San voters at Omega base (who were mostly ex-SWATF members and their dependents), and people from Angola at Delta base, both in western Caprivi. Using the same method of calculation for their numbers as for Owambo, we reach an estimate of security employees of 1,870. Observers established that places surrounding military bases were inaccessible to SWAPO during campaigning and commented on the strong DTA support apparent there, expecting that voters were bound to vote DTA.

The predominance of Kavango people in the region (85.1 percent in 1981) belies any ethnic bloc analysis. Clearly the Kavango people were divided in their vote. One possible explanatory thesis may lie in one of the important campaign issues: land. In a situation of land shortage where access to land was controlled by chiefs, people could have read their chances of increasing access in various ways. A party that promised to shore up the power of the chiefs might have ensured that those who were confident of their chief's continued patronage might well have been keen to give support to DTA and perhaps even anxious about what this might have meant for them under a SWAPO government pledging to change the present system. Those who recognized the local nature of their exploitation and powerlessness, as well as the national picture in which they were consigned to the land within the reserves, might well have been attracted to the promises of SWAPO.

### Caprivi

The ED's population was also one dominated by one ethnic group, but the Caprivi who constituted 98 percent of the population were an amalgam of three tribes. This was the fourth largest ED. The area covered by the ED had been a key territory for SADF activities, which prevented open local SWAPO organization and restricted PLAN military activity and recruitment after 1978. Caprivi is remote and distant from the capital, and SWAPO supporters experienced a great deal of intimidation during the campaign period, and SWAPO rallies were disrupted by DTA (*The Namibian*, 27 September 1989).

No data exist to determine whether party votes were split along ethnic lines between Mafwe and Masubia tribes. However, there is no history of a political alliance of the two parties with different tribes, which share common forms of social and economic organization. Angolan/Zambian immigrant voters came into Caprivi, too, but their number is unknown.

Caprivi is an area with considerable agricultural potential. It has already been earmarked for a number of commercial projects growing exotic crops. It may be that an analysis of the politics around access to land would help to shed light on the balance of support for SWAPO and DTA. The local population has become divided between those who live in the town of Katima Mulilo (estimated at around 50 percent of total Caprivi [Adams and Werner, 1990: 125]) and those who manage to obtain some proportion of subsistence from the land, commonly combined with some form of migrant labor in Katima Mulilo, a small group of whom have emerged as an elite group of commercial farmers. All these people at present have inalienable rights of access to land through customary tenure, allocated through tribal chiefs. Perhaps people voted on the instruction of chiefs. But again, no data exist of urban versus rural voting differences.

Caprivi differs from Kavango in one important respect: the existence of commercial farmers may have translated into an anti-SWAPO vote. Local perceptions of how the parties' campaign promises would affect the land situation in Caprivi were in any case allegedly affected by disinformation; SWAPO was thought to be interested in changing customary land tenure into state ownership with individual leasehold, and DTA talked about individual freehold (Adams et al., 1990: 132–133). As the land issue could thus have had a detrimental effect on both parties, we cannot be confident in using this analysis to explain the results.

Caprivi's remoteness from the rest of the country and separation even from neighboring Kavango have served so far only to ensure the continued ignorance of outsiders of local politics. Since independence the area has reputedly been named as a targeted area (along with Rehoboth) for South African support for a separatist movement such as MNR in Mozambique, or UNITA in Angola, to be led by Mishake Muyongo, allegedly already in discussion with Pretoria for assistance in setting up a separate Caprivi republic (Anon, 1989: 21). As with the MNR in Mozambique, an explanation of such a development, if the movement becomes a reality, would have to do more than show the extent of South African action; it would also have to account for the attraction of such organization to the local people. Current explanations of local politics do not do this.

*Kaokoland*

Kaokoland forms the fourth border region in the north, although it was a much smaller ED, holding only 1.9 percent of the total registered voters. It is an extremely arid, sparsely populated area of the country, whose inhabitants remain very isolated from any other part. Even during the election campaign it was unusual for a newspaper to reach the main town of Opuwo. SADF and Koevoet had controlled the whole area very tightly throughout the war, recruiting the local population into the army and as irregulars, which became a primary source of income for the population of nomadic pastoralists.

Kaokoland was certainly a DTA stronghold; it gained 65.5 percent of the local vote, and most commentators predicted such a pattern. The degree of dependence of most of the population on the previous administration (the patron image of DTA), the repression of SWAPO before 1989, and intense intimidation during the election were commonly thought to be sufficient explanation for a strong DTA victory. In addition, the ethnicity analysis is brought to bear here as the population are 94 percent Herero, generally expected to sustain loyalty to DTA.

SWAPO gained less support here than anywhere else in Namibia: a mere 10.7 percent of the Kaokoland vote. SWAPO had not been able to open an office before April 1989 and was able to campaign at all only with great difficulty, having at first been met with obstacles imposed by chiefs (Chapter 6). What is difficult to explain here is which elements voted for SWAPO at all, as there had been such a heavy clampdown on SWAPO organization and such extreme difficulties in SWAPO campaigning.

NPF had its greatest ED percentage success in this area, perhaps because of traditional loyalties to Katjiuongua, who was considered to be a high-ranking Herero (an Mbanderu chief from the royal house of Maharero) (Wellmer, 1990: 6).

## The North-Central Commercial Farming and Mining Areas

### Tsumeb

Tsumeb is a mining town surrounded by white commercial farms (the ED extended up to and included the Etosha salt pan and game area). This ED is close to Ovamboland and was under heavy security during the war years as guerrilla activity extended down to the white farming area in what has been called the "death triangle" of Tsumeb, Grootfontein, and Otavi, so named because of the effectiveness of white farmer–police cooperation in attacking guerrilla movements and SWAPO organization in the area.

The white commercial farms held employees in semifeudal conditions, and everywhere in the country workers living in these conditions were assumed to vote for DTA as a result of some mix of ignorance and various kinds of intimidation by their employers. Mining areas, such as Tsumeb town, however, delivered a relatively high SWAPO vote. These factors may explain the contrasts between the results for Tsumeb and Grootfontein, which contains the white farm areas but no mines.

### Grootfontein

Grootfontein, with its rail terminal and airfield, had been the point of departure for contract workers being flown down to the Consolidated Diamond Mine in Oranjemund. More recently, it furnished a SADF base. The ED included the town of Otavi and the Kombat copper mine on the road between it and Grootfontein (the mine employed a much smaller number of workers than the mines in Tsumeb), and so the lower vote for SWAPO in the ED does not undermine the workers-for-SWAPO thesis. In the far east the electorate included Bushmen in the Tsumkwe region, but

these were only a tiny proportion of the total ED, although they were widely assumed to have voted for DTA. The farmworkers here, as in most parts
of the country, were from various ethnic groups, according to the 1981 census, and so if they did all vote for DTA, this would suggest that there was
some factor other than simply ethnicity at work—perhaps employer influence. As in Tsumeb, the proportion of UDF support was less than the proportion of Damara in the total population.

*Hereroland*

Of the population of the ED, 89 percent were Herero (the 1981 census,
however, showed that only 38 percent of Herero lived here, 20 percent in
Kaokoland, 12.9 percent in Windhoek, and 28.7 percent in the south). Land
under communal tenure was allocated through headmen and chiefs, so there
was a group of people who had more direct power over others than that
gained simply through dispensing largesse from the public purse. This factor was thought to have had more influence here than in other parts of the
country. DTA was assumed to be the major beneficiary, although the picture was complex as there had been a history of "collaboration, competition
and conflict between SWAPO leaders and Herero leaders" (Wellmer, 1990:
6).

The local affiliate, NUDO, was a powerful element of DTA (see
Chapter 2), and many respected members of the community had participated in, and benefited from, the second-tier administration. DTA's sizable
64.2 percent of the vote apparently derived in particular from the poorest of
the community. Despite the more radical rhetoric of SWAPO, its supporters
were reportedly the better off and the educated (interview with SWAPO,
Gobabis, October 1989). DTA was also able to play on the detainees issue,
in that a considerable number of young people had joined PLAN, and
SWAPO was slow in responding to requests as to the whereabouts of relatives during the campaign period.

SWAPO's very small vote, only 15.3 percent, seemed to have come
from concentrated areas of support. Chief Munyuku in Epukiro was well
known as a SWAPO supporter, and the electoral breakdowns showed that
the highest SWAPO vote was indeed in Epukiro, where SWAPO polled
approximately 500 of its 1,025 votes (interview with UNTAG office,
Okakarara, November 1989). A young SWAPO teacher in Okakarara
whose father was a DTA supporter told us that "young people support
SWAPO. The older generation are DTA." Student boycotts in Okakarara in
1988 coupled with the fact that most SWAPO officials interviewed were
from the younger generation reinforced this impression of SWAPO's support deriving largely from the youth vote.

NPF, which managed to gain 12.6 percent of the vote (18.1 percent of
NPF's national vote), had participated in the interim government and had

traditional roots in this part of the country. Support for DTA, SWAPO, *and* NPF came through similar mechanisms: loyalty for, or the attractions of, well-established Herero leaders. Each party had such a figure, backed up by traditional political allegiances—NUDO figures channeling support to DTA; a long line of Herero figures who supported SWAPO (e.g., Mburumbu Kerina in the early 1960s, Peter Katjavivi among current leaders); and SWANU figures yielding support to NPF. But difficulties in assessing the relative strength of these traditional loyalties (i.e., a "following my leader" vote) are compounded by the additional factors of generational split (along collaborationist-liberationist lines but further confused by the detainees issue) and the specific appeal of party campaign promises (with DTA playing on the patron image). All make a far more complex political mosaic than any simple ethnic analysis would suggest.

### Gobabis

The Gobabis ED included a large number of white farms as well as part of the Herero reserve to the north of Gobabis and Aminius reserve in the south. Thus, the kinds of explanations we look to in order to understand the results are drawn from a combination of the complex factors underlying voting patterns in the Herero reserve (although Gobabis itself was only 10.1 percent Herero in the 1981 census) and the conditions of white farming areas with their varied ethnic composition. Circumstantial evidence suggests that much of the 65.9 percent DTA vote did come from farmworkers; UNTAG reported that many came into the polling booths with the DTA section of the ballot paper cut out to remind them who they were to vote for, and some handed this to the electoral officer as if this action constituted voting.

Electoral breakdowns suggest that most of the SWAPO voters (only 13.9 percent) were in Gobabis itself rather than on the farms or in the Herero reserve. Thus, these voters were probably teachers, students, nurses, and other workers who would have been familiar with SWAPO activity in the town, in contrast to the peasants voting at other polling stations. There was also a substantial 10.9 percent of the vote for ACN, no doubt from many farm owners, regardless of whether they urged their employees to vote DTA or ACN.

### Okahandja

Okahandja was another small ED, which included the Ovitoto reserve for Herero (10 percent of the area but only 5 percent of the population in 1981), the town of Okahandja itself (the central residential and business area and the black and coloured townships), and surrounding white commercial farms. According to the 1981 census, this area was inhabited by a mixed cross section of Namibians from all ethnic groups, including about one-fifth Owambo/Kavango workers. It thus resembled the neighboring Gobabis in its ethnic diversity, but it delivered a much smaller DTA vote (41.3 percent), although still more than SWAPO (35.9 percent).

UDF managed 11.0 percent of the vote, but in 1981 Damara, thought to be the natural constituency of UDF, constituted 21.1 percent of the population of Okahandja district, so it is likely that more than half the Damara voted for another party, perhaps mainly the half on the farms rather than the half in the town. Moreover, as the proportions of Damara people were roughly the same in Gobabis and Okahandja, ethnic voting is even more insufficient as an explanation of both results.

## Otjiwarongo and Outjo

These are white towns surrounded by white-owned farms; most of the white shopkeepers and businesspeople in these towns also have farms. The white population was about 20 percent in 1981. It was a frontier area during the war, so there was a great deal of anti-SWAPO feeling among whites. The strong DTA vote in both towns (42.8 percent and 45.6 percent, respectively) and significant ACN votes were therefore not unexpected. These parties perhaps also benefited from the sizable Bushman population in Outjo. SWAPO had problems campaigning on the farms (interviews with UNTAG office, October and November 1993), as elsewhere. Indeed, there were perhaps higher levels of intimidation in Outjo than in most areas apart from the north: there was graffiti suggesting the presence of "Wit Wolves," and the UNTAG office was bombed in September 1989. Once again, if this was the case, it represented an example of intimidation having a very different effect from that in Owambo. More than half of SWAPO's support in the black townships must have come from non-Owambo people, for the 1981 census indicated that there were very few Owambo in these two townships, although more in Otjiwarongo than in Outjo. The substantial UDF vote (15.1 percent in Otjiwarongo, 21.9 percent in Outjo) can in part be explained by the fact that these two towns are on the edge of Damaraland—Kamanjab was included in the Outjo electoral district, for example, and roughly one-third of its population was Damara in 1981 (although this meant that UDF did not claim all Damara votes).

## Damaraland, Karibib, and Omaruru

Damaraland is one of the most arid and poorest areas in central Namibia, being close to the Namib Desert. It became a reserve only in the 1950s after the state accepted that settler farming had failed, having damaged the environment in the process. Damaraland ED also included Arandis, the Black township of the Rossing mine.

Given the influence of the Damara Council, the core of UDF, and the prominence given to the detainees issue, the Damara people were expected to vote for UDF en masse. And indeed this was the one ED where any third party had a majority (52 percent). This level of support for UDF implied political roots in the community. CIMS observers point to structural intimidation in Damaraland, as pressure was exerted upon the population to vote for the administration that was responsible for jobs and livelihoods. Many old people were dependent on the Damara second-tier administration for their pensions; administration employees were also expected to support the hand that fed them (or claimed to feed them) as the incident at Dibasen Secondary School indicated, when sixteen SWAPO teachers lost their jobs to unqualified but more politically acceptable staff. The lack of viable alternative sources of income, because of the aridity and relative scarcity of land, intensified such dependence. Given that 67.3 percent of the population of the district were Damara in 1981, not all Damara automatically voted for UDF.

*Karibib and Omaruru*

DTA got its majorities most probably from its constituency of white farmers and their farmworkers. The SWAPO vote in these two districts seems to have come again from mineworkers: from the large number of mines scattered around Karibib, the newly opened Navatchab gold mine. Both areas bordered on Damaraland ED and had sizable minorities of Damara (about one-quarter in the 1981 census), which presumably accounts for the UDF proportions.

The labor force in Karibib in 1981 was a smaller proportion of the Karibib population than the SWAPO vote in 1989, so it is likely that SWAPO support came from other peoples, too. The remainder of the SWAPO vote in Karibib was thought to have come from education establishments such as a secondary settlement center at Otjimbingwe and the Lutheran Paulineum Seminary, whose principal was also the head of the SWAPO center.

## The Center

*Rehoboth*

This ED had its own history in that it was an area of land granted by the Germans to the Baster people, which they have retained through periods of land deprivation elsewhere in the police zone. However, in 1981 Rehoboth's ethnic composition was only roughly 63 percent Rehoboth Basters, with 14 percent Nama and 10 percent Damara, many of whom were workers on the larger Baster farms. It tends to be dismissed as an oddity with its own local parties (the ruling one in the district forming the core of FCN). However, the results show a considerably higher vote for DTA than for FCN (29.3 percent), even though this ED gave that party virtually all its national total, and a substantial vote for SWAPO (17.6 percent). The DTA vote no doubt derived from the local influence of the Rehoboth DTA Party, headed by Ben Africa, even though this was the local (sizable) opposition.

## Swakopmund

The Swakopmund ED was the fifth largest and included the town itself, the black and coloured townships of Mondesa and Tamariskia, surrounding white farms, and the voters from Walvis Bay. In 1980 there was a population of approximately nineteen hundred in Walvis Bay (Moorsom 1984: 8). In 1981, 32.7 percent of the population in Swakopmund were white. Their votes, together with those of whites from Walvis Bay, can be presumed to have gone largely to ACN and DTA, which together took 28.4 percent of the vote here.

The SWAPO majority vote here was considerable (58.0 percent). It was expected that many of the coloured population would vote for UDF (it got 7.3 percent), together with some of the Damara population of Mondesa, but it is clear that large numbers of them, along with other groups, voted for SWAPO. Owambo people alone could not have delivered the SWAPO vote as a generous estimate of the maximum number of Owambo who would have been eligible to vote was nine thousand (derived from Moorsom, 1984), or about 35 percent of the voters. SWAPO got 58 percent. Nonetheless, the fact that SWAPO obtained a high result here does not undermine the strong possibility that many people from Walvis Bay were in effect prevented from voting, as described in earlier chapters. Swakopmund's result reinforces our thesis that SWAPO's vote outside the north was concentrated in towns and other centers of employment where SWAPO had been active but that in this and other such contexts they were not solely Owambo.

## Windhoek

Windhoek was the second-largest ED, with more than 110,000 registered voters, 15 percent of the national total. It is perhaps the most difficult to analyze because of its complex composition in socioeconomic and ethnic terms. The ED includes the administrative and commercial city area with its surrounding, still almost exclusively white, residential suburbs; the large African township, Katutura, some miles away; the colored township, Khomasdal, between them; and an extensive surrounding rural and periurban area containing white-owned commercial farms, plus a few smaller mines.

Most registered voters in Windhoek town were no doubt white suburbanites (but may have also included domestic servants, although some of them may have registered in Katutura if they were not resident at their place of work or may not have registered at all). Windhoek proper plus the surrounding farms, as opposed to the townships, had 43 percent of the registered voters, higher than these areas' share in the 1981 population (40 percent). Together with a few hundred farmers, the 28.7 percent of the district population that was white in 1981 were professionals, businesspeople, and officials. The relative proportion of whites among the population most probably was reduced in the 1980s by the immigration of Africans from the countryside, by whites' own emigration as a result of a stagnant economy, by the threat that independence posed (to the most racist among them), and by their lower fertility. Against that their lower fertility and the resulting age pyramid would tend to mean that they would form a higher percentage of those older than eighteen than of the total population including children. The actual proportion of whites in the registered electorate was substantially increased by South Africans who flew into the capital so as to be on the electoral roll. However, reports of the actual voting suggest many of these may well have come to vote just across the southern border, and this may be one reason the turnout of voters in Windhoek compared to number registered was only 92.2 percent, almost the lowest in the country (although it may have also reflected some apathy, especially among coloureds).

Taking these several factors that could have inflated the white population into account, its proportion of the actual voters was likely to have been more than the 28.7 percent of the 1981 total population. But in trying to explain the white vote and the overall result, it seems logical to suppose that the party set up to protect white interests, ACN, would get its 4.9 percent of the Windhoek vote from whites. If all the remaining 25 percent of the electorate that was white had voted for DTA, then the nonwhite population of Windhoek would have contributed only a further 11 percent to the DTA vote—that is if the African and Coloured populations together were about 70 percent of the electorate, only about 15 percent of them would have voted DTA. If that was so, then DTA got far less support from the nonwhite electorate in Windhoek than it did nationally, where it scored 25 percent. The alternative explanations would be that either the white population (even with South African extras) had declined as a percentage of the adult population much more than we have assumed or that a significant proportion of whites voted for SWAPO.

The pattern suggested by these extrapolations, that SWAPO attracted a larger share of the African voters in Windhoek than it did in the largely rural, rest of the country, is also implied by other calculations. If that part of the Windhoek population that was Owambo (17 percent), Damara (16 percent), Herero (9 percent), Nama (6 percent), and Baster (5 percent) peoples, according to the 1981 census, had voted for the two main parties in the same proportions as did these populations found in the EDs of Ovamboland, Damaraland, Hereroland, Keetmanshoop, and Rehoboth, then (if we add in, say, half the 5 percent of the population that had other ethnic origins) SWAPO would have got only approximately 26 percent of the Windhoek vote, whereas it actually received almost 46 percent. Again these census proportions show not only that the voting returns cannot be explained by simple ethnic group exclusivity but also that SWAPO got a significantly higher percentage of the non-Owambo African people in the city than it did in their areas of origin—or it got significant numbers of votes from coloureds and whites. Another way of presenting these findings is to point out that the DTA and ACN vote combined (40.9 percent) was a lower proportion of the whole than the coloured and white populations as proportions of the total population (42.4 percent). If this kind of circumstantial evidence suggests that SWAPO is more of a workers' party in the big towns than simply ethnic in its support, it can also be said, given that perhaps as much as 60 percent of the adult African population of Windhoek is male, that male members of all ethnic groups were more likely to vote for SWAPO than women.

Windhoek's African population was consigned to the Katutura township a few miles from the commercial center and white suburbs. In terms of the 1981 census, it accounted for 40 percent of the population of the district, but the normal rapid urbanization process of the 1980s further fueled by people, especially from the north, displaced by the war had no doubt increased its relative share of the district population by 1989. This is only reflected to a small extent in the fact that 42.7 percent of those who registered in the ED did so in Katutura. Many more Katutura residents may have registered at their places of work.

Apart from being a separate township, Katatura's internal structure also reflected the apartheid pattern of town administration. There had been provision of large, barracklike single men's hostels for migrant workers, although most of these had been closed or demolished in recent years with the relaxing of influx control regulations. But the historic pattern of reproducing ethnic residential segments of streets, each under a chief, still persisted and could be dramatically seen during the campaign: in the Owambo location a forest of SWAPO flags were flying from most roofs, while the Herero location, for instance, had fewer flags and was more mixed. The figures just quoted imply that Katutura residents gave stronger support across the ethnic divisions than might have been expected on the basis of voting patterns in their areas of origin.

Khomasdal contained 15.7 percent of the total census district population in 1981 yet reportedly only 8 percent of Windhoek's total registered voters there. This apparent discrepancy may be explained in part by the possibility that many of the Khomasdal community voted close to their places of work in other parts of the city, thus making even speculation difficult about the Khomasdal voting profile. Khomasdal's residents are almost exclusively coloured or Rehoboth Basters (in 1981, 70.5 percent were coloured; 24.4 percent, Baster). These communities have historically constituted a labor force in a structurally somewhat privileged position compared to black workers. Politically they have often been characterized as conservative and reluctant to challenge the administration that secured them certain relative privileges while denying them others. If there was conservatism and also ambiguity among some of them about African majority rule, there were also a small but visible number of radical intellectuals in Khomasdal. Often these had been associated with SWAPO in the past but had broken with it as a result of the detainees issue, or other reasons, and were now found in some small groups affiliated to UDF and NNF. But the latter particularly were unable to attract significant votes; and UDF's significant 7.2 percent may have come from other Africans, not just coloured voters. The Baster population of Khomasdal was the likely basis for FCN's 1.4 percent of the vote—a proportion that would fit with the presumption that 30 percent of the Baster people in the capital voted FCN, the same proportion as in the Baster homeland of Rehoboth.

The surrounding periurban and rural area of the ED contained some 160 commercial farms but almost 10 percent of the 1981 population. This sizable adult population was made up, in addition to the few hundred white farming families, largely of farmworkers. The likelihood of the latter voting the way their employers voted was indicated when we observed voting at two temporary polling stations open for the day—one of these was in the freshly whitewashed barn of one farm. Groups of workers were driven up by their boss and paraded in. Also in this scattered population outside the town were a few small mines. One of these disused mining compounds, where we also observed voting, had been used as a demobilization camp for former members of the coloured battalion and their families, who were still allowed to occupy the houses under the management of their former (white) officer. The whole community made no secret of its support for DTA.

## The South

This area includes the electoral districts of Bethanie, Karasburg, Maltahöhe and Mariental, Keetmanshoop, and Lüderitz. Lüderitz is an isolated area at the extreme edge of the southern border with South Africa. It has a fishing industry and is surrounded by mines and so has been an important center of employment for Owambo contract workers. The first four EDs were sparsely populated white ranching areas. The Keetmanshoop ED included a similar district plus the Namaland reserve.

The south is the least densely populated part of the country but contains a proportionately high white population, which varies between 15.5 percent and 25 percent of the total population in the EDs. Whites might be an even higher percentage of registered voters, as they would be more heavily represented among adults than among children. Unlike the north, black Nambians in the South were forced off their land and moved into reserves, and like the Herero people further north, the Nama people here suffered violent repression in response to resistance in the early days of colonial rule, which killed 35–50 percent of the population (compared with 75–80 percent Herero—see Chapter 2). The Nama reserve was placed not at the margins of the country, like Hereroland, Damaraland, and Bushmanland, but in barren areas close to settler farms in order to provide a captive labor supply that supplemented those workers and their dependents (of many different ethnic groups, but mostly Nama, especially within the area covered by Maltahöhe ED) who were not typically migrants but lived on the farms all the time. But there is still a degree of interdependence between the population within Namaland and those of the farming districts. In these arid lands peasant survival depends on earnings from migrant labor and livestock production (goats, sheep) in the reserve. Men from the reserve seeking employment were for many years directed by the state into farm employment, rather than to the mining, fishing, and other employment sectors, whose labor was more often provided by people from Owambo communities. Many people in the south have a keen collective identity as farmers who had their land stolen by Germans and further denied them by South Africans and who want their lands back or at least sufficient land to make farming viable. In recent years the differences between poor and wealthy households within Namaland have increased, with a small number of wealthy herders obtaining greater benefit from the poor-quality land of the reserve (Adams et al., 1990).

Farmworkers here are even more intensely isolated because of the sparser population and the often smaller number of employees per farm. The density of the population is also reflected in the fact that there is only a tiny urban population. Both these facts have historically inhibited the opportunities for political organization. However, there was considerable political organization by, and support for, SWAPO in the south, dominated by the important Nama leader Hendrik Witbooi, and it was conventional SWAPO wisdom that "the south went over overwhelmingly to SWAPO" after the intensified implementation of bantustanization in the mid-1970s (SWAPO, 1981: 274).

Insofar as these reasons for thinking that SWAPO had been able to count on support in the south in the past were correct, plus the general expectation that SWAPO held some appeal for all workers and the land hungry, who would benefit from radical change, the election result suggested that SWAPO *lost* support. The common explanation for such a failure was the detainees issue and the way in which SWAPO handled criticisms leveled at it, for it developed a specifically southern dimension. And yet Witbooi, running SWAPO's campaign in the south, not only explicitly

chose to play down the issue but also chose as his main theme reconciliation, fueling fears that SWAPO would try to cover up the whole issue if it
could.

Another hypothesis suggests that such turning away from SWAPO
may have been only characteristic of Namaland, if at all, but argues that in
the south generally there is no inevitable identity of interests between those
represented by the SWAPO leadership and the majority of southerners. The
predominance of farmworkers among the population would tend to
decrease SWAPO's chances.

In other parts of the country, most pertinently Hereroland, a history of
land theft and a high level of political consciousness around land issues do
not automatically translate into a vote for SWAPO, and so the assumption
that it "should have done" here is perhaps also false. Whether this is
because of disinformation about SWAPO's campaign pledges coupled with
SWAPO's restricted access to the population, the actual rejection of
SWAPO for other reasons than the land issue, or greater positive support
for other parties requires further examination.

Coloured people in the south would have no automatic loyalty to
SWAPO; in 1981 they comprised 19 percent of the population here. As
they are mostly urban residents who do not have land (although Rehoboth
Basters are a different case), any general appeal around the issue of land
would hold no attraction. Moreover, as elsewhere in the country, members
of the coloured community who have employment in urban areas have
experienced preferential positions vis-à-vis black southerners, granted on
the basis of their race, which some might be reluctant to give up, as implied
by a SWAPO program.

Crucial, then, to any explanation of voting in these huge regions is the
extent to which there ever was effective support for SWAPO on the ground
in the south. This is an important issue for any postindependence research
agenda. Evidence of resistance to the colonial state does not automatically
translate into support for SWAPO. In fact, the southern experience of colonialism, certainly after the mid-1970s, was profoundly different from that
of SWAPO's heartland in the north, and opposition was not overtly led by
SWAPO. Community resistance to land theft predated SWAPO's formation. From the late 1970s, southern politics incorporated far more opposi-
tional political elements within the system rather than via armed struggle
against it than there had been in the war-torn north. SWAPO would have to
have been a different sort of organization (from SWAPO in the north) to
have been relevant here to the struggles of local people, both with a different program and with a type of political organization not overdetermined
by the hierarchical/militaristic political organization of guerrilla war conditions.

The significant numbers of people who did vote for SWAPO in the
south cannot be explained by the presence of Owambo people. They consti-

tuted a lower proportion of the total population in much of the south in 1981 than the SWAPO share of the vote in 1989. The south is a complex political mosaic that cannot be explained simply by the presence of farms, whose workers in several of these EDs constituted less than half the population in 1981, or by ethnic allegiances because, in spite of the preponderance of Nama and coloured people recorded on the census, there are significant proportions of other groups.

Maltahöhe, one of the smallest EDs, constitutes a small town off the main road surrounded by farms. Most of the Nama here do not have a different political history from Nama elsewhere in the south. Yet DTA did not receive a majority. No obvious explanation for this unusual result immediately suggests itself, except the possibility that SWAPO mobilization was particularly good in this place. Perhaps the Nama's very isolation made them less accessible to the DTA bandwagon of free food and entertainment and to anti-SWAPO propaganda.

Lüderitz, with its sizable SWAPO majority (63.9 percent), seems to have received support from Owambo contract workers in the mining and fishing industries. The CDM diamond mine at Oranjemund employs approximately nine thousand workers, of whom about one-third are at home in Owambo at any given time. At Rosh Pinah zinc mine, there are another five hundred or so employees (interview with Hans Glittenberg, UNTAG director for the south, October 1989). Examination of the electoral breakdown for Lüderitz by polling station reveals that the votes of the two mines and of Benguela black township together gave SWAPO this high majority. Lüderitz ED had the highest concentration of industrial workers anywhere in Namibia—largely from the Owambo region—and is thus quite different from other EDs in the south. The SWAPO share in Lüderitz is the largest that it gained, excluding Ovamboland. Ethnic and working-class explanations may thus conflate here.

Elsewhere in the south, there is no clear ethnically based explanation for DTA's votes; in any one area the DTA vote was from a larger proportion of the electorate than any one ethnic group (based on 1981 figures).

The UDF vote was high compared with other areas outside Damaraland and corresponded roughly to the proportion of the population defined as Damara in 1981. This may be where the UDF vote came from, as predicted by the ethnic bloc analysis, but this does not explain why people voted in this way. One of the main explanations for this Damara-UDF voting in Damaraland itself would also apply here: people relying on the Damara authority for their pensions and jobs. A stronger case can be made for the link with the detainees issue, as PUM's prominence as a member of UDF was considerable.

ACN received 37.2 percent of its national vote here, with Karasburg alone delivering 20.3 percent, which was the largest proportion from any one ED. Why whites here voted so heavily for ACN, rather than DTA, is perhaps explained by the presence of many of the white South Africans who came to the country only to vote. A common explanation offered for white voting preferences regarding DTA and ACN is that those who could not accept the changes implied by independence chose ACN and those who felt their privileges could still be protected voted for DTA. This would explain why many South Africans voted for ACN.

A final point worthy of note is that NNF had targeted the south as its stronghold, yet it failed to obtain enough votes even for one seat in the CA. Subsequently, NNF suggested that campaigning about women's equality and the land issue did not affect voting patterns and that the land issue lost it votes among the Herero population (interview with Abrahams, February 1990).

# List of Acronyms

| | |
|---|---|
| ACN | Action Christian National |
| ACTUR | Action Front for the Retention of Turnhalle Principles |
| AG | administrator-general |
| ANC | African National Congress (of South Africa) |
| BDP | Botswana Democratic Party |
| CA | Constituent Assembly |
| CANU | Caprivi National Union |
| CANU-UDF | Caprivi National Union-United Democratic Front |
| CCM | Chama Cha Mapinduzi (Tanzania) |
| CCN | Council of Churches in Namibia |
| CDA | Christian Democratic Action |
| CIMS | Churches Information and Monitoring Service |
| CIVPOL | UNTAG supervisors of police |
| COSATU | Council of South African Trade Unions |
| DTA | Democratic Turnhalle Alliance |
| ED | electoral district |
| FAPLA | Angolan People's Liberation Party |
| FCN | Federal Convention of Namibia |
| FLS | Frontline States |
| FNLA | National Front for the Liberation of Angola |
| FRELIMO | Front for the Liberation of Mozambique |
| FSWA | Friends of South West Africa |
| GDP | gross domestic product |
| GSSA | Government Senior Staff Association |
| IDAF | International Defence and Aid Fund for Southern Africa (London) |
| JMC | joint monitoring commission |
| KANU | Kenya African National Union |
| MNR | Mozambique National Resistance |
| MPC | multiparty conference |
| MPLA | People's Movement for the Liberation of Angola |
| NANSO | Namibian National Students' Organisation |
| NANTU | Namibian National Teachers' Union |

| | |
|---|---|
| NCC | Namibia Communications Centre |
| NDIIA | National Democratic Institute for International Affairs |
| NDP | National Democratic Party |
| NIP | Namibia Independence Party |
| NNDP | Namibian National Democratic Party |
| NNF | Namibia National Front |
| NPLF | Namibia People's Liberation Front |
| NUDO | National Unity Democratic Party |
| NUNW | National Union of Namibian Workers |
| OAU | Organization of African Unity |
| OPO | Owambo People's Organization |
| PAC | Pan-Africanist Congress |
| PC | Parents' Committee |
| PCC | Political Consultative Council |
| PLAN | People's Liberation Army of Namibia |
| PR | proportional representation |
| RSA | Republic of South Africa |
| SA | South Africa |
| SADC | South African Development Community |
| SADCC | Southern African Development Coordination Conference |
| SADF | South African Defense Force |
| SAMI | South African Military Intelligence |
| SG | Secretary-General |
| STV | Single Transferable Vote |
| SWA | South West Africa |
| SWABC | South West African Broadcasting Corporation |
| SWANU | South West African National Union |
| SWAPA | South West African People's Alliance |
| SWAPO | South West African People's Organization |
| SWAPOL | South West African Police |
| SWATF | South West African Territorial Force |
| TANU | Tanzanian African National Union |
| UDF | United Democratic Front |
| UNHCR | United Nations High Commissioner for Refugees |
| UNIP | United National Independence Party (Zambia) |
| UNITA | National Union for the Total Independence of Angola |
| UNSCR | United Nations Security Council Resolution |
| UNSGSR | United Nations Secretary-General's Special Representative |
| UNTAG | United Nations Transition Assistance Group |
| WCG | Western Contact Group |
| WRP | Workers' Revolutionary Party |
| ZANLA | Zimbabwe African National Liberation Army |
| ZANU | Zimbabwe African National Union |
| ZAPU | Zimbabwe African People's Union |

# References

Abrahams, K., 1990, "The Democratic Opposition in Theory and Practice," *The Namibian Review,* 5 February.

Adamichin, A.L., 1981–1990, "The Settlement of Conflict Situations in the Light of New Political Thinking: A Soviet Point of View," in *UNESCO Yearbook on Peace and Conflict Studies,* New York, Greenwood.

Adams, F. and Werner, W., 1990, *The Land Issue in Namibia,* Namibia Institute for Social and Economic Research, Windhoek, University of Namibia.

anon, 1989, "Namibia: Manipulating a Compromise Solution," *Southern Africa Dossier,* Maputo, May.

Asante, S. and W. Asombang, 1989, "An Independent Namibia? The Future Facing SWAPO," *Third World Quarterly,* 11.3, July.

Balch, J. and Scholten, N., 1990 "Namibian Reconstruction and National Reconciliation: Putting the Horse Before the Cart," *Review of African Political Economy,* 49.

Baran, P., 1957, *The Political Economy of Growth,* Harmondsworth, Penguin.

Barber, J. and Barrett, J., 1990, *South Africa's Foreign Policy: The Search for Status and Security, 1945–88,* Cambridge, Cambridge University Press.

Belikov, I., 1991, "Soviet Scholars' Debate on Socialist Orientation in the Third World," *Millenium,* 20, 1.

Bender, G., 1989, "Peace-making in Southern Africa: The Luanda-Pretoria Tug-of-War," *Third World Quarterly,* 11.2, April.

Berat, L., 1991, *Walvis Bay: Decolonization and International Law,* New Haven and London: Yale University Press.

Bley, H., 1971, *South-west Africa Under German Rule 1894–1914,* London, Heinemann/Evanston, Northwestern University Press.

Brown, S., 1989, "Interview with 'Mistake'," *Vyre Weekblad,* Johannesburg, October.

Buitjenhuis, R., 1982, *Essays on Mau Mau: Contribution to Mau Mau Historiography,* Leiden, African Studies Centre.

Cawthra , B., 1986, *Brutal Force: The Apartheid War Machine,* London, International Defence and Aid Fund for Southern Africa.

The Chamber of Mines of Namibia, 1991, *Mining in Namibia,* Windhoek, Chamber of Mines, 1991.

Charney, C., 1987. "Political Power and Social Class in the Neocolonial and African State." *Review of African Political Economy* 38.

Chen, B., ed. 1990. *Exporting Apartheid: Foreign Policies in Southern Africa, 1978–1988.* London: Macmillan.

Christian Democratic Action. 1982. *Constitution of the Christian Democratic Action for Social Justice.* Namibia: Christian Democratic Action.

CIMS. 1989. Weekly reports from monitors.

———. 1990. *"We Saw It All": CIMS Observers Reports,* ed. D. M'Passou. Katutura: CIMS.

Clarence-Smith, G., and R. Moorsom. 1977. "Underdevelopment and Class Formation in Ovamboland, 1844–1917." In *The Roots of Rural Poverty in Central and Southern Africa,* ed. R. Palmer and N. Parsons. London: Heinemann.

Cliffe, L. 1980. "Generations in the Zimbabwe Nationalist Movement." Paper presented at the Review of African Political Economy Conference, Leeds.

———. 1986. "National Liberation Struggles and 'Radicalisation' in Southern Africa." Paper presented at of Review of African Political Economy Conference, Liverpool.

———. 1988. "Prospects for Agrarian Transformation in Zimbabwe." *Leeds Southern African Studies* 7 (June).

Cock, J., and L. Nathan. eds. 1989. *War and Society: The Militarization of South Africa.* Cape Town: David Philips.

Cole, K. 1990. "Namibia, SWAPO and Socialist Development." School of Development Studies, University of East Anglia, unpublished ms.

Committee of South African War Resisters. 1985. "The South African Military Occupation of Namibia," in *Namibia, 1884–1984: Readings on Namibia's History and Society,* ed. B. Wood. Lusaka: UN Institute for Namibia.

Crocker, C. A. 1981. *South Africa's Defense Posture: Coping with Vulnerability.* Washington Papers 9, 84. Beverly Hills: Sage.

Cronje, G., and S. Cronje. 1979. *The Workers of Namibia.* London: International Defence and Aid Fund for Southern Africa.

Cullinan, S. 1982. "SWAPO and the Anti-Colonial Struggle." *Work in Progress* 23.

Davidson, B. 1981. *The People's Cause: A History of Guerrillas in Africa.* London: Longman.

Davies, R. 1989. "South African Regional Policy Before and After Cuito Cuanavale." In *South African Review 5,* ed. G. Moss and I. Obery. Johannesburg: Ravan Press.

Davies, R., and D. O'Meara. 1985. "Total Strategy in Southern Africa: An Analysis of South Africa's Regional Policy Since 1978." *Journal of Southern African Studies* 11, 2 (April).

Deutschmann, D., ed. 1989. *Changing the History of Africa.* Melbourne: Ocean Press.

Dollie, N., ed. 1989. *A Political Review of Namibia—Nationalism in Namibia.* Windhoek.

Drechsler, H. 1980. *Let Us Die Fighting: The Struggle of the Herero and Nama Against German Imperialism (1984–1915).* London: Zed Press.

Dropkin, G., and D. Clark. 1992. *Past Exposure: Revealing Health and Environmental Risks of Rossing Uranium.* London: Namibia Support Committee and PARTIZANS.

Du Pisani, A. 1986. *SWA/Namibia: The Politics of Continuity and Change.* Johannesburg: J. Ball.

Economist Intelligence Unit. 1990. *Namibia Country Profile, 1990–1991 Annual Survey of Political and Economic Background.* London.

Ellis, J. 1979. *Elections in Namibia?* London: British Council of Churches/Catholic Institute for International Relations.

———. 1981. "The Church in Mobilization for National Liberation." In *Namibia: The Last Colony,* ed. R. H. Green, M.-L. Kiljunen, and K. Kiljunen. London: Longman.

Ericsson, M. 1992. "Namibian Mining Industry," In *Raw Materials Report.* Sweden.

Eriksen, T. L. 1989. *The Political Economy of Namibia—An Annotated Critical Bibliography.* 2d ed. Uppsala: Scandinavian Institute of African Studies, for UNIN.

Evans, G. 1990. "Walvis Bay: South Africa, Namibia and the Question of Sovereignty." *International Affairs* 66, 3.

First, R. 1963. *South West Africa.* Harmondsworth: Penguin.

Fraenkel, P. 1984. *Pretoria's Praetorians: Civil-Military Relations in South Africa.* Cambridge: Cambridge University Press.

Fraenkel, P., and R. Murray. 1985. *The Namibians of South West Africa.* London: Minority Rights Group, 4.

Freeman, L. 1991. "Contradictions of Independence: Namibia One Year After." Ottowa: Dept. of Political Science, Carlton University, unpublished ms.

Frostin P., O, Katjavivi, and K. Mbuende. 1989. *Church and Liberation in Namibia.* London: Pluto Press.

García Márquez, G. 1977. "Operation Carlota." *New Left Review,* no. 101–102.

Geldenhuys, D. 1982. "The Destabilisation Controversy: An Analysis of a High-Risk Foreign Policy Option for South Africa." *Politikon* 9, 2.

———. 1984. *The Diplomacy of Isolation.* Johannesburg: Macmillan.

Gibson, G., T. Larson, and C. McGurk. 1981. *The Kavango Peoples.* Wiesbaden: Franz Steinerverlag.

Gordon, R. J. 1977. *Mines, Masters and Migrants: Life in a Namibian Compound.* Johannesburg: Ravan Press.

Gottschalk, K. 1987. "Restructuring the Colonial State: Pretoria's Strategy in Namibia." In *Namibia in Perspective,* ed. G. Totemeyer, V. Kandetu, and W. Werner. Windhoek: Council of Churches in Namibia.

Green, R. H., M.-L. Kiljunen and K. Kiljunen, eds. 1981. *Namibia: The Last Colony.* London: Longman.

Grundy, K. 1986. *The Militarization of South African Politics.* London: I. B.Tauris.

———. 1991. "Namibia's First Year of Independence." *Current History* 90, 556.

Hamutenya, G. H., and H. L. Geingob. 1972. "African Nationalism in Namibia." In *Southern Africa in Perspective: Essays on Regional Politics,* ed. C. P. Potholm and R. Dale. New York: Free Press.

Hanlon, J. 1986. *Beggar Your Neighbours: Apartheid Power in Southern Africa.* London: J. Currey.

Harvey, C., and J. Isaksen, eds. 1990. *Monetary Independence for Namibia.* Windhoek: Namibian Economic Policy Research Unit.

Heitman, H.-R. 1986. *South African War Machine.* London: Guild.

———. 1990. *War in Angola—The Final South African Phase.* Gibraltar: Ashanti.

Herbstein, D., and J. Evenson. 1989. *The Devils Are Among Us: The War for Namibia.* London: Zed Press.

Hooper, J. 1988. *Koevoet! The Inside Story.* Johannesburg: Southern Book.

Huntington, S. 1968. "The Bases of Accommodation." *Foreign Affairs* 46.

IDAF. 1980. *Namibia: The Facts.* London: International Defence and Aid Fund for Southern Africa.

———. 1982. *Apartheid's Army in Namibia: South Africa's Illegal Military Occupation.* London: International Defence and Aid Fund for Southern Africa.

Jabri, V. 1990. *Mediating Conflict: Decision-making and Western Intervention in Namibia.* Manchester: Manchester University Press.

Jaster, R. 1985. *South Africa in Namibia: The Botha Strategy.* London: Macmillan.

———. 1988. *The Defence of White Power: South African Foreign Policy Under Pressure.* London: Macmillan.

———. 1990. *The 1988 Peace Accords and the Future of South-western Africa.* Adelphi Papers 253. London: Brassey's International Institute for Strategic Studies.

Kaakunga, E. 1990. *Problems of Capitalist Development in Namibia: The Dialectics of Progress and Destruction.* Abo: Abo Academy Press.

Katjavivi, P. 1988. *The History of Resistance in Namibia.* London: J. Currey.

Kiljunen, K. 1981. "National Resistance and the Liberation Struggle." in *Namibia: The Last Colony,* ed. R. H. Green, M.-L. Kiljunen, and K. Kiljunen. London: Longman.

Konig, B. 1983. *Namibia: The Ravages of War.* London: International Defence and Aid Fund for Southern African.

Kramer, M. 1991. "Soviet Foreign Policy After the Cold War." *Current History* 90.

Lan, D. 1985. *Guns and Rain: Guerrillas and Spirit Mediums in Zimbabwe.* London: J. Currey.

Landis, E. 1988. "Namibia in the International Context: The Frustration of Independence." In *Namibia, 1884–1984: Readings on Namibia's History and Society,* ed. B. Wood. Lusaka: UN Institute for Namibia.

Lee, R. 1986. "The Gods Must Be Crazy, But the State Has a Plan: Government Policies Towards the San in Namibia." *Canadian Journal of African Studies* 20, 1.

Leebaert, D., and T. Dickinson, eds. 1992. *Soviet Strategy and New Military Thinking.* New York: Cambridge University Press.

Legal Assistance Center. 1989. Report of Events on 1 April 1989 by an Eye-Witness Observer, Windhoek.

Leonard, R. 1983. *South Africa at War: White Power and the Crisis in Southern Africa.* Westport: Lawrence Hill.

Leys, C. 1975. *Underdevelopment in Kenya: The Political Economy of Neo-Colonialism.* London: Heinemann.

———. 1989a. "The Security Situation and the Transfer of Power in Namibia." CIDMAA Report. Montreal: September.

———. 1989b. "The Security Situation and the Transfer of Power in Namibia." *Review of African Political Economy* 45–46.

Lipton, M. 1986. *Capitalism and Apartheid: South Africa, 1910–86.* Aldershot: Wildwood House.

Lister, A., 1987. "Prospects for Peace in Namibia at the Start of 1987." In *Namibia in Perspective,* eds. G. Totemeyer et al.

Manning, P. 1989a. "Namibia's Independence: What Has Happened to Resolution 435?" *Review of African Political Economy* 44.

Manning, P. 1989b. *The United Nations Plan for Elections in Namibia Envisaged in UN Security Council Resolution 435 (1978).* London: Southscan Occasional Paper.

Manning, P., and R. H. Green. "Namibia: Preparations for Destabilization," in Phyllis Johnson and David Martin, eds., *Destructive Engagement* (Harare: Zimbabwe Publishing House for the Southern African Research and Documentation Centre, 1986), pp. 111–138.

Mokopakgosi, B. T. 1992. "Conflict and Collaboration in South-Eastern Namibia: Missionaries, Concessionares and the Nama's War Against German Imperialism 1880–1908." In *People and Empires in African History: Essays in Memory of Michael Crowder,* ed. J. F. Ade Ajayi and J. D. Y. Peel. London: Longman.

Moorsom, R. 1979. "Labour Consciousness and the 1971–72 Contract Workers Strike in Namibia." *Development and Change* 10, 2.

————. 1982. *Agriculture: Transforming a Wasted Land.* London: Catholic Institute for International Relations.

————. 1984. *Walvis Bay: Namibia's Port.* London: International Defence and Aid Fund for Southern Africa.

Moss, G., and I. Obery. 1989. *South African Review 5.* Johannesburg: Ravan Press.

Munslow, B. 1983. *Mozambique: The Revolution and Its Origins.* London: Longman.

NADEL Observers' Report 1990. National Association of Democratic Lawyers, Report on Namibian Elections 1989, Johannesburg, South Africa.

Namibia Peace Plan Study and Contact Group. n.d. "An investigation into the extent of impartiality of the South West Africa Broadcasting Corporation" (radio and television news), Windhoek.

NCC Documents. 1989. *Namibian Essential Documents: The United Nations' Independence Plan, 1976–89.* Windhoek: Namibian Communications Center.

NDIIA. 1990. *Nation Building: The UN and Namibia.* Washington, D.C.: National Democratic Institute for International Affairs.

Ngavirue, Z. 1972. "Political Parties and Interest Groups in South West Africa: A Study of Plural Societies." Ph.D. diss., Oxford University.

Norval, M. 1989. *Death in the Desert: The Namibian Tragedy.* Washington, D.C.: Selous Foundation Press.

Oden, B. 1991. "Namibia's Economic Links to South Africa." *Current African Issues 14.* Uppsala: Nordiska Afrikan Institut.

Odendaal Commission. 1964. Report of the Commission of Enquiry into South West Africa Affairs, 1962–63. Republic of South Africa: Capetown.

Oholson, T. 1989. "The Cuito Cuanavale Syndrome: Revealing SADF Vulnerabilities." In *South African Review 5,* ed. G. Moss and I. Obery. Johannesburg: Ravan Press.

Oloya, J. J. et al. 1984. *Agricultural Economy of Namibia: Strategies for Structural Change.* Lusaka: UN Institute for Namibia.

O'Meara, D. 1982. "Muldergate and the Politics of Afrikaner Nationalism." *Work in Progress* 22.

Pankhurst, D. 1992. *The Land Issue in Namibia.* Bradford University: Department of Peace Studies.

Pilgrim, C. M. 1990. "Some Legal Aspects of Trade in the Natural Resources of Namibia." *British Yearbook of International Law 1990.* Oxford: Oxford University Press.

Price, R. 1984. "Pretoria's Southern Africa Strategy." *African Affairs* 83 (January).

————. 1991. *The Apartheid State in Crisis: Political Transformation in South Africa, 1975–1990.* Oxford: Oxford University Press.

Putz, J., H. von Egidy, and P. Caplan. 1990. *Namibia Handbook and Political Who's Who.* Postelection ed. Windhoek: Magus.

Ranger, T. 1985. *Peasant War and Guerrilla Consciousness in Zimbabwe.* London: J. Currey.

Rees, M., and C. Day. 1980. *Muldergate.* Johannesburg: Macmillan.

Rueschemeyer, D., E. Stevens, and J. Stevens. 1992. *Capitalist Development and Democracy.* Cambridge: Polity.

Saivetz, C. R., ed. 1989. *The Soviet Union in the Third World.* Boulder: Westview Press.

Saul, J. 1979. *The State and Revolution in Eastern Africa.* London: Heinemann.

Saul, J. S., and S. Gelb. 1986. *The Crisis in South Africa.* London: Zed Press.

Schmidt-Jortzig, E. "The Constitution of Namibia: An Example of a State Emerging Under Close Supervision and World Scrutiny." *German Yearbook of International Law* 34. Berlin: Dunker Und-humboldt.

Seery, B. 1989. "Security Council Resolution 435 and the Namibian Independence Process." In *South African Review 5,* ed. G. Moss and I. Obery. Johannesburg: Ravan Press.

Serfontein, J. 1976. *Namibia?* London: R. Collings.

Simon, D. 1983. "The Evolution of Windhoek." in *Perspectives on Namibia: Past and Present,* ed. C. Saunders. Cape Town: Centre for African Studies.

————. *Independent Namibia One Year On.* Conflict Studies 239. London: Research Institute for the Study of Conflict and Terrorism.

————. 1993. "Geo-political Transition and State Formation: The Changing Political Geographies of Angola, Mozambique and Namibia." *Journal of Southern African Studies* 19, 1.

Simon, D., and R. Moorsom. 1987. "Namibia's Political Economy: A Contemporary Perspective." In *Namibia in Perspective,* ed. G. Totemeyer, V. Kandetu, and W. Werner. Windhoek: Council of Churches in Namibia.

Smith, S. 1986. *Namibia: A Violation of Trust.* Oxford: Oxfam.

Steenkamp, W. 1983. *Borderstrike: South Africa into Angola.* Woburn, Mass.: Butterworth.

————. 1989. *South Africa's Border War, 1966–1989.* Gibraltar: Ashanti.

Stiff, P. 1985. *Taming the Landmine.* Alberton, South Africa: Galago.

————. 1989. *Nine Days of War: Namibia—Before, During, and After.* Alberton, South Africa: Lemur Books.

Stockwell, J. 1978. *In Search of Enemies: A CIA Story.* New York: Norton.

SWA/Namibia Today. 1988. Windhoek: Dept. of Governmental Affairs.

SWANU. 1976. *Basic Documents of the South West African National Union.* Stockholm: Pogo Print.

SWAPO. 1978. *Information on SWAPO: An Historical Profile.* Lusaka: SWAPO Department of Information and Publicity.

SWAPO. 1981. *To Be Born a Nation: The Liberation Struggle for Namibia.* London: Zed Press.

Szeftel, M. 1991. "Manoeuvres of War in South Africa." *Review of African Political Economy* 51.

Tamarkin, M. 1990. *The Making of Zimbabwe: Decolonization in Regional and International Politics.* London: F. Cass.

Tapscott, K. 1990. "The Situation of Returnees in Ovamboland." Windhoek: Namibian Institute for Social Research.

Thirion, P. W. 1985. *Commission of Inquiry into Alleged Irregularities and Misappropriations of Property in Representative Authorities and the Central Authority of South West Africa.* (Thirion Commission). 8th Interim Report.

Tjonneland, E. N. 1992. *Southern Africa After Apartheid: Challenges, Prospects and Implications for Development Aid.* Final Report. Bergen: Chr. Michelsen.

Totemeyer, G. 1978. *Namibia, Old and New: Traditional and Modern Leaders in Ovamboland.* London: C. Hurst.

Totemeyer, G., V. Kandetu, and W. Werner. eds. 1987. *Namibia in Perspective.* Windhoek: Council of Churches in Namibia.

TWIN. 1989. *This Week in Namibia.* Washington, D.C.: Lawyers' Committee on Civil Rights Under the Law, 27 August–25 September.

UN Mission. 1989. *Report of the United Nations Mission on Detainees.* Windhoek: 11 October.

UNIN. 1986. *Namibia: Perspectives for National Reconstruction and Development.* Lusaka: UN Institute for Namibia.

Urquhart, B. 1987. *A Life in Peace and War.* New York: Harper and Row.

Weiland, H. 1989. "Tables from Attitude Survey." Freiburg: Arnold Bergstraesser Institute, mimeo.

Wellmer, G. 1990. "Notes on Namibia's Transition to Independence." *Southern Africa Dossier* (Maputo) (April).

Werner, W. 1987. "Ethnicity and Reformism in Namibia." In *Namibia in Perspective,* ed. G. Totemeyer, V. Kandetu, and W. Werner. Windhoek: Council of Churches in Namibia.

Wiehann, N. 1989. *Report of the Commission of Inquiry into Labour Matters in Namibia.* Part 1. Windhoek: Wiehahn Commission.

Wolpe, H. 1988. *Race, Class and the Apartheid State.* Paris: Unesco.

Wood, B. 1991. "The UN Plan for Namibia and Its Initial Implementation." In *News from Africa's Last Colony.* London: Namibia Communications Center.

———. 1992. "Preventing the Vacuum: Determinants of the Namibia Settlement." *Journal of Southern African Studies* 17.4.

———. ed. 1988. *Namibia, 1884–1984: Readings on Namibia's History and Society.* Lusaka: UN Institute for Namibia.

World Bank. 1991. *World Development Report.* Oxford: Oxford University Press.

Ya-Otto, J. 1981. *Battlefront Namibia: An Autobiography.* New York: Lawrence Hill.

Zartman, W. 1985. *Ripe for Resolution.* Oxford: Oxford University Press.

# Index